Leibniz on God and Religion

ALSO AVAILABLE FROM THE SAME AUTHOR

The Shorter Leibniz Texts, translated by Lloyd Strickland
Leibniz Reinterpreted, by Lloyd Strickland

ALSO AVAILABLE FROM BLOOMSBURY

The Bloomsbury Companion to Leibniz, edited by Brandon C. Look
The Bloomsbury Companion to Metaphysics, edited by Neil A. Manson and Robert W. Barnard
Leibniz: A Guide for the Perplexed, by Franklin Perkins
The Science of Right in Leibniz's Moral and Political Philosophy, by Christopher Johns

Leibniz on God and Religion

A Reader

**Translated and edited by
Lloyd Strickland**

Bloomsbury Academic
An imprint of Bloomsbury Publishing Plc

B L O O M S B U R Y
LONDON · OXFORD · NEW YORK · NEW DELHI · SYDNEY

Bloomsbury Academic
An imprint of Bloomsbury Publishing Plc

50 Bedford Square
London
WC1B 3DP
UK

1385 Broadway
New York
NY 10018
USA

www.bloomsbury.com

BLOOMSBURY and the Diana logo are trademarks of Bloomsbury Publishing Plc

First published 2016

Translated material, introduction and bibliography © Lloyd Strickland, 2016

Lloyd Strickland has asserted his right under the Copyright, Designs and Patents Act, 1988, to be identified as author of this work.

'On the true Mystical Theology' was transcribed and translated by Julia Weckend, and 'Brief explanation of Revelation' was translated by Daniel J. Cook. In addition, an early translation of 'The story of Bileam' by Daniel J. Cook was revised and edited for this collection.

All rights reserved. No part of this publication may be reproduced or transmitted in any form or by any means, electronic or mechanical, including photocopying, recording, or any information storage or retrieval system, without prior permission in writing from the publishers.

No responsibility for loss caused to any individual or organization acting on or refraining from action as a result of the material in this publication can be accepted by Bloomsbury or the author.

British Library Cataloguing-in-Publication Data
A catalogue record for this book is available from the British Library.

ISBN: HB: 9781472580610
PB: 9781472580627
ePDF: 9781472580641
ePub: 9781472580634

Library of Congress Cataloging-in-Publication Data
Leibniz, Gottfried Wilhelm, Freiherr von, 1646-1716.
[Works. Selections. English. 2016]
Leibniz on God and religion : a reader / edited by Lloyd Strickland.– 1 [edition].
pages cm
Includes bibliographical references and index.
ISBN 978-1-4725-8061-0 (hb)-- ISBN 978-1-4725-8062-7 (pb)– ISBN 978-1-4725-8063-4 (epub)– ISBN 978-1-4725-8064-1 (epdf) 1. Religion. 2. God. I. Strickland, Lloyd, 1973- editor. II. Title.
B2558.S77 2016
200–dc23
2015019663

Typeset by Fakenham Prepress Solutions, Fakenham, Norfolk NR21 8NN

This book is dedicated to
Pete Clarke (340 and out – at the time of writing anyway!)
and
Nick Stone (3102 and counting – can you believe it?)

Contents

Acknowledgements xi
Abbreviations xii
Introduction: Leibniz – Theology and Practice 1
About the Texts and Translations 13
Recommended Further Reading 15

1 The *Catholic Demonstrations* 21

1. Sketch of *Catholic Demonstrations* (1668–9 (?)) 21
2. On transubstantiation (1668–9 (?)) 35
3. On the demonstration of the possibility of the mysteries of the Eucharist (autumn 1671 (?)) 42
4. A proposal to revive the *Catholic Demonstrations* (late 1679 (?)) 47

2 The Existence and Nature of God 53

(A) The Existence of God 53
1. A proof of the existence of God from his essence (January 1678) 53
2. There is only a single God (1685–6 (?)) 61
3. If a necessary being is possible, it follows that it exists (March 1689–March 1690 (?)) 63
4. God is the sufficient reason for the world (29 December 1692/ 8 January 1693) 64
5. On Reverend Father Lamy's demonstration of the existence of God (late June 1701) 66

(B) The Nature of God 69
1. God is not the soul of the world (summer 1683–winter 1685/6 (?)) 69
2. Rationale of the Catholic faith (mid-1680s (?)) 70
3. On the true Mystical Theology (mid-1690s (?)) 79
4. Review of Lüttichau's *Pansophia* (4 September 1696) 84
5. Ancient and modern understandings of God (30 April 1709) 90

3 Reason and Faith 93

1. What needs to be done to defend the Christian religion (10/20 February 1670) 93
2. On the *Treatise of Religion against the Atheists* (1677–9 (?)) 94
3. Dialogue between a theologian and a misosophist (2nd half 1678–1st half 1679 (?)) 96
4. Specimen of *Catholic Demonstrations*, or, Apology for the faith through reason (July 1683–March 1686 (?)) 103
5. An outline of a natural theology (29 September/9 October 1697) 108
6. The use of reason in theology (6 October 1706) 110
7. On the Greeks as the founders of a sacred philosophy (1 July 1714) 113

4 Ethics and the Love of God 121

1. Letter concerning Steno and Spinoza (March 1677 (?)) 121
2. Dialogue between Theophile and Polidore (summer–autumn 1679 (?)) 127
3. Aphorisms concerning happiness, wisdom, charity and justice (summer–winter 1678/9 (?)) 137
4. Dialogue between Poliander and Theophile (mid-1679 (?)) 141
5. Critical remarks on William Penn and the Quakers (March 1696) 148
6. The true theology (10/20 December 1696) 153
7. On the disinterested love of God (9/19 (?) August 1697) 157
8. On the public good (2/12 February 1700) 162
9. The essence of piety (18 March 1705) 163

5 The Bible 165

1. Short commentary on the judge of controversies, or, The balance of reason and the textual norm (1669–71 (?)) 165
2. Brief explanation of Revelation (January 1677) 174
3. On the Revelation of St John (30 June/10 July 1691) 186
4. The story of Bileam (early September 1706) 187

6 Miracles and Mysteries 195
1. The devil cannot prophesize (3 March 1680) 195
2. On the threefold God (1680–4 (?)) 196
3. On the person of Christ (1680–4 (?)) 199
4. On the Trinity (autumn 1685 (?)) 202
5. Some thoughts on the Trinity, occasioned by the reading of Stephen Nye's *Considerations on the Explications of the Doctrine of the Trinity* (1693–end 1695) 203
6. On miracles and mysteries (August–September (?) 1697) 209
7. Hasty comments on the book *Christianity not Mysterious*, written 8 August 1701 210

7 The Churches and their Doctrines 225
1. On the host (October 1677) 225
2. On Scripture, the Church and the Trinity (1680–4 (?)) 227
3. On God and the Church (autumn 1685–spring 1686 (?)) 232
4. Suppositions (autumn 1685–spring 1686 (?)) 236
5. On the certainty of salvation (17/27 March 1695) 239
6. On the authority of the Pope (1705) 241
7. Exposition of the doctrines and practices authorized by the Roman Church (1705 (?)) 244

8 Grace and Predestination 253
1. On freedom, fate and God's grace (spring–winter 1686/7 (?)) 253

9 Sin, Evil and Theodicy 271
1. The author of sin (1673 (?)) 271
2. On the goodness of God's works (autumn 1684 (?)) 273
3. Genuine dialogue (25 January 1695) 274
4. Can the bad outcomes of wicked actions be ascribed to wickedness? (after 1695 (?)) 282
5. On God and man (December 1705 (?)) 286
6. On the composition of a stirring theological poem, 'Uranius' (3 September 1711) 299

10 The Afterlife 303

(A) Resurrection and Purgatory 303
1. On the resurrection of bodies (21 May 1671) 303
2. On purgatory (January 1677) 308
3. St Augustine's opinion on purgatory (6/16 December 1694) 311
4. On the time of purification (not later than spring 1698) 315
5. Whether purgatory is an article of faith (4/14 January and 2/12 February 1700) 316
6. On the valley of Jehoshaphat (1715 (?)) 318

(B) Salvation and Damnation 319
1. On the damnation of the innocent (4/14 September 1690) 319
2. On the imagination of the future life (not later than spring 1698) 320
3. On the salvation of pagans (not later than spring 1698) 323
4. Blessedness and punishment (21 February 1705) 324
5. Preface to Ernst Soner's book on eternal punishment (1708) 325

11 Non-Christian Religions 327
1. On a small book entitled *Seder Olam* (1694) 327
2. On the Jesuit mission in China (18 January 1700) 332
3. On an intellectual exchange with the Chinese (18 August 1705) 334
4. On the Mohammedans and Socinians (2 December 1706) 337

Index 345

Acknowledgements

This volume was first planned and conceived in 2007, and work on it has taken place intermittently in the intervening years. Over that time, many debts of gratitude have been incurred, and I am pleased to be able to record these here. My thanks are due to the following:

Four anonymous referees sourced by Bloomsbury, for their helpful suggestions regarding the content, presentation and scope of this volume.

Daniel J. Cook, for allowing me to publish his translation of version 1 of 'Brief explanation of Revelation', and for allowing me to revise and annotate his translation of 'The story of Bileam'. Dan also looked over drafts of many of the texts in this volume, making numerous suggestions regarding readability, and read over the introductory essay as well.

Julia Weckend, for taking on the unenviable task of transcribing and translating the horrendously messy manuscript to 'On the true Mystical Theology', and for doing so with such great humour and patience. I hope you think the result was worth it; I think it's great.

Paul Lodge, for his thoughtful comments on the introductory essay.

Harry Parkinson, Peter Pike, John Thorley and Geert de Wilde, for checking some of my translations, and for making corrections and suggesting improvements.

Karen Sieben, for sorting out some problems I was having with Leibniz's Greek.

Birgit Zimny of the Gottfried Wilhelm Leibniz Bibliothek, Hanover, for providing me with many of the manuscripts translated in this volume.

Nora Gaedeke, Stephan Meier-Oeser and Stefan Lorenz, for their help in deciphering some of the words and passages in the manuscripts that had eluded me.

Colleen Coalter from Bloomsbury, for commissioning the project.

Liza Thompson from Bloomsbury, for seeing the book through to publication.

Abbreviations

In the notes, commonly cited editions of Leibniz's writings are referred to using the following conventions:

A = *Sämtliche Schriften und Briefe*, ed. Deutsche Akademie der Wissenschaften, 8 series, each divided into multiple volumes (Berlin: Akademie Verlag, 1923–).

CP = *Confessio Philosophi: Papers concerning the Problem of Evil 1671–1678*, trans. R. C. Sleigh, Jr (New Haven: Yale University Press, 2005).

DSR = *De summa rerum*, ed. and trans. G. H. R. Parkinson (New Haven: Yale University Press, 1992).

Dutens = *G. G. Leibnitii Opera Omnia*, ed. L. Dutens, 6 vols (Geneva, 1768).

G = *Die Philosophischen Schriften*, ed. C. I. Gerhardt, 7 vols (Hildesheim: Georg Olms, 1978).

Grua = *Textes inédits*, ed. G. Grua, 2 volumes with successive pagination (Paris: Presses Universitaires de France, 1948).

GW = *Briefwechsel zwischen Leibniz und Christian Wolf*, ed. C. I. Gerhardt (Halle: H. W. Schmidt, 1860).

H = *Theodicy*, trans. E. M. Huggard (Chicago: Open Court, 1990).

Klopp = *Die Werke von Leibniz*, ed. O. Klopp, 11 vols (Hanover: Klindworth, 1864–84).

L = *Philosophical Papers and Letters*, ed. and trans. L. Loemker (Dordrecht: D. Reidel, 1969, 2nd edn).

LTS = *Leibniz and the Two Sophies*, ed. and trans. L. Strickland (Toronto: CRRS, 2011).

NE	= *New Essays on Human Understanding*, ed. and trans. J. Bennett and P. Remnant (Cambridge: Cambridge University Press, 1996, 2nd edn).
PW	= *Philosophical Writings*, ed. and trans. M. Morris and G. H. R. Parkinson (London: Everyman, 1973).
SLT	= *Shorter Leibniz Texts*, ed. and trans. L. Strickland (London: Continuum, 2006).
WOC	= *Writings on China*, ed. and trans. D. J. Cook and H. Rosemont, Jr (Chicago: Open Court, 1994).

Introduction: Leibniz – Theology and Practice

Those who know something of Leibniz's work are well aware of the central place accorded in it to God. Yvon Beleval once claimed that no matter which part of Leibniz's thought one begins with, one soon reaches God.[1] And this is no exaggeration. To take just one example, in writings expounding his discovery of binary arithmetic, Leibniz explicitly sought to show how the discovery related to God, and how it was thus of great importance to theology.[2] We can understand this better if we consider Leibniz's insistence that, in spite of his great achievements in other fields of learning, in particular mathematics, his chief concern was in fact theology.[3] And we can in turn better understand his privileging of theology if we consider that Leibniz was, first and foremost, a practical man: more than most, he possessed the impulse to do whatever he could to improve the human experience, and throughout his life he held the fervent belief that religion afforded the means to do this. For religion, he believed, had great practical value not only for society in general, but also for individuals, both in this life and the life to come. This belief defines Leibniz's approach to religion as a whole and is the connecting thread that binds together his three signature projects in theology, namely the *Catholic Demonstrations*, Church

---

[1] See Y. Beleval, *Leibniz: Initiation à sa philosophie* (Paris: Vrin, 2005, 6th edn), p. 241.
[2] He believed that binary arithmetic, which was capable of generating all natural numbers from 0 and 1, perfectly symbolized the creation of the universe from nothing by the one God, and thus was able to convince non-believers of the core Christian belief in the creation of the universe from nothing. See for example p. 336; G. W. Leibniz, *Mathematische Schriften vol. 7*, ed. C. I. Gerhardt (Berlin: A. Asher, 1863), p. 239/SLT, p. 39; A I 19, pp. 404f.
[3] See p. 49 and A II 1 (2nd edn), p. 761. Given this, it is surprising that in the critical edition of Leibniz's writings, the Akademie edition, there is no series devoted to his voluminous theological writings. The eight series of the Akademie edition are: General, political and historical correspondence (series I); Philosophical correspondence (series II); Mathematical, scientific and technical correspondence (series III); Political writings (series IV); Historical and linguistic writings (series V); Philosophical writings (series VI); Mathematical writings (series VII); Scientific, medical and technical writings (series VIII). Leibniz's theological writings are scattered throughout these series, with most to be found in series I, II, IV and VI.

reunification and the promotion of the doctrine of optimism. A survey of these projects will make this clear.

The *Catholic Demonstrations*

Let us begin with the *Catholic Demonstrations*, Leibniz's earliest theological project, dating from the late 1660s and early 1670s, while he was working for the ecumenically-minded Catholic court of Mainz. It was conceived as a systematic apology for the Christian faith, built upon the framework of Catholicism. According to Leibniz's detailed sketch, after a prolegomena consisting of the first principles of the various branches of philosophy, the *Demonstrations* proper was to begin with philosophical proofs of the existence of God (part 1), then a demonstration of the immortality of the soul (part 2), before moving on to demonstrate the possibility of Christian mysteries, such as that of the Trinity, the Incarnation and the Eucharist (part 3), and then finally demonstrate the authority of the Catholic Church and Scripture (part 4).[4] Driven on by rigorous and irrefutable reasoning, drawn as much from the work of others as Leibniz's own ideas, the *Catholic Demonstrations* was designed to uphold the central doctrines of Catholicism, and show Christianity 'to be thoroughly holy and thoroughly rational',[5] making it a truly universal religion acceptable to all humans *qua* rational creatures.

Although Leibniz was himself a Lutheran, his decision to base the *Demonstrations* around Catholicism is not a surprising one. The central assumption of the ecumenism of Leibniz's day – reflected in the *Catholic Demonstrations* – was that the Protestants would have to come back to the Catholic fold. And Leibniz saw this as perfectly feasible: he entertained the belief that the differences between Catholics and Protestants were not as great as was often thought, and in some cases there was only the appearance of the two sides holding conflicting views. Hence when sketching out some thoughts on the Eucharist for the *Catholic Demonstrations*, Leibniz insisted that, when understood properly (that is, through the lens of his own philosophy), the Catholic doctrine of transubstantiation turned out to be identical to the Protestant (Lutheran) doctrine of the real presence.[6]

---

[4] See pp. 22–35.
[5] p. 50.
[6] See p. 44.

Although not conceived as a direct contribution to the Church reunion efforts that were beginning to stir at the time, especially in Mainz, the value it would have had for them is clear enough, as, if realized, the *Catholic Demonstrations* would have had the potential to unite all Christians, philosophically and doctrinally. However, the project was never finished; indeed, it was barely even started. Aside from a very ambitious plan,[7] Leibniz wrote only a handful of short texts in support of it, and these took the form of preliminary studies rather than finished chapters (these included texts on grace,[8] the Eucharist[9] and the Incarnation).[10] The project was abandoned in 1672, following the death of its chief patron, Baron Johann Christian von Boineburg (1622–72).

Some years later, Leibniz revisited the *Catholic Demonstrations*, pitching it in 1679 to his employer at the time, the Catholic Duke of Hanover, Johann Freidrich, in the hope that it would win his support. However, the Duke died shortly after hearing of the project, and the *Catholic Demonstrations* project died at the same time. Never one to be deterred, Leibniz went on to conceive and pursue something along the same lines in the mid-1680s, producing numerous drafts on topics relating to a rational defence of the Catholic faith, or various aspects thereof.[11] Although these writings, like those of the *Catholic Demonstrations*, were not intended as formal contributions to Church reunification, they were certainly written in its shadow, and Leibniz may have thought of them as connected to it, at least tangentially.

Church Reunification

That Leibniz would seek to provide a philosophical framework that could, in theory at least, promote reconciliation between Catholics and Protestants, was entirely in keeping with his irenical aims. For Leibniz was a fervent supporter of Church reunification, and was involved in the reunion efforts that took place in the last three decades of the seventeenth century. But

---

[7] See pp. 22–35.
[8] See A VI 1, pp. 535–6.
[9] See A VI 1, pp. 501–17. Two of these texts are included in this volume: 'On transubstantiation' (pp. 35–42) and 'On the demonstration of the possibility of the mysteries of the Eucharist' (pp. 42–6).
[10] See A VI 1, pp. 532–5.
[11] See for example pp. 70–9 and pp. 103–8.

in spite of his name being so closely associated with Church reunion,[12] Leibniz had no official role in any of the proceedings or in the documents produced. The principal discussions were held in the late 1670s and 1680s, following the warm reception given in Hanover to the Bishop of Tina, Cristobal de Rojas y Spinola (c. 1626–95), who had met with Germany's various territorial leaders to gauge the possibility of Church reunification. As the Hanoverians – for whom Leibniz worked as counsellor and librarian from 1676 until his death in 1716 – had been receptive to the idea, Spinola returned to the duchy again in 1683 and held further talks with a Protestant delegation headed by Gerhard Wolter Molanus (1633–1722), the Abbé of Loccum. As the negotiations proceeded, other interested parties joined the fray, such as France's chief theologian and Bishop of Meaux, Jacques-Bénigne Bossuet (1627–1704). However, Spinola's attempts to generate wider support among the heads of German states were coolly received. Leibniz's input in the reunion effort at this time was limited to behind-the-scenes advising and counselling, and attempting to generate support for the enterprise through his acquaintances and correspondents. But as efforts floundered, he took on a more active role in the 1690s, pressing the case for reunion through his correspondences with Paul Pelisson (1624–93), the court historian of Louis XIV, and Bossuet. To the latter, Leibniz urged that the Council of Trent (1545–63) – which had been prompted by the Protestant Reformation, and ultimately reinforced the schism between Catholics and Protestants – be superseded by a new council acceptable to all sides,[13] but Bossuet was unsympathetic to the idea, insisting that Trent was not up for negotiation.[14] The impasse could not be broken, and further setbacks, such as Pelisson's death in January 1693, Spinola's death in 1695 and Bossuet's withdrawal from the correspondence with Leibniz the same year, led to the reunion plans being quietly abandoned.[15] [16]

---

[12] One scholar calls Leibniz 'the greatest supporter of Church unity that the world has yet known'. G. J. Jordan, *The Reunion of the Churches: A Study of G. W. Leibnitz and His Great Attempt* (London: Constable, 1927), p. 31.
[13] See for example, A I 9, pp. 116–45.
[14] See for example A I 9, p. 153.
[15] Even after formal plans for reunification were dropped, Leibniz continued to be motivated by irenicism; for example, he sought a way to accommodate the Catholic doctrine of transubstantiation within his philosophy, most notably in his correspondence with Des Bosses. See *The Leibniz-Des Bosses Correspondence*, trans. and ed. B. C. Look and D. Rutherford (New Haven: Yale University Press, 2007).
[16] The best account in English of Leibniz and Church reunion is still Jordan, *The Reunion of the Churches*.

Optimism

The last of the three theological projects that epitomizes Leibniz's attitude towards religion is the promotion of his doctrine of optimism, that is, his (in)famous claim that since a perfect God acts in the most perfect way, he has created the best of all possible worlds. It was utilized very often to defend God's justice in the face of objections drawn from the existence, character and prevalence of evil in the world. Leibniz argued that the evil that exists is simply part and parcel of the best, and cannot be removed without detriment to the whole. This doctrine was one that Leibniz had endorsed since his youth,[17] and he promoted it throughout his life, in his correspondence[18] and also in a book published late in life, the *Theodicy*.[19] In part due to his tireless promotion of the doctrine, optimism became very popular in the Republic of Letters, being echoed in the work of many of the leading lights of the eighteenth century, such as Lord Henry Bolingbroke (1678–1751),[20] Christian Wolff (1679–1754),[21] Alexander Pope (1688–1744),[22] Voltaire (1694–1778)[23] and Immanuel Kant (1724–1804) (though in the case of the latter two, their initial enthusiasm for the doctrine ultimately gave way to a fierce opposition).[24]

Religion and Practice

As noted earlier, the connecting thread that binds all of the aforementioned projects was Leibniz's fervent belief in the practical value of religion, both for society in general and for the individual. This is more obvious in some cases than in others. That Leibniz should see practical value in

---

[17] See for example A VI 3, p. 125/CP, p. 49.
[18] See for example A II 1 (2nd edn), p. 186/CP, p. 3.
[19] G. W. Leibniz, *Essais de Theodicée sur la bonté de Dieu, la liberté de l'homme, et l'origine du mal* (Amsterdam, 1710). English translation: *Theodicy*, trans. E. M. Huggard (Chicago: Open Court, 1990).
[20] See H. St. John Bolingbroke, *The Works of Lord Bolingbroke* (Philadelphia: Cary & Hart, 1841), pp. 365ff.
[21] See C. Wolff, *Theologia naturalis scientifica pertractata*, 2 vols (Frankfurt, 1736–7).
[22] See A. Pope, *The Poems of Alexander Pope*, ed. J. Butt (London: Methuen & Co. Ltd, 1963), pp. 501ff.
[23] Voltaire, *The Portable Voltaire*, ed. B. R. Redman (Harmonsworth: Penguin, 1949), pp. 74f.
[24] I. Kant, *Theoretical Philosophy 1755–1770*, trans. and ed. D. Walford and R. Meerbote (Cambridge: Cambridge University Press, 1992), pp. 71ff.

religious unity is hardly surprising: he knew only too well that the religious divisions of his age were responsible for many of Europe's political and social problems. The greatest causes of misery in the Europe of his day were not earthquakes or other natural disasters, but wars, persecution and intolerance, which were often grounded in religious differences, at least ostensibly.[25] As Leibniz saw it, to solve Europe's religious differences was thus to lay the groundwork for the political and social harmony of the European peoples, who would thence sing from the same hymn sheet, so to speak.

Arguably, however, Leibniz's vision for religious union did not stop at Europe's borders, and he entertained hopes for something even more ambitious, namely the religious union of the whole of mankind. Nowhere is this more apparent than in his attitude towards the Chinese. From the information about China that began to trickle back to Europe in the late seventeenth century, Leibniz sought to identify features common to Christian and (ancient) Chinese religious thought, on which to base a dialogue that would, he hoped, ultimately lead to religious convergence between the Europeans and Chinese of his day.[26] The feasibility of a dialogue was grounded in the fact that, in Leibniz's view, the ancient Chinese religion was 'quite in accord with *natural theology*' and indeed, in essence, 'pure Christianity, insofar as it renews the natural law inscribed in our hearts'.[27] Hence for Leibniz, religion was – or at least could be – a great unifier, not through the sort of forced conversions advocated by the Christian missionaries of the day, but through dialogue between cultures.

Leibniz's sense of the practical benefits of religious union is thus clear enough. But he also saw great practical benefits in promoting his vision of Christianity as a universal religion with a strong rational backbone. He believed that the promulgation of such a religion had the potential to defeat atheism (or at least to make atheism a rationally indefensible position), inspire a genuine love of God above all things and so open up the ultimate benefit of religion – namely, personal salvation – to all. The first part of this process, namely the move from philosophy to piety, was made possible by virtue of reason; as Leibniz insisted, 'A pagan philosopher can love God above all things, since reason can teach him that God is an infinitely

---

[25] For example, the Thirty Years War (1618–48), which ended shortly after Leibniz's birth, and the revocation of the Edict of Nantes (1685).
[26] See p. 335.
[27] Dutens IV, p. 188/WOC, p. 105.

perfect and a supremely lovable being.'[28] Of course, while reason of its own accord *can* teach every pagan that God is supremely lovable, in some cases it clearly has not done so (else there would be no pagans); in these cases, however, they can be convinced that God is supremely lovable if presented with the reasoning for it that they have not worked out themselves. In these ways, then, reason may lead to piety, that is, a genuine love of God above all things, which Leibniz tended to suppose would be sufficient for eternal salvation.[29] For Leibniz, then, salvation is not the preserve of a small minority fortunate enough to know and understand a core of vital (revealed) truths, but rather the upshot of a life lived in accordance with a genuine love of God, which anyone could potentially obtain.[30]

But according to Leibniz, the benefits of belief in truths about God were not just to be found in the afterlife, but in some cases could be felt very keenly in this life too. Thus he noted that belief in his doctrine of optimism, being as it was a successful defence of God's justice, had a number of 'practical consequences', namely:

> *First*, it follows that the world is governed in such a way that a wise person who is well informed about it will have nothing to find fault with … *Second*, every wise man should be content, not only by necessity, and as it were by a forced patience, but with pleasure and a kind of extreme satisfaction, knowing that everything will happen in such a way that the interests of each individual person persuaded of this truth will be looked after with every possible advantage … *Third*, we should love God above all things, since we find everything with greater perfection in him than in things themselves, and since his goodness is as valuable to us as our omnipotence … *Fourth*, by means of these opinions we can be happy in advance here below, before enjoying everything God has prepared for us.[31]

Hence a successful theodicy is not merely an intellectual achievement, but one with the potential to have a dramatic effect on the lives of those who understand the import of it. Such people have every reason to feel

---

[28] p. 142.
[29] See for example pp. 142–3, p. 154, and A I 6, pp. 78–9. In some texts, Leibniz suggests that a sincere love of God is not, by itself, sufficient for salvation, but that those who have it will be given whatever grace or other aids are required in order to be saved. See, for example, p. 247, p. 323; also Klopp IX, p. 304/LTS, p. 399; G VI, p. 157/H, p. 177.
[30] Hence Leibniz insists (p. 211), 'it is evident that a truly Christian theology is practical, and that the principal aim of Christ was to inspire sanctity of will rather than to plant notions of secret truths into the intellect'.
[31] p. 135.

contentment and satisfaction in this life, even if they suffer inconveniences or come up against other troubles.³² I have elsewhere termed this Leibniz's 'philosophy of contentment'.³³ He presented it often in his work,³⁴ and needless to say, practised what he preached, claiming

> I know no one happier than I am, because God gave me this understanding, as a result of which I envy no king; and I am certain that God takes special care of me, that is, that he has destined my mind for immense joys, in that he has opened to me such a certain and easy way of happiness.³⁵

Religion was thus, to Leibniz, the means by which one could bring about not just peace between different groups, cultures and nations, but also peace of mind to individuals in this life, and eternal happiness in the next.

Leibniz's Religious Views

Clearly, Leibniz's writings on religion need to be placed in this context, and approached in the knowledge that Leibniz was committed first and foremost to practice, with theory or speculation taking a supporting role; as he indicated to one correspondent, 'my aim has been not to pack the shops with books filled with nothing but air, but where possible to achieve something useful through them'.³⁶ The upshot of this is that Leibniz's writings sometimes appear to be shaped more by pragmatic or prudential considerations than by personal conviction. It has been suggested (for example) that Leibniz's interest in the Eucharist was motivated not by personal curiosity, but by his viewing it as a puzzle whose solution would satisfy others and – more importantly – contribute towards religious harmony in Europe.³⁷ His attempts to work out a satisfactory metaphysics of the resurrection of the same body seem similarly motivated, not least

---

³² For further information, see D. Rutherford, 'Leibniz and the Stoics: The Consolations of theodicy', in E. J. Kremer and M. J. Latzer (eds), *The Problem of Evil in Early Modern Philosophy* (University of Toronto Press: Toronto, 2001), pp. 138–64; LTS, pp. 40–8.
³³ See LTS, p. 34.
³⁴ See for example A VI 3, pp. 668–9/SLT, pp. 166–7; G VI, pp. 30–1/H, pp. 54–5, and G VI, pp. 267–8/H, pp. 282–3; A VI 4, p. 485; A VI 4, pp. 1535–6/L, p. 305.
³⁵ A VI 3, p. 477/DSR, p. 31. See also A I 17, p. 200.
³⁶ A II 1 (2nd edn), pp. 136–7.
³⁷ C. Wilson, *Leibniz's Metaphysics* (Manchester: Manchester University Press, 1989), p. 301. See also U. Goldenbaum, 'Spinoza's Parrot, Socinian Syllogisms, and Leibniz's Metaphysics: Leibniz's Three Strategies of Defending Christian Mysteries', *American Catholic Philosophical Quarterly* 76 (2002): 556–7.

because in his essay devoted to the topic, Leibniz states quite bluntly that there are no scriptural grounds to believe that it will be the same body that is resurrected.[38] The solution he goes on to offer, therefore, is not necessarily one that he would personally endorse; instead, it is for those who do believe in the resurrection of the same body. Perhaps the clearest example of all of Leibniz putting practical considerations over personal belief when working on religious matters comes from his commentary on the New Testament book of Revelation. Leibniz begins his study by noting that some in Europe had interpreted the prophecies of Revelation as pertaining to the present age, and were attempting to hasten the start of the Second Coming of Christ by fulfilling these prophecies themselves, a process that often involved creating civil unrest.[39] Concerned by this, Leibniz saw the need for 'a special interpretation of the *Revelation* that will cut off these dangerous thoughts once and for all'.[40] He thus suggested that Revelation and its prophecies be interpreted not as applying to the present day, or even to the future, but to events that had already taken place in the first century AD, that is, in the time of John, the book's author. As he very candidly explained, he was putting forward such a principle of interpretation not because it was the best, or because it was most correct, but because it was most conducive to social harmony and the public good.[41] What Leibniz's own views may have been on the meaning of Revelation are unknown.

Consequently, Leibniz's willingness to defend (on practical grounds) doctrines and positions to which he was apparently not personally committed means that determining his own religious views is no easy matter.[42] This is only compounded when one acknowledges certain circumstances of his life. By birth he was a Lutheran, although he was uncomfortable with the term.[43] He was presented with numerous opportunities to convert to Catholicism – often with the promise of personal advancement attached – but chose not to

---

[38] See pp. 305–6.
[39] For example, the Fifth Monarchists of England.
[40] p. 175.
[41] See p. 175.
[42] Similarly, when Leibniz disagreed with the teachings of other religions, or particular interpretations of Christian teachings, it was often on practical grounds rather than for rigid doctrinal reasons. Hence he criticizes various Christian splinter groups for being sectarian and divisive rather than for any serious error in doctrine. See for example p. 153 and p. 156. He reserved the same ire for those of the mainstream branches of Christianity who engaged in sectarianism and who condemned those of different faiths. See for example A I 14, p. 743.
[43] See A I 7, p. 257.

take them.⁴⁴ In spite of his apparent commitment to Lutheranism, Leibniz did not attend church often, and his scanty church attendance, along with his refusal to take communion,⁴⁵ earned him a reputation in Hanover as a non-believer. Locals playfully referred to him as 'Glaubenichts', that is, one who believes in nothing.⁴⁶ While it seems farfetched to suppose Leibniz had no religious beliefs at all, it is far from clear what beliefs he did have. This has led scholars to wildly different interpretations of Leibniz's religiosity. In the nineteenth century, Charles William Russell suggested that Leibniz was in fact a Catholic, at least privately.⁴⁷ More recently, Stuart Brown and Shelby Hunt have suggested that Leibniz was a deist,⁴⁸ and George MacDonald Ross has described him as a pagan metaphysician.⁴⁹ Meanwhile, Allison Coudert has emphasized Leibniz's sympathy with the Kabbalah,⁵⁰ and Maria Rosa Antognazza has sought to show the depth of Leibniz's Christian beliefs.⁵¹ While some of these suggestions are very much overdrawn, being based on a consideration of a relatively narrow range of Leibniz's writings, all enjoy some textual support. It is thus no wonder that Richard Popkin once asked: 'Do we have to have two, or maybe three, or four Leibnizes to make him compatible …?'⁵² While that undoubtedly goes too far, it does emphasize the difficulty in ascertaining the personal views of someone who was prepared to put his name to doctrines he did not himself hold if he felt it was in the public interest to do so. Perhaps, then, Leibniz's most deeply held belief was not in this or that religious creed or doctrine,

---

⁴⁴ See for example A I 6, p. 229; A II 2 (2nd edn), p. 227.
⁴⁵ See *Leibniz und Landgraf Ernst von Hessen-Rheinfels*, ed. C. von Rommel, 2 vols (Frankfurt, 1847), II: p. 107.
⁴⁶ In the Hanoverian dialect, 'Glaubenichts' was pronounced 'glöwenix', which gave rise to the pun on Leibniz's name common in Hanover at the time: 'Leibniz glöwenix': Leibniz believes in nothing. See *Aus den Briefen der Herzogin Elisabeth Charlotte von Orléans an die Sophie Kurfürstin von Hannover*, ed. E. Bodemann, 2 vols (Hanover: Hahn, 1891), II: p. 292.
⁴⁷ C. W. Russell, 'Protestant Evidence of Catholicity', *The Dublin Review* 10 (1841): 429.
⁴⁸ See S. Brown, 'The Regularization of Providence in Post-Cartesian Philosophy', in R. Crocker (ed.) *Religion, Reason and Nature in Early Modern Europe* (Dordrecht: Kluwer, 2001), p. 3; Shelby D. Hunt, *Controversy in Marketing Theory: For Reason, Realism, Truth, and Objectivity* (New York: M. E. Sharpe, 2003), p. 33.
⁴⁹ G. MacDonald Ross, 'Leibniz and the Origin of Things', in, M. Dascal and E. Yakira (eds), *Leibniz and Adam* (Tel Aviv: University Publishing Projects Ltd, 1993), p. 252.
⁵⁰ See A. Coudert, *Leibniz and the Kabbalah* (Dordrecht: Kluwer, 1995). Coudert stops short of saying that Leibniz was a Kabbalist, but claims that he was sympathetic to – and strongly influenced by – Kabbalistic doctrines.
⁵¹ See M. R. Antognazza, *Leibniz on the Trinity and the Incarnation* (London: Yale University Press, 2007).
⁵² R. H. Popkin, *The Third Force in Seventeenth-Century Thought* (Leiden: Brill, 1992), p. 282. It should be noted that Popkin's question was intended to be rhetorical.

but in what religion could and should be, namely a force for good, bringing people together and enriching their lives. To that ideal, at least, Leibniz's commitment was certain, and unwavering.

About the Texts and Translations

It is often noted (and lamented) by scholars that Leibniz left no magnum opus that laid out the whole of his philosophical system. It is noted much less often, if at all, that he left no great, definitive work detailing his theological system either (if indeed he had such a thing). While Leibniz did write lengthy works in which he expounded his theological views, namely the so-called *Examen religionis christianae* of 1686,[1] and the *Theodicée* of 1710, neither can plausibly be considered the definitive source of Leibniz's theological views, nor indeed can any single work of the 50,000 writings that remain to us of his Nachlass. Instead, Leibniz's theological system is scattered among his writings like fragmentary tesserae, and has to be reconstructed accordingly. To assist with this task, seventy-one of these pieces are collected together in this volume.

In the early stages of planning this volume I decided that it should focus on the philosophical side of Leibniz's theology, interpreted quite broadly to cover not just the existence and nature of God, but also other areas in which philosophy and theology intersect (at least for Leibniz), such as the interpretation of Scripture, ethics, certain doctrinal issues like the Trinity and the afterlife, reactions to non-Christian religions, etc. Notably absent from this volume are any of Leibniz's writings connected with Church reunion efforts, by which I understand efforts to reunite the Catholic and Protestant Churches, and those to reunite the different Protestant sects. The chief reason for not including such writings is that it would have been impossible to do them justice here: a relatively small selection from them totalling c. 12,000–15,000 words (which is all that I could have devoted to them in this volume) seemed pointless. To do justice to the reunion writings would require a large volume devoted just to them, and it is to be hoped that such a volume may be available in English before too long.

---

[1] A VI 4, pp. 2356–455. English translation: *System of Theology*, ed. and trans. C. W. Russell (London: Burns & Lambert, 1850).

In any case, it is not just writings concerned with Church reunion that have been omitted. Even leaving the reunion writings aside, Leibniz's writings on God and religion are voluminous, and choosing which writings to include and which to omit was not an easy task. I have sought to favour those that, together, would enable a reader to get a well-rounded understanding of Leibniz's practical theology, broadly understood, and (where relevant) to track diachronic changes in his thinking. I do not doubt that arguments could be had about whether such-and-such a text should have been included in place of one of those I have selected, but this is inevitable: with any anthology, there are bound to be disagreements about the relative importance of certain texts. The only way around this is to produce not a selective anthology, but a volume that includes everything of relevance (or, indeed, everything). In the case of Leibniz's writings on God and religion, this would be prohibitively large.

This volume is presented as a scholarly edition, in which the texts have been carefully translated from the most reliable sources, usually the original manuscripts, or, where this was not possible (because the manuscripts had been lost), from the best available source. I have sought to capture all philosophically-interesting deletions and marginalia.

Some of the writings in this volume are drawn from Leibniz's correspondence, but at the suggestion of anonymous reviewers secured by the press I have given these descriptive titles so that it is clear what these writings are about. So, for example, Leibniz's letter to John Toland of 30 April 1709 is here given the title 'Ancient and modern understandings of God' (pp. 90–1), which I take to be a fair description of what is discussed. Each text is prefaced with a short introduction detailing its source and, where known, background information regarding its composition.

Recommended Further Reading

Only English-language works are mentioned.

Works by Leibniz

Many of the standard English-language anthologies of Leibniz's philosophical works contain one or more texts concerning God and religion. The following volumes, however, contain texts entirely concerned with those subjects:

Leibniz, G. W. (1990), *Theodicy*, trans. E. M. Huggard, Chicago: Open Court.
Leibniz, G. W. (2005), *Confessio Philosophi*, trans. Robert C. Sleigh, Jr, New Haven: Yale University Press.
Leibniz, G. W. (2011), *Dissertation on Predestination and Grace*, trans. Michael Murray, New Haven: Yale University Press.

Works on Leibniz

Books: Authored

Adams, R. (1994), *Leibniz: Determinist, Theist, Idealist*, Oxford: Oxford University Press.
Antognazza, M. R. (2007), *Leibniz on the Trinity and the Incarnation: Reason and Revelation in the Seventeenth Century*, trans. Gerald Parks, New Haven: Yale University Press.
Antognazza, M. R. and Hotson, H. (1999), *Alsted and Leibniz on God, the Magistrate and the Millennium*, Wiesbaden: Harrassowitz.
Carlson, A. (2001), *The Divine Ethic of Creation in Leibniz*, New York: Peter Lang.
Jordan, G. J. (1927), *The Reunion of the Churches: A Study of G. W. Leibnitz and His Great Attempt*, London: Constable.

Poma, A. (2013), *The Impossibility and Necessity of Theodicy: The "Essais" of Leibniz*, trans. Alice Spencer, Dordrecht: Springer.

Strickland, L. (2006), *Leibniz Reinterpreted*, London: Continuum.

Books: Edited

Coudert, A. P., Popkin, R. H. and Weiner, G. M. (1998), *Leibniz, Mysticism and Religion*, Dordrecht: Kluwer.

Dascal, M. and Yakira, E. (1993), *Leibniz and Adam*, Tel Aviv: University Publishing Projects Ltd.

Jorgensen, L. M. and Newlands, S. (2014), *New Essays on Leibniz's Theodicy*, Oxford: Oxford University Press.

Articles and chapters

Adams, R. M. (1994), 'Leibniz's *Examination of the Christian Religion*', *Faith and Philosophy* 11: 517–46.

Almond, I. (2006), 'Leibniz, Historicism, and the "Plague of Islam"', *Eighteenth Century Studies* 39: 463–83.

Anfray, J.-P. (2002), 'God's Decrees and Middle Knowledge: Leibniz and the Jesuits', *American Catholic Philosophical Quarterly* 76: 647–70.

Antognazza, M. R. (2002), 'Leibniz on Religious Toleration: The Correspondence with Paul Pellisson-Fontanier', *American Catholic Philosophical Quarterly* 76: 601–22.

Antognazza, M. R. (2013), 'Natural and Supernatural Mysteries: Leibniz's *Annotatiunculae subitaneae* on Toland's *Christianity not Mysterious*', in W. Schröder (ed.), *Gestalten des Deismus in Europa*, Wiesbaden: Harrassowitz Verlag, 29–40.

Backus, I. (2013), 'G. W. Leibniz and Protestant Scholasticism in the Years 1698–1704', in J. J. Ballor, D. S. Sytsma and J. Zuidema (eds), *Church and School in Early Modern Protestantism*, Leiden: Brill.

Bardon, A. (2001), 'Leibniz on the Epistemic Status of the Mysteries', *Philosophy & Theology* 13: 143–58.

Blumenfeld, D. (1974), 'Leibniz's Proof of the Uniqueness of God', *Studia Leibnitiana* 6: 262–71.

Blumenfeld, D. (1995), 'Leibniz's Ontological and Cosmological Arguments', in N. Jolley (ed.), *The Cambridge Companion to Leibniz*, Cambridge: Cambridge University Press.

Blumenfeld, D. (1995), 'Perfection and Happiness in the Best Possible World', in N. Jolley (ed.), *The Cambridge Companion to Leibniz*, Cambridge: Cambridge University Press.

Brown, G. (1988), 'Leibniz's Theodicy and the Confluence of Worldly Goods', *Journal of the History of Philosophy* 26: 571-91.
Brown, G. (1995), 'Miracles in the Best of all Possible Worlds: Leibniz's Dilemma and Leibniz's Razor', *History of Philosophy Quarterly* 12: 19-38.
Brown, G. (2005), 'Leibniz's Mathematical Argument Against a Soul of the World', *British Journal for the History of Philosophy* 13: 449-88.
Brown, S. (1998), 'Soul, Body and Natural Immortality', *The Monist* 81: 573-90.
Brown, S. (2007), 'Leibniz and Robert Boyle: Reason and Faith: Rationalism and Voluntarism', in P. Phemister and S. Brown (eds), *Leibniz and the English-Speaking World*, Dordrecht: Springer.
Carlin, L. (2002), 'Reward and Punishment in the Best Possible World', *The Southern Journal of Philosophy* 60: 139-60.
Cook, D. J. (1990), 'Leibniz: Biblical Historian and Exegete', in I. Marchlewitz and A. Heinekamp (eds), *Leibniz' Auseinandersetzung mit Vorgängern und Zeitgenossen*, Stuttgart: Franz Steiner Verlag.
Cook, D. J. (2008), 'Leibniz on Creation: A Contribution to his Philosophical Theology', in M. Dascal (ed.), *Leibniz: What Kind of Rationalist?*, Dordrecht: Springer.
Cook, D. J. (2008), 'Leibniz: The Hebrew Bible, Hebraism and Rationalism', in D. J. Cook, H. Rudolph and C. Schulte (eds), *Leibniz und Das Judentum*, Stuttgart: Franz Steiner Verlag.
Cook, D. J. (2009), 'Leibniz on "Prophets", Prophecy, and Revelation', *Religious Studies* 45: 269-87.
Cook, D. J. and Strickland, L. (2011), 'Leibniz and Millenarianism', in F. Beiderbeck and S. Waldhoff (eds), *Pluralität der Perspektiven und Einheit der Wahrheit im Werk von G. W. Leibniz*, Berlin: Akademie Verlag.
Davidson, J. D. (2005), 'Video Meliora Proboque, Deteriora Sequor: Leibniz on the Intellectual Source of Sin', in D. Rutherford and J. A. Cover (eds), *Leibniz: Nature and Freedom*, Oxford: Oxford University Press.
Fouke, D. (1994), 'Emanation and the Perfections of Being: Divine Causation and the Autonomy of Nature in Leibniz', *Archiv für Geschichte der Philosophie* 76: 168-94.
Fouke, D. C. (1992), 'Metaphysics and the Eucharist in the Early Leibniz', *Studia Leibnitiana* 24: 145-59.
Franklin, J. (2002), 'Two Caricatures, II: Leibniz's Best World', *International Journal for Philosophy of Religion* 52: 45-56.
Garber, D. (2009), 'Leibniz, Theology and the Mechanical Philosophy', in V. Alexandrescu (ed.), *Branching Off: The Early Moderns in Quest for the Unity of Knowledge*, Bucharest: Zeta Books.
Goldenbaum, U. (1999), 'Transubstantiation, Physics and Philosophy at the

Time of the *Catholic Demonstrations*', in S. Brown (ed.), *The Young Leibniz and His Philosophy*, Dordrecht: Kluwer.

Goldenbaum, U. (2002), 'Spinoza's Parrot, Socinian Syllogisms, and Leibniz's Metaphysics: Leibniz's Three Strategies of Defending Christian Mysteries', *American Catholic Philosophical Quarterly* 76: 551–74.

Griffin, M. V. (1999), 'Leibniz on God's Knowledge of Counterfactuals', *The Philosophical Review* 108: 317–43.

Hillman, T. A. (2013), 'Leibniz and Luther on the Non-Cognitive Component of Faith', *Sophia* 52: 219–34.

Hillman, T. A. and Borland, T. (2011), 'Leibniz and the Imitation of God: A Criticism of Voluntarism', *Philosophy & Theology* 23: 3–27.

Jespers, F. P. M. (2008), 'Universal Religion, Contingency, and Truth in Leibniz', in D.-M. Grube and P. Jonkers (eds), *Religions Challenged by Contingency: Theological and Philosophical Approaches to the Problem of Contingency*, Leiden: Brill.

Kremer, E. J. (2001), 'Leibniz and the "Disciples of Saint Augustine" on the Fate of Infants who Die Unbaptized', in E. J. Kremer and M. J. Latzer (eds), *The Problem of Evil in Early Modern Philosophy*, Toronto: University of Toronto Press.

Kulstad, M. (2002), 'Exploring Middle Ground: Was Leibniz's Conception of God ever Spinozistic?', *American Catholic Philosophical Quarterly* 76: 671–90.

Laerke, M. (2010), 'The Golden Rule: Aspects of Leibniz's Method for Religious Controversy', in M. Dascal (ed.), *The Practice of Reason: Leibniz and His Controversies*, Amsterdam: John Benjamins Publishing Company.

Lee, S. (2004), 'Leibniz on Divine Concurrence', *The Philosophical Review* 113: 203–48.

Lodge, P. (2016), 'Theodicy, Metaphysics, and Metaphilosophy in Leibniz', *Philosophical Topics*, forthcoming.

Lodge, P. and Crowe, B. (2002), 'Leibniz, Bayle, and Locke on Faith and Reason', *American Catholic Philosophical Quarterly* 76: 575–600.

Lin, M. (2011), 'Leibniz's Philosophical Theology', in B. C. Look (ed.), *The Continuum Companion to Leibniz*, London: Continuum.

Losonsky, M. (2012), 'Locke and Leibniz on Religious Faith', *British Journal for the History of Philosophy* 20: 703–21.

Mercer, C. (2002), 'Leibniz on Knowledge and God', *American Catholic Philosophical Quarterly* 76: 531–50.

Moll, K. (1999), '*Deus sive harmonia universalis est ultima ratio rerum*: The Conception of God in Leibniz's Early Philosophy', in S. Brown (ed.), *The Young Leibniz and His Philosophy*, Dordrecht: Kluwer.

Murray, M. J. (1995), 'Leibniz on Divine Foreknowledge of Future Contingents and Human Freedom', *Philosophy and Phenomenological Research* 55: 75–108.

Murray, M. J. (2002), 'Leibniz's Proposal for Theological Reconciliation Among the Protestants', *American Catholic Philosophical Quarterly* 76: 623–46.

Nelson, E. S. (2009), 'Leibniz and China: Religion, Hermeneutics, and Enlightenment', *Religion in the Age of Enlightenment* 1: 277–300.

Newlands, S. (2014), 'Leibniz on Privations, Limitations, and the Metaphysics of Evil', *Journal of the History of Philosophy* 52: 281–308.

Pactwa, D. P. (2009), 'Leibniz's God: Cosmic Calculator and his Freedom of Willing the Best of all Possible Worlds', *Bijdragen, International Journal in Philosophy and Theology* 70: 304–36.

Phemister, P. (2007), 'Leibniz and God's Freedom to Create', *Revue Roumaine de Philosophie* 51: 3–19.

Ribas, A. (2003), 'Leibniz' *Discourse on the Natural Theology of the Chinese* and the Leibniz-Clarke Controversy', *Philosophy East and West* 53: 64–86.

Riley, P. (1983), 'Leibniz' Unpublished Remarks on the Abbé Bucquoi's Proof of the Existence of God (1711)', *Studia Leibnitiana* 15: 215–20.

Rudolph, H. (2008), 'The Authority of the Bible and the Authority of Reason in Leibniz's Ecumenical Argument', in M. Dascal (ed.), *Leibniz: What Kind of Rationalist?*, Dordrecht: Springer.

Rudolph, H. (2010), 'Leibniz vs. Jablonski: An Intestine Struggle on Uniting the Protestant Camp', in M. Dascal (ed.), *The Practice of Reason: Leibniz and His Controversies*, Amsterdam: John Benjamins Publishing Company.

Rutherford, D. (2001), 'Leibniz and the Stoics: The Consolations of Theodicy', in E. J. K. and M. J. Latzer (eds), *The Problem of Evil in Early Modern Philosophy*, Toronto: University of Toronto Press.

Schmaltz, T. M. (2010), 'Malebranche and Leibniz on the Best of all Possible Worlds', *The Southern Journal of Philosophy* 48: 28–48.

Sleigh, Jr, R. C. (1996), 'Leibniz's First Theodicy', *Noûs vol. 30 supplement: Philosophical Perspectives, 10, Metaphysics*: 481–99.

Sleigh, R. (1994), 'Leibniz on Divine Foreknowledge', *Faith and Philosophy* 11: 547–71.

Sleigh, Jr, R. C. (2001), 'Remarks on Leibniz's Treatment of the Problem of Evil', in E. J. K. and M. J. Latzer (eds), *The Problem of Evil in Early Modern Philosophy*, Toronto: University of Toronto Press.

Strickland, L. (2006), 'Leibniz on Whether the World Increases in Perfection', *British Journal for the History of Philosophy* 14: 51–68.

Strickland, L. (2009), 'Leibniz on Eternal Punishment', *British Journal for the History of Philosophy* 17: 307–31.

Strickland, L. (2009), 'Leibniz, the "Flower of Substance", and the Resurrection of the Same Body', *The Philosophical Forum* 40: 391–410.

Strickland, L. (2010), 'False Optimism? Leibniz, Evil, and the Best of all Possible Worlds', *Forum Philosophicum* 15: 17–35.

Strickland, L. (2010), 'Leibniz's Philosophy of Purgatory', *American Catholic Philosophical Quarterly* 84: 531–48.

Strickland, L. (2011), 'Leibniz's Universal Rational Religion', in H. Breger and J. Herbst (eds), *Natur und Subjekt*, Berlin: Akademie Verlag.

Strickland, L. (2011), 'Taking Scripture Seriously: Leibniz and the Jehoshaphat Problem', *The Heythrop Journal* 52: 40–51.

Strickland, L. (2016), 'Leibniz's Harmony between the Kingdoms of Nature and Grace', *Archiv für Geschichte der Philosophie*, forthcoming.

Vailati, E. (2002), 'Leibniz on Divine Concurrence with Secondary Causes', *British Journal for the History of Philosophy* 10: 209–30.

Wampler, E. (1996–7), 'God, Beauty, and Evil in Leibniz's Best of all Possible Worlds', *Proceedings of the Heraclitean Society* 18: 133–42.

Webb, M. O. (1989), 'Natural Theology and the Concept of Perfection in Descartes, Spinoza and Leibniz', *Religious Studies* 25: 459–75.

1

The *Catholic Demonstrations*

1. Sketch of *Catholic Demonstrations* (1668–9 (?))[1]

Manuscript:

M: LH I, 7, 6 Bl. 44–5.

Transcription:

A: A VI 1, pp. 494–500.

During his time at the Catholic court of Mainz, working for Baron Christian von Boineburg (1622–72), Leibniz undertook a grand theological project, the so-called *Catholic Demonstrations*, intended to be a systematic apology for the Christian faith built upon the framework of Catholicism. The following text is the plan of the *Catholic Demonstrations* project. It is not an easy text to read, in part because much of it is in note form rather than good prose; the text is also replete with names of authors whose works are to be discussed, most of which are unknown today. Nevertheless, the plan offers important insights into the young Leibniz's beliefs and activities *vis-à-vis* religion; the plan also reveals the sheer scale of the project, and indeed of Leibniz's ambition, which underwrote it. As it happens, Leibniz did not come close to completing the *Catholic Demonstrations*; indeed, he scarcely even started it, as only a handful of short pieces were ever written for it, and these were of

---

[1] Author's title. From the Latin. Complete.

the form of preliminary studies rather than finished chapters (these studies included texts on grace,[2] the Eucharist[3] and the Incarnation).[4]

The manuscript consists of the main plan on the left hand side of the page, and marginal notes on some of the parts of the plan on the right (this structure is duplicated here). The main plan cannot have been written earlier than 1668 because it mentions Becher's *Methodus Didactica* (1668), while the marginal notes cannot have been written earlier than 1669, since they mention Mauritius's *Consiliorum chilonensium specimen* (1669).

SKETCH OF CATHOLIC DEMONSTRATIONS

The prolegomena will cover the Elements of Philosophy. That is, the first principles of Metaphysics (on Being), of Logic (on mind), of Mathematics (on space), of Physics (on matter) and of Practical Philosophy (on the state).

In the Elements of Philosophy, words will be used in their popular sense, not Scholastic sense, in order not to give rise to harsh-sounding and scandalous conclusions, which is the beginning of Jansenism.

Part I. Demonstration of the Existence of God.
Chapter 1. Demonstration from this principle, that there is nothing without a reason.
Chapter 2. Demonstration from this principle, that motion cannot take place without continuous creation.
Chapter 3. Demonstration from this principle, that there is no origin of motion in bodies.
Chapter 4. Demonstration from this principle, that there is no origin of solidity in bodies.
Chapter 5. Demonstration of the infinite probability, or moral certainty, that the beauty of the world arises from a mind.

This can be held back for Part 3, Chapter 13.

The Scholastics have multiplied terms without necessity, but we are largely able to do without them for philosophizing solidly. NB – no common opinion from Scholastic theologians is to be explicitly condemned, although those may be cited from which there follows an opinion that should be condemned. Each *Index Expurgatorius* should be consulted, and a reason for the

---

[2] See A VI 1, pp. 535–6.
[3] See A VI 1, pp. 501–17. Two of these texts are included in this volume: 'On transubstantiation' (pp. 35–42), and 'On the demonstration of the possibility of the mysteries of the Eucharist' (pp. 42–6).
[4] See A VI 1, pp. 532–5.

Chapter 6. The paralogisms committed by some in the demonstrating of God's existence, especially Descartes,⁶ Ward⁷ (Hogelande is to be considered here)⁸ and Valerianus M.⁹
Chapter 7. The paralogisms of atheists against the existence of God. Vanini in his dialogues.¹⁰ The authors of the book on the three imposters.¹¹

Part II. Demonstration of the Immortality of the Soul, or of Incorporeality.

Chapter 1. From the immediate experience of thought.

Chapter 2. From the infinite replicability of reflection, because every sensation is an enduring reaction (see Hobbes),¹⁴ but this is not so in bodies.¹⁵

decision should be given, where appropriate.⁵
La Philosophie Chrestienne ou les mystères de la Foy prouez par raisons naturelles (Paris, 1639), a book reported in a catalogue which Schönwelterus has given me, among the unbound books, in quarto, no. 44.

Doctrinae antiquae de natura animae (London, 1654), by C. Gaderus, in duodecimo,¹² in *Catalogus Ubbenii.*¹³
NB. Just as angles do not make a point divisible, so ideas do not make God or a mind divisible. For points really are situated in an angle, as minds are in a point.
Minds are not conscious of all their own actions, for otherwise they would reflect on any reflection whatsoever, and could not make progress.

---

⁵ The *Index Expurgatorius* was a list of books prohibited to Roman Catholics unless the errors they contained were corrected.
⁶ See René Descartes, *Principia philosophiae* (Amsterdam, 1644).
⁷ See Samuel Ward, *Tentamen de Dei existentia et animae immortalitate demonstranda* (Oxford, 1642).
⁸ See Cornelius van Hogelande, *Cogitationes, quibus Dei existentia item animae spiritualitas et possibilis cum corpore unio demonstrantur* (Amsterdam, 1646).
⁹ See Valerianus Magnus, *Concussio fundamentorum fidei catholicae, jactata ab H. Conringio* (Straubing, 1645).
¹⁰ See Lucilio Vanini, *De admirandis naturae reginae, deaeque mortalium, arcarás liber IV* (Paris, 1616).
¹¹ See [Anonymous], *Liber de tribus impostoribus* (written 1598). The three imposters were the three Abrahamic religions: Judaism, Christianity and Islam.
¹² See C. D. L. H. Gaderus, *Doctrinae antiquae de natura animae et diverso ejus diversis temporibus statu nova instauratio, quae ad exercitationes* (London, 1654).
¹³ See *Catalogus variorum et insignium librorum, praecipue theologicorum (cum appendice aliorum) Martini Ubbenii* (1661).
¹⁴ Leibniz probably has in mind here Thomas Hobbes, *De corpore*, IV.25.2.
¹⁵ bodies. | ¶ Chapter 3. Corollaries from this: explanation of the origin of the soul through traduction. Chapter 4. How the mind may be in a place, and how it acts on the body. | *deleted*.

Chapter 3. From the wonderful construction of dreams.

Therefore one is conscious of one's own actions when one wills them.
NB. What Colomies reports in his *Opuscula* about the dream of Gilbert Gaulmin, who was working on a Greek poem.[16] Add *Prima Scaligerana*, on Brugnolus,[17] likewise the short history of Johann de la Marre in *Guieti vita*,[18] which I believe was prefixed to Boeckler's edition of Terence.[19]

Chapter 4. From the thinking of incorporeal things.

Chapter 5. On ἐξ αὐτοκινήσεως,[20] following Plato.

NB. A History of Miracles is to be compiled from extant public records. Add Jordan's *De eo quod Divinum aut Supernaturale*,[21] Mauritius's *De denunciatione sagarum* and *Consiliorum*,[22] Heer's *Observationes*.[23] Barthelemy Faye.[24] Silvestro Pietrasanta's *Thaumasia*,[25] although it is wonderfully fabulous. Add de la Mare from Dijon, where similar.

---

[16] Paul Colomies, *Opuscula* (Paris, 1668), p. 98.
[17] See J. J. Scaliger, *Prima Scaligerana* (Utrecht, 1670), pp. 23–4.
[18] See Johann Albrecht Portner, *De Francisci Guieti vita* (1657).
[19] See Publius Terentius, *Sex comoediae cum annotationibus J. H. Boecleri* (Strasbourg, 1657).
[20] 'self-motion'.
[21] See Hieronymus Jordan, *De eo quod Divinum aut Supernaturale est in morbis humani corporis* (Frankfurt, 1651).
[22] See Erich Mauritius, *De denunciatione sagarum* (Tübingen, 1664); *Consiliorum chilonensium specimen, sive responsa de jure XXX* (Kiel, 1669).
[23] See Henri de Heer, *Observationes Medicae oppido rarae in Spa et Leodii animadversa* (Lüttich, 1645).
[24] Barthelemy Faye, *Energumenicus ejusdem Alexicacus* (Paris, 1571).
[25] See Silvestro Pietrasanta, *Thaumasia verae religionis contra perfidiam sectarum* (Rome, 1644).

Chapter 6. The demonstration by the most illustrious Kenelm Digby, in the book on the immortality of the soul.[26]

Part III. Demonstration of the Possibility of the Mysteries of the Christian Faith.

Chapter 1. The extent of God's eternity, against Boëthius, and Scholastics on eternity, age, time.
Chapter 2. The extent of omniscience, against middle knowledge.
Chapter 3. The extent of omnipotence, against Wycliffe and Hobbes.
On the mere possibility of future things.
Chapter 3.[27] Explanation of the composition of ideas in God and another mind, with the help of the centre point, following the views of Johannes Michaelius in his book *de Visu*.[28]

Chapter 4. The extent of God's omnipresence, and the multipresence of any other mind whatsoever, against Conrad Vorstius, and the Scholastics on the impletive, circumscriptive and definitive 'where'.[29]
Chapter 5. The possibility of triunity, indeed its necessity, through the composition of that which understands, that which is understood and the act of understanding.

Regarding a single philosophical and theological truth, against the Averroists, Hofmann and Slevogt.
All these are mere hypotheses. And a hypothesis is nothing other than the giving of a possible cause, i.e. an explanation of a possible mode.

How God knows all things, and how all properties are contained in a definition, can be wonderfully illustrated with the example of number, for instance he who knows that 3 is 1 + 1 + 1.

---

[26] See Kenelm Digby, *Demonstratio immortalitatis animae rationalis, sive tractatus duo philosophici* (Paris, 1655).
[27] The duplication in chapter numbers is Leibniz's own, and presumably a mistake.
[28] See Johannes Michaelius, *Oculi fabrica, actio, usus, sive de natura visus* (Lyon, 1649).
[29] 'It is known that there are three ways something is said to be in a place, namely circumscriptively, definitively and repletively. Something is said to be in a place circumscriptively when a beginning, middle and end in place can be attributed to it, or when its parts are commensurate to the parts of the place, and in this sense alone is a body in a place. Something is said to be in a place definitively insofar as it is here and not elsewhere, and in this sense angels are in a place ... Something is said to be in a place repletively because it fills the place, and in this sense it is said that God is in every place because he fills every place.' Albertus de Orlamunde, *Summa naturalium*, 1.11, in Albertus Magnus, *Opera omnia*, ed. Auguste Borgnet, 38 vols (Paris, 1890), vol. 5, p. 455.

ἐξ ἑνὸς, πάντων καὶ πανθένώσει.³⁰ *From the agreement of universals with a third thing.* How the third thing may arise, and how it has proceeded from individuals.

Chapter 6. An outline of the same thing with regard to space: from the point, the line and the surface; and with regard to body, from matter, shape and motion.

Chapter 7. Warding off the darts of the Socinians.

Chapter 8. The procession of the Holy Spirit from the Father and the Son, against the Greeks.

Chapter 9. A harmonious explanation is given for why only the second person of the deity was incarnated.

Chapter 10. How God may be the Father, the source of the deity, and yet be coeternal with the other persons: the Father is prior in nature, not in time.

Chapter 11. That *ad intra* actions are divided, but *ad extra* works are undivided.³¹

Chapter 12. The possibility of creation, from its necessity in all those things that are moved. Part I chapter 2.

Chapter 13. The nature of angels.

Chapter 14. The origin of the first human mind explained by means of a separated portion of divine breath.³²

NB. The origin of the first mind from God, educted from active potency, the origin of the first body from nothing, educted from objective potency. The origin of the world from chaos, and an explanation of the seven days according to the hypothesis of Descartes and Regius.³³

---

³⁰ 'from one comes also complete unification'.

³¹ The distinction between God's internal actions, or relations with himself ('ad intra'), and his external actions, or relations with things outside of him ('ad extra'), has been common in the discussions of the Trinity since the time of Augustine. See Augustine, *De Trinitate*.

³² The description is reminiscent of Genesis 2.7, in which God breathes life into man, but the phrase Leibniz uses here ('divinae particulam aurae') is in fact from Horace, *Satires*, II.2.79.

³³ On several occasions Descartes had indicated his interest in producing a reconciliation of his

Chapter 15. The propagation of the human mind through traduction from God, explained with a new argument from the divisibility of an indivisible point.
Chapter 16. Freedom of minds, and the necessity of bodies. Against the predeterminators on this matter, and this should be continued.
Chapter 17. To what extent men are obligated to God, and God to men; men by strict right, condignly; God by right, broadly speaking, i.e. congruously. Thomas Bradwardine,[34] Juan Caramuel.[35]
Chapter 18. That God is absolutely not the cause of the evil of guilt, but is the *per accidens* cause of the evil of punishment. Jacob Martini and Jakob Thomasius.[36]
Chapter 19. That the forbidden fruit in Paradise was a poison that has destroyed the image of God and introduced original sin. R. Otreb and Thomas Albius.[37]
Chapter 20. On the essence and propagation of original sin, against Flacians, Manicheans, Gnostics and Platonists.
Chapter 21. On the cause of sin, against Philippe de Mornay and Eilhard Lubinus.[38]
Chapter 22. On the Incarnation of the Son of God.

Explanation of auxiliary grace, which in no way detracts from free will. On the end of life etc. NB. Auxiliary graces no more detract from freedom than taking advice constrains one's deliberating.

---

philosophy with the first chapter of Genesis, which details the first seven days of the world. See *Œuvres de Descartes*, ed. C. Adam and P. Tannery, 12 vols (Paris: Léopold Cerf, 1897–1910), IV: p. 698; René Descartes, *The Philosophical Writings of Descartes*, trans. John Cottingham, Robert Stoothoff, Dugald Murdoch and Anthony Kenny, 3 vols (Cambridge: Cambridge University Press, 1984–91), III, p. 172 and p. 349.

[34] See Thomas Bradwardine, *De causa Dei contra Pelagium et de virtute causarum ad suos Mertonenses libri III* (London, 1618).

[35] See Juan Caramuel Lobkowitz, *Theologia moralis fundamentalis, praeterintentionalis, decalogica, sacramentalis, canonica, regularis, civilis, militaris* (Frankfurt, 1652).

[36] See Jacob Martini, *Tractatus de causa peccati* (Wittenberg, 1641), and Jakob Thomasius, *An Deus sit causa peccati per accidens* (unpublished manuscript).

[37] See Rudolfo Otreb [pseudonym; real name: Robert Fludd], *Tractatus Theologo-Philosophicus* (Oppenheim, 1617), and Thomas White, *A Catechism of Christian Doctrin* (Paris, 1659, 2nd edn). White went by several names, Thomas Anglus and Thomas Albius being the most common.

[38] See Philippe de Mornay, *De veritate religionis christianae liber* (Antwerp, 1583), and Eilhard Lubinus, *Phosphorus, de prima causa & natura mali* (Rostock, 1601).

Chapter 23. On Noah's ark. Joannes Buteo and Gaspar Schott.[39]
Chapter 24. On the Tower of Babel. Bochart's *Phaleg*.[40] Duret on languages.[41] Besold on languages,[42] Thomas Albius's *Tractatus*,[43] Becher's *Methodus Didactica*.[44]
Chapter 25. On Lot's wife, turned into a pillar of salt.
Chapter 26. That aside from one Incarnation, it is probable that no divine miracles have taken place (angelic miracles are another matter), but that the appearance of them arises perhaps from the ordinary course of nature determined beforehand to this end.
Chap. 27. On the congruence of the Incarnation, or: why God was made man. St Anselm's book, *Cur Deus homo*?
Chapter 28. On the mode of the Incarnation, against the Arians and Nestorians.
Chapter 28a. On the same against the Eutychians.
Chapter 29. Against the Lutheran communication of certain properties, of deity in humanity, or against the Ubiquitarians.
Chapter 30. On the Tübingen-Giessen Ταπεινοσιγραφίας controversy.[46]

How in the feeding of the 5000 the part is greater than the whole. It is explained from the nature of growth and development. See Boyle's experiment about the tree thriving in the watery vessel, in *The Sceptical Chymist*.[45]

On the nature of subsistence, against the Scotists; life is subsistence that is apparent. NB. All things are constantly moved.

---

[39] See Joannes Buteo [pseudonym; real name: Jean Borrel], *De arca Noe* in *Delphinatici opera geometrica, quorum tituli sequuntur* (Lyon, 1554).
[40] See Samuel Bochart, *Goegraphia sacra, seu Phaleg et Canaan, cui accedunt variae dissertationes philologicae, geographicae, theologicae &c* (Caen, 1646).
[41] See Claude Duret, *Thresor de l'histoire des langues de cet univers* (Cologne, 1613).
[42] See Christoph Besold, *De natura populorum* (Tübingen, 1619).
[43] See Thomas White, *Sonus buccinae: sive tres tractatus de virtutibus fidei et theologiae* (Cologne, 1659).
[44] See Johann Joachim Becher, *Methodus didactica, das ist, gründlicher Beweiss dass die Weg und Mittel, welche die Schulen bisshero ins Gemein gebraucht die Jugend zur Erlernung der Sprachen* (Munich, 1668).
[45] See Robert Boyle, *The Sceptical Chymist* (London, 1661).
[46] Leibniz is referring here to the dispute between Balthasar Mentzer, a theologian from Giessen, and three theologians from Tübingen, namely Lukas Osiander, Melchior Nicolai and Theodor Thummius, about the presence of Christ in the Eucharist. Leibniz refers to the debate using the title of one of Thummius's books, namely Ταπεινωσιγραφια sacra, h.e. Repetitio sanae et orthod. doctrinae de humiliation Jesu Christi (Tübingen, 1623).

Chapter 31. Against the communication of properties of the Theopaschites, of humanity in the deity.
Chapter 32. Against the monothelites.
Chapter 33. Against the Aphthartodocetes.
Chapter 34. The possibility of transubstantiation, against the meaning of Berengar and Zwingali; and on Lutheran consubstantiation, with which it is reconcilable. The real elevation of the mind into heaven, of the more recent Calvinists. And how accidents may be preserved when a substance is changed, and how the species remaining in the bread and wine are real and not only apparent, as is the colour of a rainbow. And resolving all the difficulties of the Scholastics in this matter, on the quantitative mode etc.

At this point, the matter of the Sacrifice.
In the Eucharist, not only the mass and species remain. For properly speaking, the mass is not a substance, as even the Scholastics themselves testify. And there is no need to require the absence of one matter and the presence of another, because two bits of matter are similar in every respect. Cardinal de Lugo explains the conversion through a sheer succession in the function of the other,[47] likewise Veronius.
The species of Christ cannot be present, otherwise many accidents of the same kind, like for example the many instances of whiteness of the Christ's body and the bread, would be in the same subject at the same time. Because matter, according to Thomas, is not a Being, and according to us it is mass itself, namely that which fills up space, which the Scholastics have considered as a quantity, namely an accidental one. They agree with the Nominalists, who maintain that matter does not differ from quality. If the bread's matter and the substantial form ceases to be

---

[47] Cardinal de Lugo, *Disputationes Scholasticae et Morales*, disp. 7 sect. 1.

present, and Christ's matter and substantial form begins to be present, it follows that there is not transubstantiation but a mere substitution of one in the place of the other, which has itself been annihilated. For transmutation may be either that transubstantiation or transaccidentation: of course there is no change unless there is a common subject remaining. For if there is no common subject, there will be the annihilation of one and the succession of the other.

Chapter 35. The possibility of the immaculate conception of the Virgin Mary; the probability of Christ.

Chapter 36. That Christ merited salvation by his active obedience, and that with his passive obedience (such as his work of supererogation) given to us (because it can benefit even those who do not want it), he made amends for the sins of mankind: Piscator.[48]

Chapter 37. How Christ through the temporal passion makes good the eternal punishment of the damned, against the Socinians. This cannot be explained according to the infinity of the subject. But insofar as every punishment of the damned is privative in itself (to which, being infinite, one positive is equivalent), it is positive by accident.

Chapter 38. That men deserve the amendatory punishment of purgatory, with all sins being so to speak impurities. But those who die in a state of mortal sin die incorrigible (and thus it is by accident that

Add Digby and Thomas Anglus.[49]

---

[48] See Johannes Piscator, *De justificatione hominis coram Deo* (Herborn, 1699).
[49] See Digby, *Demonstratio immortalitatis animae rationalis*.

the place of cleansing becomes hell to them by their own will).

Chapter 39. Because there is a difference between mortal sin and venial sin, which is that the former is voluntary, the latter inadvertent.

Chapter 40. Therefore he who dies in mortal sin dies in a willing state of pugnacity, rebellion and enmity towards God. And it is said that he who gets himself in that state is confirmed in it more and more.

Chapter 41. He who dies in a state of venial sin, and recognizes it after death by his mind being illuminated, he suffers voluntarily, which to him is purgatory, and here he suffers on account of the love arising out of friendship and contrition; if someone guilty of a mortal sin is displeased on account of being deprived of eternal happiness, then he suffers out of attrition.

Chapter 42. The difference between attrition and contrition, i.e. between love arising out of friendship and love arising out of concupiscence. And the principle of love is beauty, from which ultimately arises the pleasure of the mind.

NB. Authors should be referred to about the salvation of formal heretics who do not acknowledge the power of the Church. Perhaps the contrite are freed from the punishment of loss, and the attrite without the sacrament from the punishment of sense. It is said that he who dies without repentance dies in mortal sin. He who dies in mortal sin is damned. He who does not die in mortal sin, if he is a Christian who is purged, he is saved through Christ's passion. Whether perhaps a non-Christian may be punished only by the punishment of loss, where he is abandoned by God, as children are.

He who is aware of sin, wills it, and is also a Christian who dies in mortal sin, is not saved unless the Church remitted the sin unto him. But in the meantime, if he is otherwise repentant, he is not damned. Therefore although the use of the sacraments is necessary for eternal salvation, nevertheless it is not necessary for avoiding eternal death. The grief of him who cannot have a priest, as for example a separatist Lutheran, takes the place of the sacrament. NB. Nor is he damned.

Chapter 43. Mortal sin is changed into venial by a true faith, namely the merit of Christ, for the removal of venial sin in purgatory. How does this happen? Evidently because Christ has not strictly speaking made satisfaction for our punishment, and God does not strictly speaking punish but gives us the merit of Christ.

Faith is material, just as heresy is material. Chapter 44. The essence of true faith is practical, in the will, a wonderful precaution for atheists to be brought back to the right path. Here also Herbert's *De religion gentilium*.[50]

Chapter 44a. That perhaps some (even if we pass over God's secret judgements) of the pagans in sin are punished with pain of loss alone; and that punishment (as in the case of children) does not inevitably bring with it pain of sense, namely in the case of those who do not attain the knowledge, even after death, that there is some eternal blessedness (as also in the case of innocent children).

The excommunicated are, in effect, only so in name.

Chapter 45. Why in the fathers has the pain of loss not caused the pain of sense? By the hope for better things, namely faith in Christ. Chapter 46.[51] Those who die with attrition and absolution have their mortal sin changed into venial. Contrition is equivalent to the sacrament and attrition. Chapter 47. The more we suffer for venial sin in this life, the less we suffer for it in the future life, at the time when in an intermediate state, or rather, the more we have restored in terms of good, i.e. we have attained so much good that would not have existed without the evil that preceded it, with an advantage being drawn out of adverse circumstances, just as Adam's sin is called 'happy' by some.

---

[50] See Herbert of Cherbury, *De religione gentilium, errorumque apud eos causis* (Amsterdam, 1663).
[51] 46 | If those who die in mortal sin without the absolution of the priest are truly penitent, they are at any rate not saved but perhaps are not damned either. | *deleted*.

Chapter 48. Explanation of the intermediate state of separated souls using a new argument, which is consistent with the principles of the Jews.

Chapter 49. The pain of the soul: melancholy brings about the greatest bodily pain. And it occurs both in purgatory and in hell. On the other hand, the beatific vision brings about bodily pleasure.

Chapter 50. God punishes no one otherwise than privatively, insofar as he does not bestow happiness upon them. In this way, the cruelty of eternal punishment is undermined.

Chapter 51. The beatific vision, i.e. the gazing upon God face to face, is the contemplation of the universal harmony of things because God, i.e. the Mind of the universe, is nothing other than the harmony of things, or the principle of beauty in them.

Chapter 52. The beatific vision and bodily pleasure, and the knowledge of the blessed, and conversely the ignorance and bodily pain of the damned, increases to infinity, but the beatific vision increases because at that time he who recognized beforehand the parts and their harmony now recognizes the parts of the parts, since the continuum is divisible to infinity.

Chapter 53. The same numerical body that has or has not sinned will experience joy or pain.

Chapter 54. The separated soul can have the beatific vision before its body is restored. Lateran Council.[53]

Chapter 55. The studies of chemists about the purification of this world through fire.

NB. There is no ultimate end, and beatitude does not consist in the appetite being inactive but in not being impeded in its progress to ever further ends. Hobbes.[52] The reason the beatific vision increases continuously is because as the world is moved more, things are increasingly divided.

---

[52] See Thomas Hobbes, *De homine*, XI.
[53] This appears to be a mistake. Leibniz is presumably thinking of the Council of Florence (1438–45), and the bull 'Laetentur coeli' issued 6 July 1439. See *Enchiridion symbolorum definitionum et declarationum de rebus fidei et morum*, ed. Heinrich Denzinger, no. 693.

Chapter 56. It is not necessary that we
establish that the whole universe is destroyed
on the last day. It is sufficient that it be
destroyed in part, evidently this great planet.
See Vossius, *De cometis*,[54] and
Copernicus, *De orbibus magnis*.
Chapter 57. Some have conjectured
(imaginatively more than accurately)
that angels are the men of an earlier world,
the saved are the good and the damned are
the devils. Some would have it thus even now.

*Part IV. Demonstration of the Authority of
the Catholic Church. Demonstration of the
Authority of Scripture.*
Chapter 1. Demonstration of the theoretical
infallibility of the Catholic Church, drawn
from the great number of Christians,
insofar as it appeals to tradition, i.e. the truth.
Chapter 2. Demonstration of the practical
infallibility of the Catholic Church, drawn
from a civil person [*una persona civilis*],
insofar as it makes decisions as a Judge.
Chapter 3. The Catholic Church has the
supreme active power over all Christians,
except insofar it commands violence and
disparages those who are passive. Which it
cannot do.
Chapter 4. The council of bishops represents
the Catholic Church.
Chapter 5. The Roman pontiff has the right
to convene a council and to make proposals
therein. This can happen not only through
the congregation of the council in one place,
but also through the circulation of encyclical
letters. The Roman pontiff has the right of a
guide.
Chapter 6. The Roman pontiff has the
supreme presumptive active power in the
world, i.e. he is the vicar of Christ. Thus it

However, the book by
Petrus Ostermann should be
inserted (Mainz, 1642,

---

[54] Leibniz is probably thinking here of Gijsbert Voet's *De cometis*, in volume 5 of his *Selectarum disputationum theologicarum* (Utrecht, 1669).

has come about that the Church has been given supreme power over sins, namely the power to absolve and to retain them. Therefore the Universal Church has the supreme active power. Whoever has supreme active power is a civil person. A civil person is one who has a single will. One who has a single will can reach a conclusion about every event. The will of a group cannot be certain unless there is someone who proposes, and there is the right of speaking.

containing the Recesses of the Empire),[55] published by Nicolas Heill.[56] The title *On the chief bishop and the other bishops*, § *However, he who now occupies the seat of Peter should as chief Bishop have thus used his power not for destruction, but for edification.* Therefore he has only presumption.

2. On transubstantiation (1668–9 (?))[57]

Manuscript:

M: LH I 2, 3b Bl. 1–9 and 12.

Transcription:

A: A VI 1, pp. 508–13.

This is one of the first texts Leibniz wrote for the *Catholic Demonstrations* project; it contains a reference to the plan of the project (see no. 1) and so was likely written around the same time. A few small parts of the manuscript are now illegible, and these are indicated with an ellipsis: …

On transubstantiation

With God's help, we have undertaken to show the possibility of the transubstantiation of bread and wine into the body of Christ, who suffered

---

[55] A Recess of the Holy Roman Empire was the document containing all of the decisions ratified by the Imperial Diet.
[56] See Petrus Ostermann, *Aller dess Heiligen Römischen Reichs gehaltener Reichs Tag Ordnung Satzung und Abschied sampt andern Kayserlichen und Königlichen Constitutionen* (Mainz, 1642).
[57] Author's title. From the Latin. Complete.

for us; the Catholic Church teaches that this transubstantiation happens at the time of consecration. Therefore it is to be demonstrated: (1) that the bread and wine, having lost their own substance, acquire the substance of Christ's body, (2) and are everywhere numerically identical with it; (3) that only their species or accidents remain; and (4) that the substance of Christ's body is present in all places where the species of consecrated bread and wine exist.

This proof depends upon the interpretation of the terms 'substance', 'species' or 'accidents', and 'numerical identity', which we shall obtain from the notions of these things received by the Scholastics, albeit explained clearly.

(I)

1. *Substance* is being subsisting in itself.
2. *Being subsisting in itself* is that which has a principle of action within itself. For, taken as an individual, being subsisting in itself, i.e. this or that substance, is a *suppositum*. (Indeed, the Scholastics customarily define a *suppositum* as a substantial individual.) Now actions pertain to *supposita*. Thus a *suppositum* has within itself a principle of action, i.e. it acts. Therefore a being subsisting in itself also has a principle of action within itself. Q.E.D.
3. If that which has a principle of action within itself is a body, it has a principle of motion within itself. Indeed, every action of a body is motion. Because every action is a variation of essence, every action of a body is therefore a variation of the essence of body. Now the essence or definition of a body is being in space. Therefore, a variation of the essence of body is a variation of existence in space. And variation of existence in space is motion. Therefore every action of a body is motion. Q.E.D. Aegidius Romanus's *Theoremata de hostia* should be consulted.[58] The Jesuit William of Paris, *De sacramentis*.[59]
4. No body, when separated from a concurring mind, has a principle of motion within itself, as was demonstrated in part I of the *Catholic Demonstrations*, where the existence of God is demonstrated.
5. Therefore no body, when taken as separated from a concurring mind, is a substance.
6. Whatever is not substance is accident, i.e. species.

---

[58] Aegidius Romanus, *Theoremata de hostia consecrata* (Bologna, 1481).
[59] William of Auvergne [also known as William of Paris], *De sacramentis* (thirteenth century).

7. Therefore body, when separated from a concurring mind, is accident, i.e. species.
8. Whatever is taken with a concurring mind is substance; whatever is taken as separated from it is accidents. Substance is union with mind. Thus the substance of the human body is union with a human mind, while the substance of bodies devoid of reason is union with the universal mind, i.e. God. The idea is the union of God with creature.
9. Therefore the substance of body is union with a sustaining mind.
10. A substance in union with a concurring mind is transubstantiated by the union of the concurring mind being changed.
12. [60] Therefore bread and wine as bodies, when the concurring mind is changed, are transubstantiated into the body of Christ, i.e. assumed by Christ (inasmuch as a special concurrence of the mind of Christ, which assumes the bread and wine in body ... is substituted in place of the general concurrence, which the universal mind or God bestows upon all bodies). Q.E.D.

(II)

13. If a body consecrated and assumed by the mind of Christ has the same concurring mind as the glorified body of Christ, who suffered for us,
14. it has numerically the same substantial form, or substance, as the body of Christ, who suffered for us, by no. 9.
15. Therefore the bread and wine in transubstantiation have acquired numerically the same substance as the body of Christ, who suffered for us. Q.E.D.

(III)

16. A body that is only transubstantiated is not changed in any other way than in the substantial form, or idea, of the concurring mind, by no. 9.
17. All the qualities, i.e. accidents or species, can remain in that wherein nothing is changed other than the concurring mind.
   For mind is compatible with all accidents; it does not bestow essence upon them, or deprive them of essence, just action.
18. Therefore all accidents or species are preserved in the transubstantiated bread and wine: extension, consistency, colour, flavour, etc., can remain. Q.E.D.

---

[60] There is no number 11 in the manuscript.

(IV)

19. Every mind lacks extension. Part II of the *Catholic Demonstrations*.
20. Whatever lacks extension is not coextensive with space.[61]
21. Whatever is not coextensive with space is not in a place by itself.
22. Therefore mind is not in a place by itself.
23. Mind acts upon a body which is in space.
24. To that extent, then, it can be said to be in space by operation. St Thomas.
25. Every action of a mind is thought.
26. Mind can think of many things at the same time.
27. Therefore mind can, by operation, be in many places at the same time.
28. Therefore the mind of Christ can at the same time bestow operation, action or subsistence upon Christ's glorified body as well as upon the species of consecrated bread and wine, and upon various different species in various places on the earth.
29. Therefore the mind of Christ can be present everywhere in the species of consecrated bread and wine.
30. The mind of Christ, concurring with his glorified body which suffered for us, is his substance, by no. 9.
31. Therefore the substance of the glorified body of Christ can be present everywhere in the species of bread and wine. Q.E.D.[62]

Comments

These philosophical theses of ours differ not at all from the received philosophy. For nature is the principle of motion and rest even for Aristotle. And substantial form is nature, strictly speaking, for him. Hence Averroes and Angelus Mercenarius, and Jacob Zabarella, hold that substantial form is the principle of individuation.[63] Those who locate the nature of subsistence in the union of matter and form, with Murcia,[64] agree with this as well.

---

[61] Here Leibniz added as a marginal note: 'Here it is to be demonstrated, against Descartes, that space and extension really differ from body, because otherwise motion would not be a real being, and a vacuum would be necessary.'

[62] Here Leibniz added as a marginal note: 'Ideas are unions of mind and body, just as angles are unions of a point with lines. Ideas are the same as the substantial forms of things. Thus ideas are in God as every action is in an agent, and as creation is in God. If someone asks whether an idea is created or not, one will be forced to answer, is a created thing a creature or not?'

[63] See for example Archangelus Mercenarius, *Dilucidationes de principio individuationis* (Padua, 1571), and Jacopo Zabarella, *De rebus naturalibus libri XXX* (Frankfurt, 1607).

[64] See Francisco Murcia de la Llana, *Selecta circa octo libros physicorum Aristotelis* (Ingolstadt, 1601).

What more need I say? Plato himself with his soul of the world in the *Timaeus*,[65] Aristotle with his agent intellect diffused throughout all things in *Metaphysics* and *Physics*,[66] the Stoics thinking that the substance of the world is God, Averroes propagating the … Intellect of Aristotle,[67] Fracastorius and Fernelius … origin of forms:[68] all agree in this: substance, nature, principle … I think these things have been disentangled in such a way that, when the Philosopher has been accurately investigated in the work of more recent people, I have no doubt for a future demonstration.[69]

I imagine our Scholastics will be perplexed, not with regard to the matter itself but with regard to the words. For I can hear them speaking like this: 'What? You who presume to demonstrate the possibility of transubstantiation, do you think you will satisfy the Church with terms used capriciously? On the contrary, you must use the terms "substance", "transubstantiation", "accident", "species" and "identity" in the sense the Council of Trent is likely to have favoured, and it has doubtless favoured that which is customary among the chorus of Scholastics. Unless you adhere to this, you will expropriate the words of the Church, and therefore you will display the mind of a heretic.'

Well said, O Scholastics! But your warning comes too late, since this matter has already been taken into consideration. For neither the conception of identity, nor that of transubstantiation, nor of accidents or species, is an innovation, which is clear from the demonstration set out earlier. For there I demonstrate the numerical identity of substance from the numerical identity of substantial form, which is consistent with the principles of the most renowned of the Scholastics and Aristotelians, and likewise of those philosophers for whom substantial form is the principle of individuation. I define 'transubstantiation' as a change of substantial form. I call 'species' whatever can be thought about in a real body separated from substantial form, namely matter taken with its accidents. I call 'substance' a being subsisting in itself. The horde of Scholastics agrees that a being subsisting in itself is the same as a 'suppositum'. For a *suppositum* is a substantial individual (in the same way that a person is a rational substantial individual), i.e. a certain substance in particular. And the

---

[65] See Plato, *Timaeus*, 34a–40d.
[66] See for example Aristotle, *Metaphysics*, XII.7. However, the *loci classici* about the agent (or active) intellect are to be found in *De anima*, III.5.
[67] See Averroes, *Long Commentary on the De Anima of Aristotle* (twelfth century).
[68] See for example Girolamo Fracastoro, *De sympathia et antipathia rerum liber I* (Venice, 1546).
[69] Leibniz is here referring to Aristotle, who was often called 'the Philosopher' by Scholastic thinkers.

School has generally established it as characteristic of a *suppositum* that it is denominated by action; from this comes the rule that actions belong to *supposita*. It is clear from this that the *suppositum*, substance, being subsisting in itself – which are all the same – is defined correctly in the sense likewise accepted by the Scholastics, as that which has a principle of action within itself, for otherwise it will not act but instead be an instrument of an agent. A further consequence of this is that substantial form is itself the principle of action, namely of motion in bodies. To make the harmony more apparent, the same understanding of substantial form emerges from another principle of Aristotle and the Scholastics. For Aristotle himself, and the most prominent of his followers, have intimated that substantial form is nature. Nature is the principle of motion and rest. Therefore, substantial form – in the Aristotelian sense as well – is the principle of motion and rest.

Perhaps opponents will make a different objection which is not to be ignored, namely that it follows from this hypothesis that there is one substantial form for all bodies, by which I mean the concurring divine mind. But this does not follow, for even if the divine mind is the same, nevertheless the concurring divine mind is not.[70] For the divine mind consists of the ideas of all things.[71] Therefore, since the idea of thing A is one thing, the idea of B another, the result is that one idea of the divine mind concurs with thing A, another with thing B. That the composition of the divine mind from ideas does not constitute parts is elsewhere demonstrated with the example of a point. Therefore Plato's 'idea' is the same as Aristotle's substantial form. Hence it is apparent that there is not one substantial form for all bodies but a different one for different bodies, for as the disposition of matter is varied, so too is the form and the idea, and from the form and the idea proceeds a body's motion and rest.

It is to be shown from the hypothesis of those who think matter is mass that they do not require it to be a substance, whereas those who think matter is anything insensible do require it to be a substance.

It should be demonstrated from the general consensus of philosophers

---

[70] Here Leibniz added as a marginal note: 'Therefore it is not changed by the disposition species have to corruption.'

[71] Here Leibniz added as a marginal note: 'St Thomas also thinks that the sacrament could have been celebrated at the time the soul of Christ was separated [from his body]. I don't know whether this is true. But perhaps it is; for it could be understood as separated from it in the same way that it is now separated from the host, namely with suspended action.' Leibniz is presumably thinking of Aquinas's *Summa Theologiae*, III, Q76, art. 1, ad 1.

that the substance of a thing does not fall under the senses. Therefore it is necessary that the word 'mind' means something different from what is today adopted by 'sense', otherwise it would fall under the senses. The substance of each thing is not mind so much as an idea of a concurring mind. In God there are infinite, really diverse, ideas, and yet God is indivisible. God's ideas are the substance of things, but not their essence. God's idea is not the substance of things which are moved by the mind.

In an idea there is contained ideally both passive and active potentiality, both active and passive intellect. There is matter in the idea to the extent that the passive intellect concurs, and form to the extent that active intellect does so. NB. Bread and wine are not transessentiated but transubstantiated. Somewhere in the breviary it is said that the body of Christ is made bread and wine, but this is metonymical. The language of the Council of Trent should be rigorously heeded: that bread and wine are not substance but substantiated being. It is less correctly said that man is a substance, and this is foreign to the use and nature of speech, and a modification of the abstract into the concrete. Therefore it cannot be tolerated except by metonymy.

The usefulness of these demonstrations in theology and philosophy is as follows:

In theology they are useful against atheists in such a way that, even if it seems to them that Catholic tradition is shown by the Reformed to imply contradiction, they do not then think it follows that the Christian religion is false; the demonstrations are useful against the Reformed in such a way that they do not think they have demonstrated that Catholic tradition implies contradiction; and they are useful for the peace of the Church in such a way that it is apparent that Church dogmas are not as crude as appears from the foolish writings of some.

The demonstrations are useful for philosophy, so that we not be further frightened by its renewal, or that the article of transubstantiation be overturned through fear.

We must start with the examinations of others who have done the same before us, both that of the Scholastics in particular as well as generally that of all who have held that the same mass of body can be in several places, which completely and utterly implies contradiction.

Milletière, who reduced it to a certain extraordinary form of words, has been sufficiently refuted by Daillé.[72]

That of Bonartes, who thought that the body was transformed internally and thus that only the outermost accidents deceive sight and are intentional species.[73] From which it follows … that we do not receive the substance of the body of Christ but that of another.

Nor that of Descartes to Father Dinet, whose view amounts to the same thing.[74]

Nor of Thomas Anglus (for which see articles 7 and 12)[75] that it is 'augmentation' and bread and wine have been added to body with this sole distinction from natural augmentation, namely that it is not discontinuous, that it is not dispersed, but that it retains its accidental qualities.

Descartes is refuted in the works of Théophile Raynauld.[76]

3. On the demonstration of the possibility of the mysteries of the Eucharist (autumn 1671 (?))[77]

Manuscript:

M: LH I 2, 3a Bl. 1–8.

Transcription:

A: A VI 1, pp. 515–17.

The following appears to be one of the last texts Leibniz wrote in support of the *Catholic Demonstrations* project before it was abandoned following the death of Boineburg, Leibniz's employer, in 1672. The text ends with Leibniz expressing the

---

[72] See Jean Daillé, *Adversus Milleterianam de conciliandis religionibus sententiam disputatio* (London, 1637).
[73] See Thomas Bonartes Nordtano, *Concordia Scientiae cum Fide e difficillimis philosophiae et theologiae Scholasticae quaestionibus* (Cologne, 1659).
[74] See René Descartes, *Fourth Set of Replies*, in *The Philosophical Writings of Descartes*, II: pp. 173–8.
[75] See Thomas Anglus's preface to Kenelm Digby, *Demonstratio immortalitatis animae rationalis*.
[76] Théophile Raynauld, *Opera Omnia*, 20 vols (Lyon, 1665–9).
[77] Author's title. From the Latin. Complete.

wish to report his findings to the renowned Catholic theologian and philosopher Antoine Arnauld (1612–94), which he did in a letter written November 1671;[78] it is therefore likely that this text was written shortly before that letter.

On the demonstration of the possibility of the mysteries of the Eucharist

To demonstrate the possibility of something is the same as to explain some *hypothesis* or possible mode (possible, i.e. clearly and distinctly intelligible) whereby, once it is assumed, it follows that the thing comes to pass: alternatively, it is the same as to show by which method a given problem could be constructed, at least by God. Thus to show that an ellipse is equal to a circle is a problem that can be constructed and solved by a geometer, but to move the Earth from its place, to reduce a given body to nothing and to transubstantiate bodies while preserving their appearance are all problems that can only be put before God. Therefore, even if we cannot solve these in practice, we are nevertheless able to do so purely by contemplation, i.e. we can demonstrate clearly and distinctly a possible mode, which I now intend to do for the mysteries of the Eucharist.

The mysteries of faith are astonishing or paradoxical revealed propositions, such as 'God is threefold' and 'God was made man'. When I say 'revealed', I mean that the conclusion is not known by demonstration, either on account of the obscurity of the human mind, as with the *Trinity* (for otherwise, given a vision of the divine essence, a demonstration of the Trinity will be given, i.e. it will be clearly and distinctly evident from the divine essence itself that Trinity necessarily follows), or because they are facts, as with the *Incarnation* (which, because it depends upon God's will, can be known only by God' revealing it).

When I call them 'astonishing' or 'paradoxical', I mean they seem impossible at first glance. Therefore, just as it is up to faith to grant their truth by revelation, so it is up to reason to acknowledge their possibility by demonstration. But while faith is necessary for all, demonstration of possibility is useful only to the wise; in their case, either their genius drives them towards a deeper investigation of things and they seek to satisfy themselves to the extent that the human mind can progress, or their public duty calls them to vindicate the truth against the attacks of atheists, infidels and heretics. As such people not only harp on about impossibilities and implied

---

[78] A II 1, pp. 275–87.

contradiction but also set these things forth, there can be no more proper or profound way of resisting them than by the demonstration of possibility; for just as a clear definition saves a thousand distinctions, so also a clear definition saves a thousand responses. Once the method of possibility is clearly laid out, it is immediately apparent that all alleged impossibilities depend upon a false hypothesis and a contested opinion that is not understood, and so they are not relevant to the matter in hand.

The mysteries of the Eucharist are *the real presence* and *transubstantiation*. They are encapsulated in these two propositions: 1. The one and same body of Christ (which suffered on the cross for us) is really present, in its own substance, wherever there is a Eucharist Host. 2. In the Eucharist Host, the substance of the body of Christ is under the appearance of the bread.

The Augsburg Confession grants only the first proposition;[79] the Roman Church adds the second, and with the most careful phrasing of the Council of Trent.[80]

At some time when I, who belong to the Augsburg Confession, was working on demonstrating the possibility of a real presence, I happened upon transubstantiation at the same time (completely beyond my hope), and indeed found that in the details and in the final analysis transubstantiation and real presence amount to the same thing, and hence that the dispute in the Church only exists because one side has not understood the other.

Therefore, I say, transubstantiation, properly understood, as conceived by the Council of Trent, and as I have explained it according to the principles of St Thomas above all, is not opposed to the Augsburg Confession, and in fact follows from it.

There remain other disputes about the Eucharist between the followers of the Roman Church and those of the Augsburg Confession, and since these relate to practice, I do not make them mine. They depend upon these two questions in particular: 1. Whether the real presence and transubstantiation (which I shall show to be the same thing) are momentary, and

---

[79] Augsburg Confession article X: 'Of the Lord's Supper we teach that the Body and Blood of Christ are truly present and are distributed to those who eat in the Lord's Supper. We reject those who teach otherwise.'

[80] Council of Trent session XIII, chapter IV: 'And because that Christ, our Redeemer, declared that which He offered under the species of bread to be truly His own body, therefore has it ever been a firm belief in the Church of God, and this holy Synod doth now declare it anew, that, by the consecration of the bread and of the wine, a conversion is made of the whole substance of the bread into the substance of the body of Christ our Lord, and of the whole substance of the wine into the substance of His blood; which conversion is, by the holy Catholic Church, suitably and properly called Transubstantiation.'

do not last beyond the moment of use, i.e. sumption, as the Augsburg Confession teaches; or whether, having begun at the time of consecration, they last until the corruption of the outward appearance, as the Roman Church claims. Each of the two answers to the proposed question is equally possible, and it depends solely on the will of God which he will have preferred. 2. Whether the Host should be worshipped with *cultus latria*;[81] this is also settled by the answer to the first question, for if the Host is the body of Christ only for the moment of use, it should not be worshipped until it has been taken.

Hence I am quite certain that the Augsburg Confession has not in any way differed from the Roman Church in this matter except about questions related to practice and worship, and that it has not rejected transubstantiation except that which should begin from consecration and end in corruption, and hence for the meantime it should command *cultus latria*.

But dragging myself away from these questions, it will have sufficed to have shown that the real presence and transubstantiation (of whatever duration they may be, this not affecting the essence of the matter) amount to the same thing, and to have demonstrated the possibility of each at the same time.

No one in the public eye has thus far demonstrated a possible means of transubstantiation (not wishing to repeat myself, but it is likewise regarding the real presence). The Scholastics have tried but without success, and philosophy has been so distorted for their own interests that learned men tolerate those monstrous and fictitious entities, received in particular by Scholastics who struggle to explain transubstantiation; such things are gradually disappearing from the new philosophy.

In our time, a few have tried to unite [these ideas] with the new philosophy: Descartes,[82] Thomas Bonartes,[83] Emanuel Maignan,[84] and Thomas Anglus[85] but all without success.

Arnauld, the most skilled and most learned man of the new philosophy, often challenged by Claude who harps on about the impossibilities in this

---

[81] The highest form of worship, which should be directed solely at God.
[82] See René Descartes, *Fourth Set of Replies*, in *The Philosophical Writings of Descartes*, II: pp. 173–8.
[83] See Thomas Bonartes Nordtano, *Concordia Scientiae cum Fide e difficillimis philosophiae et theologiae Scholasticae quaestionibus* (Cologne, 1659).
[84] See Emanuel Maignan, *Cursus philosophicus concinnatus ex notissimis cuique principiis Tomus 1* (Toulouse, 1653).
[85] See the preface added by Thomas Anglus [real name: Thomas White] to the Latin translation of Kenelm Digby's *Two Treatises* (1645): *Demonstratio immortalitatis animae rationalis, sive Tractatus duo philosophici* (Paris, 1651).

subject, did not have the courage to venture here, content to crush resistance with the consensus of the ancients.[86]

But Claude, following Aubertin, Blondel and Daille,[87] whenever in any somewhat clearer place is overwhelmed by those mystical figures of speech, he retreats unharmed into the thickets of impossibility, as if holding a shield before him, and cries out that this interpretation is necessary unless we prefer to entangle ourselves willingly in contradictions and monstrosities of meaningless words. Thomas Hobbes, powerful in his eloquence, repeats the same arguments in his *Leviathan* (in the part about the Kingdom of Darkness),[88] and his book can both harm and benefit more than a hundred others.

Nor is there hope in this world of the new philosophy that Hercules will be disarmed, and that gainsayers can be fully convinced by the judgement of wise Catholics, unless its possibility should be deduced from the new philosophy itself. This is the only way to bring the controversy to a complete end.

The matter is commonly almost given up as hopeless, and hence among the pious and the wise, and especially among our princes, it must be treated all the more seriously as the greater is their concern for the salvation of the people.

This one thing I desire, that with regard to an argument of such importance, it may become an opportunity for speaking in person with that excellent man Arnauld, to whom I know that hardly anything more pleasing can be reported.[89]

---

[86] Jean Claude (1619–87) was a Protestant minister who had a fractious exchange about the Eucharist with Antoine Arnauld. Claude initiated the exchange with his *Réponse aux deux traittez intitulez La perpetuité de la foy de l'eglise catholique touchant l'Eucharistie* (Charenton, 1667), a popular work that was reprinted numerous times in the years that followed. Arnauld responded with his *La perpetuité de la foy de l'Eglise catholique touchant l'Eucharistie, deffendue contre le livre du Sieur Claude, Ministre de Charenton* (Paris, 1669). This elicited a further response from Claude, in the form of *Réponse au livre de Mr Arnaud, intitulé La perpetuite de la foy de l'eglise catholique touchant l'Eucharistie défendue* (Quevilly, 1670). Arnauld then responded in turn, with his *Reponse Generale Au Nouveau Livre de M Claude* (Paris, 1671).

[87] Edme Aubertin (1595–1652) published a number of works on the Eucharist, including *L'Eucharistie de l'ancienne église* (Geneva, 1633) and *Anatomie du liure publié par le sieur de la Milletiere pour la transsubstantiation* (Charenton, 1648); David Blondel (1591–1655) wrote *Esclaircissements familiers de la controverse de l'eucharistie, tirez de la parole de Dieu, & des escrits des SS. Peres* (Quévilly, 1641); Jean Daille (1594–1670) wrote *Joannis Dallaei adversus Milleterianam de conciliandis religionibus sententiam Disputatio, Divisa in Partes duas: quarum prior est de Primatu, de Eucharistia, justificatione, Sanctorum invocatione, & precibus pro mortuis. Altera de Natura, & Gratia, & aeterna Praedestinatione* ([no place], 1637). All three were Protestant clergymen.

[88] Thomas Hobbes, *Leviathan, or, The Matter, Forme & Power of a Common-Wealth Ecclesiasticall and Civill* (London, 1651). Leibniz is referring to the book's fourth and final part ('Of the Kingdome of Darknesse').

[89] Leibniz subsequently reported his view to Arnauld in a letter written at the start of November

4. A proposal to revive the *Catholic Demonstrations* (late 1679 (?))[90]

Manuscript:

M: LBr F 12 Bl. 150-1 u. 161-2.

Transcription:

A: A II 1, pp. 756-9.

Leibniz abandoned the *Catholic Demonstrations* project following Boineburg's death in 1672, but revisited it later in the decade, raising it with his employer at the time, Duke Johann Friedrich of Hanover (1625-79), in the following letter, hoping to win support for its revival. There exist two different drafts of Leibniz's letter; the following is the second of the two, which is presumably closer to the version Leibniz would have sent.[91] The Duke, however, died shortly after hearing of Leibniz's plans (he died on 18 December 1679), and thus the project was shelved a second time, though Leibniz was to conceive and pursue a similar project in the mid-1680s (see for example 'Specimen of *Catholic Demonstrations*, or, Apology for the faith through reason', pp. 103-8).

Your Grace

Your Serene Highness has done me favours which excuse me from making requests of him at the present time; I now have an opportunity to do one for him, which he will use as he sees fit.

Having examined the controversies with the late Baron von Boineburg, I found that there were only three or four passages in the Council of Trent that troubled me, and to my mind were in need of an interpretation that does not conflict with the words or the sense of the Church as I believe it to be, nor also with the common opinions of Scholastics, and especially of monks. And as these people have a great influence over people's minds

---

1671; see A II 1, pp. 275-87. Arnauld did not respond.
[90] Editor's title. From the French. Complete.
[91] For the first draft of the letter, see A II 1, pp. 750-5/L, pp. 259-62.

– consider the sentence they passed on Galileo – I desired, in order to be safe and to proceed with sincerity, that a declaration from Rome be procured, indicating that these interpretations at least contain nothing that is contrary to the faith.

Mr Boineburg was delighted with this proposal, and when I travelled to France he gave me letters for Mr Arnauld, believing that his view would carry great weight. But Mr Boineburg's death took away my hope of succeeding via this path, and from that point onwards I thought of Your Serene Highness, inasmuch as Mr Boineburg had already intended to speak to you of it.

Now on the assumption that these declarations could be obtained, I had drawn up the plan of an important work under the title *Catholic Demonstrations*, consisting of three parts: the *first* would contain demonstrations about *God and the soul*, since indeed I have some startling ones. The *second* would contain proofs of *the Christian religion*, and of the possibility of our principal mysteries, particularly of the Trinity, the Incarnation, the Eucharist and the resurrection of bodies. The *third* part is about *the Church* and its authority, about the divine right of the Church hierarchy and about the limits of secular and ecclesiastical power, the difference being that all men as well as churchmen themselves owe to sovereigns an outward and passive obedience, that is, at least an unreserved irresistibility and sufferance towards external goods, following the practice of the first Christians, who would not obey the impious orders of Emperors, but who endured them all. In exchange, all men and even sovereigns owe to the Church an inward and active obedience: that is, they must do everything the Church commands, and believe everything it teaches, though it will never command anyone to resist sovereigns, and will never teach anything that implies contradiction. For these are the only two exceptions. Upon these principles I clearly explained the most difficult questions.

This great work (great not because of its size, but because of its matters) would be preceded by the demonstrated elements of the true philosophy. For in order to judge of demonstrations in matters of fact and morality, there must be a new part of *logic*, namely the art of weighing probabilities and of estimating which side the balance inclines when there are probabilities on both sides. *Metaphysics* also needs to be pushed forward in order that we may have clear notions of God, soul and person, and of the nature of substance and accidents. For I re-establish demonstratively and explain intelligibly the substantial forms that the Cartesians claim to have eradicated as inexplicable chimeras, to the detriment of our religion, whose mysteries would be nothing but impossibilities if the nature of body consisted only in extension, as Descartes claims. This point of my metaphysics will be infinitely agreeable to the Jesuits and other learned theologians. Likewise, without having some deeper insight into *physics* one could not resolve the difficulties that arise against the history of creation, the deluge and the resurrection of bodies. Lastly, the true *morality* should be demonstrated so that we know what justice is, and likewise justification, freedom, pleasure, beatitude and the beatific vision. And for the conclusion, there is nothing so in conformity with the true politics and the happiness of humankind (even here below and in this life) than my proposal about the irresistible power of sovereigns over external goods, and of God's dominion over souls through the Church. For I seem to recall mentioning on other occasions that nothing is more necessary for peace than the power of sovereigns, and nothing is more useful for the general good than the authority of the Church, which forms a body of all Christians united by the bonds of charity, and which can hold in a sacred respect the greatest powers on earth, while they are also sensitive to the reproaches of conscience. This is why every good man must desire that the lustre of the Church be everywhere restored, and that the spiritual power of its true ministers over the faithful be recognized a little more than is often done by those who would pass for the most Catholic.

But before giving these theological and philosophical demonstrations, and to anticipate those who are prejudiced against these sorts of works (thinking that their authors are superficial souls), I had the intention of first distinguishing myself and of setting myself apart from the crowd with the mathematical discoveries I have made: these discoveries, according to the greatest men in these matters that our age has to offer, can be compared with some of the finest ones Galileo and Descartes have given us. One cannot dispute the merit of an author in mathematics like one can in other matters, and this is why I remained so long in France, in order to improve myself in this area, and I have not dwelled on these sciences for their own sake, but in order to make them serve the advancement of piety.

Lastly, in order to put the finishing touch to my plan, and to make my demonstrations irrefutable, despite their being about matters not ordinarily thought to be susceptible to irrefutability, I wanted to offer essays on this new language, or characteristic, which will mean that every bit of reasoning will be like an arithmetical calculation for the easy discovery of truths and for irresistibly establishing the truths that have been discovered.[92] This

---

[92] Leibniz is referring here to his work on developing a formal language of thought (the universal characteristic), the terms of which would, when combined in accordance with a kind of logical

language, or writing, will be able to be taught in a few days for ordinary use, and, so long as it is introduced among the missionaries, it will quickly spread throughout the world because of its ease of use and its enormous value in the commerce of nations. And where it is established, piety and reason will not fail to reign in souls of the highest calibre, since in the end men usually sin because of false reasoning, and since at that time one will not be able to make mistakes in reasoning without making solecisms against the rules of this language. Thus aside from miracles and other extraordinary aids from on high, I do not think a more potent way can be found for advancing the Christian religion, since in the way I explain everything in my work on the *Demonstrations*, I show it to be thoroughly holy and thoroughly rational. I don't think one can find a more important and more agreeable proposition for the Congregation for the Propagation of the Faith. But the declarations I desire on certain points of the Council [of Trent] are necessary first of all, for since I think that the contrary implies contradiction, my characteristic or language would one day refute the contrary, in spite of myself and the whole world. After all, since the truth alone forms the rules of this language, we cannot be biased and turn things around as happens in other languages.

But in order to obtain these declarations, we must undoubtedly act with much adroitness in order that it not be known where the requests come from, and that the authority of the person who puts in the requests is such as to ensure they get an unprejudiced and fair examination; for sometimes a person rejects from the outset, and scorns the most innocuous and important things. There is nothing so easy for Your Serene Highness than to assist in a way that would be judged most appropriate. And the matter is made all the more easy since the Pope today looks to be a good man,[93] enlightened and fair-minded, and since he has shown his zeal by condemning some unreasonable propositions of a false morality,[94] and his moderation by approving the exposition of the faith published by the Bishop of Condom,[95] which is the most moderate I have yet seen.

---

calculus, generate and determine propositional truths in matters such as ethics and metaphysics. For examples of some of Leibniz's writings on this language, see A VI 4, pp. 156–60/PW, pp. 1–4; A VI 4, pp. 527–31/PW, pp. 5–9.

[93] Innocent XI (1611–89) had been Pope for three years at the time of writing, having been elected in September 1676. He had pushed for higher moral standards both within the clergy and the faithful. Perhaps more importantly from Leibniz's perspective, Innocent XI was sympathetic to reunification efforts.

[94] In 1679, Innocent XI condemned 65 propositions from (mostly Jesuit) writings that were deemed to display moral laxity.

[95] Jacques-Bénigne Bossuet, *Exposition de la doctrine de l'Eglise catholique sur les matieres de controverse* (Paris, 1671).

Further, there is also an important reason which surpasses all those I have mentioned, and which obliges me to break my silence. It concerns Your Serene Highness in particular, who will perhaps receive great satisfaction from it, and I shall speak of it in due course. Nevertheless, I am sincerely,

Your Grace

2

The Existence and Nature of God

A. THE EXISTENCE OF GOD

1. A proof of the existence of God from his essence (January 1678)[1]

Manuscripts:
M1:   LH IV, 1, 13a Bl. 3 (first draft).
M2:   LH IV, 1, 13a Bl. 4 (second draft).
M3:   LH IV, 1, 13a Bl. 1–2 (third draft).

Transcriptions:

A1:   A II 1 (2nd edn), pp. 585–6 (following M1).
A2:   A II 1 (2nd edn), pp. 586–7 (following M2).
A3:   A II 1 (2nd edn), pp. 588–91 (following M3).

The following pieces were drafted for one of Leibniz's correspondents, Henning Huthmann (?–1729). Following a face-to-face discussion about Leibniz's proof of a necessary being, Huthmann wrote to Leibniz in January 1678: 'I can respond to the argument recently proposed, and at the same time can show that existence cannot be deduced from any concept of essence. Whenever I get some free time, and it is agreeable for me to come, I shall very swiftly appear, and most lucidly reveal

---

[1] Author's title (taken from the third draft). From the Latin. Complete.

my opinion.'² Leibniz sketched out the first of the following pieces on the back of Huthmann's letter.

[First draft]

If a necessary being is possible, it actually exists.

For let us suppose that it does not exist; from that I shall argue in the following way:

A necessary being does not exist, according to the hypothesis.

Whatever does not exist, it is possible for it to not-exist.

It is falsely said of whatever can possibly not exist that it cannot not-exist.

Of whatever it is falsely said that it cannot not-exist, it is falsely said that it is necessary. For necessary is that which cannot not-exist.

Therefore it is falsely said that a necessary being is necessary.

This conclusion is either true or false.

If it is true, it follows that a necessary being implies contradiction, or is impossible, because contradictory things are demonstrated from it, namely that it is not necessary. For a contradictory conclusion can be shown only with regard to a thing that implies contradiction.

If the conclusion is false, it is necessary that something in the premises is false, yet the hypothesis can be the only false thing in the premises, namely that a necessary being does not exist.

Therefore we have concluded that a necessary being is either impossible or exists.

Therefore if we define God as being from itself, or a being from whose essence existence follows, or a necessary being, it follows that if God is possible he actually exists.

It should be noted here that a conclusion which implies contradiction can be true, namely if it is about an impossible thing. For example, a square circle is not a circle. This proposition is true, although it is contradictory, for it is legitimately proved from truths in this way: a square is not a circle, a square circle is a square, therefore a square circle is not a circle.

---

² A II 1 (2nd edn), p. 584.

[Second draft]

Proposition

If a necessary being is possible, it actually exists.

Demonstration

For let us suppose that it does not exist; from that I shall argue in the following way:
A necessary being does not exist, according to the hypothesis.
Whatever does not exist, it is possible for it to not-exist.
It is falsely said of whatever can possibly not exist that it cannot not-exist.
Of whatever it is falsely said that it cannot not-exist, it is falsely said that it is necessary.

Therefore

It is falsely said that a necessary being is necessary.
 Since this conclusion is contradictory, and contradictories can be shown only when a thing implies contradiction, it follows either that a necessary being implies contradiction, i.e. is not possible, or that if it is possible, a contradictory conclusion cannot be formed from it, and it is necessary that something in the premises is false, which can be nothing other than the hypothesis itself, namely that a necessary being does not exist.
 Therefore the hypothesis should be rejected, and hence:
If a necessary being is possible, it will actually exist.

Corollary

Since we define *God* as being from itself, or a being from whose essence existence follows, or a necessary being, there follows this remarkable proposition:
If God is possible, he will actually exist.
 Which was to be demonstrated.
This proposition is the pinnacle of modal theory.

Scholium

Because God is also defined as the most perfect being, and existence is in fact numbered among the perfections, it is indeed correctly said from this that God is a being whose essence includes existence. Yet from this it cannot be demonstrated, as the Cartesians think, *that God exists*, but only this: *that God exists, assuming he has some essence*, that is, assuming he is possible.

And this proviso is beautifully obvious especially from our demonstration laid down here. For if contradictory conclusions (such as in this case that *a necessary being is falsely said to be necessary*) should be always false, then something was also false in our premises, and hence this one: *a necessary being does not exist*. Therefore we should have had demonstrated that a necessary being, or God, exists. However it should be observed (which as far as I know has not been observed) that contradictory propositions can be true, if they are expressed of impossible things, i.e. things implying a contradiction. For example, with regard to a four-sided circle, it can be proved by a legitimate inference that it is not a circle, because a four-sided thing is rectilinear, while a circle is not rectilinear. At any rate, then, we have shown either that God is impossible or that he actually exists. I think this is of great importance, since it is easier to show the possibilities of things than their existence, and each and every thing is considered possible until the contrary is proved. Yet it is not surprising that the Cartesians, who thought they had absolutely proved existence in this way, have not won approval, since in the same way in which they prove God's existence, it can be shown that man exists. For let us assume some concept, *a necessary man*, which we signify by A. I say that A exists, which I prove by means of the Cartesians' method, for A's essence includes existence, by hypothesis. But the response will be that it is uncertain whether there is such an essence, that is, whether it can be properly imagined and distinctly conceived, or whether A is possible.

[Third draft]

January 1678

A proof of the existence of God from his essence

(1) The possible existence or possibility of anything, and the essence of that same thing, are inseparable (that is, if one of them exists in the region of ideas or truths, or of realities, the other also exists in it. That is, given the truth of the existence of one, the truth of the other exists, for truths exist even if things do not exist and are not thought to exist by anyone ...)

Therefore, with that assumed

(2) The possible existence or possibility of God, and the essence of God, are inseparable (for the essence of a thing is the specific ground of its possibility).

Now, however

(3) The essence of God and his actual existence are inseparable.³ ⁴ See the proof of this under 'NB' and 'NB NB'.

Therefore it must be concluded

(4) The possible existence or possibility of God, and his actual existence, are inseparable.

Or, which is the same thing

(5) Assuming God is possible, it follows that God actually exists.⁵

The third proposition is proved in this way:
(3) The essence of God and his actual existence are inseparable.

NB I prove this firstly, for
((1)) The essence of God and supreme perfection are inseparable (*ex hypothesi*, for we suppose the essence of God contains supreme perfection).
((2)) Supreme perfection and every perfection in kind are inseparable.
((3)) Actual existence is a perfection in kind.

---

³ inseparable | (because we define God as a necessary being, or that being from whose essence existence follows, or that being whose essence and existence are inseparable. Nor is it supposed in this that God exists; instead it is supposed only that in the region of ideas or truths some essence is to be found with which existence is necessarily connected, and to which we bestow the name of God) | *deleted*.

⁴ In the margin Leibniz wrote here: 'If a necessarily existing being is possible, it will certainly exist, for if a necessarily existing being does not exist it will be impossible because it implies contradiction that there is something that necessarily exists and yet does not exist. Therefore the issue comes down to this, that we show that a necessary being, or an essence from which existence follows, is possible. (The whole issue comes down to this formula: *If a necessarily existing being is possible, it actually exists*. For if it will not exist it is certainly possible that it does not exist. Therefore it is impossible that it is necessary, i.e. that it is not able to not exist. Therefore an actually non-existing necessary being is impossible. Therefore if a necessary being is possible, it will actually exist.) A necessary being is proved by that to exist and to be possible at the same time, because otherwise all things are contingent. If all things are contingent then they were able to be otherwise for a similar reason, i.e. it is false that there is nothing without a reason. If a necessarily existing being is possible, then its essence can be understood to include necessary existence. If that essence is A, I say that the being endowed with essence A exists. For if it does not exist it is not necessary that it exists. Therefore its essence does not include necessary existence, which is contrary to the hypothesis, for it either implies impossibility or it is impossible. Therefore if a being endowed with essence A does not exist, it will be impossible. But essence A includes necessary existence. Therefore if a necessarily existing being does not exist it will be impossible, or if a necessary being is possible, it exists. Which was to be demonstrated.'

⁵ exists. | ¶ If anyone should desire a more ample or more distinct proof of the third proposition, it is possible to satisfy him | *deleted*.

Therefore
The essence of God and his actual existence are inseparable.

But since this argument can be tightened into an abbreviated form, and the mention of perfection can be removed,
NB NB   I therefore prove it, secondly, in this way:

((4)) The essence of God[6] includes necessity of existence (for by the name of God we understand some necessary being).

((5)) One whose essence includes necessity of existence has an essence that is inseparable from existence (for otherwise any given thing is only possible or contingent).

Therefore
The essence and existence of God are inseparable.

Therefore we have finally concluded:
If God is possible, he actually exists, and now all that needs to be proved is that a most perfect being, or at any rate a necessary being, is possible.

Comments
(1) This argument has found it very hard to get assent among men, because it is without an example, which is not surprising since only the essence of God has this privilege that existence can be deduced from it *a priori* without supposing any actuality or any experience; this is because God is also the first being, or being from itself, or a being from whose essence existence follows. But he who does not reflect on this, even if he may feel himself convinced, and even if he does not have any solid response to this argument, will nevertheless always suspect some deception in it, and will scarcely be able to trust himself and his own reasoning, as tends to happen with all paradoxical conclusions.
(2) Cartesians work with conceptions or ideas alone, but they do not adequately bring out the force of this argument, as I have learned from experience, when they have compared their argument with mine. That is why they have not noticed that they are only able to conclude that God exists by supposing his possibility. For they believe that from their argument it is proved absolutely that God exists, which is false.

---

[6] God | and necessary existence are inseparable (for we suppose or define God as a necessary being | *deleted*.

(3) Essences, truths or objective realities of concepts do not depend either on the existence of subjects or on our thinking, but even if no one were to think about them and no examples of them existed, nevertheless in the region of ideas or truths, as I would say, i.e. in reality, it would remain true that these possibilities or essences actually exist, as do the eternal truths resulting from them.

(4) Eternal truths are not to be considered in this argument as hypothetical things that suppose actual existence, for otherwise we would have a circular argument. That is, from the supposed existence of God his existence would be proved. Of course in saying that the essence of God includes existence, it should not be understood to mean that if God exists he necessarily exists, but in this way: in reality, with no one thinking about it, it is unconditionally, absolutely and simply true that the essence and existence of God are inseparably connected in that region of essences or ideas.

(5) As in the region of eternal truths, i.e. in the realm of ideas that exists in reality, there subsist unity, the circle, power, equality, heat, rose, and other realities or forms or perfections, even if no individual entities exist and there were no thinking about these universals; so also there is found, among other forms or objective realities, *actual existence*, not as is found in the world or in examples, but as some kind of universal form which, if inseparably connected with some other essence or form in the realm of ideas, results in a being necessarily existing in actuality.

(6) In order that a possible objection against our argument may be more easily removed, we should consider that all those who grant that God is a necessary being must also grant that some argument similar to ours can be made about God. For he is necessary, or being from itself, whose existence necessarily follows from his essence, or is inseparable from it, therefore there must be some such argument through which the actual existence of God can be deduced from a consideration of his essence or possible existence alone, such that anyone who considered the essence of God perfectly would clearly see *a priori* that necessary existence follows from it. Therefore all the objections usually raised against our argument at first glance (namely that actualities cannot be deduced from possibilities, and others of that kind) immediately fail, for the same objections (as I have shown) can also be made against that argument which holds that anyone who considers the essence of God would understand that existence follows from it. Therefore it is evident from this that anyone who wants to attack our superior argument

must make some specific objection against it, which may not even be an objection to the argument just mentioned. But since our superior argument is not concerned with particulars, the only objection that can therefore be made against it is this: it may be denied that the concept of God, either as the supremely perfect being or a necessary being, is possible. For this point alone could not be an objection to someone who specifically considered the essence of God and noticed that existence followed from it, since every essence that we perceive distinctly does not imply a contradiction, but is possible. Therefore this alone remains to be done to demonstrate the existence of God, that his possibility, i.e. of the supremely perfect being or at any rate the necessary being, is demonstrated. For either it should be said that the necessary being is an impossible fiction, or it should be admitted that anyone who understands its specific nature (whatsoever it may ultimately be) will also understand, from the essence alone, i.e. *a priori,* that it has within it necessity of existence, or the inseparability of essence and existence.

(7) Spinoza reasons thus, following Descartes: 'to say that something is contained in the nature or concept of a thing is the same as to say that it is true of that thing' (just as it is contained in the concept of a triangle, or follows from its essence, that its three angles are equal to two right angles). 'But necessary existence is contained in the concept of God in the same way. Therefore it is true to say of God that there is necessary existence in him, or that he exists.'[7] To this argument, and others like it, it can be objected that all those propositions are conditional, for to say that three angles equal to two right angles are included in the nature or concept of a triangle is to say only that if a triangle were to exist, then it would have this property. So in the same way, even if it be granted that necessary existence is part of the concept of God, still the only thing that will be inferred from that is that if God exists, then he will have this property (of necessary existence), or that if God exists, he exists necessarily. Our argument, however, does not suffer from this difficulty, but proves something more, namely that if God is merely possible, he necessarily exists in actuality.

---

[7] Leibniz is here quoting the proof of Proposition 5 from Spinoza's *Renati Descartes Principiorum philosophiae pars I et II, more geometrico demonstratae* (1663). See Spinoza, *Complete Works*, trans. Samuel Shirley (Indianapolis: Hackett, 2002), p. 133.

2. There is only a single God (1685–6 (?))[8]

Manuscript:

M: LH I 6, 3a Bl. 7.

Transcription:

A: A VI 4, pp. 2211–12.

In 1686 Leibniz wrote a lengthy theological treatise which has since become known as *Examen religionis christianae* [*An examination of the Christian religion*] but which Leibniz himself left untitled and unpublished.[9] The work is a detailed systematic theology from an avowedly Catholic perspective. Why Leibniz wrote such a work is unclear. It can be dated to April–October 1686 on the basis of the watermark of the paper used; this means it was composed in the aftermath of negotiations between senior Catholics and Protestants regarding Church reunification. This in turn might suggest it was intended as a platform for further reunion discussions, but the work is too sympathetic to Catholicism to be acceptable to Protestants. Another possibility is that the work was drawn up as Leibniz's personal statement of faith, perhaps to see how his views would be received by Catholics. However, it is claimed that the work contains views which Leibniz elsewhere appears to reject.[10] Whatever its provenance, the themes of the *Examen religionis christianae* and the topics treated therein were clearly very important to Leibniz during the first half of the 1680s, as he wrote numerous shorter texts on them. The following piece is one of those shorter texts that Leibniz penned on the way to writing the *Examen religionis christianae*.

1) *It is certain that there is only a single God.* This is why those who say that there are three divine persons do not understand or must not

---

[8] Editor's title. From the French. Complete.
[9] A VI 4, pp. 2356–455. English translation: *System of Theology*, ed. and trans. C. W. Russell (London: Burns & Lambert, 1850).
[10] For details, see Robert Adams, 'Leibniz's Examination of the Christian Religion', *Faith and Philosophy* 11 (1994), pp. 517–46.

understand the word 'person' in the way it is generally understood, otherwise there would be three Gods. This is why they compare the three persons of the same divine substance with the three faculties located in one and the same soul, as are the power of acting, knowledge and the will.

2) *It is also true that Jesus Christ is an actual man*; this is against those who thought that the divinity took the place of his soul, and who confused the divine nature with human nature, attributing to one what belongs to the other.

Moreover, it should be agreed that only eternal and omnipotent God deserves a religious adoration. This is why[11] one should only adore this fullness of the divinity that Holy Scripture says dwells in Jesus Christ.[12]

3) *There is a very close union between the divine nature and the humanity of Jesus Christ*.[13] This union does not consist merely in the agreement or conformity of views, but also in a real influence, presence and intimate operation. And it seems that this union is as perfect as can be had between creator and creature.

4) *Everything that is said about the Trinity and the Incarnation should be explained in such a way that it does not clash with the divine perfections or the honour due to the supreme being.* For as we do not sufficiently understand what the terms 'person', 'nature' and 'union' mean with regard to God, it is acceptable to give them a sense that is reasonable and worthy of God.

5) *Nevertheless the safest thing to do is to keep to the formulas that God himself has revealed.* And for this reason it would be good for theologians to abstain from all expressions not authorized by Scripture and the perpetual tradition of the Catholic Church.[14]

6) And as for practice, it is important to recommend to men that our supreme love should only be concerned with what is divine and eternal, whereas often it is the human nature of Jesus Christ, and the knowledge we have of him according to the flesh, that holds our affection.

---

[11] why | when one adores Jesus Christ one declares that one adores only the divinity which dwells in him | *deleted*.

[12] An allusion to Colossians 1.19.

[13] *Christ*. | Jesus Christ is called the son of God, | *deleted*.

[14] Church. | As for practice, it is important to recommend to men that they not become overly attached to the humanity of Jesus Christ. | *deleted*.

3. If a necessary being is possible, it follows that it exists (March 1689– March 1690 (?))[15]

Manuscript:

M: LH IV 6, 9 Bl. 6.

Transcription:

A: A VI 4, p. 1636.

The provenance of this short piece is unknown. On the basis of the watermark of the paper, it is possible that it was written during Leibniz's stay in Italy, from March 1689 to March 1690.

This proposition, 'if a necessary being is possible, it follows that it exists', is the pinnacle of modal theory, and marks the first transition from possibility to being, or from the essences of things to existences. And because such a transition is necessary (otherwise nothing would exist), it even follows that a necessary being is possible, and indeed exists. And of course, if there were no necessary being, no reason could be given for the existence of things, nor would there be a cause for why something exists. Or, to put it more concisely, it is necessary that something exists, and therefore a necessary being exists. It must be seen whether this consequence is sufficient. For it seems to follow from this that at least some beings are necessary in a second way. But this second necessity must be founded upon some absolute necessity.

---

[15] Editor's title. From the Latin. Complete.

4. God is the sufficient reason for the world (29 December 1692/ 8 January 1693)[16]

Manuscript:

M: LBr F 16 Bl. 8.

Transcription:

A: A I 9, pp. 14–16.

Leibniz occasionally made a record of philosophical discussions he had, and the following piece is ostensibly a record of a conversation with his patroness, Electress Sophie of Hanover (1630–1714).

Summary of what I said in a conversation with Madam the Electress of Brunswick-Lüneberg, in Hanover 29 Xbr 1692

The principle of motion is one of the ways of leading us to the divinity. It is true that every body which is in motion is pushed by another body which, being in motion itself, is also pushed by another. And it always continues like this to infinity, or rather until a first motion is reached.[17] But this first motion could not have its origin in bodies, since a body only ever pushes after having been pushed. We must therefore have recourse to a higher cause. But even if there was no first motion, and even if it were supposed that the chain of causes, or of bodies which push each other, continues to infinity, we would still be obliged to look for the true cause of motion in something incorporeal, which must be found outside the infinite sequence of bodies. In order to understand it better, let us employ a fiction and imagine not only that the world is eternal, but also that there is a monarchy or eternal commonwealth in this world, and that in the

---

[16] Editor's title. From the French. Incomplete: the second half of the text, which concerns a proof for the existence of unities, has not been translated.

[17] reached. | But even if it were supposed that this should carry on to infinity, one would not find any sufficient reason | *deleted*; this deletion is not noted in transcription A.

archives of this commonwealth a certain sacred book has always been kept, the copies of which have been renewed from time to time. It is evident that the reason why this book says what it does is that it has been copied from another book which is identical but older, and the one which is the source of the latter is itself the copy of another, even older copy, and this carries on forever without there ever being an original, but always copies of copies. With this supposed, it is evident that one will never find in all these copies any sufficient reason for what is found in the book. Now in place of the fiction of the book, one has only to take a species, for example that of birds, and, supposing it to be eternal, it is clear that every bird is a copy of another one, and nevertheless in the whole sequence of birds one never finds the reason why there are birds rather than some other species, and I mean a sufficient reason.[18] And in place of birds or of some other species, one has only to take the motions which actually exist, which are also in some way the copy or consequence of some preceding motions, and so on to infinity, without there ever being found, in the whole of this infinite sequence of effects or copies, a sufficient or original reason. However nothing ever happens without there being a sufficient reason for it. Therefore the sufficient reason for the whole sequence of mutable things is found outside of this sequence and must consist in something immutable, which also has so much influence on all these copies that it is, properly speaking, the perpetual original of them, and this could only be found in the divinity.[19]

---

[18] reason | beyond which there is nothing further to ask for | *deleted*; this deletion is not noted in transcription A.

[19] Compare Leibniz's formulation of this argument in a paper written on 23 November 1697, 'On the ultimate origination of things': 'Let us imagine that the book of the elements of geometry has always existed, one always copied from another; it is evident that, even if a reason can be given for the present book from a past one, from which it was copied, nevertheless we shall never come upon a full reason no matter how many past books we assume, since we would always be right to wonder why such books have existed from all time, why books existed at all, and why they were written in this way. What is true of books is also true of the different states of the world; for a subsequent state is in a way copied from a preceding one (although according to certain laws of change). And so, however far back you go to earlier states, you will never find in those states a full reason why there should be any world rather than none, and why it should be such as it is.' G VII, p. 302/SLT, p. 31.

5. On Reverend Father Lamy's demonstration of the existence of God (late June 1701)[20]

Manuscript:

M: LH XI 1, 6 Bl. 5–6.

Transcription:

A: A I 20, pp. 247–8 (partial transcription only).

This piece is an extract from a letter sent to François Pinsson in late June 1701; the final draft of it was published in the September/October 1701 issue of *Mémoires pour l'histoire des sciences et des beaux arts* (sometimes referred to as the *Journal de Trévoux*), of which Pinsson was the editor.[21] The piece was written in response to an essay by François Lamy (1636–1711) on the Cartesian demonstration for the existence of God, published in the January/February issue of the same journal.[22]

[First draft][23]

I have often spoken of my opinion on the demonstration of the existence of God put forward by Mr Descartes, following St Anselm,[24] and I have shown that it is not a sophism, but an imperfect demonstration. For it supposes the possibility of God, and if this were also demonstrated then

---

[20] Editor's title (taken from the title given to the piece by Pinsson, the editor of the journal in which it appeared). From the French. Incomplete: those parts of the letter not connected with this topic, and so not published by Pinsson under this title, have not been translated.

[21] 'De la demonstration du R. P. l'Amy', *Mémoires pour l'histoire des sciences et des beaux arts* (September/October 1701), pp. 203–7.

[22] François Lamy, 'Lettre du Pere L'Amy Benedictin de la Congregation de S. Maur à M. l'Abbé Brillon Docteur de la Maison de Sorbonne, pour la défense d'une Demonstration Cartesienne de l'Existence de Dieu, attaquée par ce Docteur dans le Journal des Savans du 10. Janvier 1701', *Mémoires pour l'histoire des sciences et des beaux arts* (January/February 1701), pp. 187–217.

[23] None of the material from the first draft is recorded in transcription A.

[24] The original argument can be found in Anselm's *Proslogion*, II–III, and the third of Descartes's *Meditations*.

his existence follows,²⁵ and we would have an absolutely finished demonstration, in accordance with *a priori* rigour. It is a great privilege of the divine nature to need only its possibility, or essence, in order to exist. So without saying anything about 'the perfect being', it is sufficient to say that the being which exists through its essence (*ens a se*)²⁶ exists if it is possible, which makes the argument even simpler and more independent²⁷ and almost an identity, as are the first corollaries derived from a definition. For since essence is nothing other than the foundation of possibility, the definition of 'being from itself', or God, namely: '*ens a se* is that which exists through its essence', could be changed into this: '*ens a se* is that which actually exists if only it is possible'. So if God is possible, he exists. Those who imagine that existence cannot be proved through ideas, notions, essences or possibilities alone deny that this definition is possible. But if they were only to reflect on what has just been said they would understand.²⁸

[Final version]

I have already explained elsewhere my opinion on the demonstration of the existence of God given by St Anselm and revived by Descartes,²⁹ the substance of which is that what contains all the perfections, or is the greatest of all possible beings, also includes existence in its essence, since existence is among the perfections, and since otherwise something could be added to it. I hold the middle ground between those who take this reasoning to be a sophism, and the opinion of Reverend Father Lamy explained here, who takes it to be a finished demonstration.³⁰ So I grant that it is a demonstration, but an imperfect one, which requires us to presuppose a truth that likewise deserves to be demonstrated. For it is tacitly supposed that God, or rather the perfect being, is possible. If this point were also appropriately demonstrated then it could be said that the existence of God would be demonstrated geometrically, *a priori*. And this confirms what I

---

²⁵ follows | necessarily | *deleted*.
²⁶ 'being from itself'.
²⁷ independent |, and at the same time shows that I was right to say that the reality of ideas is nothing other than their possibility. God is more than possible, since he is necessary. But at issue here is what is lacking for a geometrically rigorous demonstration, which would require the proof of this possibility | *deleted*.
²⁸ understand | that if the being from itself were impossible, all other beings would be impossible too, since beings through others suppose some being from itself | *deleted*.
²⁹ See G. W. Leibniz, 'Meditationes de cognitione, veritate, et ideis', *Acta Eruditorum* (November 1684), pp. 537–42. English translation: L, pp. 291–4.
³⁰ Lamy, 'Lettre du Pere L'Amy Benedictin', pp. 187–217.

have just said,[31] that we can reason perfectly about ideas only by knowing their possibility: geometers have taken heed of this, but the Cartesians not enough. Yet it may be said that this demonstration is still considerable, and so to speak presumptive, for every being should be considered possible until its impossibility is proved. However I doubt that Reverend Father Lamy had grounds to say that the demonstration was adopted by the School, since the author of the marginal note rightly remarks there that St Thomas rejected it.[32] Be that as it may, an even simpler demonstration could be put together by not mentioning perfections at all, so as to avoid the objection of those who would take it upon themselves to deny that all perfections are compatible, and consequently that the idea in question is possible. For in saying merely that God is a being from itself, or primitive being (*ens a se*),[33] that is, a being that exists through its essence, it is easy to conclude from this definition that such a being, if it is possible, exists; or rather that this conclusion is a corollary which is immediately derived from the definition and hardly differs from it at all. For as the essence of a thing is only that which constitutes its specific possibility, it is quite clear that for a thing to exist through its essence is for it to exist through its possibility. And if the *being from itself* were defined in even narrower terms, by saying that it is the being which must exist because it is possible, it is clear that the only thing that could be said against the existence of such a being would be to deny its possibility. On this subject we could also lay down a proposition which would be among the most considerable of the doctrine of modalities, and one of the best fruits of all logic, namely that *if the necessary being is possible, it exists*. For 'the necessary being' and 'the being through its essence' are merely one and the same thing. Thus the argument taken from this angle appears to be solid, and those who claim that actual existence can never be inferred from notions, ideas, definitions or possible essences alone, in fact fall back into what I have just said, that is, they deny the possibility of the being from itself. But what is remarkable is that this very approach helps to make them see that they are wrong, and ultimately fills the gap in the demonstration. For if the being from itself is impossible, all *the beings through others* are also impossible, because they

---

[31] said I that every reasoning about ideas presupposes their reality I *deleted*. This is not recorded in transcription A.

[32] The marginal note reads: 'It is not agreed that the whole School had adopted this demonstration, which was rejected by Saint Thomas.' *Mémoires pour l'histoire des sciences et des beaux arts* (January/February 1701), p. 188.

[33] 'being from itself'.

ultimately exist only through the being from itself. And therefore nothing could exist. Which is absurd. This reasoning furnishes another important modal proposition, equal to the preceding one, and which together with it completes the demonstration. It could be expressed like this: *if the necessary being does not exist, there is no possible being.* It seems that this demonstration had not been taken so far until now; however I have also endeavoured elsewhere to prove that the perfect being is possible.[34]

I had no intention, Sir, other than to write to you in a few words some short reflections on the *Memoirs* you sent me, but the variety of the matters, the passion of meditation and the pleasure that I took from the generous intention of the Prince who is the patron of this work,[35] carried me away. I beg your pardon for this verbosity, and I am sincerely, etc.

B. THE NATURE OF GOD

1. God is not the soul of the world (summer 1683–winter 1685/6 (?))[36]

Manuscript:

M: LH I 20 Bl. 208.

Transcription:

A: A VI 4, p. 1492.

The provenance of this piece is unknown. The Akademie editors speculate that it may have been written in connection with Leibniz's discussions of substances and body between 1683 and 1686.

---

[34] See for example A VI 3, pp. 572–4/DSR, pp. 91–5.
[35] Louis Auguste, Duke of Maine (1670–1736), who established the *Mémoires pour l'histoire des sciences et des beaux arts* in 1701.
[36] Editor's title. From the Latin. Complete.

It can be demonstrated that *God is not the soul of the world*, for the world is either finite or infinite. If the world is finite, then God, who is infinite, certainly cannot be said to be the soul of the world; but if the world is assumed to be infinite, it is not one being, i.e. one body in itself (just as it has been demonstrated elsewhere that the infinite in number and in magnitude is neither one nor whole). Therefore no soul can be understood in it. Certainly an infinite world is no more one and whole than infinite number, which Galileo has demonstrated is neither one nor whole.[37]

There are also other arguments, such as this one: that God is the continuous producer of the world, but the soul is not the producer of its own body.

2. Rationale of the Catholic faith (mid-1680s (?))[38]

Manuscript:

M: LH I 3, 7c Bl. 3–4.

Transcription:

A: A VI 4, pp. 2313–23.

In the mid-1680s, following discussions about Church reunion that had taken place in Hanover, Leibniz wrote a series of apologies of the Christian faith, some of which concentrated on using arguments supplied by the natural light, that is, by reason.[39] In these pieces, Leibniz is concerned above all to show that the dogmas of the Catholic Church are in harmony with reason, perhaps in an effort to lay solid metaphysical foundations for the reunion of the Churches. The following piece is part of this series, but in spite of that, and its title, it is more a work of natural theology, the conclusions of which are in keeping with Catholic doctrine. It has been

---

[37] Leibniz may here be referring to 'Galileo's paradox', which suggests that notions such as 'equal', 'greater' and 'less' apply to finite sets but not infinite ones. See Galileo Galilei, *Dialogues concerning Two New Sciences*, trans. Henry Crew and Alfonso de Salvio (New York: Dover, 1954), pp. 31–3.
[38] Author's title. From the Latin. Complete.
[39] See also 'Specimen of *Catholic Demonstrations*, or, Apology for the faith through reason (this volume, pp. 103–8); 'Apologia fidei catholicae ex recta ratione', A IV 3, pp. 226–33.

aptly described as Leibniz's 'philosophical creed'.[40] The paper bears no watermark, but the themes of the piece were ones Leibniz revisited often between 1683 and 1686, suggesting it is from that period.

Rationale of the Catholic faith

On the one God

1) *God is the most perfect substance.*[41]

To whom, of course, all perfections can be attributed, and regarding whom all imperfections should be denied. For whatever perfections are understood formally in other things are attributed eminently to God, being careful to conceive of them as purged of every imperfection. But a perfection is nothing other than an attribute which involves no limitation, like being, acting, living, knowing and being able, to which a limitation is added in creatures, from which there results: being made, being acted upon, dying, learning what is not known and being impeded. Consequently the latter ones cannot be said of God, but the former ones can, as long as they are understood in a way utterly without qualification, so that his essence is maximally full, and independent, his action so universal that all things depend upon him, his life extends to eternity, his knowledge to omniscience and his power to omnipotence. It is evident that this notion of God is accepted both by distinguished ancient philosophers with sublimity of thoughts and by the whole of the Catholic Church, nor do Protestants disagree with it. Only Socinians and certain Remonstrants (among whom Conrad Vorst is famous for his execrable published book *de Deo*)[42] imagine a kind of God circumscribed by limits, and they say many things about him that are unworthy of his highest divinity, evidently because, having plunged themselves into the contemplation of finite things, they do not grasp these sublime concepts and therefore consider them as impossible. But it should be known that an absolute concept is always prior to and simpler than a limited one, from which it follows that the concept of God is evident to those who contemplate eternal truths with a mind diverted from the senses, even if this concept can no more

---

[40] A VI 4, p. LXXVI.
[41] substance. | This is the concept or definition of God received in the Catholic Church. | *deleted*.
[42] Conradus Vorstius, *Tractatus theologicus de Deo, seu Disputationes decem de natura et attributis Dei* (Steinfurt, 1610).

be perceived by the imagination and the senses than can colour be heard or a sound tasted.

2) *God exists.*[43]

This is demonstrated both *a priori* and *a posteriori*. *A priori*, or from God's essence or his possibility, that is, from the very concept of the most perfect being. For God is he who has every single perfection. Moreover, existence is also a perfection, for obviously a being from itself – one whose essence involves existence, or one which is a necessary being – is more perfect than one which is only contingent. But if the concept or essence of God involves existence, existence can certainly be predicated of God. Anselm of Canterbury first put forward this argument in his book against a foolish man.[44] The existence of God is proved *a posteriori* from the existence of finite contingent things, the reason for which cannot be given except by coming to a necessary being, which has the reason for its existence in itself and hence has no limit, inasmuch as a limit can only be supposed from without. The existence of God is particularly confirmed through the most beautiful arrangement of things, and especially from the nature of the mind. Consequently, when Socinius denied – against Holy Scripture and the opinion of the Catholic Church – that God can be discovered by the natural light of creatures, he did so wrongly.

3) *God is eternal.*

This follows from the fact that his essence involves existence. Therefore his existence is necessary, and that which is necessary is eternal.

4) *God is unique.*

For if there are many, they will differ, and indeed they will differ in their

---

[43] *exists.* | ¶ Anselm first put forward the simplest argument for the existence of the divine in his *Liber contra insipientem*. God is without doubt something greater or more perfect than which cannot be thought. But a being whose essence involves existence is more perfect than one whose essence does not involve it. Consequently existence necessarily follows from the essence or concept of God; moreover, whatever follows from the concept of something can actually be predicated of it, like trilinearity with regard to a triangle. Consequently, existence can be predicated of God, i.e. God exists. This argument is suspected of a sophism because it concludes too abruptly. And St Thomas looks for something in it, which interpreters have not understood well enough. For he observes that this argument supposes that there is a God in the nature of things. This should not be understood as though the argument were supposing God actually exists, but at any rate it does suppose that the essence of God has a place in the nature of things, as does the essence of a rose in winter, i.e. it supposes that God is possible. This, then, is the privilege of the divine nature, that its existence follows from its possibility or essence alone, i.e. that its essence involves existence, or that it is from itself. But as a result, if it is not first demonstrated that God is possible, the argument is incomplete. However, we have explained well enough in the preceding that the concept of God is possible. Therefore we hold that he exists. | *deleted*. Leibniz is referring to Aquinas' *Summa Theologiae* I.q2.1 reply to objection 2.

[44] St Anselm, *Liber contra insipientem*.

perfections, because nothing else is understood in God, and so each one of them is lacking some perfection, contrary to the definition of God.

5) *God is incorporeal*

Since every body has a boundary which makes a shape. Consequently, the pagans who worshipped the sun and stars made the gravest of mistakes. And Macrobius tries to show that the sun at any rate is considered everywhere as the highest God, and that it goes back to the mystical theology of the ancients.[45] This error is supported by an ignorance of the true system of the world, for whoever considers the whole world to be in the form of a globe which encloses several spheres within itself, the outermost of which is the surface bearing the stars, which is itself the form of a crystalline orb adorned with nails of gold, will easily convince himself that the sun, whose supreme beauty and power is evident, is either God or God's body, or at least his seat, unless someone prefers, with Aristotle, that God be bound to the outermost sphere.[46] But he who knows that the fixed stars are, as it were, just so many suns, and that there is no noble body in the world, will unquestionably realize that God is an ultramundane intelligence, to speak with Martianus Capella,[47] and that his seat is everywhere, and limit nowhere. But if someone[48] were to think that God is an infinite body whose members are all other bodies, a view to which those who, with the Stoics, make God the world or nature seem to incline, that person should consider that even if it were granted that there is a greater number of bodies than any assignable number, a single infinite whole still cannot be constructed from them, just as any single infinite number cannot be understood as composed from unities exceeding any number, as was shown elsewhere. And so God will always be something outside and beyond the aggregates of bodies.

6) *God is a mind, and is separate from every body.*

Obviously God has bodily attributes only eminently, for although God is not in space, he is still present, and although he is devoid of motion, he still moves. On the other hand, mental attributes belong to God formally,

---

[45] Macrobius, *Saturnalia* I.17.
[46] Aristotle, *De mundo* 397b25.
[47] Leibniz may be referring to Martiani Capella, *De Nuptiis Philologiae et Mercurii libri IX. emendati et Scholiis illustratis* (Basel, 1597), IX.910, although here Capella refers to 'extramundane intelligences' rather than 'ultramundane' (though both 'extra-' and 'ultra-' mean 'beyond').
[48] someone | were to imagine that God is a fire or aether spread throughout everything, he would not have an adequate consideration of the fact that there is in the world no body of the utmost subtlety. | *deleted*.

because mental attributes, like knowing, willing and being able, involve no imperfection. Therefore nothing prevents an infinite mind from being conceived, namely one which does not receive its thoughts from elsewhere, for even we do not discover eternal truths by sensation and experience; instead they flow from the very nature of the mind, and of concepts or ideas, which Plato maintained were actually one's own reminiscences.[49] And the more perfect each mind is, the less need it has to acquire knowledge through experience. Therefore the most perfect mind will conceive all things *a priori* and from itself, in the manner of eternal truths. Moreover, from the fact that he is the author of the world, it is obvious that God is not a mind which informs some body like ours does, and that he cannot be called the Soul of the World. Besides, the world is either finite or infinite. If it is finite, an infinite mind will not be the soul of a finite body, but if the world is infinite, it does not constitute some single infinite whole, as we mentioned a little earlier, nor can it thus be considered as an animated body.

7) *God is omniscient.*

For he knows the possibilities or the essences of things from a consideration of his own intellect which, since it is the most perfect, expresses all things – at any rate those which can be thought – by their ideas. On the other hand, he knows the contingent or actual existences of all things besides himself from a contemplation of his own will or of his free decrees, the first of which is that from many possibilities he chooses that which is more perfect, or better.[50] Yet there remains the difficulty urged by some

---

[49] See Plato, *Meno*, 82–6.

[50] better. | But whether it is the better does not depend upon God's will: such a thought is a dangerous doctrine since it means that even justice would be said to depend upon God's choice, in which case it will not be an attribute of God but only what God has willed of things.

Yet that which is a *perfect* good does not depend upon God's will but on the ideas in his intellect, likewise with what is true and false, equal or unequal, commensurable or incommensurable. And to think that goodness and justice derive not from the actual notions of things but from the sheer choice of a legislator, and therefore that every law is positive, is a dangerous opinion which removes the merit of justice from God, just like the preacher of tyranny in Plato makes justice that which pleases the powerful. For why should God be praised for those things he made with beauty, perfection and justice if they are to be called beautiful and just only because he made them, if it didn't matter what he would make and if even the opposites of the things he has made that are now called base might also have been called just if only they had been produced?

From which it is evident how God's knowledge does not introduce a necessity into things, since he knows necessary things in a different way from how he knows contingent things, even if both kinds of knowledge are certain and *a priori*. For necessary truths can be demonstrated from concepts or possible essences alone, while contingent truths are known for certain from the hypothesis of God's free decrees or those of another mind which has its own choice. Therefore two opposites do not in fact cease to be possible in themselves even if God chooses by reason of his

against divine omniscience, namely how can God know what another mind will choose according to the pleasure of its own free will? And this no less concerns those who think that we can choose without any reason, for what knowledge can there be of a thing which is completely indifferent? But those who understand, with Aristotle and Thomas, that the will is never led to anything except under the rule of the greater good, or at least of the apparent greater good – they solve the problem without difficulty, for since God foresees contingent things from his own free decrees, he will also know from those what the state of a free mind deliberating about some choice will be at any given time, i.e. how the arguments for each side will appear to it. Therefore he knows on which side of those presented the greater good or evil will be found, and hence what a mind will freely but certainly choose. From this it is also straightforwardly obvious how God knows what any free mind would choose if it were to find itself in any situation which nevertheless will not actually occur, and indeed God is unable not to see on which side the reasons will be more impressive or make a stronger impression. But of those who have been unwilling to make so much use of a natural explanation on account of certain prejudices of the School, some are compelled to doubt whether God is able to know such things, even though this is unworthy of God and contrary to Holy Scripture itself, while others, because of this difficulty, devise some form of God's knowledge which is scarcely consistent with divine perfection, for it should not be thought that God knows anything by way of perception or sight (like we do), such that he cannot see an *a priori* reason for his own knowledge from the nature of the thing itself and from the connection between subject and predicate, that is, from the ideas of his own intellect. For although God does not engage in reasoning, he always sees and discovers the reasons in himself, otherwise there would be something independent of him.

8) *God is omnipotent and the creator and conserver of all things.*

All things originate from God: the essences of things from his intellect, the existences of things from his will. And from this it is obvious that the power or virtue of acting is a perfection, and is therefore to be attributed to God, and in fact in the highest degree, but not to the extent that he can do something contradictory or absurd, as certain enthusiasts seem to

---

own pleasure which is better; but another mind chooses that which appears better. Therefore those people who think – and this is not without danger to weaker minds – that all things happen by a fatal necessity, and who consider impossible anything which neither was, is or will be, are in error, confusing the certain with the necessary. | *deleted*.

think. Moreover, God creates things, conserves them and concurs with them in their operation. And indeed, conservation is nothing other than a continued creation, since things in existence always depend upon God absolutely, as much in their development as at the beginning; for it should not be said, in respect of God, that a thing is produced from a preceding thing, but from nothing, since it can be said that nothing remains of the preceding thing which is not also itself produced anew. Therefore, so far from matter being eternal, it consists, on the contrary, in a momentary flux, and even if some creatures were assumed to have always existed, the world could still not be called eternal. Moreover, in this continuous production of things consists God's concurrence with creatures' operations, because God continuously bestows upon them the substance, force and all requisites of operation, even if the operation itself is not God's but the creature's.

9) *God is good, or just.*

This follows from his wisdom, for justice is nothing other than a soul's consistent inclination, worthy of the wise, towards the goods and evils of others. Therefore it is to be considered as certain that those who could understand the secret economy of the whole of providence will discover that no one can justly complain and that nothing better can be wished for, because those who know are unable not to love God above all things, even if they are not yet granted distinct knowledge of the divine plan and the beatific vision. But what is good, perfect and just, i.e. worthy of the wise, does not depend on God's will, but on his essence, i.e. on the ideas in his intellect, as is the case with what is possible or impossible, equal or unequal, and commensurable or incommensurable. In fact it is a very dangerous opinion of those who consider that the just and the good derive not from the actual notions of things but from the sheer choice of a legislator, and who make every law positive, just like the preacher of tyranny in Plato, who defines justice as that which pleases the powerful.[51] On this basis there would be no notion of justice in itself, nor would justice be something attributed to God, nor would God differ from a tyrant except in terms of power. And why, I ask, would God be praised for the beauty and perfection of the things he had made or for the justice of his own decrees; how would he have seen that what he made was good if it didn't matter what he would make,[52] if anything he would have made

---

[51] See Plato, *Republic*, 338c–39a.
[52] Leibniz's point that God saw that what he made was good clearly recalls Genesis 1.10, 1.12, 1.18, 1.21, 1.25 and 1.31.

would be, by that very fact, beautiful, good and just, even those things which are now considered wicked? Lastly, how can he be said to have acted wisely and as befits the most perfect mind if, in that which he produces, it happens as though by a kind of fated lot rather than reached by a definite rule of choice?

10) *God's foreknowledge and providence do not destroy free will, nor is God the cause of sin, nor is the misery of the wretched to be imputed to him.*

Even though it was concluded from the previous article that no one can complain about God, it is still useful to address the objections which have been considered by men everywhere and from antiquity, and which have given occasion to the gravest heresies. The first objection is that we must necessarily sin and be wretched if God has foreknown it from eternity. The response is that God knows that this is certain but it is not necessary, for he knows what you will freely choose. But a second, more serious objection follows from providence or predetermination, namely how can it be said that I choose anything freely if in choosing I depend upon God, if my mind is inclined to one side by him, i.e. if the series of things grounded in God makes it so that false but impressive reasons appear before my deliberating mind, by which it is impelled to choose? The response should be that false reasons do in fact incline the mind to choose, but they do not necessitate, speaking with the Scholastics, since whoever is of good will would always be able to avoid the sin, which in fact only consists in an evil will. But you will urge again that it is strange that God should bestow a good will on one person while he casts another into those circumstances which give rise to an evil will. For although it has to be admitted that an evil will is sufficient for the punishment of a criminal, no matter how it originated, nevertheless parents are blamed when they raise their children badly, as is a commonwealth which causes the corruption of its own citizens. We shall reply that in fact the mass of men in Adam was already corrupted, and therefore thanks should be given to God for saving some rather than blame directed against him for abandoning the others. But the reply will be that in the beginning it was possible for the mass of men not to be corrupted, and hence that the same difficulty returns with regard to the sin of Adam himself; and, further, that we do not have the freedom of sticking to the sublapsarian position,[53] but must necessarily go back in time beyond the fall, unless we

---

[53] Sublapsarianism is a position held by some Calvinist theologians. It holds that God decreed (1) to create man such that he was able to fall, (2) to permit man to fall, (3) to provide the means of salvation to all, and (4) to elect some to salvation and to condemn the rest. It is a doctrine about the logical order of God's decrees rather than their temporal order (because God is held to be outside time).

want to pretend that there is no difficulty. And in general, God would have been able to prevent every sin if he had wanted to, and indeed this cannot be denied. But because he has permitted sin, it is to be held as certain that it was introduced for reasons most important to his own wisdom. Indeed, it should be thought that there is a greater perfection of things with sin permitted than with it excluded, even if this is not immediately obvious to us who cannot observe the secrets of things. Accordingly, Paul appealed to the depth of divine wisdom,[54] and certain pious and shrewd men were induced to call Adam's fault a happy one, which caused the mystery of the Incarnation to obtain.[55] But the cause of sin is not to be traced back to God's will, since it always aims at the most perfect and, on account of its benevolence and especially on account of its most abundant love for humans, it has not disregarded anything which the condition of making things perfect demands. Instead, the cause of evil is to be traced back to non-being, or privation, that is, to the natural limitation or weakness of things, or even – which comes back to the same thing – to the original imperfection which is earlier than original sin itself. This original imperfection performs the same role for orthodox supralapsarians in safeguarding the justice of God as original sin does for the sublapsarians,[56] and it causes every created mind to be inclined to judge from only a small number of things observed unless it is supported either by experience of a preceding error or by divine grace. Moreover, this limitation and imperfection depends on the ideas or essences of things, not on God's will, and hence it happened that God would assist some with grace and would abandon others to their natural weakness, the eternal cause of his own glory, that is of the greater good in general, with the election in Christ made not out of sheer choice or because of the worth of those chosen, but with consideration for achieving a greater perfection of the whole. And this greatest perfection would not be obtained except by repeatedly permitting those things that can appear to be evil or less excellent in themselves, in the way that a harmony becomes better by the inclusion of occasional dissonances. Whoever gives proper consideration to these things

---

[54] An allusion to Romans 11.33: 'O the depth of the riches both of the wisdom and knowledge of God!'

[55] Leibniz is probably thinking of these lines from the Exsultet, the Easter proclamation of the Catholic Church: 'O truly necessary sin of Adam, which was erased by the death of Christ! O happy fault, that merited so great a Redeemer!'

[56] Supralapsarianism holds that God decreed (1) to elect some to salvation and condemn the rest, (2) to create human beings, i.e. the elect and the condemned, (3) to permit man to fall, and (4) to save the elect. As with sublapsarianism, it is a doctrine about the logical order of God's decrees held by some Calvinist theologians.

will always acquiesce to the divine will, will adore the power and love the goodness of the creator: knowing that these thoughts entering the mind of a soul and impelling each one to the best duties of faith and charity come from the divine spirit, and therefore that those who are thus affected are by that very fact in a state of grace, and that God turns all things into good for the one loving him.[57] And so the pious man will be a stranger to the errors which greatly detract from divine dignity and which turn the souls of men away from the love of the most beautiful and most beneficent substance; such are the errors of the Socinians and certain Remonstrators who diminish God's knowledge and the dependence of all things on God in order that they may look out for his justice and human freedom. Then on the other hand there are the errors of others who, in order to preserve God's greatness, trace all things back to his will, and do away with every concept of justice by concluding that God's commandments are impossible to keep, and that sins are necessary. These people are not afraid to make God the author of sins, as though sins were evil not by nature but by law; or as though the Lord of all things would be able to make decisions regarding his own creatures by some sheer choice, without any consideration for the previous arrangements of things which he has foreseen, and for the idea of good and justice itself. Impartial judges will perhaps conclude that we have dealt adequately with both types of error not by avoiding the difficulty or by changing the state of the question, as is often done, but by way of a frank and clear explanation.

3. On the true Mystical Theology (mid-1690s (?))[58]

Manuscript:

M: LH I, 5, 1 Bl. 1.

Transcription:

VON: Franz Vonessen, 'Zwei Kleine Philosophische Schriften', in *Antaios*, ed. Mircea Eliade and Ernst Jünger (Stuttgart: Ernst Klett Verlag, 1966), VIII/2: pp. 128–33.

---

[57] An allusion to Romans 8.28.
[58] Author's title. From the German. Complete. Translated by Julia Weckend.

In 1694, Leibniz began corresponding with André Morell (1646–1703), an antiquarian and numismatist, who was also an ardent supporter of the cobbler-turned-mystic Jakob Böhme (1575–1624). Morell often tried to get Leibniz to read Böhme's works and look favourably upon his views, though his efforts met with limited success, as Leibniz had little patience for the sort of mystical theology taught by Böhme. Indeed, he even claimed that Böhme 'often did not understand himself', let alone the things he wrote![59] The following piece is possibly inspired by his exchanges with Morell, which cover some of the same ground;[60] the text itself appears to be Leibniz's attempt to invest the idea of a mystical theology with 'a good sense' (i.e. to find an acceptable way of understanding it), and thus to wrest it back from people like Böhme.

On the true Mystical Theology

Every[61] perfection in creatures flows immediately from God (such as essence, power, existence, magnitude, knowledge, will).

The concomitant[62] shortfalls flow from creatures themselves, their limits or *non plus ultra*, thus leaving[63] boundaries in their wake (in the form of limits to essence, resistance to power, passion in existence, restriction in magnitude, obscuring of knowledge and a wavering of the will).

The inner light alone, which God himself kindles in us, has the power to grant us our first knowledge of God. Through such apprehension alone do we attain a clear grasp of essence and truth, so that neither further evidence of truth, nor further explanation of such essences, will be required.

Many a person is learned but not enlightened since[64] he follows not God or the light but merely his earthly teacher, or continues believing his external senses and thus keeps on dwelling on imperfect things.

This light does not arrive from the outside, even though external teachings also can – and on occasion must – provide us with the opportunity to catch a glimpse of it. Among the external teachers there are two that best awaken

---

[59] Grua I, p. 79. See also A I 15, p. 560, where Leibniz casts doubt on Böhme's ability to express his thoughts adequately. Leibniz did eventually praise Böhme's humility and meekness; see A I 17, p. 474.
[60] See especially A I 15, pp. 558–62, and A I 16, pp. 161–5. Both are from 1698.
[61] Every | (α) highest good | (β) worthiness | *deleted*.
[62] concomitant | imperfection | *deleted*.
[63] leaving | finiteness | *deleted*.
[64] since | this inner light is God's eternal word. | *deleted*.

the internal light: the book of Holy Scriptures and the experience of nature. Yet neither helps if the internal light does not participate.

This inner light is the eternal word of God in which lies all wisdom,[65] all light, indeed the archetype of each and every being and the source of all truth. Without this light's illumination nobody has the true faith; and without true faith nobody will be blessed.

The light fills the heart with clarity and reassurance, not with fantasies and mad stirrings. There are some who imagine a world of light in their brain, reckon they see splendour and magnificence and are surrounded by many thousands of tiny lights. But that is not the true light, only a heating of the blood.[66]

When confronted with the true light, one is convinced that it is of God, and not of the devil or flesh. Just as the sun is proof of itself, so is this light.

All creatures are from God and nothingness. Their self-being is from God, their non-being from nothingness. This is also born out in numbers in a wonderful way, and the essences of things are like numbers.[67]

No creature can be without non-being, or else it would be God. Even angels and saints must have it.[68]

True self-knowledge means to clearly distinguish between one's self-being and one's non-being.

We come to recognize God through recognizing perfections. The divine perfections are concealed in all things but only a very few know how to find them therein. Knowledge of God is the beginning of wisdom. The divine qualities are the grounds for the proper ordering of knowledge. Even though they are prior to other things, and other things develop from them, they still will be discovered first and through themselves, and other things through them. God is the easiest and the hardest to know: the first and easiest when following the path of light, the hardest and last on the path of shadows.

---

[65] wisdom, | the model of all knowledge, the reasons for all truth | *deleted*.

[66] Leibniz's desire to give physical explanations of apparently mystical phenomena can be seen in his discussion of Rosamund Juliane von der Asseburg (1672–1727?): he argued that her visions and prophecies were a product of her imagination, which in turn had been shaped by her closeted, religious upbringing. See A I 7, pp. 33–7/LTS, pp. 75–80, and A I 7, pp. 45–52/LTS, pp. 86–94.

[67] Leibniz often took his discovery of the binary system, in which all numbers derive from 1 and 0, to serve as an analogy for creation, in which all things are derived from God and nothingness. See for example G. W. Leibniz, *Mathematische Schriften vol. 7*, ed. C. I. Gerhardt (Berlin: A. Asher, 1863), p. 239/SLT, p. 39.

[68] it. | It is enough for them to recognize their own self-being to lift themselves above their non-being. | *deleted*.

Most of our knowledge and inventions [*tichten*] belong to the path of shadows, such as historical accounts, languages, cultural and natural practices. There is in fact some light along with the shadow, but only a few can distinguish them. Just as the findings from Roman Antiquity and similar human traditions are of value to us, but of no use to someone enslaved[69] in[70] barbarism, the latter still understands to make use of natural resources such as the potentials in herbs so that he knows, for example in places like Turkey, how to prepare chickpea meal [*erbs schrot*]. This shows that systematic knowledge [*wißenschaft*] accumulated through such natural practices in turn only serves in this world, towards alleviating this life's immediate needs. But this cannot make the very same knowledge complete, nor advance it, when it removes God from this world.

In the meantime, these findings have their great use and reward indeed, not just for[71] the immediate needs of life and human societies, but also because they act as tools [*werckzeuge*] for the removal of obstacles from the path of light. Sensory delights and the contemplation of shadow plays should only be used out of necessity and as a tool, without stopping there.

Within our self-being there lies an infinity, a footprint, indeed an image of the omniscience and omnipotence of God. Each individual self-state [*selbststand*], such as I or you, is a unified, indivisible, imperishable being, which does not just consist of three parts – soul, mind and body; there are[72] more things which immediately belong to the one being, as if incorporated in it. Even though each individual self-state is without parts, there are other things imprinted in it without taking up space there themselves.

Each and every being contains everything, although with varying degrees of clarity.[73]

Bodies are the mere work of God, minds are in fact the kingdom of God. God is more intimately related to me than the body. Bodily things are mere fleeting shadows, glimpses,[74] phenomena [*gestalten*], real dreams. The essential truth is solely in the mind, even though inexperienced people mistake appearances for dream, and what is tangible for truth.

Sin is not from God; instead, in some creatures original sin arose from their non-being and thus out of nothingness.

---

[69] Reading 'keinen schlaven' (M) in place of 'keinen Pflanzer' (VON).
[70] in | America | *deleted*.
[71] Reading 'dienend' (M) in place of 'dringend' (VON).
[72] are | other things not belonging to it | *deleted*.
[73] clarity. | Corporeal self-beings belong to | *deleted*.
[74] glimpses, | are like phenomena, not like self-beings | *deleted*.

God permitted sin because he knew how to bring about a greater good out of evil.

Only the evil themselves have suffered a loss through sin. God's creation as a whole has not lost but gained through it.

God's will to power is not unconstrained, but he wants everything for a reason and according to what is best. His election through grace has its origin in the anticipated merits of men, and is therefore based neither on their foreseen faith, nor on anticipated deeds, but on many higher reasons. For, whether a person believes, or else thinks and acts virtuously, is also contained in God's pre-election of him in Christ.

God desires the welfare of and the best for all creatures. But he neither chooses one in preference to another out of[75] will to power as though choosing without a reason and because they merely spring to mind; nor does he choose according to their achievements or merits; nor does he choose what is likely the best for them individually (though they only get to be the best they can through him); instead, the overall best arises because of their very creation.

For a lesser thing combined with another lesser can often bring about something better overall than the composition of some other two which individually are nobler than any one of the former. Herein lies the secret of the election through grace and the untying of the knot. (*Duo irregulariae possunt aliquando facere aliquid regularius quam duo regularia.*)[76]

The denial of the self is the hatred of the non-being which is part of us; and the love of the origin of our self-being, that is, God.

To crucify the old Adam, and to draw close to Christ; to let Adam die away and to find a life in Christ; all these amount to this: to deny non-being and to cling to self-being.

He who knows to favour the inner light before sense appearances [*sinbilden*], or self-being before non-being, loves God above all things. He who merely fears God loves himself and his non-being more than God.

Faith without knowledge is not derived from divine spirit, but only from dead letter or hollow sound.

Faith devoid of light does not bring about love, but only fear or hope, and is not living.

He who does not act according to faith does not truly believe even when he boasts of it.

---

[75] Here VON adds 'blindem' [blind] which is not present in M.
[76] 'Two irregular things can sometimes make something more regular than can two regular things.'

It is lamentable that so few people know what light and faith, love and life, Christ and blessedness are.[77]

The teachings of Christ are spirit and truth, but many turn it into flesh and shadow. Most people are not seriously engaged, they have not tasted truth and are caught up in shrouded unbelief.

Let each person prove to himself[78] whether he has faith and life. If he finds certain joys and pleasures greater than those that come from his love for God and the fulfilment of his will, then he does not know Christ sufficiently and does not feel the promptings of the Holy Spirit.

Scripture provides us with a beautiful test whether a person loves God, namely when he loves his brother,[79] and makes efforts to help and to serve him. Whoever does not do so boasts wrongly of enlightenment, or of Christ and the Holy[80] Spirit.

4. Review of Lüttichau's *Pansophia* (4 September 1696)[81]

Manuscript:

M: LBr 153 Bl. 19–22.

Transcription:

A: A I 13, pp. 227–32.

The following is a review of Wolf Heinrich von Lüttichau's *Pansophia, oder, Grund aller Weisheit: in Erkäntnüss Gottes nach seinem Wesen, vermittelst der Vernunffts-Kräffte gesuchet / von W.H.V.L.O.L.* (Berlin, 1696). Leibniz sent his review to the editor of the *Nouveau Journal des sçavans*, Etienne Chauvin, who published it in the September/October 1696 issue of that journal (pp. 398–407). The only surviving copy of this text is Leibniz's draft, which is translated here. There are a few differences between Leibniz's draft and the version of the text published in

---

[77] are. | Most people think of Christ's spirit in terms of carnal thoughts and works. | *deleted*.
[78] himself | if he wants to know whether he follows the rightful path | *deleted*.
[79] See Matthew 22.37-9; Mark 12.29-31; Luke 10.27
[80] Reading 'des Heiligen' (M) in place of 'seines' (VON).
[81] Editor's title. From the French. Complete.

the *Nouveau Journal des sçavans*, though these were probably Chauvin's stylistic changes to the (no longer extant) fair copy that Leibniz despatched. At any rate, the differences between Leibniz's draft and the version of the text published by Chauvin are insignificant.

Report on Mr Lüttichau's book, sent to Mr Chauvin

I have still not noticed, Sir, whether your journal has mentioned a very good German book published in Berlin some months ago, the author of which is a gentleman from the neighbouring country. A great Prince told me of this book some months back,[82] and I have seen it myself recently. As it deals with an important subject and in a very good way, it is worthy of a review, all the more since it has had the approval of Mr Strimesius, an able theologian and philosopher from Frankfurt on the Oder.[83] The title means: *Pansophia, or, the foundation of all wisdom, consisting in the knowledge of God, according to his essence, and in the knowledge of man, according to his nature; the whole thing researched by means of the powers of reason by W.H.V.L.O.L.*[84] The work has two parts; the first concerns the knowledge of God, and boils down to showing the following 8 propositions: 1. that God is the primary essence, or essence itself, 2. that he is the supreme Excellency, and the most perfect being, 3. that he contains the perfection of all beings, 4. that he is a holy substance, and unique, 5. that he knows everything, and is everywhere, 6. that he is all-powerful, 7. that he is just and true, 8. that he is supremely good and worthy of being loved. Appended to each proposition is the use that it can have in the practice of Christian virtues, together with devout prayers aroused by meditation, the power and eloquence of which is apparent.

The author shows that one could not know God better than by the name he gave himself when speaking to Moses; he called himself: *the one who is*.[85] And as the names God gives to things are the best, this notion will be anterior to that of the perfect being which Descartes and Henry More[86] and

---

[82] According to Leibniz's *Tagebuch* entry of 21/31 August 1696, this great Prince was Anton Ulrich (1633–1714), Duke of Brunswick-Wolfenbüttel. See Leibniz, *Geschichtliche Aufsätze und Gedichte*, ed. Georg Heinrich Pertz (Georg Olms: Hildesheim, 1966), p. 201.
[83] Johann Samuel Strimesius (1648–1730), who was at the time Associate Professor of Theology at Frankfurt an der Oder, contributed a foreword to Lüttichau's book.
[84] The acronym stands for Wolf Heinrich von Lüttichau, Obrist-Leutnant.
[85] Exodus 3.14.
[86] Henry More (1614–87), a philosopher and poet, one of the so-called 'Cambridge Platonists'.

other able authors have employed.[87] And the reason the author gives for this is that the essence or nature of a thing consists in the fundamental conceptions that have to be employed to form the notion of it, to which affections or properties are afterwards joined. In this matter the order of nature should be followed rather than an arbitrary order. Now according to the author, supreme perfection presupposes in God something anterior, which he calls being the primary Essence of all beings, or the Being of Beings, *Ens Entium*,[88] which contains the plenitude of all the others. So it seems that he still differs a little from those who maintain that the primary notion of God is *ens a se* [being from itself], that which is from itself, wherefrom they infer that he is the source of others, although ultimately these notions agree well enough. As for *perfection*, the author maintains that it consists in an addition, or multiplication, such that a thing is all the more perfect when there are more additions in it, like in numbers, and that each thing is perfect to the extent that it is a being. He infers from this that the being which contains the whole plenitude of beings also contains all the degrees or all the additions of perfection. A musician, no matter how skilful he is, is never perfect. But if abstract music could appear before us, it would be perfect. Now the author says that these ideas or these abstract universals really subsist in God along with their eternal truths, whatever the Peripatetics may say about it. So he takes the side of the Platonists. It is true that Thomas Aquinas and several other Peripatetics seem not too far away from this view. He also proves that there is only one God by maintaining that it is not permitted to grant several infinites. *Likewise*, that there is only one single abstract universality of being. And when he speaks of divine knowledge, he holds with some learned theologians and philosophers that the Word is the archetype world of ideas, and that there is no hypothesis which better explains the eternal generation of the Son of God. And on that issue, he very correctly remarks that Descartes was wrong to take essences and truths as something arbitrary which depends on God's will.[89] Moreover, the author grounds God's presence on the dependence that all the other beings have on him, and grounds his justice on order or proportion. And all that is said in a very good sense. He adds that God could not cause more harm to his creature than he has done good to it.

He refutes those who claim that it is better to be in misery than not to

---

[87] Cf. Descartes, *Meditations* V; Henry More, *An Antidote against Atheism* (London, 1655), ch. III.
[88] 'Being of beings'.
[89] See for example Descartes, *The Philosophical Writings of Descartes*, II: p. 291, and III: p. 23.

be at all, and says that this opinion was only invented to support an even worse one, namely that God can bring himself to damn innocent creatures eternally. And for this reason he does not want to grant that simple being contains an intrinsic goodness.

The second part, which concerns the knowledge of man, boils down to the following propositions: 1. that man is a creature of God, 2. that he is an intelligent creature, 3. that his nature inclines him to love, 4. that his love (in the state of corrupted nature) is contrary to order. The author maintains with the Scholastics that conservation is a continual creation, and he holds with the Platonists and Father Malebranche that we see all things in God,[90] from which he draws the consequence that truth and philosophy are something nobler than is thought. He also says that we always think of the universal being, just as we are always inclined to the general good. And the void is, in his view, the occasional cause of motion, the particular efficient cause of which is the impulsion of one body by another, although the universal cause of this motion is God himself, who always conserves the same quantity of it, according to Descartes (whose error in this matter, however, has recently been discovered).[91] He likewise thinks that the void or privation is the occasional cause of the moral motion of love, that temporal goods are the particular efficient cause of it, but that God, or the general good, is the universal cause, which has given a certain measure or quantity of this motion to the intellectual world too. And just as we see in God all the things we see, it must be the case that we likewise love in God everything we love. And although Father Malebranche claims that we are necessarily inclined only towards the general good, our author nonetheless thinks that we are even necessarily inclined to the particular good, according to its degree of goodness known to us. He explains this with the comparison of a balance, although elsewhere he seems to infer that it is not necessary that man exists, since if the creator loved him with a necessary love, it would be the supreme degree of love. In the state of corrupted nature man has become his own creature, by changing the order of love, and our author shows that one could not be a sinner without folly and that one never chooses evil except by a false judgement, by taking it

---

[90] Nicolas Malebranche (1638–1715), philosopher and Oratorian. See Nicolas Malebranche, *The Search after Truth*, trans. Thomas M. Lennon and Paul J. Olscamp (Cambridge: Cambridge University Press, 1997), pp. 230ff.
[91] Leibniz is referring here to one of his own essays, the 'Brevis demonstratio erroris memorabilis Cartesii', originally published in the March 1686 issue of *Acta eruditorum*, pp. 161–3. English translation: L, pp. 296–301.

for a good. He also remarks that in the event that one could not properly explain how the sin of the first man was communicated – without injustice – to posterity, one would be obliged to have recourse to the hypothesis of pre-existence. Finally, he makes fun of those who believe that ignorance is the mother of devotion, and that both erudition and insight are enemies of piety; he does not think that this deserves a serious refutation. It is not knowledge and insight but rather ignorance and passion that make men impious and malicious.

So that, Sir, is the substance of this work. You can judge how much importance I attach to it by the trouble I have taken to give you this report on it – I hardly ever do this except when some new discovery is concerned. But I think it is right to commend these kinds of writings, and to point out all their merit in order to encourage the distinguished persons of our nation, when they are masters of their time, to follow the example of foreigners a little more than they have done until now, and not to leave meditation only to those learned by profession, who are often prevented by their occupations from giving their minds free reign. I am also delighted that these matters have begun to be treated in Germany, for as I said to you recently, the German language is the touchstone of solid thoughts, since it does not suffer from the chimeras of the vulgar school.[92]

I hope, however, that the author of this fine treatise will permit me to add some minor reflections. Mr Strimesius has rightly admired the research done here on the formal notion of God. But as few people have properly understood in what consists the difference between formal notions and properties, I will add a word on what I have said about that before, in the *Acts* of Leipzig, when discussing ideas.[93] I hold, then, that real notions which serve as the foundation of *a priori* demonstrations, are those which carry the proof of possibility with them. So every predicate, of which it can be doubted from the outset (leaving experience aside) whether it is possible or not, is only a property, and can give only nominal definitions.[94]

It can be doubted whether perfection consists in addition, and whether it is formed by composition, like numbers, since it appears that it is formed by the negation of limits instead. It also seems that simple being does

---

[92] A I 12, p. 626.
[93] Leibniz is referring here to his essay 'Meditationes de Cognitione, Veritate et Ideis', published in the November 1684 issue of *Acta eruditorum*, pp. 537–42. English translation: L, pp. 291–4.
[94] 'This gives us, too, a means of distinguishing between *nominal definitions*, which contain only marks for discerning one thing from other, and *real definitions*, through which the possibility of the thing is ascertained.' A VI 4, p. 589/L, p. 293.

contain an intrinsic goodness, for even if everyone were to agree that it is better to be nothing than to be miserable, it is also still true that it is better to be something than to be nothing, all other things being equal; that is, leaving good fortune and bad fortune aside. I find some soundness in what the author says about ideas and eternal truths, the original reality of which could only be in God, which I am accustomed to call the region of essence and the basis of truths. However, I do not know if God is strictly speaking the universal and abstract being according to how these terms are understood among philosophers. But it is not necessary to go over this in detail here – it is sufficient that it is good in the author's sense.

In a certain sense it can truly be said that we see all things in God, and that he is our immediate external object. I hold, however, that there is also always something in us which corresponds to the ideas which are in God as well as to the phenomena which occur in bodies, and this means that when the received philosophy talks of certain species it is not entirely as wrong as is thought. But it is mistaken about the origin of these species, and elsewhere I have explained the commerce of substances, the manner in which we are aware of external things, and the union of two substances as different as the soul and the body;[95] the profound search for these things having led me and as it were forced me to the discovery of new principles as different on this point from those of the School as from those of the Cartesians and of Reverend Father Malebranche.

I wholeheartedly subscribe to what was said of the use of true knowledge: ignorance is the mother of crimes. And one could not have a solid virtue without being enlightened at least on the major point of wisdom. Perhaps it would be appropriate to push the practical consequences of this doctrine a little further. As our perfection consists in the knowledge and the love of God, it follows that we are advanced in perfection to the extent that we penetrate eternal truths, and that we have zeal for the general good. So those who are truly enlightened and well-intentioned work, with all their power, for their own instruction and for the good of others, and if they have the means for it, they try hard to procure the increase in the enlightenment of men, in Christian virtue and public happiness. This is the touchstone of true piety.

---

[95] Leibniz is referring here to his essay 'Système nouveau de la nature et de la communication des substances', published in the 27 June and 4 July issues of the *Journal des Sçavans* (1695). English translation: SLT, pp. 68–77.

5. Ancient and modern understandings of God (30 April 1709)[96]

Manuscript:

M: LBr 933 Bl. 13–14.

Transcription:

T: John Toland, *A collection of several pieces of Mr. John Toland, now first publish'd from his original manuscripts: with some memoirs of his life and writings*, 2 vols (London, 1726): II, pp. 384–7.

This piece is an extract from a letter to the Irish-born philosopher John Toland (1670–1722), with whom Leibniz had a sporadic correspondence in the last decade of his life. The letter was occasioned by Toland sending Leibniz a copy of a book he had recently published, *Dissertationes duae, Adeisidaemon et origines Judaicae* (The Hague, 1709). Leibniz's page references are to this book.

You often mention, Sir, the opinion of those who believe that there is no other God, or no other eternal being, than the world, that is, matter and its interconnection (as you explain on p. 75), without this eternal being having intelligence (p. 156). In your view, this is an opinion that Strabo attributes to Moses (p. 156), and you yourself attribute it to the philosophers of the east, and especially to those of China (p. 118). And you even say (p. 115) that one can compare it with (albeit equivocally) the perfect being, the Alpha and the Omega, what was, is and will be; what is all in all,[97] in which we move and live and have our being,[98] as Holy Scripture puts it. But as this opinion (which you point out is one you yourself reject) is as pernicious as it is poorly founded, it would be wished, Sir, that you would relate it only

---

[96] Editor's title. From the French. Incomplete: parts of the letter on other topics have not been translated.
[97] The description of God as 'all in all' is to be found in 1 Corinthians 12.6 and 15.28, and Ephesians 1.23.
[98] An allusion to Acts 17.28.

alongside a suitable refutation, which you will perhaps give elsewhere. But it would always be better not to administer the antidote after the poison. And to speak the truth, it does not appear that the majority of those ancients and moderns who have talked about the world as a God have thought this God devoid of knowledge. You know that Anaxagoras joined intelligence with matter. The Platonists conceived a soul of the world, and it appears that the doctrine of the Stoics also came back to that, so that in their view the world was a kind of animal, or the most perfect living being possible, whose individual bodies were only its members. It seems that Strabo also understands it thus in the passage that you quote. Even the Chinese, and other Orientals, conceive certain spirits of heaven and of the earth, and perhaps there are even among them some who conceive a supreme spirit of the universe. So the difference between all these philosophers (especially the ancients) and the true theologian would consist in the fact that, according to us and the truth, God is beyond the corporeal universe, and is its author and master (an extramundane intelligence), whereas the God of these philosophers is only the soul of the world, or even the animal that results from it. Nevertheless their Whole (πᾶν) was not without intelligence, any more than our supreme being. Madam the Electress[99] is accustomed to quote and to praise especially the passage of Scripture that asks if it is reasonable that the author of the eye does not see, and that the author of the ear does not hear:[100] that is, that there is no knowledge in the first being from which comes the knowledge in the others.

And strictly speaking, if there is no universal intelligence in the world, then it will not be possible to conceive it as a substance truly one: it will be merely an *aggregate*, an assemblage, as would be a flock of sheep or even a pond full of fish. Thus to make it an eternal substance that deserves the name of God would be to play with words, and to say nothing using fine words. The errors disappear when one gives sufficient consideration to the oft-neglected results of this great principle, which holds that everything has a reason which determines why it is thus rather than otherwise: this obliges us to go beyond everything material, because the reason for the determinations could not be found there.

---

[99] Electress Sophie of Hanover (1630–1714), Leibniz's patroness.
[100] Psalms 94.9: 'He that planted the ear, shall he not hear? he that formed the eye, shall he not see?'

3

Reason and Faith

1. What needs to be done to defend the Christian religion (10/20 February 1670)[1]

Manuscript:

M: Augsburg, *Staatsbibliothek*, Cod. Aug. 20, 408, Nr. 296, Bl. 415–16.

Transcription:

A: A II 1 (2nd edn), p. 55.

The following is an extract from a letter to Gottlieb Spitzel (1639–91), a Protestant clergyman with leanings towards pietism. He and Leibniz corresponded between 1669 and 1672.

Since it is a task of the greatest magnitude to demolish entirely and finally everything that can be objected to the Christian religion, especially when the matter contains the most serious knotty points of exegetical, historical, scholastic and polemical theology, it is reasonable to pursue abridgements until there arises someone who brings an end to such a huge enterprise in a just work. That is, the truth of natural religion should first be demonstrated precisely, namely the existence of most powerful

---

[1] Editor's title. From the Latin. Incomplete: the remaining parts of the letter have not been translated.

and most wise being, that is, God, and then the immortality of our soul. The route to victory will be shorter once this is done, since it is in accordance with reason that God has revealed a true religion to mortals, and none of the others can be compared with the rationality of the Christian one. Although, in case some trace of resistance should remain, I should like there to arise at some point someone who, instructed in all kinds of learning, and history, and languages, and with reinforcements of philosophy on his side, after throwing light on all of the harmony and beauty of the Christian religion, and after driving away the clouds of innumerable objections against its doctrines, text and history, reports a complete, unqualified victory.

2. On the *Treatise of Religion against the Atheists* (1677–9 (?))[2]

Manuscript:

M: LBr F 12 Bl. 107.

Transcription:

A: A II 1 (2nd edn), pp. 675–6.

The following is an undated draft of a letter to Leibniz's employer at the time, Duke Johann Friedrich. As it concerns Maudit's *Traité de la religion contre les Atheés*, published in 1677, it cannot have been written earlier than that, and it must have been written prior to the Duke's death at the end of 1679.

Your Grace,

I have read the *Traité de la religion contre les Atheés*.[3] It says ordinary things very well, and can have an effect on libertines such as one ordinarily encounters, who are libertines more by inclination rather than by reasoning. But it is not suitable for persuading people who reason with care, who will

---

[2] Editor's title. From the French. Complete.
[3] Michel Mauduit, *Traité de la religion contre les athées, les déistes et les nouveaux pyrrhoniens* (Paris, 1677).

prefer a completely bare thought, as is proposed by Mr Pascal,[4] than one dressed up in so many useless words. For wanting to take pen in hand in order to write out some extracts, I found no worthwhile ones in it, which is a sure sign that a book lacks substance.

The basic thought of this work is, in fact, already in Cicero, who, when talking about the immortality of the soul, says that he does not want anyone to remove this error from his mind, if it is one.[5] For he says: if it is a truth then I can hope for immense goods from it, and if I am mistaken then I do not have to fear that one day the dead will make fun of me. Whereas those who take the opposite view, in order to obtain here some small advantages, put at risk that which is infinitely more considerable. The author of *L'Art de bien penser* (i.e. Mr Arnaud) has written a chapter specially, which says, in substance, the same thing.[6]

But to speak the truth on the matter: this argument does not conclude anything about what people should believe, but only about what they should do. That is, it proves only that those very people who do not believe either in God or an immortal soul should act as if they do believe while they are unable to demonstrate that these things do not exist. For there are two entirely separate issues: to know what is most certain in practice, and to know what is most probable in belief. This is a distinction the casuists themselves have quite correctly drawn. For often one is obliged to follow the most certain, even though it is not the most probable. Thus we need other reasons to convert the atheists, since these ones are suitable for persuading them only to live as others do and not to make them believe. Moreover, belief is not a voluntary thing, so all exhortations are pointless. There is a need for reasons, and it is not possible that the soul could surrender itself to anything else. Indeed, we are not lacking true reasons to uphold religion,[7] and I am annoyed that there are so few people who make use of them as they should.

---

[4] Blaise Pascal (1623–62), a renowned mathematician and inventor of calculating machines who turned to theology and philosophy after experiencing an intense religious experience in 1654.
[5] Cicero, *Cato major de senectute*, 23.56: 'But if I am wrong in thinking the human soul immortal, I am glad to be wrong; nor will I allow the mistake which gives me so much pleasure to be wrested from me as long as I live.'
[6] The reference is to Antoine Arnauld and Pierre Nicole, *La loquige, ou l'art de penser* (Paris, 1662), pt. 4 chapter 12 ('Some rules for the right direction of reason in the belief of events which depend on human faith').
[7] religion | . Our author does not make too much use of them, and he contrives opinions in order to attack them. For example, the maxim that he says (on p. 138) reigns among the impious, namely that 'one should not believe anything one does not understand', | *deleted*.

3. Dialogue between a theologian and a misosophist (2nd half 1678–1st half 1679 (?))[8]

Manuscript:

M: LH I 3, 2 Bl. 1–4.

Transcription:

A: A VI 4, pp. 2212–19.

The provenance of this piece is unknown. Its dating is based on the watermark of the paper.

Dialogue between a theologian and a[9] *misosophist*[10]

M. Oh Theologians, will you never cease being foolish using reason in those matters where it is becoming to be wise rather through faith?

T. We shall not cease using reason until God ceases to be wise or man ceases to be rational.

M. *The wisdom of man is foolishness before God,*[11] and in the divine sphere, man's reason is an instrument of error, rather than an instrument of understanding.

T. A proud wisdom is foolishness before God, for it is confused by God, who humbles the proud;[12] and the man who will desire to scrutinize the mysteries by reason will be overwhelmed by glory and be blinded by that great splendour, but for the man who seeks God with a sincere heart, God illuminates his reason for him so that he may see his wonders. And just as we do not look directly at the sun but either in water or through coloured

---

[8] Author's title. From the Latin. Complete.
[9] *a | sceptic | deleted*.
[10] A misosophist is a person who hates wisdom.
[11] 1 Corinthians 3.19.
[12] Cf. 1 Corinthians 1.17-31.

glass, likewise a man – whom either a pious disposition or the necessity of defending the faith calls to a more profound contemplation of divine matters – will not gouge out the eyes of reason, for then he will see nothing; instead he will examine by means of Holy Scripture (by whose intervention the great efficacy of the heavenly rays is accommodated to our weakness) as it were through a veil laid over the holy of holies. But this veil shall be lifted only when we shall no longer look upon God in a mirror or as an enigma, but face to face.[13]

M. So you think reason should be joined with faith.

T. Why not, if reason convinces us of our faith? For in what other prerogative are we superior to the Mohammedans?

M. We have true miracles; they do not.

T. A great deal of reasoning is required to prove miracles we have not seen; indeed, even if we see them with our very own eyes, we still need to do a lot of weighing up to ensure we are not deceived. Besides, you know that the miracles of Scripture need another criterion in turn, namely doctrine, since the antichrist too will conjure up signs which will deceive even the elect (if that were possible).[14] Moses said that a prophet who teaches contrary to the law must not be believed, even if he gives signs.[15]

M. I concede that miracles are to be examined according to the standard of doctrine, but of revealed doctrine, I say, not natural.

T. Doesn't the first revelation itself depend upon miracles?

M. Yes it does.

T. Then those first miracles at least: must they not require another, earlier revelation?[16] What do you say to that? Why do you hesitate?

M. I don't know how you have trapped me and backed me into a corner.

T. You will act in a more noble way if you admit that the trap came not from me but from you.

---

[13] Cf. 1 Corinthians 13.12.
[14] A paraphrase of Matthew 24.24: 'For there shall arise false Christs, and false prophets, and shall shew great signs and wonders; insomuch that, if it *were* possible, they shall deceive the very elect.'
[15] An allusion to Deuteronomy 13.1-3.
[16] revelation | (of which there isn't one, because we have already assumed the first revelation) | *deleted*.

M. Your arguments are so strong that I would be compelled to agree with you, if I had not learned that all reasonings with regard to the divine sphere should be distrusted.

T. All reasonings, even with regard to the human sphere, are doubtful, that is, they are not to be accepted before careful examination, especially in an important matter.

M. And if no objection to your most recent argument now occurs to me, nevertheless nor will you have any response to my argument.

T. Which is?

M. That with the analysis of faith into reason being granted, every instance of faith will be human, not divine.

T. The most important authors who have written about the analysis of faith[17] have resolved this difficulty very well. For on the one hand there is the human analysis of faith with regard to the motives of credibility, an analysis made in accordance with history and reason by examining and confirming histories; and on the other, there is the divine analysis of faith, which is made in accordance with the effective operation of the Holy Spirit in our hearts.

M. But that internal declaration of God is sufficient without rational arguments, for many people believe in accordance with the simplicity of their own heart, even if they know no rational reasons for believing.

T. I agree that many people, with the singular benevolence of God adapting itself to the capacity of all, possess a true faith without having any convincing reasons for it, and that these people can be saved. But our religion would be wretched if it lacked persuasive arguments, and it would not be preferable to that of the Mohammedans or the pagans since no reason could be given to those who asked for one, nor could the faith be defended against impiety or even against the doubts which often make pious men anxious.

M. There is something in what you say. Yet I had thought it was safer to banish every reasoning from theology, since I believed that human principles prove nothing certain in the divine sphere.

---

[17] faith |, like Gregory of Valencia from the Society of Jesus, Holdenus from the Sorbonne, and others | *deleted*.

T. If that were so, not even God's existence could be proved by rational arguments.

M. God's existence should actually be proved by revelations and miracles.

T. But I have told you that revelations and miracles should be examined by reason.

M. But what do you say to this argument, *that human principles are not appropriate for the divine sphere*?

T. I answer that there are principles common to the divine and human sphere, and that theologians have very readily observed this. Indeed, I agree that physical principles pertain only to the human sphere, for example that iron does not float in water, or that a virgin does not give birth, for through the absolute power of God, which is beyond nature, the opposite can be brought about; but metaphysical principles are common to the divine and human spheres, because they concern truth and being in general, which is common to God and created beings. Such is the metaphysical principle that the same thing cannot be and not be at the same time, or that the whole is greater than the part. The same goes for *logical principles* or syllogistic forms, which even God and the angels will acknowledge to be true.

M. But God and angels do not need logic.

T. Certainly God doesn't use logic, perhaps angels do – they do not need syllogisms, yet they will not therefore scorn them. I do not do arithmetic with counters, because I know that all things are better solved with a pen, but I do not therefore scorn counters, or regard them as false.

M. I shall never concede to you that our metaphysical principles are true before God.

T. Then that principle, that the same thing cannot be and not be at the same time, is not valid before God or in the divine sphere?

M. Indeed it is not.

T. None of the holy fathers or learned theologians will agree with you.

M. Even if the learned do not stand on my side, at least the pious will.

T. Let's see how pious your claims are: with that principle (about contradictory things not being permitted at the same time) removed from the divine sphere, we shall be able to accept and reject the deity or the Trinity at the same time; and in the same way, we shall be able to be pious and atheists, Catholics and Arians, at the same time.

M. I believed that *no word is impossible with God*,[18] therefore contradictions will not be impossible for God either.

T. If no word is impossible for God, it will even be possible for him to destroy himself, to sin, and other things of that kind.

M. All things are possible for God, except those which are contrary to his perfection.

T. Fine, very well, but contradictions are also contrary to his own perfection, for they would make God absurd, and would make him assert the true and false at the same time, and pursue and forgo his own aim at the same time.

M. I shall admit (because you urge so) this principle of contradiction even in the divine sphere, but I shall not admit that we are able to judge correctly which things are contradictions in the divine sphere.

T. If we have eyes and memory then we are also able to judge about contradiction. For it is at any rate a requisite that the subject and predicate of a contradictory proposition are the same, i.e. that the words are the same in both and the sense of the words is the same. Whether the eyes will judge that the words are the same in both, or whether we understand the same thing in both by the words, our memory or consciousness will tell us, so that only attention is required.

M. I shall perhaps grant this in the simplest arguments, in which a contradiction is readily apparent, but not in the more difficult arguments.

T. In more difficult arguments we need only have more attention: a long chain of syllogisms can be examined no less surely than a brief argument, for we only have to examine each syllogism separately according to its form and content. Therefore we just require more time and patience with many syllogisms than with a few.

M. But it seems unworthy to me that logic has so much validity in the divine sphere.

T. Do you think that grammar is more worthy than logic? And yet

---

[18] Cf. Luke 1.37.

everybody agrees how useful grammar is in explaining a sacred text. And indeed if you reject syllogisms, you reject all reasonings, for all reasonings are always syllogisms, at least imperfect ones, like enthymemes, in which some proposition or sign is implicitly understood. But imperfect ones cannot be more certain than the perfect. In fact the forms of syllogisms are clearly demonstrated with mathematical certainty from that principle of contradiction you admitted.

M. We can be saved without logic.

T. I agree, for we can also be saved without reasonings, and we are able to reason without syllogisms. Yet we are unable to comprehend and uphold the foundations of faith without reasonings; and we cannot easily elicit the truth in very difficult matters or convince an obstinate opponent without logical skills.

M. The Holy Fathers scorned that subtle method of reasoning in theological matters.

T. Some did, not all. For St Augustine can be justly called the Father of Scholastic Theology, from whom the Master of the Sentences[19] and St Thomas have derived a great deal.

M. Those who argue the most, are most lacking in faith.

T. Sometimes this is true of those who do it the most, but never of those who do it well.

M. It is safest just to believe whatever the Church believes. You know that short story by Bellarmine, about the person who debated in a contest with the devil.[20]

T. I suppose you are joking, since that story is ludicrous. Nor do I think you will use the same circular argument as he did, namely 'I believe whatever the Church believes, and the Church believes what I believe'.[21] In addition, it is necessary to establish the Church on firm reasons.

---

[19] Peter Lombard (c. 1100–1160) taught theology at Notre Dame and was, briefly, Archbishop of Paris. His highly influential *Libri quatuor sententiarum* [Four books of sentences] earned him the title 'Master of the Sentences'.
[20] Robert Bellarmine, *De arte bene moriendi* (Antwerp, 1620), II.9. English translation in *Spiritual Writings*, trans. John Patrick Donnelly and Roland J. Teske (New Jersey: Paulist Press, 1989), p. 354.
[21] Cf. A VI 6, p. 521/NE, p. 521: 'Cardinal Bellarmine even believed that there is nothing superior to that childlike faith in which one submits to an established authority, and he reports with approval

M. I have always been pleased by the modesty of those who humbly profess that they believe without any inquiry.

T. Believe me, often those who speak like that in earnest are either very simple (and God is nonetheless able to give them the true faith, since they have done what is incumbent on them) or true hypocrites and secret atheists. Pomponazzi was accustomed to speak like this,[22] and Vanini,[23] who, declining to respond to objections with this excuse, have forsaken the cause of God. For when they introduced serious problems they pretended that they were yielding to the authority of the Church and that these problems were not obstacles. There is no greater enemy of religion and piety than he who asserts faith contrary to reason, which is to prostitute faith before the wise. Even great Popes and councils and faculties of theology, with the observed skill of hypocrites, have forbidden twofold truths which conflict with each other, one divine, the other human, from being established.[24]

M. You almost persuade me that I should trust that human reason, when properly grasped, never conflicts with the revealed divine faith, and that the word of God, which has been written or handed down, does not differ from the natural law engraved in our hearts since birth (as Paul attests).[25]

T. Since I seem to have reduced you to a more moderate position, I shall in turn concede something to you, so that we may shake hands and be more readily united. For as I believe that our natures were created for meditating, and that those burning with a true passion for piety should not be the least dissuaded from the contemplation of divine things, since noble things can be elicited by which piety may be aroused, the faith defended and propagated and the glory of God exalted, so in turn I am very displeased by those barren logic-choppers and wretched debaters who know nothing

---

the words of a dying man who kept the devil at bay by means of this circle which he was heard to recite over and over: "I believe whatever the Church believes. The Church believes what I believe."

[22] Pietro Pomponazzi (1462–1524/5), an Italian philosopher who argued that not only was there no rational demonstration for the immortality of the soul, but also that philosophy showed the soul to be material and naturally mortal. He also put forward a naturalistic interpretation of miracles, which in his view were merely events brought about by a concatenation of natural causes.

[23] Lucilio Vanini (1585–1619), an Italian philosopher who wrote under the name 'Julius Ceaser'. Although ordained as a priest he developed a naturalistic philosophy in his published works, arguing that the soul was mortal and God the manifestation of nature. Following the condemnation of his book *De Admirandis Naturae Reginae Deaeque Mortalium Arcanis* (Paris, 1616), he was arrested on suspicion of atheism and subsequently executed.

[24] The doctrine of twofold truth was condemned in session 8 (held 19 December 1513) of the Fifth Lateran Council (1512–17).

[25] An allusion to Romans 2.15: 'Which shew the work of the law written in their hearts.'

of the profound and the solid, but who, bickering over useless frivolities and getting involved in insane quarrels, let the truth slip away and offend charity. It was better that these people be saved by simple faith than that they be condemned by an ostentatious but empty and hollow theology; but those who have come via true reasonings and profound meditations to a clear acquaintance of the truth – their faith rests on firm foundations and is conspicuous by an effective charity. Consequently, we should be wary not of sound reasoning but of the empty sophistical reasoning of deceivers, and we should believe as certain that no one on the Earth is closer to heaven than one who, imbued with the profound truths of mystical theology, rejoices in the feeling of divine love, especially if he also spreads his own happiness to others; for it should be considered as demonstrated that, as every person in this mortal life advances further in the knowledge and love of God (this love surely follows from true knowledge) and is the cause of a greater good, so will he persist there with a greater glory.

4. Specimen of *Catholic Demonstrations*, or, Apology for the faith through reason (July 1683–March 1686 (?))[26]

Manuscript:

M: LH I 3, 7b Bl. 1–2.

Transcriptions:

A: A VI 4, pp. 2323–7 (following M).

This piece recalls (in both title and content) the 'Catholic demonstrations' project of the 1660s and 1670s, and appears to be a preface to a much longer work on the same theme, a work which was apparently never written. It belongs to a series of writings from the mid-1680s in which Leibniz sought to defend Christian doctrines,

---

[26] Author's title. From the Latin. Complete.

especially those endorsed by Catholicism, by means of reason.[27] The watermark of the paper suggests the piece was written between July 1683 and March 1686.

Specimen of Catholic Demonstrations, *or, Apology for the faith through reason*

The Christian faith does not rest upon ordinary reasoning, but upon the testimony of the Catholic Church received from miracles and martyrs, and passed on to us by the unbroken tradition and writings preserved in the Church. Yet amazingly, a remarkable consensus about the true philosophy of our religion moves the soul of men who are pious and who have entered into the secrets of the sciences, for there is the clearest indication that the same God is both the maker of the nature of things and the author of the grace granted to us through Christ. However, we have entered those times in which many people abuse both their own natural abilities and the insights of the sciences, either by rejecting incorporeal substances (which is most surely atheism) and directly destroying providence; or at any rate by undermining the Christian religion, by pronouncing as impossible the Trinity of persons in one God, the Incarnation of the Word and other mysteries which go beyond human comprehension; or lastly by doing damage to the Church, as when they attack the sacrament of the body and blood of Christ, and when they think about the justification and election of men and the whole economy of our salvation in such a way that is unworthy of divine greatness and justice. Since there are those who do these things, devout and educated persons must be careful lest the Christian commonwealth, which is the one most in keeping with reason, comes to harm through the perverse employment of reason. And indeed it would be desirable that men should exercise their natural abilities in matters useful for life, where there is a large enough space for their activity, rather than in matters of faith, where simplicity is the safest course.

Yet because it is not possible to avoid conflict nowadays, and our bold adversaries either mock our humility or interpret it as hypocrisy, and see themselves as victorious and insult those who yield, to the great detriment of souls and scandal of the simplest folk, necessity compels us to engage in close quarter combat.

---

[27] See for example 'Rationale of the Catholic faith' (this volume, pp. 70–9), and 'Apologia fidei catholicae ex recta ratione', A IV 3, pp. 226–33.

And so, at the last Lateran Council, Christian philosophers were strongly urged to make every effort to illuminate the truth of faith through sound reason, and to strive to undo the arguments of their adversaries.[28] And if only Augustines and Aquinases were alive today, in whom wisdom manifested itself in piety to the same extent that solidity manifested itself in subtlety. If such guardians were present in our age, I believe they would have ensured that the more each person should admire the beauty of Christian dogmas, the more enlightened he would be. Yet even though we are not their equals, it will not for that reason seem that we should despair, as long as we keep in mind that the cause of God is what concerns us,[29] and that there is often more boldness than wisdom in our opponents. Moreover, I should say what, above all, has persuaded me to take on a task which would more properly be entrusted to others, given such an abundance of outstanding men. Indeed, I deliberated long and hard before undertaking this task,[30] not being unaware of its difficulty, but I overcame my hesitations following frequent encounters with men I met on my travels, and at courts, who were intelligent but corrupted by their licentiousness. No small number of these had some taste for mathematics and had been enticed by the charms of some new philosophy, which seemed to offer them some facility to speak on any occasion about the most serious questions, and at first they looked down on my naivety. But when they saw that I was not ignorant of those new teachings, and when they were able to tolerate and even praise the fact that I had penetrated a little more deeply into the interior of geometry than is usual, they began to be genuinely surprised and to criticize me for feeding on acorns after fruit had been discovered. For they had so established that final causes should be done away with, as they were not natural but moral, and were invented by ourselves when we considered nature using our natural abilities; they had established that all possibles are brought forth from the bosom of matter by some kind of necessary order, and so that what we invent for ourselves about the plan and choice of providence is worthless; they had established that God either does not exist, or is nothing other than that power which brings forth all possibles by a necessary order, and that this order depends upon the laws of mathematics; they had also

---

[28] Leibniz is referring here to session 8 (held 19 December 1513) of the Fifth Lateran Council (1512–17).
[29] us, | (and he even inspires the tongues of babes to praise him) | *deleted*. Leibniz is alluding here to Psalm 8.2.
[30] task, | for although I have some training in divine and human studies, I nevertheless knew how deep | *deleted*.

established that our minds are either corporeal or are extinguished with our bodies, or at any rate forget everything, and, according to some, return to the soul of the world.[31] I, on the other hand, maintained that even final causes may be referred to efficient causes, when of course the agent is intelligent, for then he is moved by knowledge of the goal; and that even moral causes are natural, for they are obtained from the nature of the mind. And so, if all things are directed by mind, then the production and preservation of all things will not be necessary and blind, but free and full of purpose. From this the elements of piety and justice immediately proceed.

Nor do I reject the laws of mathematics in physics, and I willingly acknowledge that the actions of bodies on each other are in turn varied according to their size and shape, but the very substance of a body, and what it does and has done to it with regard to other bodies, that in truth involves notions quite different from size and shape, and [to grasp it] we must return to the ancients, who established certain substantial forms. At first the able-but-licentious moderns ridiculed these ideas, as if they did not perceive them sufficiently clearly and distinctly. Gradually they became unsettled and brought to a sort of suspicion. In the end some gave up when they recognized that the true notion of body had previously been completely unknown to them, for it consists not in extension but in the force to act and be acted upon, that is, in the power to move and resist, even though size and shape controlled and restrained that power, which was by its own nature undefined. For I showed them that the very laws of mechanics flow not from geometrical principles but from metaphysical ones, and that if all things were not directed by mind, they would be quite different from what we experience. Nor can any given body be understood as an *unum per se*,[32] indeed it would be nothing more than an aggregate of points, which is impossible unless it was held together by some kind of substantial form, which is sort of analogous to the soul, namely the first actuality or force of acting, joined to each and every body by the will of the creator, the exercise of which is limited by the obstacles of other bodies. Such a thing is what the ἐντελέχεια[33] of Aristotle has indicated more than expressed.

Moreover, I reminded them that thought, or the force to act with respect to oneself, is given to minds alone among these forms or souls. From this

---

[31] Although Leibniz suggests that these views were held by 'no small number' of philosophers, he is in fact describing doctrines advanced by Spinoza (1632–77).
[32] 'a true unity, a genuine individual'.
[33] 'entelechy'.

there follows not only perpetual subsistence, such as there is in fact for all substances (which do not perish, but are changed), but also a perpetual knowledge of itself, in which consists immortality and true life. Further, I showed that matter does not consist in extension any more than force does in action, and therefore, just as force is that from which action follows unless something prevents it, so matter is the force in any body to be acted upon or to resist, from which there follows a particular extension of the body, unless the author of things wills otherwise. And hence a way is opened for us to defend the Sacrament of the Eucharist.

I know that all these things will seem very absurd to those who have now put their names to the new sects in philosophy; there will also perhaps be some who will not consider what follows to be worth reading. But they should know that I too was once disposed in almost the same way, when the charms of seductive new matters enticed me as a young man. And I considered these things not in passing, but, like many, saw them as suitable even for defence and illumination. But, as my meditations continued, and I cleared my mind of rubbish, I began to consider all things more seriously and deeply, and at first those dogmas were suspect to me, and in the end they proved to be false, when new light was shone on them. And the same thing happened to me as happens to one who, having been wandering in a wood for a long time, suddenly emerges into an open plain, and realizes that, contrary to every expectation, he has returned to that place from which he first strayed into the wood, and got lost.

I understood, of course, that the views of the ancients should not be overturned but explained and made firm, views which today are rejected and despised for no other reason than that their meaning and force is not known. And in truth I was only cured when I sought a criterion for truth other than the one which is tossed around everywhere by people today, namely that whatever is clearly and distinctly perceived is true.[34]

I understood, of course, that it is prone to misuse, and is worthless unless marks of 'clear' and 'distinct' are identified. For everybody thinks that he understands clearly and distinctly whatever has impressed itself strongly upon him, and if he appeals to the inner testimony of the spirit then all debate at once ceases with him, and an incurable error remains in his mind.

---

[34] The criterion of truth mentioned here is that advanced by Descartes at the start of his third Meditation, where he writes: 'So I now seem to be able to lay it down as a general rule that whatever I perceive very clearly and distinctly is true'. See Descartes, *The Philosophical Writings of Descartes*, II: p. 24.

Thus there is need for everybody to have not private marks of the truth, but public ones, no more so in religion than in philosophy. Few notions are observed distinctly by us; the things we perceive clearly are for the most part confused. Yet this does not prevent many truths becoming known to us, by experience in the case of confused notions, and by demonstration in the case of distinct ones (at least insofar as they are distinct). And for the most part the benevolence of providence has provided us with a way from those few distinct notions to an unravelling of even the confused ones, if only we should use the true analysis, which I think is still unknown among so many who vaunt their analytics.

5. An outline of a natural theology (29 September/9 October 1697)[35]

Manuscript:

M: LBr 730 Bl. 74.

Transcription:

A: A II 3, pp. 382–3.

From a letter to Vincent Placcius (1642-99), a jurist and Professor of Philosophy at Hamburg, with whom Leibniz corresponded on a more or less regular basis between 1676 and 1699:

    For many years now I have thought long and hard about a natural theology which is in harmony with right reason and does not detract in any way from revealed religion and divine honour. And so I entered into the arguments, as the matter seems sufficiently within my powers. God ought to be considered in two ways: physically and morally. Physically, as the ultimate reason for things, in respect to every perfection that things contain; and morally, as the monarch of the most perfect commonwealth, such as is

---

[35] Editor's title. From the Latin. Incomplete: those parts of the letter on a different topic have not been translated.

that City of Minds (so to speak) of the whole universe. With that laid down, practical theology is nothing other than the jurisprudence of the universal commonwealth (whose ruler is God), insofar as this theology deals with our duties in this commonwealth. And from this in turn is resolved that knotty problem of predestination, which has provoked men to produce various answers. The resolution is that God would not permit sin or evil unless he could obtain a greater good from evil. It should even be held as certain that no one is damned except by himself, and indeed that he perseveres in the state of misery only by his own will. To my mind, many other excellent things may be said which have not been sufficiently considered or explained by theologians, and which are nevertheless not contrary to the sound theology we have received. Certainly I do not agree with the Socinians who think that there is no need for satisfaction or vengeance in God; but on the contrary, I declare that, aside from the correction of the sinner and the example set for others, one can and should consider in the punishment the harmony itself that is ultimately satisfied by a just vengeance. And so I think that in the commonwealth of the universe there is no good deed without reward, and no sin without punishment. Therefore, if one should remove from anger its imperfection, which consists in the accompanying clouding of reason and the feeling of pain, and one leaves in it only the will to punish, it can be attributed to God, as per the example of Holy Scripture. Of course sin is not an evil for God, or for the universe (because of the correction which attends it, which thereby procures a greater good), but only for the sinner. Of course, all the passions can be attributed to God (except those which include in themselves something bad, like the envy that the ancients so foolishly attributed to their gods), if one takes them for rational inclinations separated from the confusion of the senses. However perhaps it will be possible to use more refined expressions, through which you will best consider him.

6. The use of reason in theology (6 October 1706)[36]

Manuscript:

M: LBr 445 Bl. 45.

Transcription:

GR: Grua I. pp. 64–8.

From a letter to Isaac Jacquelot (1647–1708), court Chaplin to the French colony in Berlin, with whom Leibniz corresponded between 1702 and 1706 (what follows is in fact the last of Leibniz's letters to Jacquelot):

I am delighted to learn that you are replying to Mr Bayle,[37] and have no doubt that you will do it as you have before,[38] that is, by avoiding what may offend. For this is an individual of such great merit, and who can render so many services to Letters and even, if he wants to apply himself, to religion, that it is right to handle him with tact; that is why I am quite angry about the great quarrel he had with Mr Le Clerc,[39] another excellent man, and one very capable of giving us his insights. Both should concentrate their efforts on instructing us on a number of things and on advancing towards each other from their respective sides without offending each other and without muddling personal disputes with the discussion of things. It would also be hoped that able men desire to devote their intelligence and their knowledge to edifying truths rather than to paradoxes and error, whether in the form of objections or otherwise.

---

[36] Editor's title. From the French. Incomplete: a short passage on another subject has not been translated.
[37] Pierre Bayle (1647–1706), man of letters and sometimes journal editor, best known for his *Dictionnaire historique et critique* (Amsterdam, 1697). Leibniz is referring here to Isaac Jacquelot's *Examen de la théologie de M. Bayle* (Amsterdam, 1706).
[38] Jacquelot's *La Conformité de la foy avec la raison* (Amsterdam, 1705) was in part an attack on Bayle.
[39] See Jean Le Clerc, *Bibliothèque choisie: Pour servir de suite à la Bibliothèque universelle*, Tomes IX, X (Amsterdam, 1706); [Pierre Bayle], *Réponse pour Mr Bayle à Mr Le Clerc, au sujet du 3. et du 13. article du 9. tome de la Bibliothèque choisie* (Rotterdam, 1706).

For myself, far from being angry that an able and well-intentioned man makes specious objections against the truth, I take pleasure in seeing and examining them, since these sorts of objections always serve to clarify the matter and to throw a new light on it; but I wish that they were put in Latin books, or ones read only by people advanced in learning, like the Scholastics, especially when dealing with truths about which it is important that the public be persuaded.

Nevertheless I find that Mr Bayle makes objections out to be stronger than they are, as though he likes the idea that there are invincible objections that can be opposed to the truth. The *Réponse aux Questions d'un Provincial*,[40] and the response that has just been made on his behalf to Mr Le Clerc in explaining the précis of the doctrine of the first book,[41] seems to me to admit of some difficulty when it says there, on page 18:

> that the way of bringing man's moral and physical evil into harmony with the attributes of the infinitely perfect unique principle of all things, is beyond all philosophical insights, such that the objections of the Manicheans leave open difficulties that human reason cannot resolve.[42]

For if the way of bringing evil into harmony with the perfection of God means giving the detail of the reasons that led him to permit the evils, then this way could be inexplicable, because it perhaps depends upon the universal harmony which encompasses infinity. And nevertheless the objections raised against the permission of evil can and must be susceptible of a good solution, for it is not necessary that whoever responds to an objection demonstrate his thesis *a priori* and thoroughly explain everything obscure and difficult it contains. Yet it is necessary that people who are gifted and capable of application be able to find a way to respond to objections; otherwise there would be no more obscurity in this respect, because it would be *clear* that the thesis is false, and it would be wrong to hold for certain what is refuted by an objection to which one cannot adequately respond. For what is a demonstration other than an invincible argument, that is, an argument whose form is good, and whose matter consists in propositions that are either evident or proved by similar arguments until one comes to evident propositions alone? Thus to say that what reason or

---

[40] Pierre Bayle, *Réponse aux Questions d'un Provincial*, 3 vols (Rotterdam, 1706). Leibniz made notes on this book (see Grua II, pp. 491–4), which is his principal target in the *Theodicy* (1710).
[41] Bayle, *Réponse pour Mr Bayle à Mr Le Clerc*.
[42] Bayle, *Réponse pour Mr Bayle à Mr Le Clerc*, p. 18.

revelation teaches us could be subject to invincible objections, would be to want there to be demonstrations for and against, because reason teaches us by an invincible objection that what it refutes is false.

I believe most of those who have spoken at length about the use of reason in theology, such as Vedelius,[43] Musaeus[44] and others, will ultimately agree with what I have just said. It is true that whoever is completely persuaded of a truth is not in any way obliged to examine all the objections that may be made against it, and even that it would be wrong for most people to try to do that. It is also true that one should not distance oneself from the letter of the text when the contrary reasons are only probable. But everyone agrees that reason and revelation could not teach an absurdity.

In the question of the origin of evil, whoever would want to bring an invincible objection against God's goodness and wisdom would have to prove, for example, that evil could be avoided without losing some more considerable amount of good. But in order to prove this thesis, it would not be enough to say that someone else could not prove the contrary, or that they could not show the connection of these evils with the greater goods, because it is enough to be able to say that this connection is possible until the opposite is proved. And one should resist trying to prove the opposite, inasmuch as it would lead to an absurdity, namely that God would not have acted in accordance with the most perfect wisdom. For as it is true that there is an infinitely perfect God who has permitted evil, we should say with St Augustine that he did it for a greater good,[45] although it be beyond the forces of human reason to show *a priori* and in detail in what this good consists. For it is sufficient to know broadly and *a posteriori* that that must be the case, because evil has actually occurred and God exists.

If someone is of another opinion, and claims that the truth can admit of difficulties consisting in invincible objections, he loses the means of acquiring knowledge, or rather he recognizes two contradictory truths. I am therefore of the opinion that one can and must reply to the objections of the libertines, atheists, infidels and heretics, and I entirely agree with the recommendations the last Lateran Council makes to Christian philosophers, in urging them to apply themselves to address the poor reasons of

---

[43] See Nicolaus Vedelius, *Rationale theologicum seu de necessitate et vero uso principiorum rationis ac philosophiae in controversiis theologicis* (Geneva, 1628).
[44] See Johannes Musaeus, *De usu principiorum rationis et philosophiae in controversiis theologicis libri tres* (Jena, 1644).
[45] See for example St Augustine, *Enchiridion ad Laurentium liber unus*, I.100: 'a good being would not permit evil to be done, unless in its omnipotence it can make a good from the evil'.

the Averroists and those other Peripaticians who in those times maintained that the immortality of the soul was true according to faith, and false in philosophy.[46] And I strongly commend your plan to take up the defence of faith against objections drawn from modern philosophy.

7. On the Greeks as the founders of a sacred philosophy (1 July 1714)[47]

Manuscript:

M: LH 39 Bl. 54–7 (lost since 1945).

Transcription:

PR: Patrick Riley, 'Leibniz, Platonism, and Judaism: The 1714 Vienna lecture on "the Greeks as Founders of a Sacred Philosophy"', in *Leibniz und das Judentum. Studia Leibnitiana Sonderhefte 34*, ed. Daniel Cook, Hartmut Rudolph and Christoph Schulte (Stuttgart: Steiner, 2008), pp. 109–13.

This piece is a lecture Leibniz delivered to the newly-formed Academy of Sciences in Vienna.

The Greeks themselves have acknowledged that they derived many things from barbarians. Plato taught in *Cratylus* that the origin of the Greek language is to be sought in foreign lands, that is, in Celto-Scythia,[48] traces of which survive today, especially in Germany. And amongst others, 'pyr', that is, 'fire' (a word whose origin was sought by Plato), is evidently German (learned men have observed countless others of this sort). The alphabet was brought to the Greeks from the Phoenicians by Cadmus:

'Phoenicians first –
if we credit the tale – dared

---

[46] See p. 102 n.24.
[47] Editor's title (taken from the German title given to the piece in the Ritterkatalog). From the Latin. Complete.
[48] See Plato, *Cratylus*, 409d–e.

to make words permanent,
using signs and crude characters.'[49]

The Greeks are reported to have derived geometry from the Egyptians because the boundaries of fields were being obscured by the floods of the Nile. On account of that, the people devoted their efforts to inventing a means which would give the measurements of fields, whereby the lost boundaries could be restored.

The Arabs and their neighbours, the Chaldeans and Egyptians, reflecting upon the heavens, discovered the science of stars. And so from them there arose astronomy, which was later sullied by astrological superstitions. The Greeks came upon this science later, but made it more accurate. Hipparchus counted the stars for posterity, while Eratosthenes was he

'who for all mankind surveyed the circuit of the skies.'[50]

Solon and Pythagoras and other wise men among the Greeks who had travelled to the east brought back from there mathematical sciences and history, that is, the memory of antiquity. About which that Egyptian priest said to Solon that the Greeks are ever children because they are ignorant about past times.[51]

But now, leaving aside the other sciences, theology is the matter at hand, and the question is: in theology, how much do the Greeks owe to barbarians, and how much have they added? By 'theology' here is meant not that superstitious, mythological and idolatrous theology of the gentiles, but true theology, partly natural and partly revealed. Natural theology is that which, like all the other sciences, originates from the seeds of truth embedded in the mind by God, their author. Revealed theology is that which has been drawn from those ancients to whom God has manifested himself more intimately, and has been propagated by tradition. Both kinds existed among the people of the east before they reached the Greeks. But the most important aspect consists in those doctrines which were once recognized not so much by entire nations (if you except the Hebrews) as by wise men: that is, that there is one God, author and governor of all things, and that human souls are not extinguished by death, but after this life come to

---

[49] Lucan, *Pharsalia* III, 220–1. Translation from Lucan, *Pharsalia*, trans. Jane Wilson Joyce (Ithaca: Cornell University Press, 1993), p. 63.
[50] Virgil, *Eclogue* III.41.
[51] An allusion to Plato, *Timaeus*, 22b.

another one in which they receive rewards or suffer punishments depending on whether this life has been lived well or ill.

As regards the unity of God, this was accepted not only by the Israelites, but also by the Chaldeans in Abraham, and by the Arabs in Job, and insofar as we can follow the conjecture, was approved by the most ancient wise men of China. Hence Fu xi, who simultaneously ruled and philosophized among them more than three thousand years ago, in order to show that all things were derived by God from nothing, wrote all numbers by using only two characters: one signifying unity, the other signifying nothing.[52] The Chinese themselves lost the meaning of this hieroglyphic writing, but I have revived it, and reduced it to a certain kind of arithmetic.[53]

This doctrine of the unity of God was peculiar to the wisest people among the Greeks and Romans. Plato (as he himself implies in the *Timaeus*) taught it as if it were in secret, in order not to imperil himself in the manner of Socrates.[54] He established that the supreme God had created inferior beings and granted them immortality, and so the inferiors of that God were nothing other than those beings we call angels.[55] Antisthenes, in Book 1 of Cicero's *De natura deorum*, said that there is one God in nature, but many according to popular belief.[56]

I come to the other main part of natural theology, which teaches that souls are not extinguished by the death of a man but are preserved for rewards and punishments. The monuments of the ancients prove that this doctrine was long established among peoples of the east and the west. A certain man of our time, not unlearned but not of the highest calibre, wanted to persuade us that the entire doctrine of the immortality of the soul derived from the fictions of the Egyptians, and that to them we owe the fare of Charon for those crossing the river, to them we owe Cerberus, and the belief about those left unburied being excluded from the place of rest, and about the judges in the underworld.[57] I would readily admit that the fables about the underworld came to the Greeks from the Egyptians and were elaborated and reworked by the Greeks; however, I find that the essence

---

[52] For further details, see Leibniz's 'Dialogue on the natural theology of the Chinese', in Dutens IV, pp. 207–10/WOC, pp. 132–8.
[53] Leibniz is referring here to his invention (or 'rediscovery', as he thought) of binary arithmetic.
[54] See Plato, *Timaeus*, 29e-30c. See also Letter XII, 363b.
[55] Presumably a reference to Plato, *Timaeus*, 39e–40e.
[56] See Cicero, *De natura deorum*, I.32.
[57] Leibniz is referring here to the second of John Toland's *Letters to Serena* (London, 1704), pp. 19–68 (entitled 'The history of the soul's immortality among the heathens'), especially pp. 40–9.

of the doctrine about the immortality of souls was much earlier and more widespread. For the most ancient Brahmins of India believed that we pass from death to a better life, as Strabo claims in Book XV.[58] With regard to the Thracians, Mela (in Book II) and Solinus (in chapter 10) revealed that some believed that souls return, while it seemed to others that souls proceeded to happier places.[59] As regards the Celtic Druids, this is best known from Caesar (Book VI of *De bello gallico*), Strabo (Book IV) and Lucan (Book 1):

> 'Hence, their men
> are bent on charging at swords; their minds readily accommodate
> death, and, since life will return, caution to them is cowardice.'[60]

Also well known is the belief of northern peoples about the souls of brave men dining with Odin, about which we have Bartholi's learned dissertation.[61] But the thinking of these (and other) people seems to have been that of the Siamese today, that certain souls will return in bodies for a long time yet, while others, having at last completed their cycle, reach a blessed resting place and divine abodes. Indeed, Pythagoras very clearly encouraged the doctrine of the immortality of souls brought from the east, and spread it to the people of Greece and Italy, but he added the fiction of metempsychosis. For it is a bad habit of common people to desire embellishments of fictions, and to be less affected by an unadorned truth.

These dogmas of natural theology were supplemented with something divinely revealed to the friends of God, which was afterwards propagated among the people by tradition. The formation of the abundantly furnished world from disordered chaos is one example of this. Moses clearly taught this doctrine. The Phoenicians derived it from Moses and spread it to the Greeks. They relate that there was a certain Phoenician writer, Sanchuniathon, some of whose writings were translated into the Greek language by Philo of Byblos, where Moses' doctrine concerning the origin of the world is outlined to some extent.[62] In addition, it is said in Moses and Sanchuniathon that the spirit of the Lord, having moved over the waters, brought forth things from that.[63] On account of this, Thales of Miletus (who was of Phoenician origin according to the testimony of Herodotus) taught that Mind had formed all

---

[58] See Strabo, *The Geography*, XV.1.59.
[59] See Pomponius Mela, *De situ orbis libri III*, II.18; Gaius Julius Solinus, *De mirabilibus mundi*, X.
[60] Lucan, *Pharsalia*, I.460-2. Translation from Lucan, *Pharsalia*, trans. Joyce, p. 19.
[61] Thomas Bartholinus, *De causis contemnendae mortis* (Copenhagen, 1689).
[62] See Philo of Byblos, *The Phoenician History*.
[63] See Genesis 1.2.

things from water, as Cicero claims in Book 1 of *De natura deorum*.[64] So Anaxagoras was not the first to think that all things were confused to begin with, and then were ordered by Mind. The entire opinion received by the Greeks is captured in the most elegant verses of Ovid, to whom God is:

'That artificer of things, the founder of a better world.'[65]

And in the same way the view reached the Greeks that man had been formed by God from muddy earth: indeed Prometheus, whose name means divine providence, 'molded [man] in the image of the all-controlling gods'.[66] The distinction between the Sabbath and the other days of the week was given to people from the most ancient times, and Hesiod already knew the holy seventh day: 'ἐβδομον ἱερον ἡμας'.[67]

It is also evident that it was through Moses that people learned of the punishment of that great flood, imposed on the human race for being immersed in sin, and that one person, along with his family, was saved from it. The Hebrews along with Berosus the Chaldean called this person 'Noah', according to Josephus's *Contra Appionem*, Book 1;[68] the Assyrians called him 'Sisithrus', according to the testimony of Abydenus in Book IX chapter 12 of Eusebius's *Praeparationis*,[69] while the Greeks called him 'Deukalion', as is apparent from Lucian's *De Dea Syria*;[70] And Plutarch likewise uses this name when discussing the doves released from the ark, in his book on whether terrestrial or aquatic animals are cleverer.[71] Moreover, Nicholas Damascenus, in the book by Josephus already cited, also related that the ark was brought to rest on the mountains of Armenia.[72]

Thus it was observed by the learned a little while ago that the fable of the three brothers born to Saturn originated from the three sons of Noah dividing the world.[73] They modelled Saturn on Noah, and also corrupted the story of a naked father mocked by his son into the fable of the Father

---

[64] See Cicero, *De natura deorum*, I.25.
[65] Ovid, *Metamorphoses*, I.79.
[66] Ovid, *Metamorphoses*, I.83.
[67] 'The seventh day is holy'. See Eusebius, *Evangelicae Praeparationis*, XIII.12.13.
[68] See Flavius Josephus, *Contra Appionem*, I.19.
[69] See Eusebius, *Evangelicae Praeparationis*, IX.12.2.
[70] See Lucian, *De Dea Syria*, §13.
[71] See Plutarch, *De sollertia animalium*, §13.
[72] See Flavius Josephus, *Contra Appionem*, I.19.
[73] An allusion to Genesis 9–10. Although Leibniz uses the plural for 'the learned' (eruditi) here, he seems to have in mind one person in particular, namely Urbain Chevreau (1613–1701), as much of this paragraph is based on claims made by Chevreau in his *Chevraeana. Seconde partie* (Paris, 1700), pp. 88ff.

castrated by Jove.[74] For it seems to them that Ham, or Cham, is Jupiter, who is also called Hammon; Japeth was considered to be Neptune because, amongst other things, Greece and the western islands were of his lot; while Pluto, the god of the underworld, was based on Shem, because Semites and especially the Hebrews hated the other races whom they abhorred through superstition.

The future transformation of the world through fire, intimated in sacred writings, was also related by Hystaspes the Persian in the Second Apology of Justin Martyr, and was known to the philosophers and poets of Greece.[75] According to Clement of Alexandria's *Stromata* V, Heraclitus and the Stoics said that the world will be purged by fire.[76] There exists a particular dissertation, written by a learned man, about the Stoic conflagration of the world. And that was well known to Ovid:

'And he recalled the Fates foretold a time
When sea and land and heaven's high palaces
In sweeping flames should burn, and down should fall
The beleaguered bastions of the universe.'[77]

The actual mystery of the Most Holy Trinity was already known to the ancient Hebrews, but was propagated more by tradition than by explicit writing, and eventually it was made visible to the people by Christ through a sort of subtle beam of light. I do not know how it had already reached the Greeks in Plato. For he, in his letter to Dionysius, supposes three principles in the divine nature: the father, the mind (which our John calls λογον)[78] and the spirit, which Christians call the Holy Spirit.[79] The seeds of this doctrine already seem to have been scattered by the Pythagoreans, who attributed the ternary number to God; about this, see the beginning of Aristotle's *De caelo*,[80] and Servius on Virgil's *Eclogue* VII,[81] and especially Plotinus

---

[74] Leibniz is referring here to Noah being seen naked by Ham, one of his sons, as related in Genesis 9.22. In Greek mythology, Saturn was castrated by his son, Jove. However a different account is given in Cicero, *De natura deorum*, III.62.
[75] See Justin Martyr, *Second Apology*, §20.
[76] See Clement of Alexandria, *Stromata*, V.14.
[77] Ovid, *Metamorphoses*, I.256-8. Translation from Ovid, *Metamorphoses*, trans. A. D. Melville (Oxford: Oxford University Press, 2009), p. 8.
[78] 'logos'.
[79] Leibniz is perhaps thinking of Plato, Letter II to Dionysius, 312e-313a. But it is difficult to be certain, because Plato does not explicitly advance the view Leibniz here attributes to him.
[80] See Aristotle, *De caelo*, 268a10-15.
[81] Leibniz's reference is slightly amiss; the relevant passage from Maurus Servius Honoratus's *Commentary on the Eclogues of Vergil* can be found at VIII.75.

(though already instructed by Christians) in his book on the three primary hypostases.[82]

These examples may suffice as evidence of the sacred wisdom propagated by barbarians (as they are called), especially those from the east to the Greeks, although it is possible to supplement them with many more. Now we must consider whether the Greeks added anything of great importance. And in the first place, it is sufficiently apparent that among the Greeks there were no divine revelations by which they might be correctly taught or instructed in something of great importance; indeed, these things were not even mentioned. Indeed, Pythagoras boasted that the transmigration of souls was revealed to him, and given by God so that he might remember his previous states. But this was false, and no one doubts that it is mythological. Yet if he had spoken the truth, he confirmed only that the miracles worked by Apollonius of Tyana and others – miracles received from the east and vaunted by later Pythagoreans and Platonists – are evidently groundless, and even if they were true they reveal nothing worthy of being known by mortals.

And so the only thing that remains to be discussed is whether the Greeks contributed anything to the amplification and illustration of natural theology which could be acquired from the nature of things by the power of man's natural abilities. But although I doubt whether the Greeks discovered anything completely new in theology, I nevertheless think that they expressed more distinctly certain things which had been explained more obscurely by eastern peoples. Indeed, Moses spoke about God in such a way as to make it sufficiently apparent that that most important thing which he said of himself, 'I am who I am', placed the source of essence beyond any contamination of the body;[83] but yet he did not express such a great truth eloquently in the manner of a dogma. With regard to souls, eastern peoples too did not speak in such a way that makes it plain that they are immaterial. Of course the wise men in Eastern populations were used to images, and were content to teach of a single supreme author of things and most just director of souls; but about the nature of God and the soul their philosophizing was inadequate.

But on the other hand, the Greeks first advanced a certain metaphysics (inasmuch as it is based upon philosophy) and they clearly recognized incorporeal substances in God and in other minds. This is apparent from

---

[82] See Plotinus, *Enneads*, V.1.9.
[83] An allusion to Exodus 3.14.

what is related of the Pythagoreans, and from what is reported about Anaxagoras, but especially from Plato and Aristotle, whose writings survive, and who also gave the reason for immateriality. For Plato recognized that the principle of motion could not be corporeal and that therefore the soul is τὸ αὐτὸ χίνητον,[84] the principle of motion, self-animated.[85] Aristotle also sought in incorporeal substances the principle of both motion and also thought. And not only did he put heavenly intelligences (which were believed in back then) in command of the world,[86] but also he knew that the active intellect existing in man is something different from the body, and separable.[87]

So to conclude, it should be said that even great truths about divine matters have been derived from the barbarians, but that a kind of sacred philosophy, in which the nature of divine and spiritual matters is not only more clearly explained but also demonstrated with admirable arguments, has been derived from the Greeks. So therefore God, who initially used the Hebrew race as an instrument of his supreme providence, instructed men (who were still rather uncultivated, and scarcely informed about the precepts of the sciences) through the revelations of prophets; but later he kindled a new light in the human race. He did this by infusing the Greek mind with the pursuit of wisdom, so that divine truths might be fortified with certain demonstrations against all the doubts of men, who must go onwards to progress over generations towards a greater subtlety of thinking.

Recited in the Academy, Vienna, 1 July 1714.

---

[84] 'self-moved'.
[85] See Plato, *Phaedrus*, 245c–e.
[86] See Aristotle, *Metaphysics*, 1072a19–b3.
[87] See Aristotle, *De anima*, 430a23–5.

4

Ethics and the Love of God

1. Letter concerning Steno and Spinoza (March 1677 (?))[1]

Manuscript:

M: LH I 4, 7 Bl. 17–22.

Transcription:

A: A VI 4, pp. 2197–202.

In this piece, written for an unidentified correspondent, Leibniz takes a critical look at the contents of a letter sent by Nicolas Steno (1636–86), the Apostolic Vicar in Hanover, to Spinoza, shortly before the latter's death.

Another letter to the same[2]

After I wrote to you, I read at my leisure the final letter by Mr Steno, *De vera philosophia ad novae philosophiae reformatorem*.[3] I understand that it is addressed to the late Mr Spinoza, who departed this life several weeks ago.[4] Spinoza was a man of profound meditation, and he had the talent of

---

[1] Editor's title. From the French. Complete.
[2] Leibniz does not identify the recipient of the letter.
[3] 'to the reformer of the new philosophy, concerning true philosophy'. An English translation of this letter (written in Florence in 1675) from Nicholas Steno to Spinoza can be found in *The Correspondence of Spinoza*, ed. and trans. A. Wolf (London: Frank Cass & Co. Ltd, 1966), pp. 324–34.
[4] Spinoza died 21 February 1677.

explaining himself clearly. I have been informed that he left some writings full of rather extraordinary opinions: judging from what survives to us of his work, I do not doubt that there are several excellent thoughts among a great number of scarcely acceptable and very false assertions. Initially he had hitched himself to the opinions of the renowned Descartes, in the way that his disciples usually do, i.e. unreservedly. But having thought deeply about his leader, he began to notice that he had even more to say. I know that it is quite difficult for the Cartesians to rid themselves of the prejudice regarding their master's infallibility, at least with regard to his principal assertions. They do not give any attention to that, and I do not see another way of disabusing them than that of making them reduce the discourses of this author to the form of a rigorous demonstration. I think it was in this way that Mr Spinoza began to be disabused, when he attempted to prove Mr Descartes's *Principles* by means of demonstrations. I don't know whether his own demonstrations will be any better, since in the book we have of his entitled *Renati des Cartes principiorum philosophiae pars I et II more Geometrico demonstratae per Benedictum Spinosam*,[5] and in the appendix he calls *Cogitata Metaphysica*,[6] I see arguments where I think he went too fast, for want of observing the rigour of demonstrations. This is why we shall never have well-grounded true principles until we are minded to adopt the utmost rigour in the form of the argument. Geometers themselves sometimes depart from this, since they see that there is no danger in doing so owing to the shapes which make up for the lack of words; but when the object of reasoning is immaterial, one could not be too precise.

I say this in passing, and now return to Mr Steno's letter, which is entirely moralistic, containing exhortations to rouse Spinoza's attention and to oblige him to the examination of the true Church, a matter which he rightly judged that Spinoza would hardly be concerned about unless stirred by something great.[7] Spinoza was not greatly stirred by Mr Steno's exhortation on account of the great difference between their views. And indeed, it seems to me that Mr Steno presupposes too many things to persuade a man who believed in so few.

He points out to him the advantages of the Catholic Church, which offers

---

[5] *Renati des Cartes principiorum philosophiae pars I et II more Geometrico demonstratae per Benedictum Spinosam* (Amsterdam, 1663).
[6] *Cogitata Metaphysica*. This was an appendix to *Renati des Cartes principiorum philosophiae pars I et II more Geometrico demonstratae per Benedictum Spinosam*.
[7] Leibniz is perhaps thinking of the following passage from Steno's letter to Spinoza: 'you believe that all men are dead with you, who deny the light of grace to all men, since you have not experienced it yourself', *The Correspondence of Spinoza*, p. 331.

such an easy way for all men to be eternally happy without any distinction between able people and idiots, something philosophy could not do. Spinoza will doubtless say that promises are fine, but that he has taken a vow to believe nothing without proof. Mr Steno takes it upon himself to provide it – he says that he was himself rather distant from the true path,[8] and that he was brought back from his straying by the wonders he found in the Church, namely: 1) that he spoke to people whose thoroughly ardent zeal stirred him;[9] 2) that their life edified him even more;[10] 3) that the conversion of an inveterate libertine, such as he said he had known, instantly came across to his mind as a miracle;[11] [12] 4) that the sublime thoughts of an idiot,[13] which elevated his mind to say thoroughly divine things, are hardly less admirable;[14] 5) that the monarchical government is very appropriate for the preservation of the union;[15] 6) that there are no people whose lives are more

---

[8] 'I too was stuck fast if not in altogether the same, yet in the gravest, errors', *The Correspondence of Spinoza*, p. 325.

[9] 'I have not yet come to the end of my fourth year in the Church, and yet I have already seen such great examples of sanctity that I am truly compelled to say with David: *Thy testimonies are very sure*', *The Correspondence of Spinoza*, p. 329.

[10] 'I say nothing of Bishops, nothing of Priests whose words, heard by me in ordinary conversation, as I would testify even with my own blood, were the human symbols of a divine spirit, such is the blamelessness of their life and her eloquence; nor shall I name many who have embraced a strict rule of life, about whom I would say the same thing', *The Correspondence of Spinoza*, p. 329.

[11] 'I hold it the greatest of all miracles that those who have spent thirty or forty years or more in every licence of their desires should as it were in a moment of time turn away from their wickedness and become the most holy examples of the virtues, examples such as I have seen with these eyes and clasped for joy with these hands, and which have often moved me to tears for myself and others', *The Correspondence of Spinoza*, pp. 329–30.

[12] In a draft of this letter, Leibniz wrote in the margin here: 'When Bonacorsi, chevalier of Malta, was in the bordellos (houses of pleasure), he learned through the recounting of another debauchee this sermon by the Frenchman Father Brescian, who had been in the hands of the Iroquois. He was touched by it, and from then on made general confession, and resolved himself to works of charity. This father was an apostolic man, and spoke in a stirring way. His hands had been half-eaten by the Iroquois.
A man who lived his whole life in delights suddenly resolved to become a Capuchin monk etc.'

[13] In a draft of this letter, above 'the sublime thoughts of an idiot' Leibniz wrote 'a lady from Luque'. The Luque in question is presumably the village in Southern Spain.

[14] 'I shall only adduce examples of two kinds, one of persons converted from the worst life to the most holy, the other of the ignorant, so-called in your way of speaking, but who obtained sublime notions of God, without any study, at the feet of the crucified. Of this kind I know those who are occupied with mechanical arts or bound to servile tasks, both men and women, who, through the exercise of divine virtues, have been carried to the praise of God and the understanding of the soul, whose life was holy, their words divine, and their works not seldom miraculous, such as the prediction of future events, and other things, which I pass over for the sake of brevity', *The Correspondence of Spinoza*, p. 329.

[15] 'the Christian rule, which seeks only unity of Faith, of Sacraments, and of Charity, admits of but one head, whose authority consists not in arbitrarily making any kind of innovations, which is the calumny of our adversaries, but in the fact that the things that belong to divine right, or necessary things, remain always immutable, but things that belong to human right, or indifferent things, are

saintly, and who pursue perfection more, than those who are in the Roman Church.[16] After that, he comes to Mr Spinoza's philosophy, or the philosophy of anyone else: 7) he shows him the imperfection in this, that it could not explain in what consists the union of the soul and the body, nor how the soul is aware of the actions or passions of matter, and similar things;[17] 8) that the word of God should not be rejected because it is contrary to demonstrations based on hypotheses such as those of modern philosophers;[18] 9) that it is in vain to hope for better knowledge of the nature of God, of the soul and the body than that which so many holy men have had;[19] 10) and lastly that the Catholic faith is the true philosophy.[20]

---

changed according as the Church judges it expedient for just causes, for instance, if it sees that the wicked are misusing indifferent things for the overthrow of those that are necessary. Hence in interpreting Holy Scripture and in determining the doctrines of the Faith it so acts that the doctrines and the interpretations handed down by God through the Apostles may be preserved, and new and human doctrines may be proscribed. I shall not speak of other things which are subject to his authority since it is sufficient to make this monarchy probable to you that there should be the unity of beliefs and actions which was so often taught by Christ', *The Correspondence of Spinoza*, pp. 330–1.

[16] 'seek out all the societies in the world and you will not find elsewhere that the pursuit of perfection is undertaken with such fervour or carried out with such joy as among us', *The Correspondence of Spinoza*, p. 331.

[17] 'Examine, I beg of you, all your demonstrations and bring me even one about the way in which the thinking thing and the extended thing are united, in which the moving principle is united with the body which is moved. But why do I ask you for demonstrations on these points, who will not be able even to explain to me their probable ways? Hence it comes about that you cannot explain the sense of pleasure or of pain apart from suppositions, and the stirring of love or of hate, and likewise the whole Philosophy of Descartes, however diligently examined and reformed by you, cannot demonstratively explain to me this one phenomenon, namely, how the impact of matter on matter is perceived by a soul that is united to matter', Steno to Spinoza, in *The Correspondence of Spinoza*, pp. 331–2.

[18] 'What is more alien from reason than to deny His divine words whose divine works are obvious to the senses, because they are inconsistent with the demonstrations of men made by means of an hypothesis?' Steno to Spinoza, in *The Correspondence of Spinoza*, p. 332.

[19] 'I am sure that to discover new principles explaining the nature of God, of the soul and the body is the same thing as to discover fictitious principles, since even reason teaches that it is inconsistent with the divine providence that the true principles about these things should have been hidden from the most holy men for so many thousands of years, to be first discovered in this century by men who have not even attained the perfection of moral virtues: for I should believe that only those principles about God, the soul, and the body, are true, which are preserved from the beginning of created things until this day always in one and the same society, the state of God. Among the first teachers of these principles that famous old man, who caused S. Justin to change from a worldly philosophy to the Christian philosophy, said that there *have been philosophers, ancient, blessed, just, beloved of God, who spoke under the inspiration of the Divine Spirit and prophesied that those things would come to pass which now do come to pass*. Principles put forward by such Philosophers and transmitted to us without interruption in the succession by successors like themselves, and even now to-day obvious through philosophers of the same kind to him who seeks them with a right reason, I should believe to be the only true principles, where the sanctity of life proves the truth of doctrine', *The Correspondence of Spinoza*, pp. 332–3.

[20] 'Examine the principles and the doctrines of this philosophy not in the writings of its enemies or

This, in a few words, is the substance of Mr Steno's letter. I do not know what Mr Spinoza would have said by way of response. For my part, I will frankly say what my response would be if it was up to me to make one: I would therefore say (to respond in order) 1) that those who speak in a stirring way are usually impassioned, and consequently less enlightened; 2) that quite often hypocrisy and ambition masquerade as holiness; that the pagans have not been lacking people whose lives were austere and beyond reproach; that there are people in all sects who live well, insofar as can be judged from the outside; 3) that the philosopher Xenocrates immediately converted a libertine who had come to him to ridicule him;[21] 4) that Jakob Böhme said rather amazing things for a cobbler, without thereby being of the Roman Church; 5) that the monarchical government is not always the best, although it is more capable of perfection than any other; 6) that true perfection does not consist in what many people imagine, but in the perfection of the understanding and in the mastery over the passions, things which are as rare in the Roman Church as they are elsewhere, since men usually expel one passion by means of another passion. Without mentioning those who act out of ambition, I will content myself with saying that the majority of those who have lived in a manner which is called 'holy' were driven by the fear of hell. Few people know what the love of God above all things is, even though it is the principle of true religion. This love is proportionally greater the more one is enlightened. Those who have it through a demonstration have it more firmly and more perfectly, provided that practice is in accordance with theory, which one will achieve through exercise. As for 7) the imperfection of philosophy, there is no need to go out of one's way here since it is not necessary to know everything; 8) and if one does not explain how the soul is united with the body, one is not thereby less capable of finding a number of other important propositions; although perhaps this problem is easier to resolve than is thought. To tell the truth, demonstrations based on uncertain hypotheses are themselves

---

in the writings of those who are its hangers-on, whom wickedness allies with the dead or ignorance allies with children, but in those of the masters thereof, perfect in all wisdom, dear to God and probably already sharing in eternal life, and you will acknowledge that the perfect Christian is the perfect philosopher, even if it were only an old woman, or a slave intent on servile tasks, or an ignorant man, in the world's judgement, seeking a living by washing rags. And you will exclaim with S. Justin, *I find this the one, and safe, and useful philosophy*', *The Correspondence of Spinoza*, p. 333.

[21] Leibniz is thinking of the incident in which Xenocrates converted a drunken Polemo, who had burst in while Xenocrates was lecturing on temperance. See Diogenes Laertius's 'Life of Polemo' in *The Lives and Opinions of Eminent Philosophers*, IV.

uncertain, but the demonstrations of geometry and metaphysics do not have to be of this nature, and that which contravenes these demonstrations would assuredly not be the word of God; 9) I still do not see why one cannot find new insights about the nature of God, of the body and the soul, even though most saints haven't had them. For the saints are those who, in loving God above all things, have acquired a mastery over their passions and are ready to do anything for him. Now to love God one must know him, that is, one must have some notion of what one calls 'God', and this notion must be capable of inspiring love. But just as those who have a sufficient notion of the nature of the circle do not thereby know its most beautiful properties, this can likewise happen with regard to the nature of God, since a knowledge which is passable, but real and solid, together with a genuine practice is what makes holiness, and I do not see why a man who is not holy cannot sometimes know the nature of the body and the mind better than the saints themselves. 10) Finally, I agree that the true religion is the best part of the true philosophy, which teaches us to love the most perfect of all beings, and that the eternal life consists in the knowledge of this being.

This, in a few words, is what I have to say to Mr Steno's points. I leave you to judge it, and I will stop after having made a pronouncement that seems necessary to me, which is that I assure you that very far from criticizing Mr Steno I can say that I hold him in high regard and, if I am permitted to say so, that I love him. For I believe I recognize in him a passion animated by a true charity. I am not surprised that he is put off by philosophy, because it has still not proven the strength of metaphysical demonstrations. For my part, I say with sincerity that I am very content with those I have found, since they have taught me the most satisfying truths in the world, which agree wonderfully with the Christian religion and which can give here below the foretaste of an eternal life. I wish the same good fortune to everyone, but especially to persons who deserve as much as does Mr Steno that we take an interest in their conversion. I am, Sir,[22]

---

[22] In a letter to Jean Gallois of September 1677, Leibniz made the following comments which bear on Steno's letter to Spinoza: 'We have here Mr Steno in his capacity as Bishop *in partibus* [*in the land of unbelievers*] and as Apostolic Vicar in this court, in place of the late Bishop of Marocco that His Serene Highness spoke with. I do not know if you have seen Mr Steno's letters about controversy; there is one which was addressed to Mr Spinoza. Spinoza died this winter. I saw him while passing through Holland, and I spoke with him several times and for a long time. He has a strange metaphysics, full of paradoxes. Among other things, he believes that the world and God are merely one and the same thing in substance, that God is the substance of all things, and that creatures are only modes or accidents. But I remarked that some of the so-called demonstrations he showed me are not correct. It is not as easy as one thinks to give true demonstrations in metaphysics. There

2. Dialogue between Theophile and Polidore (summer–autumn 1679 (?))[23]

Manuscript:

M: LH I 20 Bl. 61-7.

Transcription:

A: A VI 4, pp. 2228-40.

The following dialogue, which may well have been composed for Duke Johann Friedrich, was one of a series of dialogues on theological matters that Leibniz wrote in the late 1670s.

THEOPHILE.[24] For some time now I have found you a little changed, my dear Polidore, and it seems to me that you do not have your usual gaiety. Yet your affairs are as one would wish, your prudence has been assisted by fortune and of the things which men seek with such eagerness you lack nothing. You have wealth, you have acquired glory and God has given you a constitution so robust that we hope to enjoy your company for many years yet. That being the case, I cannot understand the cause of the change I see.

POLIDORE. I know that you love me, Theophile, and I have enough consideration for you to enlighten you on this point. You should know, then, that what you see in me is not sadness but the indifference I have towards many of the things which were agreeable to me before. For ever since I have obtained the things I wished for, I have recognized their vanity, and finding myself at the height of the happiness to which men aspire here

---

are some, however, and very fine ones. One could not achieve them before having established good definitions, which are rare. For example, no one has properly defined what "similar" is. And yet, prior to having defined it, one could not give natural demonstrations of several important propositions of metaphysics and mathematics', A II 1 (2nd edn), p. 568.
[23] Editor's title. From the French. Complete.
[24] At the top of the second sheet, Leibniz wrote: 'Written before the death of the late Monseigneur Duke Johann Friedrich.' The Duke died on 28 December 1679.

below, I recognize better than ever the imperfection of human nature, which is incapable of solid happiness. You know I am hardly concerned with coarse pleasures, but of late[25] I am finding more and more that the most refined pleasures attributed to the mind are only agreeable deceptions which disappear when closely examined. Is there anything in the world to which great souls are more sensitive than glory? And yet what good will it do me when I am reduced to dust? I will not for that reason stop doing things worthy of approbation, for it is my habit to do them, and I would have difficulty doing otherwise, but I shall no longer make special efforts to acquire for myself this chimerical immortality. My curiosity is thus diminished by half, and I no longer enjoy the beauties of nature and the arts; and I find even less satisfaction in these fine discourses, which often consist only in an outburst of well-ordered words. And although I recognize that there are solid sciences, like mathematics and mechanics for example, I observe that they are only of use to those who make a profession of them. For they require too much application, and since we shall lose the fruits of all our efforts in a moment, let us not burden ourselves with anything at all. Let us follow an easy style of life and arm ourselves with indifference against the deceptive charms of enterprises.

TH. I feel sorry for you, Polidore, for I see that you are depriving yourself of the greatest satisfaction of life when you are in the best position to enjoy it.[26] But I feel even more sorry for the public and for posterity, which will be deprived of those great and fine things you planned when your affairs did not also permit you to carry them out, which makes me admire the conduct of men who seek only what is far off. But I did not realize that you have changed your maxims, and that you no longer think you have cause to make an effort for the public, and that it seems ridiculous to you to work for a time when we shall no longer exist. However I think you would judge otherwise if you had good assurance that there is a great monarch of the universe, who takes everything done for the public as done to himself. And if you were convinced of the immortality of our souls, you would take an interest in the state of future centuries.

PO. If you are speaking to me as a theologian then I shall end the discussion, for I submit to the faith. But if we restrict ourselves to the limits of philosophy, I see great reasons for doubting these fine things, which serve only to allay our misery with false hopes. I admit I would like to number

---

[25] late | I have recognized that the other pleasures are merely agreeable deceptions | *deleted*.
[26] it |, and I admire the strange conduct of men who seek only what is far-off. | *deleted*.

among those who are happy with their errors, *Felices errore suo*:[27] but since I clearly see what they are, it is no longer in my power to distract myself with them.

TH. But you, who have such excellent knowledge, and have so often admired the wisdom of nature, can you doubt a governing providence[28] when you consider the machine of the universe, which proceeds with so much regularity?

PO. It seems to me it is no great wonder to see that the sun turns around its centre, that it carries and turns with it the liquid matter – called ether – which surrounds it, and consequently carries and turns some large balls called planets which float in this ether and follow its motion with greater or lesser speed in proportion to their solidity and distance.[29] And as nothing resists them, we should not be surprised if their periods are regular without any change being noticed for a long time.

TH. What you say is reasonable. Assuming the motion of this ether around the sun, as well as these balls of different solidity and volume, the rest follows mechanically. But tell me, how is it that there is a sun, an ether and planets?; could the world not have been made in a completely different way? And who made the choice of this one? And the principle of motion we observe in it – where does that come from?

PO. I think there is a soul of the world, which gives life and movement to it.

TH. You will not get away with that. Let us see: does this soul act by choice or by necessity?

PO. Perhaps by necessity.

TH. Then you have no need of a soul, and you had only to say at the outset that this form of the world and this motion are necessary. However nothing is absolutely necessary when the contrary is possible. Now there is no impossibility or contradiction in conceiving a world without a sun, and a sun positioned and moved in a completely different way from ours.

PO. I agree that the world could have been made in a thousand other ways, but this one is apparently the simplest, and nature acts via the shortest ways; therefore it was necessary for it to act in this way.

TH. If this nature or World Soul or, in a word, this mover of which you

---

[27] 'Happy with their mistake', Lucan, *Pharsalia*, 1.459.
[28] providence | ? I respond to you with the poet Claudian. | *deleted*.
[29] distance. | Imagine if you will some pieces of wax swimming in a clear vase. | *deleted*.

speak is capable of reason, I see that it will act through the ways it will consider the simplest. But otherwise I do not see how simplicity will carry the day. For as a cause always acts as much as it can and as long as it is not hindered, it must therefore be the case that all possible things generate themselves, which is not possible since there are many that are incompatible, or else that nothing generates itself.

PO.[30] It seems to me that there is a compromise position, for of all the possible ways to make the world, one has to be preferred to all the others – one which causes most things to succeed, and which, so to speak, contains a lot of essence or variety in a small volume; and which, in a word, is the simplest and the richest.

TH. I understand you. Let us imagine that there are possible beings *A, B, C, D, E, F, G*, equally perfect and candidates for existence, of which there are incompatibles: *A* with *B* and *B* with *D* and *D* with *G* and *G* with *C* and *C* with *F* and *F* with *E*. I say that one will be able to make two possibles exist together in fifteen ways: *AC, AD, AE, AF, AG, BC, BE, BF, BG, CD, CE, DE, DF, EG, FG*, or else three together in the following nine ways: *ACD, ACE, ADE, ADF, AEG, AFG, BCE, BEG* and *BFG*,[31] or else four together in this way alone: *ACDE*, which will be chosen from all the others, because one thereby obtains the most possible, and consequently these four, *A, C, D, E*, will exist in preference to the others, *B, F, G*, which will be excluded, for in taking one of them one cannot obtain four together. Therefore if there were some power in possible things to pull themselves into existence, and to come to light ahead of others, then those four would unquestionably carry the day, for in this struggle necessity itself would make the best choice possible, as we see in machines where nature always chooses the most advantageous option to lower the centre of gravity for the whole mass as much as it can. Likewise, these four possible beings would be preferred. But as possible things have no existence at all, they have no power to make themselves exist, and consequently the choice and the cause of their existence has to be sought in a being whose existence is already established and consequently necessary in itself. This being has to contain in itself the ideas of the perfections of possible things, in order to choose and produce them. And it will doubtless choose according to

---

[30] PO. | You do not frame your dilemma very well: there is a middle way, for of all possible things | *deleted*.

[31] Leibniz added here 'plures addendi' [more to be added]. And this is correct, as he omitted the combination CDE.

the degrees of perfection found in these ideas, or according to the claim that they can have to existence in the aforementioned way, that is, in the simplest or most beautiful way to make the universe, as we touched on above: namely, through which more things or more perfect things succeed, or through which the most essence and the most perfection is obtained that is possible to obtain together. For the most beautiful and the simplest is that which yields the most with the least difficulty, as for example a perfectly round ball is simpler than any other body, because it includes more mass within the same circumference than any other shape. And for this reason a body that collides with some other contrary body, for example a drop of oil in water, collects itself into a round ball in order to disturb, and be disturbed, as little as possible. It is therefore evident that the author of things will act with reason, since he acts according to the perfections of the ideas of each thing, and since he must understand and consider everything all at once in order to match all things together in the best way possible, he will have supreme wisdom and the utmost power. See now if what we have just discovered ought not to be called God.

PO. This is excellent, sound reasoning, and I am very surprised by it. After this I shall no longer be surprised at the wonderful structure of organic bodies, the smallest part of which surpasses in ingenuity all the machines men are capable of inventing. But it seems that this wisdom, which shows such an admirable economy in each animal or organic body considered separately, abandons them afterward to attack each other with the greatest confusion imaginable. A wretched sheep is torn apart by a wolf, a pigeon falls prey to some vulture, the poor flies are exposed to the malice of spiders. And what tyranny do men themselves exercise over the other animals! Among themselves they do more than wolves and more than vultures. What appearance of reason or order in all this! Or rather, since we are agreed upon the supreme wisdom of the author of things, we should say that he does not care about what we call justice, and that he takes pleasure in this mayhem just as we take pleasure in hunting beasts which kill each other. Individuals must give way, he cares only for species, some of which subsist through the misfortune of others. And our folly is presumptuous enough to imagine that he will exempt us from these universal revolutions by an immortality which is without example in nature and is all the more incredible since a beginning must be followed by an end.

TH. Your arguments are plausible, and many spiritual persons are unfortunately taken with them, but thank God there is a way of meeting them.

We have established that God made everything in the greatest perfection of which the universe is capable. And consequently each thing has or will have in itself as much perfection as it is capable of claiming in proportion to what it has already, without harming others.[32] Now as pleasure is nothing other than the feeling of an increase in perfection, it follows that God will give to all creatures as much pleasure as they are capable of, so that those who are reasonable find themselves as happy as possible, without prejudicing the harmony of the universe, which demands that, in the final analysis, there is the most perfection and the most happiness which is possible to obtain in the whole. Perhaps this cannot happen without the misery of some who deserve it.

Now of all the creatures that surround us, only the mind of man is capable of a true happiness. And it may be said that the difference of God to man is only like that of more to less, though the proportion is infinite. Man demonstrates truths; he invents machines and is capable of containing within himself the perfections of the things whose ideas he conceives. He knows this great God, he honours him, he loves him and he imitates him. He exercises dominion over some things with a detachment and an elevation like God's, though man's resolutions meet with obstacles in their execution. It may be said that, with regard to the perfection of the mind, there is a greater difference between man and other creatures which lack reason than there is between God and man. In a word, there is some fellowship between God and men. For as both are rational and have some commerce with each other, they compose a kind of City which must be governed in the most perfect way. This is why, if God is the supreme wisdom, as his admirable works show, and if wisdom seeks perfection everywhere, insofar as it is possible, it should not be doubted that the most perfect beings and the ones most similar to God are those most considered in nature, and that God had consideration for their happiness in preference to everything else. For ultimately this is possible without the order of the universe opposing it. It is true that our bodies are subject to the impact of other bodies, and consequently to dissolution. But as the soul is a substance entirely different from matter and extension, it cannot be destroyed. And that being the case, it is capable of subsisting and of being happy, despite the world's upheavals. For, provided that God leaves it a memory and thoughts, it can be happy

---

[32] others. | Now the perfection of a thing consists in the variety of operations of which it is capable, and by the force with which it can act; this power, acting without refraction, is a step towards a greater power or perfection. | *deleted*.

and unhappy, punished and rewarded, according to the laws of this City, of which God is the monarch. I can demonstrate via physical reasons that the soul is incorruptible, and that it will always think about something. But a moral argument is required to prove that the soul will remember what took place in the body, an argument which is nonetheless demonstrative provided that one keeps in mind the laws of this divine monarchy, which would otherwise not be well-governed since without memory there would be no reward or punishment. And we should not be surprised that the soul always subsists, even though it had a beginning, for as it is a substance, it could only perish by annihilation, that is, by a miracle. For even the smallest atom of matter never perishes, even though it passes through a thousand forms. Now it is clear that the mind does not have any comparison with an atom, nor even with any body whatsoever. And as the perfection of things in general always goes forward (increasing, or at least staying steady), we should not be surprised if the soul, when leaving this life, passes into a state incomparably beyond the one it had before birth. I add that God apparently wanted to leave an image of death by making us aware that the soul thinks and makes up a thousand things when dreaming, as if it were in a separate world. And I see nothing that prevents God arousing dreams in it which are agreeable and harmonious, or sad and dreadful, until it pleases him to make it re-enter an organic body worthy of it, in order that it continue to play its role among creatures.

PO. Your arguments are stirring and unanswerable, and I admit that they have made an impression on me, all the more since you have quite wonderfully anticipated the objections of those who believe that all souls are to be reunited to the soul of the universe,[33] just as the body is lost in the general mass. For as you have very well said, what is once a separate substance will always remain so, and it will carry out its own functions irrespective of whether it is united to something else. So this union of souls to the universal soul consists only in a play on words that mean nothing, as souls are not like raindrops or streams which return into an ocean, and if the comparison were correct it could be said that each atom of the raindrop does not cease to subsist in the ocean itself, and that therefore souls reunited to the universal soul, or rather to God, would not cease to have their own thoughts.

TH. If there were a way to explain and demonstrate to you in a few words some of my more profound thoughts, like for example that bodies subsist

---

[33] universe, | just as the body is reduced to dust. | *deleted*.

only with respect to minds and through minds, and that each mind is a certain expression of the universe and could not naturally cease to think or perish except with the universe, you would not only agree about providence and the immortality of the soul, for you are now convinced of that, but you would also be astonished at the blindness of those who imagine that certain of matter's motions and divisions can destroy the indivisible substances which give all action and even all existence to matter, and which receive impressions only from God. It is true that our souls could reach a state similar to that of newborn children, which indeed and with regard to morality would be worth as much as mortality, but the order of the universe will not allow so many acquired perfections to perish needlessly; on the contrary, it is by means of minds that past things are preserved, and that nothing is lost in the world. Ultimately it is through this that God is not only the principle but also the monarch of things; and as each mind is a reduplication or living representation of the whole universe, according to the degrees of each one's way of conceiving, and as God is himself a mind, and the source of all minds, it must be the case that he cares for them as much as he does the universe, and even that the universe is made in the most advantageous way, to form for the assemblage of all minds a kind of government. This government, like through the reflection of so many mirrors in which God views himself in different ways, bears the splendour of God's perfection and the satisfaction he himself receives from it, to the highest point possible.

PO. I understand the force of your arguments very well. For since God is a mind, and the most perfect of all, I see that he will be the happiest and[34] the most satisfied. But I also see that he will have commerce with other minds, and that he will have much more pleasure, if I am permitted to speak in this way, in his kingdom over minds than over his power over bodies. For if the universe is taken without minds it is just a one-off, but each mind is a new way of expressing or of representing the universe according to how God considers it, so to speak, from a certain side. And the minds which contemplate God, which reason about him and in some way reason like him, insofar as they know the truth, must doubtless have more of an effect on him than all the brute creatures, with regard to which the deft touches which God employs in the government of minds would be useless. Our commonwealths are only little diversions compared with

---

[34] and | will have all the pleasure possible. | *deleted*.

this universal monarchy, yet they are nonetheless pleasing to God just as we take pleasure in the little houses of cards we see children build. Now as God's monarchical government is established in its greatest perfection, everything reason can invent in our commonwealths must be found there in an infinitely higher degree, and as justice is nothing other than what contributes to the perfection of a society, it must be the case that God is just in the supreme degree.

TH. Since you have recognized this important point, let us draw its practical consequences. *First*, it follows that the world is governed in such a way that a wise person who is well informed about it will have nothing to find fault with, and he will not even be able to find anything more to wish for. *Second*, every wise man should be content, not only by necessity, and as it were by a forced patience, but with pleasure and a kind of extreme satisfaction, knowing that everything will happen in such a way that the interests of each individual person persuaded of this truth will be looked after with every possible advantage. For when God admits us a little further into his secrets than he has until now, then among other surprises there will also be the one of seeing the wonderful devices he has used to make us happy beyond what we would have been capable of conceiving. *Third*, we should love God above all things, since we find everything with greater perfection in him than in things themselves, and since his goodness is as valuable to us as our omnipotence.[35] For we obtain from his goodness everything we can wish for with regard to our happiness. *Fourth*, by means of these opinions we can be happy in advance here below, before enjoying everything God has prepared for us, whereas those who are malcontents expose themselves to losing voluntarily everything God has tried to give them. And it can be said that this resignation of our will to that of God, whom we have every reason to trust, follows from the genuine divine love, whereas a dissatisfaction and even sorrow in mundane matters involve something of hatred toward God, which is the greatest of misfortunes. *Fifth*, we should demonstrate the supreme love we bear toward God through the charity we owe to our neighbour. And we should make every effort imaginable to contribute something to the public good. For it is God who is the Lord, and the public

---

[35] 'et puisque sa bonté nous tient lieu de nostre toute-puissance.' In the French of Leibniz's day, 'tenir lieu de' meant 'to be worth as much as'. In this passage Leibniz is not suggesting that humans *are* omnipotent; his point is rather that God's supreme degree of goodness is ultimately as valuable to humans as the attribute of omnipotence would be if they had it. This becomes clearer in the next sentence.

good concerns him like his own, and everything we will do unto the least of his subjects, whom he has the goodness to treat as brothers, will be done unto him; so he will be all the more in favour of what will contribute to the general good. *Sixth*, we should try to perfect ourselves as much as we can, and especially the mind, which strictly speaking is what is called our 'self'. And as perfection of the mind consists in the knowledge of truths and in the exercise of virtues, we should be persuaded that those who in this life have had more ingress into eternal truths and the more transparent and clearer knowledge of God's perfection, and who consequently have loved him more and demonstrated more ardour for the general good, will be subject to a greater happiness in the other life. For finally, nothing is neglected in nature; nothing is lost with God; *all our hairs are numbered,*[36] *not a glass of water will be forgotten;*[37] *qui ad justitiam erudierunt multos fulgebunt quasi stellae;*[38] no good action without reward, no evil one without some punishment; no perfection without a series of others to infinity.

PO. These are truly fine and generous maxims, and I see that they directly combat the indifference into which I would have plunged without your help. For if God takes up the public's cause, we should not fear obliging something we cannot see, and if our souls will always be members of this commonwealth of minds, we ought to take part in that which affects posterity. Finally, if all perfections, once acquired, are preserved and multiplied in a certain way, our knowledge will not die with our bodies, and we will have no cause to regret our labours. You have restored me to life, my dear Theophile, for the idle and negligent life which I was about to lead is no better than death. I now reclaim my vigour and go back to my plans. I see that virtue and glory are not chimeras. I recognize that[39] the ordinary laments about the misery of life poison our satisfaction and greatly deceive us. Instead we must consider that we are the most perfect and happiest among the known creatures, or at least that it is entirely up to us to be so, *felices nimium sua qui bona norint.*[40] After this, no longer will we complain about nature; let us love this God who has so loved us, and let us know once

---

[36] An allusion to Matthew 10.30.
[37] An allusion to Matthew 10.42.
[38] 'They who lead many into righteousness shall shine forth as the stars.' This is a slight misquotation of part of Daniel 12.3: 'Qui autem docti fuerint, fulgebunt quasi splendor firmamenti: et qui ad justitiam erudiunt multos, quasi stellae in perpetuas aeternitates.'
[39] that | the human race is as happy as it wants to be | deleted.
[40] 'most happy, if they knew their advantages'. A slight misquotation of Virgil, *Georgics* II, 458: 'O fortunatos nimium, bona si sua norint' [O most blessed, if they knew their advantages].

and for all that the knowledge of great truths, the exercise of divine love and charity, the efforts that one can make for the general good and to relieve the ills of men, to contribute to the happiness of life, to advance the sciences and arts and everything that serves to acquire a true glory and immortalize oneself through good deeds – all of these are steps towards this felicity, which will bring us as close to God as we are capable of, and which in some way we may treat as apotheosis.[41]

3. Aphorisms concerning happiness, wisdom, charity and justice (summer–winter 1678/9 (?))[42]

Manuscript:

M: LH IV 8 Bl. 4–5.

Transcription:

A: A VI 4, pp. 2798–801.

The following is one of a series of papers that Leibniz wrote in the late 1670s in an attempt to develop an ethics derivable almost *more geometrico*, that is, in a geometrical manner.[43] Beginning with definitions of key terms, Leibniz then adds hypotheses and propositions, before deducing a number of theorems from these.

         a   b

Justice is *charity of the wise*.

              c

a *Charity* is general *benevolence*.

              d

---

[41] That is, our ultimate glorification.
[42] Editor's title. From the Latin. Complete.
[43] See also A VI 4, pp. 2792–8, and 2802–5.

c *Benevolence* is the habit *of love.*

      f   e

d *To love* is *to be delighted by the happiness* of another.

      g

b *Wisdom* is the science *of happiness.*

      h

e.g. *Happiness* is durable *joy.*

      l

h *Joy* is an impression *of pleasures,*[44] that is, a sense of present pleasures, a recollection of past pleasures and a hope of future ones.

l *Pleasure* is a sense *of perfection.*

m *One is perfected* whose power in increased.

Hypothesis
The world is governed by the wisest and most powerful monarch.

Every wise man is the friend of God.
Whoever is the friend of God, is wise.

Preliminary propositions concerning the will of God

God loves all.
God bestows on all as much as is possible.
Neither hatred, nor wrath, nor sadness, nor envy, belong to God.
God loves everyone in proportion to their perfection.
The end or aim of God is his own joy, or love of himself.
God created creatures endowed with minds for his own glory, or love of himself.
God created everything in accordance with the greatest harmony or beauty possible.
The perfection, i.e. harmony, of the universe does not allow all minds to be equally perfect.

---

[44] *pleasures* | . The word 'pleasure' cannot be explained. But the causes of pleasure can be explained. And it seems to consist in a true induction of many observations. *Pleasure* is a sense of perfection | deleted.

God loves minds in proportion to the perfection that he has given to each of them.

The question why he has given more perfection to this mind than to another is one of a number of pointless questions, such as if you were to ask whether the foot is too big or the shoe squeezing the foot is too small. And this is a mystery, ignorance of which has obscured the whole doctrine of predestination.

Theorems concerning wisdom and happiness

He who does not obey God is not the friend of God.
He who obeys God out of fear is not yet the friend of God.
He who loves God above all things is alone the friend of God.[45]
He who does not seek the common good does not obey God.
He who does not seek the glory of God does not obey God.
He who at the same time seeks the glory of God and the common good obeys God.
Whoever claims that God is not perfect does not love God sufficiently.
He who is displeased with some things in God's actions does not think God perfect.
He who thinks that God does certain things out of pleasure, having no reason, or from an irrational or unreasoning freedom, does not think God perfect.
He who thinks that God does all things in the best way possible acknowledges that God is perfect.
Whoever takes no delight from the contemplation of divine perfection does not love God.
All creatures serve the happiness or glory of God according to the degree of their perfection.
Whoever serves the happiness of God against his own will does not love God.
Whoever places his own happiness in relation to divine happiness, he alone loves God.
Whoever loves God endeavours to learn his will.
Whoever loves God obeys his will.
Whoever loves God loves all.
Every wise man endeavours to benefit all.

---

[45] God. | He who works for the glory of God, obeys God. | *deleted*.

Every wise man benefits many.
Every wise man is a friend of God.
Every friend of God is happy.
The wiser one is, the happier he is, supposing his power to be equal.
The more powerful one is, the happier he is, supposing wisdom to be equal.
Every wise man is just.
Every just man is happy.

Theorems on the justice of the wise or happy man in relation to others, or on our duties

A duty is whatever is necessary with regard to the perfectly just.
Permitted is whatever is possible with regard to the just.
A sin is whatever is impossible with regard to the just.

> To speak accurately, nothing is indifferent, i.e. every act is either a duty or a sin. Therefore indifference arises only from our ignorance.

Our duty is
- To seek wisdom
- (To seek power in proportion to the wisdom already acquired)
- To seek knowledge of God
- To seek knowledge of ourselves
- To seek knowledge of the world
- To seek knowledge useful to our perfection
- To seek knowledge of the general method
- To seek knowledge of persuading
- To seek virtue, or a habit of disposition governed by reason
- To rule all things with a certain order
- To make a summary of what is to be done
- To have one's own faculties of the mind and of one's fortune at hand and ready to act
- A. To be of use to all persons as far as possible
- B. To change nothing in established things without a sufficiently great hope of a greater good, and therefore
- B. To preserve every single thing in those things which lie in our power. From this now arises jurisprudence, or the doctrine of right, ownership, obligations and actions.
- From A follows distributive justice, i.e. that which concerns the best state.
- From B follows the doctrine of commutative justice, or of right and ownership and of the way of preserving every single thing in those

things which lie in our power, for *right* in this sense is nothing other than our means of preserving those things which are in our power, for that is permitted.

4. Dialogue between Poliander and Theophile (mid-1679 (?))[46]

Manuscript:

M: LH I 20 Bl. 68–71.

Transcription:

A: A VI 4, pp. 2220–7.

The following dialogue, which may well have been composed for Duke Johann Friedrich (Leibniz's employer at the time), was one of a series of dialogues on theological matters that Leibniz wrote in the late 1670s. The Akademie editors suggest that the character of Poliander may have been based on Nicolas Steno,[47] the Apostolic Vicar in Hanover who had converted to Catholicism in 1667 and devoted his life to theology thereafter. The character of Theophile speaks for Leibniz.

Dialogue between Poliander and Theophile

Some months ago I found myself in the same coach as an apostolic missionary, and a very honourable man of the Augsburg Confession who had held important responsibilities at the court but had withdrawn from the world to attend to his salvation. The missionary's name was Poliander; he had grown old in controversy and had almost no hesitation in directing people onto this subject. He therefore quickly latched on to Theophile (this was the gentleman's name), seeing in him a temperament to listen quietly. Poliander deployed all his rhetoric and made use of the devices common to those of his kind. Theophile defended himself with a certain modesty and

---

[46] Author's title. From the French. Complete.
[47] See A VI 4, p. 2219.

simplicity which nonetheless suggested a great measure of soundness, and an enlightened and tranquil soul.

The discussion had already lasted a whole morning, without any progress being made, when Theophile, speaking up to change the conversation a little, began like this:

Th. I am surprised, Poliander, that people are more concerned with these disputes than with the practice of piety. You agree that those who love God above all things are in a state of salvation. What more is needed? And what is the point of burdening oneself with so many difficult things?

Po. It is not sufficient to love God; one must obey his wishes, that is, the Church which is their interpreter.

Th. The one who truly loves God above all things will not fail to do what he knows to be in accordance with God's orders.[48] This is why one must begin with this love, since charity and justice are its inevitable results.

Po. A pagan philosopher can love God above all things, since reason can teach him that God is an infinitely perfect and a supremely lovable being. But in spite of that he will not be a Christian, since perhaps he will not have heard of Jesus Christ, without whom there is no salvation. So love of God is not sufficient.

Th. This question of the salvation of pagans is too difficult for me. However, I have a great fondness for the thinking of some learned and pious theologians who believe that God will enlighten all those who sincerely seek him, at least at the point of death, by revealing to them, even inwardly, what must be known about Jesus Christ. This is in accordance with the indisputable rule that[49] God does not refuse his grace to those who do what is incumbent on them.

Po. I have no desire to combat opinions which seem to me very suitable for reconciling piety with reason, and I am happy to agree with you that the love of God above all things is sufficient when the matter is understood in this way. But this love has to be true, serious, sincere and active. For we try to learn the wishes of the person whom we love and to conform ourselves to them. A true lover will look out for the slightest movements of the one who does him good. And yet you people believe you can exempt yourselves from

---

[48] orders. | ¶ Po. This is why it is sufficient to love God, since everything else is only a consequence of this love, and since one cannot love him without obeying him, inasmuch is possible | *deleted*.

[49] that | facientibus quod in se est, Deus non denegat gratiam [God does not refuse his grace to those who do what is incumbent on them] | *deleted*. The Latin expression was a medieval maxim often associated with the Lutheran Church, though also adopted by some outside of it (indeed, it predated Lutheranism).

learning the orders that God has made sufficiently well known that no one has grounds for ignorance. There is nothing as radiant and as evident as his Church, which from far enough away is as visible as a city located upon a hill. And yet you close your eyes in order not to see it.

Th. I admit that one has to learn the will of the person one loves and honours, in order to carry it out; but as there is order in all things, and as one could not be equally diligent about different concerns at the same time, I believe that our obedience has to begin with the first of his wishes, which is well enough known to us; for reason and Scripture tell us that we must love God above all things and our fellow man as our self.[50] It even appears that this love is sufficient for salvation, and that everything else is a consequence of it, in accordance with what we have just said.

Po. I assume that a person truly loves God, and I now wish to know what the one who loves God ought to do. And I maintain that the first concern we should have after the love of God should be the search for the true Church.

Th. Yes, that's fine, but you make a rather large assumption about something which is quite rare here below. For Poliander, do you suppose that people do love God above all things?[51] For my part, I maintain that few people know what the love of God is.

Po. Even if I granted you that, you couldn't draw much from it. For it may be that some people truly love God without being able to explain the nature of divine love, and quite often without knowing that what they have in their soul ought to be called divine love.

Th. What you say is true; I believe God gives this honour to many well-intentioned people, but it is always safer to act by choice and to be able to arouse this love in oneself and in others, without waiting for the chance occurrence of a fortunate circumstance. Leaving aside the fact that it is more satisfying to know what one is doing.

Po. What! In matters of grace, you attribute something to chance and something to foolish humans?

Th. I admit that every action agreeable to God happens only by his grace, but one is always more certain of obtaining it when one seeks it by suitable ways, and by choice, than when one just waits for it to occur, which is even contrary to duty. This is why someone who is warned about this sins

---

[50] Matthew 22.37-39.
[51] things? | Therefore there are very few wicked people in the world | *deleted*.

grievously when he turns his thoughts away from the concern of seeking the means to attain this love, which is the way of salvation.

Po. Perhaps the love of God is not as necessary as you think, and it is sufficient to fear him. For according to our teaching, attrition, that is, penitence performed through fear of punishment, is sufficient, together with the Sacrament of Absolution, even if one does not love God above all things, that is, even if there is no contrition, for you know the difference between these two kinds of penitence.

Th. I am surprised that an opinion as dangerous as this has been received among people who profess Christianity. The Jansenists show us its absurdity, the Holy Fathers and even the old Scholastics are ignorant of it, and since God has commanded us to love him above all things, it is quite clear that whoever does not do so is in a state of mortal sin.

Po. Don't talk to me about Jansenists, Theophile – in Rome they are considered to be heretics. As for the Fathers, we hardly study them, and in fact we do without them after having drawn many fine excerpts from them which help us to combat you. This is all the use we make of the Fathers. Besides, the ancients are eclipsed by the wonderful subtleties and curious questions of the moderns. In a word, since the Church is infallible, all the opinions which publicly prevail today in the chairs of theology can only be correct, as well as all the practices publicly received and approved by a stream of doctors. The doctrine of attrition is among them, and there is no need to seek any other proof of it.

Th. Yet there are men of piety and erudition among you who speak of reform, who try to bring you back[52] to the simplicity of doctrine and the exactitude of discipline which was apparent in the early Church.

Po. These are visionaries or ambitious men and they are scarcely better than heretics, since they have the arrogance to reform the holy Church. Really? Children reforming their mother! Is there anything so preposterous? Yet if you still insist in wishing for reformers, we have a good number of them, but they[53] are careful not to upset the opinions received by the doctors.

Th. It seems to me that you do not want reformers, taking the matter aright, since the Church and what it teaches and approves publicly are, as you see it, off limits to reform. But you want people who cherish the mode,

---

[52] back | to the discipline and the purity of the early Church | *deleted.*
[53] Reading 'ils' in place of 'il'.

and you call them reformers, as are the founders and renovators of religious orders.

Po. This is true, if you call 'mode' what we call the practice received in the Church in accordance with the century in which we live, for the Church, being infallible like it is, cannot but choose a mode which is fitting for the time. This is why when[54] hermits are in vogue, we have to rush into the Thebaid;[55] when Scholastic theology reigns, we must quibble as much as possible; when casuists take their place, there is some merit in being a casuist. For even if the casuists were wrong in reducing the number of sins,[56] they were nonetheless useful since men who believe that what they are doing is not sinful will not sin as much as when they know they are sinning. But even though the casuists reduce the number of sins which are contrary to moral virtues, in return for that they lead men to the Christian virtues, that is, they teach them to have regard for sacred ceremonies and all kinds of religious observances received today, for we should urge these things as far as we can. This is why those who introduce certain ways and modes of praying and honouring God, like rosaries, chaplets, scapulars and a thousand other sacred inventions, are the true reformers, who teach people to conform to the mode[57] which reigns in the Church, which is the interpreter of God's wishes.

Th. But you are not saying anything to me about charity or justice, and I hardly see any reformers who take up these issues, and fewer still who succeed with them in the minds of men of our time. Perhaps because this is not the mode.

Po. Be very careful about confusing these purely moral reforms with Christian reforms. Justice and charity are things we can have in common with pagans, but there have to be other pious practices to please God. That is, we need fastings, cilices,[58] disciplines, gratings, books of hours, Hail Marys and similar things, since I see nothing in the Lord's Prayer which a pagan cannot also say. This is why we attach much more importance to the Hail Mary.

---

[54] when | the Church approves and praises witnesses, martyrs and | *deleted*.
[55] The Thebaid is a desert in upper Egypt, and in early Christian times it was used as a retreat by Christian hermits.
[56] A key claim among early modern casuists was that the strict morals of the Church Fathers should yield to the laxer morals of the day.
[57] mode | of the ecclesiastical court, approved by the Church | *deleted*.
[58] A cilice is more commonly known as a hairshirt, that is, a coarse garment usually made from goat hair or horse hair, worn by penitents and ascetics for the purpose of mortifying the flesh.

Th. If we were to suppose the infallibility of the practice which reigns in your Church, I would have to agree with everything you said, Poliander. But it seems to me that this is to push infallibility a little too far, and a number of able men among you recognize no infallible Catholic doctrine other than that which comes from tradition. They give to the Church the right of witness and of guardian, and not that of arbiter. This being so, there is no need to hold fast to the practice which reigns today, but rather to that which the Church of today knows it has received from Jesus Christ and the apostles through the tradition of those who preceded modern practice.

Po. These are the fine principles of certain Sorbonists or other henchmen of France's clergy, which we consider semi-heretical. For in that way the door is open to anybody who dares to oppose what happens in the Church and who scorns its judgements unless antiquity can be shown to have been of the same opinion. This is why he will accuse the superiors of bad example, the inferiors of dissolution, the deeply religious of excess, the frequent partakers of communion of sacrilege, the Scholastics of sophistry and the casuists of licence. So he is not the cause of these people being heretics, they do everything needed for that. And if the Pope dared to excommunicate them in our time, and if they found some secular support, they would remain in the schism like Luther and Zwingali, unless they renounce this flawed principle which reduces infallibility to antiquity, and which separates it from modern practice.

Th. What you said just now is an apology for Luther and Zwingali; it is therefore the Pope's error which has brought about the schism, and which has taught us the hard way to be a little more moderate.

Po. Well, the Pope is merely waiting for a favourable time. Perhaps one day there will be some minority in France or some Cardinal minister or some King who bears a grudge against the clergy, and the court of Rome, which is shrewd, and which knows how to conceal and reveal things when required, will make some new concordat with the King, which will subjugate these restless spirits to him, at the expense of their purse.

Th. The King currently has no need of Rome's consent to obtain free gifts.[59] But let us leave the court of Rome, and all its infallibility, since you have still not proved it to me, and since lengthy discussions are required to settle this matter, as we have shown this morning. Let us return to what is more certain, namely that we must love God above all things and our fellow

---

[59] 'dons gratuits'. In Leibniz's day, this was the name given to grants made by the French clergy to their King.

man as ourselves. It is in this that the law consists. It is in this, adding to it the teaching of Jesus Christ, that the true active faith consists also. For Jesus Christ has taught us this great secret: that he has been not only the preceptor but also redeemer of mankind, to expiate our sins. The divinity that dwells in the human nature of Jesus Christ has brought about the reunion of God and men. There will be no salvation except in Jesus Christ. God will enlighten, in Jesus Christ, all those who love him, even if it happens only at the moment of death. But we do not need to wait such a long time when love is true, as we can obtain this knowledge sooner;[60] and even less do we need to defer the practice of this love, whereby God disposes us to receive from him everything we need to be saved. You call yourself an Apostolic Missionary, and we call ourselves Evangelicals: let us agree with the evangelist and apostle St John, who preached nothing other than this charity full of faith, and this divine love which bursts out through good deeds, and we will have done enough to save ourselves and to win over souls.

Po. I have no instruction at all about that from Rome. However I like your arguments, in part, and I shall give them a little more attention in the future than I have in the past. But you, who have meditated so well on divine love, fulfil your promise too. For you came to agree with me that the first thing which should be sought after this love is the true Church. This Church is the true union of all the living members of Jesus Christ, and in a word, it is the universal charity.

Th. If you put it like that, I am already on your side. But it seems to me that you demand something more, which would be difficult to grant you. You wish us to be convinced of an enormous number of things that are new and hardly certain, and to condemn absolutely all who dare to doubt them. Aside from that, you are too ceremonious, and you burden souls with so many superfluous concerns that they turn away from the one which ought to be their main concern. All this seems to me to be harmful to this universal charity. But here is the inn, and we shall speak more at our ease when we have relaxed a little from the fatigues of the journey.

End

---

[60] That is, the knowledge of Jesus Christ required for salvation.

5. Critical remarks on William Penn and the Quakers (March 1696)[61]

Manuscripts:

M1: LH I 5, 3 Bl. 7–16 [version 1]
M2: LH I 5, 3 Bl. 5–6 [version 2]

Transcriptions:

A1: A IV 6, pp. 358–60 [following M1]
A2: A IV 6, pp. 361–5 [following M2]

On 2 March 1696 Leibniz advised a correspondent that he had been reading William Penn's *An account of W. Penn's travails in Holland and Germany, anno MDCLXXII for the service of the Gospel of Christ by way of journal containing also divers letters and epistles writ to several great and eminent persons whilst there* (London, 1695, 2nd edn).[62] In doing so, Leibniz wrote out many pages of extracts from the book, and at the end of his notes he began putting down some of his own thoughts; this apparently prompted him to write some critical remarks in a separate document. Version 1, below, is the concluding (critical) part of the text that otherwise consists only of Leibniz's extracts from Penn's book;[63] version 2 appears to be an expanded and revised version of Leibniz's critical remarks.

[Version 1]

To make some reflections on this account in a few words, I find it very useful for understanding the different types of human nature, and I even approve of there being people who use extraordinary methods to draw others out of their lethargy, and for this reason they should be forgiven for using certain affected practices which seem bizarre. The world is addicted to trifling matters: people do not think about what true felicity

---

[61] Editor's title. From the French. Version 1 is incomplete: Leibniz's extracts from Penn's book have not been translated. Version 2 is complete.
[62] See A I 12, p. 445.
[63] The full text, including all of Leibniz's extracts, is available in A IV 6, pp. 341–60.

consists in. Arguments alone are not sufficient to make them go back into themselves; something is needed which stirs passions and ravishes souls, as does music and poetry. And the kind of eloquence that is accompanied by gestures also noticeable in an excellent theatrical actor – and generally in all those whose imagination is vivid, overpowering and contagious – seems to me to be found in these new preachers too. I by no means say this to criticize them, since I admit that these mannerisms are often necessary to make a strong emotional impact. It is true that I think I have noticed a little too much artifice and affectation in William Penn. There are many magnificent words which scarcely explain anything. I also do not know whether these people genuinely possess in their understanding the insight they claim for themselves. Insight is nothing other than the knowledge of great truths, but it is not in evidence here. However it is always something to be led to the good, even if it is only by a kind of passion or by a game of the imagination without the insight which ought to be in the understanding, provided that there is also an effort to acquire this true insight, without which I do not think one can have a true love of God, since one could not love something without knowing it and without noticing the beauties of what is loved. So to love God properly we must know his perfections, which the eternal truths represent to us, as by entering into the fundamentals of things we see there the great order and thoroughly wonderful universal harmony, which is with regard to the divinity what a ray is with regard to the sun. This is why I hold that the stirring ways of these extraordinary preachers are good for giving first impressions and for leading souls away from the vanity of the world, but to fill our soul to its capacity, and to make us feel and express in ourselves the force of the divine perfections, which constitute our true felicity, and do so forever, there has to be something else.

[Version 2]

The history of the journey that the famous Quakers Robert Barclay and William Penn made with their companions in Germany and in Holland in 1677, published in English with some related works,[64] seems to me to be rather useful for several reasons, but especially for understanding the

---

[64] Namely Penn's *A call to Christendom in an earnest expostulation with her to prepare for the great and notable day of the Lord that is at the door* (London, 1694).

different types of human nature, and for seeing the power of religion on souls when it is put forward in an extraordinary way. It is even apparent that these people adopt some shadow or imitation of the behaviour of the apostles at the beginning of the Church. However I find there this noteworthy difference, among others, that these early Christians demonstrated more simplicity in their behaviour, and more efficaciousness in the real improvement of their audience.[65] A more natural, and yet very forceful way of speaking is to be found in the Gospels and in the epistles of the apostles and of apostolic men, such as St Clement and St Barnabas, whose letters have been recently rediscovered.[66] But here, everything written by William Penn seems to me to be written with a great deal of artifice and reservation, in terms which are affected and mysterious and which smack a little too much of cliquishness and the intention to control others, without one finding in it enough of a useful doctrine by which to profit. The letters included here, written by the same author, are of the same character: full of magnificent words, but which do not explain anything. I do not know if he or his associates will have said something more substantial in their assemblies or *Meetings*, about which so much is said. But I am afraid that the whole thing is only a skilful way of attempting to arouse the passions through extraordinary ways of acting and speaking, and so to speak a game of an excited and contagious imagination, somewhat as there are preachers who know how to bring their audience to tears, or as there are certain arias which are moving.

I would not disapprove of these mannerisms, which are suitable for emphasizing good things, if I found them accompanied by a clear and luminous doctrine, as was that of Jesus Christ and the apostles, and by the practice of a true charity such as was seen in the early Christians. The ideas Jesus Christ gives us of God are great, but they are clear at the same time. He teaches us that God has care of everything and that everything is accounted for by him, even down to our hairs;[67] that those who love him will be eternally happy;[68] that we should only fear him since only he

---

[65] audience. | Aside from *Revelation* | deleted.
[66] Leibniz is referring here to Clement, ΠρΤζ ΚορνΦίουζ ἐπιστολή πρώτη. *Clementis ad Corinthios epistola prior. Ex laceris reliquiis vetestissimi exemplaris Bibliothecae Regiae*, ed. P. Young (Oxford, 1633), and Barnabus, Φερομένη του ἁγίου Βαρναβά ἀποστολή ἐπιστολή χαθολιχή. *Sancti Barnabae apostoli (ut fertur) Epistola catholica*, ed. H. Menardus (Paris, 1645).
[67] See Matthew 10.30; Luke 12.7.
[68] See John 10.28.

has power over souls;[69] that the slightest good will be rewarded, down to a glass of water given through charity to a poor man who is thirsty;[70] and that one must therefore rely on providence after having fulfilled one's duty.[71] And when he commends us to love above all things this great God whom he has depicted as so lovable and so good, and after him to love our neighbour as ourselves,[72] he covers both theory and practice at the same time. So now that providence has enriched our century by so many new insights, which result from the wonderful discoveries which have been made in nature and which show us its beauty more and more, we should profit from them by applying them to the ideas Jesus Christ gives us of God. For nothing could indicate the divine perfections better than the admirable beauties found in his works. I see that the majority of those who lay claim to a greater spirituality, and particularly the Quakers, try to show their distaste for the contemplation of natural truths. But in my opinion they should do just the opposite, unless they want to encourage our own laziness or ignorance. On this point I find Mr Helmont,[73] Mr Knorr,[74] Mr More and Mr Poiret[75] more reasonable than most others, although I do not want to endorse a number of their views in which they distance themselves from the Church. True love is based upon the knowledge of the beauty of the object loved. Now God's beauty is apparent in the wonders of the effects of this supreme cause. Thus the more one knows nature and the solid truths of the true sciences, which are so many rays of the divine perfection, the more one is capable of truly loving God. With Jesus Christ having laid the foundations of the love of God through the knowledge common to all men, it is for us to strengthen these great ideas day by day through the new natural insights that God has given us expressly for this purpose, and whose grace is used according to the disposition of each person. And we are ingrates if we do not profit from his generous acts. It is true that religion and piety do not depend upon the profound sciences, since they must be within the grasp of the simplest people. But those to whom God has given the time and the means of

---

[69] See Matthew 10.28.
[70] See Matthew 10.42; Mark 9.41.
[71] See Luke 17.10.
[72] See Matthew 22.37-9; Mark 12.30-1; Luke 10.27.
[73] Francis Mercury van Helmont (1614–98), alchemist, philosopher and student of the Kabbalah.
[74] Christian Knorr von Rosenroth (1636–89) was an intimate of Francis Mercury van Helmont and translator of many Kabbalistic texts.
[75] Pierre Poiret (1646–1719), a philosopher and mystic.

understanding him better, and consequently of loving him with a more enlightened love, should not neglect the opportunities for it nor, consequently, the study of nature. And those who try to distance men from this on the pretext of certain insights which they boast about, and which consist only in their over-active imagination, make us abandon what is solid in favour of chimeras, and flatter our negligence.

As knowledge of God's greatness and of the traces of his goodness and his wisdom consist principally in the contemplation of the wonderful order which is discovered in all things to the extent that one penetrates to their foundation, it is obvious that the love of God and of the divine order which results from him will also make us strive to conform to this order and to what is the best. This means that the wise are not in any way dissatisfied with what is past, knowing well that it cannot fail to be the best; but they strive to make the future as good as possible, insofar as it depends on them; knowing that if we fail in this the general order or the harmony of things will lose nothing by it, the loss in fact being ours because we will have less of a connection to it. This is why the more one loves God, the more one will strive in one's own particular way to share in the divine perfections which are widespread in things, and especially in the happiness of souls (which are the best beings we know), by contributing to our own instruction and to that of others. For all true happiness consists only and exclusively in a perpetual progression of joys coming from celestial love, or from the contemplation of the true beauties of the divine nature. This internal fondness and this inexpressible pleasure which arise from the knowledge of divine and eternal truth makes one readily detach oneself from the vanities of the world and from all perishable things. A person who has absorbed all of this will put all of his effort solely into spreading this happiness to others as well, for it is in this way that he himself most shares in the general good and in the harmony of the great order.

It is true that the Weigalians, Boehmists, Quakers, Quietists, Labadists, and other similar persons also seem to strive for these detachments from worldly vanities, but everything they say about abnegation, self-annihilation and silence, while employing a thousand fine terms, could be solid only insofar as it boils down to preferring the general good and the greatest expressions of the divine perfections to all considerations of worldly things. If there is something else, it is caprice or an idle fancy. The true sign of the spirit and grace of God is to enlighten and to make better. Several among them seem to have good views, but they lack genuine insights, throwing themselves into extraordinary ways of behaving which inspire more than they enlighten. It is a shame that their zeal is not accompanied by more knowledge, and perhaps also by more general charity, and that they do not leave behind these useless and artificial affectations of refusing the honours and expressions received among honourable people, affectations which they only seem to adopt to distinguish themselves by a singular character. Instead of that, charity should move us away from everything which smacks of the sectarian and which increases divisions.

6. The true theology (10/20 December 1696)[76]

Manuscript:

M: LBr 661 Bl. 17–18.

Transcription:

A: A I 13, pp. 397–400.

This piece is from a letter to André Morell, with whom Leibniz corresponded regularly between 1694 and 1702.

I read with pleasure how you lectured our good Abbé by teaching him the true theology, which theologians often hardly know. I have thought more about these things and for a longer time than you perhaps think. I read with pleasure and with respect the invaluable fragments of the Acts of the martyrs of the early Church. These *Acta sanctarum Felicitatis and Perpetuae*, which the late Mr Holstein first published,[77] and which some even believed were written by Tertullian, charmed me when I saw them the first time, as did the book by Martyr Hippolite,[78] which the late Mr Gudius first uncovered.[79] As for the lives of the saints, I find that the

---

[76] Editor's title. From the French. Incomplete: material on other topics has not been translated.
[77] Lucas Holstein, *Passio sanctarum Martyrum Perpetuae et Felicitatis* (Rome, 1663).
[78] Hippolytus.
[79] Leibniz is referring here to Hippolytus's *Demonstratio de Christo et Antichristo*, which was first published by Marquardus Gudius (Paris, 1661).

late Mr Arnauld d'Andilly, brother of the Doctor, made a good choice of them.[80] And as for St Teresa, you are right to esteem her works. One day I found in them this fine thought: that the soul ought to conceive things as if there were only God and itself in the world.[81] This thought gives rise to an idea which is significant even in philosophy, and I have made good use of it in one of my hypotheses.[82] I even found solid thoughts in St Catherine of Genes (she is different from the one of Siene). I forgive these people the credulities noticeable in their works, and I content myself with finding excellent things there, on the whole. Thus I am naturally led to concern myself with what should be praised in things, without paying too much attention to what can be criticized in them, especially when the praiseworthy parts prevail. I read books not to censure them but to profit from them, which means that I find some good everywhere, though not equally.

I don't know whether you saw what the late Mr Pelisson had printed of the correspondence I had with him.[83] Through the testimony of esteemed authors of the Roman Church I showed him this secret, known to few people, that according to the principles of this Church and its better theologians, one can be saved through the sincere love of God above all things, whatever communion one belongs to.[84] And I was surprised that he had no qualms about printing that in Paris. For able persons have recognized that what he said against it does not weaken the impressions that my letter can give.[85] It is not that his eloquence does not weaken everything that can come from me, when it is only about that, but the force of arguments always prevails over eloquence, however great it may be, provided that these arguments are clearly explained.

I don't know if you have seen the books of the Jesuit Father Spee, who was an excellent man.[86] The first person I heard praise this father was Johann Philipp, Elector of Mainz,[87] who recommended him to me to the

---

[80] See Robert Arnauld d'Andilly, *Vies de plusieurs Saints illustres de divers siècles* (Paris, 1665).
[81] 'remember that in the entire world there is only God and the soul'. St Teresa of Avila, *Complete Works of St Teresa of Avila* (London: Burns & Oates, 2002), p. 77.
[82] See A VI 4, p. 1581/L, p 324; G IV, p. 484/SLT, p. 74.
[83] Between 1691 and 1693 Leibniz corresponded with the court historian of Louis XIV, Paul Pelisson-Fontanier (1624–93), on matters connected with Church reunion. Pelisson published some of the exchanges, without Leibniz's consent, in his *De la tolerance des religions, Lettres de M. de Leibniz et Réponses de M. Pellisson* (Paris, 1692).
[84] See A I 6, pp. 73–83.
[85] Leibniz is thinking here of his correspondent Henri Basnage de Bauval; see Bauval's letter of 27 July 1692, A II 2, pp. 548–9.
[86] Friedrich Spee (1591–1635), poet, theologian and ardent opponent of witch trials.
[87] Johann Philipp von Schönborn (1605–73), Elector of Mainz and also Bishop of Würzburg and

point of giving me a copy of his book on the Christian virtues, *Güldenes Tugend-Buch*,[88] in which I admired everything, except for the German verses, the true taste for which is still unknown in the Roman Church. But the thoughts are so fine and profound and, at the same time, so well crafted to reach even the vulgar and unenlightened souls in the world, that I was charmed by them. He especially recognized and recommended this great secret of the effect of the true love of God. He even proposes a nice method for praising God at all moments, the solidity of which he even proves like the mathematicians. I pointed it out to Abbé Molanus,[89] who found it so beautiful that he applied it to a fountain he has in his Abbey. And he taught it to Roman Catholic Abbés, colleagues (in part) who had come to see him, being of the same order.[90] If you cannot find the book where you are, I will find it for you. This great man is also the author of the book which has caused quite a stir without it being known where it came from; for one must look after oneself, to speak properly. It is *Cautio criminalis circa processes contra sagas*.[91] I know from the mouth of this same Elector that this Father is the author. The book was translated into several languages. It was praised and refuted. Mr Becker talks about it a lot in his *Enchanted World*.[92] But no one knew to whom it should be attributed. The elector mentioned to me that this good father had admitted to him that he had accompanied to the fire a very great number of so-called criminals in his capacity of confessor; that he had thoroughly quizzed them to discover the truth, but that he could not say he had found anyone who gave him grounds to think they had truly been a sorcerer. The Elector was still a canon in Würzburg when this Father said these things to him;[93] but he was touched by them so much that as soon as he became bishop he put a stop to these proceedings, which had been only too common in Franconia.[94] I know that the late Miss de Bourignon[95] and even Mr Poiret are of another view,[96] and believe that the world is

---

Bishop of Worms.
[88] Friedrich Spee, *Güldenes Tugend-Buch* (Cologne, 1646).
[89] Gerhard Wolter Molanus (1633–1722) was Abbé of Loccum in Lower Saxony, and the principal Protestant representative during the negotiations for Church reunion, which took place in Hanover in the 1670s and 1680s. He corresponded with Leibniz from 1679 until Leibniz's death in 1716.
[90] Molanus was Abbé of Loccum, which was a Cistercian monastery.
[91] [Friedrich von Spee], *Cautio criminalis, seu de processibus contra sagas* (Rinteln, 1631).
[92] Balthasar Bekker, *De Betoverde Wereld* (Amsterdam, 1691–3).
[93] Johann Philipp was appointed canon of Würzburg in 1629, a post he held until he was made Bishop of Würzburg in 1642.
[94] A region of Southern Germany.
[95] Antoinette de Bourignon (1616–80), Flemish mystic.
[96] See Pierre Poiret, *La vie continuée de damlle. Antoinette Bourignon. Reprise depuis sa naissance, &*

teeming with sorcerers. But they should be forgiven for that in favour of the other excellent thing they say.

    I have perhaps meditated with as much application as Mr Poiret himself on what the true inner theology is. And I have even tried to respond to it through the effects. In my opinion, the touchstone of true illumination is a great ardour for contributing as much as possible to the glory of God and the general good. And I find so few people who take this to heart that it surprises me. I have made suggestions of this nature thousands of times. But I usually found that people who wanted to appear the most pious were paralysed when it really comes to doing good, instead being content to vent themselves with fine words as if God can be won over by ceremonies. I find also that few men have a true idea of the good. I only design to call a person 'good' who really makes men more perfect and the grandeur of God better known. I also find that those who are of a sectarian or schismatic humour, that is, who put distance between themselves and those who are full of good intention but do not act rightly in their opinion, could have neither charity nor illumination in its true purity. It seems to me that the late Mr Labadie,[97] the late Miss de Bourignon and William Penn, with his brethren, had that fault of being sectarian or condemnatory. Among those people who have extraordinary views I have found hardly anyone who agrees with me about this great principle of charity besides Mr Helmont,[98] in whom I have noticed a true ardour for the good, although aside from that we often have very different opinions about particular matters. You tell me, Sir, of some people in Holland of an eminent sanctity; you will do me therefore a very great favour if you will inform me of your discoveries about them. For there is nothing I value more than the acquaintance of such persons. I am not fortunate enough to know Mr Poiret. But I have seen certain things of his that have satisfied me very much. However it is true that there are others which have not satisfied me, especially what he wrote against the *Acts of Leipzig* and the excellent Mr de Seckendorff.[99] [100] But his zeal should be forgiven. If his intention is truly good, I will like and respect him very much.

---

suivie jusqu'à sa mort (Amsterdam, 1683), chapter XIV.
[97] Jean de Labadie (1610–74), a convert to the Reformed Church whose mystical writings won many followers, particularly in the Netherlands.
[98] Francis Mercury van Helmont (1614–98), alchemist, philosopher and student of the Kabbalah. Leibniz met him on numerous occasions, and assisted him in some of his publishing projects.
[99] Veit Ludwig von Seckendorff (1626–92), statesman in Saxony, and sometime private scholar.
[100] Leibniz is thinking here of Poiret's anonymously-published *Monitum necessarium ad Acta eruditorum Lipsiensia anni 1686* (Amsterdam, 1686), which responded to critical remarks Seckendorff had made in the *Acta Eruditorum* in January 1686 about one of Poiret's earlier works.

And it is among other things for the marks of good intention you give that I am with so much respect, Sir –

7. On the disinterested love of God (9/19 (?) August 1697)[101]

Manuscript:

M: LBr 685 Bl. 104–5.

Transcription:

A: A II 3, pp. 367–71.

This piece was written for Claude Nicaise (1623–1701), a scholar and Catholic priest, with whom Leibniz corresponded between 1692 and 1700. It concerns the bitter debate on quietism and the disinterested love of God that had erupted in France following the publication of *Explication des Maximes des Saints* (Paris, 1697) by the Archbishop of Cambrai, François Fénelon. Various tracts, pamphlets and books soon followed, of which Leibniz had read three, as he indicates in his letter to Nicaise of 9/19 August 1697: 'Thanks to a favour by Mr Pinsson I have received Mr de Noyon's *lettre pastorale* and the letter from Abbé de la Trappe on the subject of quietism;[102] the first is learned and eloquent, and the second explains very well the root of the matter and what must be corrected in the quietude of false mystics. Yet it seems to me that it does not concern Mr de Cambrai. I have read a report of his book in Mr de Bauval's *Histoire des ouvrages des sçavants*,[103] and I find nothing in that which seems dangerous to me. You will see more fully what I think about this matter in the attached paper.'[104] The following piece is the 'attached paper' referred to here.

---

[101] Editor's title. From the French. Complete.
[102] François de Clermont-Tonnerre, *Lettre pastorale de Monseigneur l'illustrissime et reverendissime Eveque Comte de Noyon, Pair de France, Commandeur de l'ordre du S. Esprit, Conseiller ordinaire du Roy en son conseil d'etat* (Paris, 1697); Pierre de Villiers, *Lettre sur l'oraison des quietistes. Où l'on fait voir les sources de leur illusion* (Paris, 1697).
[103] *Histoire des ouvrages des sçavants* (March, 1697), pp. 321–40.
[104] A II 3, p. 363.

The Bishop of Noyon's *Lettre pastorale* is learned and eloquent,[105] and in a word bears the character of its author. But I would have wished that he had wanted to explain himself further, since he would have taught us many fine and important things. He dissuades the reader from books filled with dangerous maxims,[106] but he does not name these books and he does not explain in what consists the 'new and semi-quietism'.[107] I imagine it must be well known in his diocese. However these generalities can still be detrimental to the truth (of which error often adopts the liveries), serving to oppress innocents and distance souls from the purest theology of true mystics, which ought to break us away from worldly things in order to lead us to God. I therefore wish that he would explain himself more amply, and that he would better indicate the boundaries of error and the truth.[108]

There are doubtless false mystics who imagine that once one is united with God by an act of pure faith and pure love, one remains united to him, as long as one does not formally revoke this union. For it is very clear that every action through which we prefer our own pleasure to that which is in keeping with God's glory or with his good pleasure (made known to us by reason and faith) is an effective revocation of the union with God, even if one does not make this express reflection on a formal revocation.[109] It is therefore an illusion to base the union with God on inaction, since it is rather through actions and the frequent exercises of divine virtues that we should maintain our union with God, in order to demonstrate and strengthen the habit of these virtues which unite us to him.

As for charity or disinterested love, about which I see awkward disputes have arisen, I think that one could not better extricate oneself than by giving a true definition of love. I believe I once did so, in the preface of the work known to you,[110] Sir, when indicating the source of justice. For *justice* is fundamentally nothing other than charity in conformity with

---

[105] de Clermont-Tonnerre, *Lettre pastorale*.
[106] de Clermont-Tonnerre, *Lettre pastorale*, pp. 5–6.
[107] The phrase is from de Clermont-Tonnerre, *Lettre pastorale*, p. 16.
[108] truth. | However the letter from the Abbé de la Trappe helps in part with this, and perhaps Mr de Noyon wanted to rely on it, which is why these two letters appear together. (α) The letter from the Abbé de la Trappe is in my view just as solid, (β) Nevertheless, I find that able theologians have | *deleted*.
[109] revocation. | Mr de la Trappe sees very well the illusion of the so-called continual union based on inaction, | *deleted*. Leibniz is referring here to de Villiers, *Lettre sur l'oraison des quietistes*.
[110] 'Praefatio codicis juris gentium diplomatici' (1693), A IV 5, pp. 50–79. Partial English translation in G. W. Leibniz, *Political Writings*, trans. Patrick Riley (Cambridge: Cambridge University Press, 1988, 2nd edn), pp. 165–76.

wisdom. *Charity* is a universal benevolence. *Benevolence* is a disposition or inclination to love, and it has the same relation to love that habit has to act. And *love* is this act or active state of the soul, which makes us find our pleasure in the felicity or satisfaction of others. This definition, as I have noted from then on, is capable of solving the enigma of disinterested love, and distinguishing this love from relationships of interest or debauchery. I remember that in a conversation I had several years ago with[111] Count ….. and other friends, in which only human love was discussed, this difficulty was raised, and my solution was found satisfactory. When one sincerely loves a person, one does not seek one's own advantage or pleasure detached from the advantage or pleasure of the person loved; instead, one seeks one's pleasure in the contentment and in the felicity of this person. And if this happiness was not pleasing in itself, but only because of an advantage to us which results from it, it would no longer be a sincere and pure love. So it must be the case that one immediately finds pleasure in this felicity, and that one finds grief in the unhappiness of the person loved. For everything that produces pleasure immediately through itself is also desired for itself, as constituting (at least in part) the object of our aims and as something which enters into our own felicity and gives us satisfaction.

This serves to reconcile two truths which appear incompatible; for we do everything for our own good, and it is impossible for us to have other feelings, although we may say we do. However we do not yet love altogether purely when we do not seek the good of the object loved for itself and because it pleases us itself, but because of an advantage for us that comes from it. But with the notion of love we have just given, it is clear how we simultaneously seek our own good for ourselves and the good of the object loved for itself: when the good of this object is immediately, finally (*ultimato*) and in itself our aim, our pleasure and our good; as happens with regard to all the things wished for because they are pleasing to us in themselves, and are consequently good in themselves, even if one were to have no consideration for the consequences; these are ends and not means.

Now divine love is infinitely above the loves of creatures, for other objects worthy of being loved in fact constitute part of our contentment or our happiness, insofar as their perfection affects us, whereas God's felicity does not constitute a part of our happiness, but the whole. He is the source of it and not the accessory, and as the pleasures of lovable earthly objects can

---

[111] with | the Italian Count | *deleted*.

have harmful consequences, only the pleasure one takes in the enjoyment of the divine perfections is surely and absolutely good, and without any possible danger or excess in it.

These considerations show in what consists the true disinterestedness of pure love, which cannot be detached from our own contentment and felicity, as Mr de la Trappe has very rightly remarked,[112] since our true happiness essentially embraces the knowledge of God's happiness and of the divine perfections, that is, the love of God. And consequently it is impossible to prefer one to the other by a thought founded in distinct notions. And to wish to be detached from oneself and from one's own good is to play with words or, if we turn to the effects, it is to fall into an extravagant quietism: it is to desire a stupid inactivity, or rather an affected and stimulated inactivity, in which under the pretext of the resignation and annihilation of the soul swallowed up in God one may proceed to libertinism in practice, or at least to a hidden speculative atheism, such as that of Averroes and of other, more ancient, thinkers, who claimed that our soul is ultimately lost in the universal spirit and that this is the perfect union with God. I find some traces of this opinion in the rather ingenious – but sometimes quite ambiguous and rather questionable – expressions of certain epigrams of a mystical author called *Johann Angelus*.[113] I don't doubt that the true mystics and guides are far removed from it, and I have especially found satisfaction in the excellent works of the Jesuit Father Spee,[114] whose merit was infinitely beyond the reputation he has acquired. However it must be admitted that precepts sufficient for stimulating the pure love of God above all things and true contrition are not always given. And even when the love of God is based on his favours, considered in a way which does not at the same time show his perfections, it is a love of an inferior degree, doubtless useful and praiseworthy, but which is nonetheless interested, and does not satisfy all the conditions of pure divine love. And according to Father Spee's principles, it would have to be related to that theological virtue called hope rather than to charity itself. Moreover, one can feel obliged to a person without respecting him, when his favours do not show his wisdom, but the love with which we are concerned here could not exist without respect.

I think that the intention of the Archbishop of Cambrai was to inspire

---

[112] See de Villiers, *Lettre sur l'oraison des quietistes*, p. 23.
[113] Johann Angelus Silesius was the pseudonym of Johann Scheffler (1624–77), a mystic and poet who converted from Lutheranism to Catholicism.
[114] In what follows, Leibniz is primarily thinking of Spee's *Güldenes Tugend-Buch*.

souls to the true love of God, and to that tranquillity which accompanies the enjoyment of it, while at the same time avoiding the illusions of a false quietude.[115] Whether he has successfully carried out his plan, I cannot yet say. However, I trust it will not be badly received, and the report I have seen of this book in the *Histoire des ouvrages des sçavants* confirms me in this thought,[116] for it seems to me that everything I have read could be interpreted favourably. However, as I learn that some exceedingly judicious people find fault with this work,[117] or ask for further clarification, I suspend my judgement on it; and while waiting for further clarification, I will always be inclined to have a good opinion of an author, especially when there is evidence of his merit from elsewhere, and I think that there is scarcely a matter that deserves to be examined more than the true love of God. I have recently learned that a young English lady called Miss Ash has exchanged some fine letters with an able theologian called Mr Norris on the subject of the disinterested love of God,[118] which is so much spoken of in France now. Nothing is more in the jurisdiction of ladies than notions of love. And as divine love and human love have a common notion, the ladies will very much be able to go deeper into this part of theology.

---

[115] Leibniz is here referring to François Fénelon (1651–1715), Archbishop of Cambrai, and his book entitled *Explication des Maximes des Saints* (Paris, 1697). As Leibniz reveals further on, he had not read Fénelon's book at the time of writing this text, merely a report on it in a journal.
[116] *Histoire des ouvrages des sçavants* (March, 1697), pp. 321–40.
[117] Most likely a reference to Jacques Bénigne Bossuet, the Bishop of Meaux, who was so incensed by Fénelon's book that six weeks after its publication he had published his own critical response to it, namely *Instructions sur les états d'oraison* (Paris, 1697).
[118] Leibniz is here referring to the letters exchanged by Mary Astell (1666–1731) and John Norris (1657–1711), which were written during the course of 1693–4. They were published in Norris's book *Letters concerning the love of God between the author of the Proposal to the ladies and Mr. John Norris, wherein his late discourse, shewing that it ought to be intire and exclusive of all other loves, is further cleared and justified* (London, 1695). Leibniz refers to Astell as 'Miss Ash' because his information on the Norris–Astell debate came from a letter of 4/14 May 1697 written by Thomas Burnett, who referred to Astell as 'Mistriss Ash' (see A I 14, p. 182). Leibniz merely repeats Burnett's mistake.

8. On the public good (2/12 February 1700)[119]

Manuscript:

M: London British Library Add. 5104 Bl. 56–7.

Transcription:

A: A I 18, pp. 376–7.

This piece is an extract from a letter to Thomas Burnett (1656–1729), a Scottish gentleman and enthusiastic supporter of the Hanoverian succession who travelled extensively throughout Europe. Leibniz enjoyed an extensive correspondence with him between 1695 and 1714. The context of the following remarks is Newton's reported unwillingness to publish his 'work on colours', that is, his *Opticks, or, a Treatise of the Reflexions, Refractions, Inflexions and colours of Light*, which was eventually published in 1704.

You know my principles, Sir, which are to prefer the public good to all other considerations, even to glory and money. I have no doubt at all that a person of Mr Newton's strength shares my view. The more one is sound, the more one has this disposition, which is the great principle of an honourable man and even of justice and true piety, since to contribute to the public good and to the glory of God is the same thing. It seems that the goal of all mankind should, in the main, simply be the knowledge and the development of the wonders of God, and it is for this reason that God has given mankind the empire of this globe.

---

[119] Editor's title. From the French. Incomplete: material on other topics has not been translated.

9. The essence of piety
(18 March 1705)[120]

Manuscript:

M: LBrF 4 Bl. 5–6.

Transcription:

Klopp: Klopp IX, pp. 117–18.

The following is an extract from a letter to Caroline of Ansbach (1683–1737), who at the time was Princess of Ansbach; later in 1705 she married Georg Augustus, the Electoral Prince of Hanover. Following the Hanoverian succession in 1714 she became Princess of Wales, and in 1727, when her husband ascended the throne of England (as George II), Caroline became Queen of Great Britain. Leibniz corresponded with Caroline from 1704 until his death.

I am convinced, not by flighty conjectures, that everything is ordered by a substance whose power and wisdom are supreme and of an infinite perfection, so that, if in the present state we were able to understand the order[121] God has placed in things we would see that nothing better could be wished for, not only in general, but even in particular for all those who share the view I have just mentioned, that is, who have a true love of God as well as the complete confidence one ought to have in his goodness. And this is what Holy Scripture teaches us, in accordance with reason, when saying that God makes everything turn to the good for those who love him.[122] Now it is quite clear that love is nothing other than the state in which one finds one's pleasure in the perfections of the object loved. And this is what happens in those who recognize and appreciate these divine perfections and the proportion, justice and accomplished beauty[123]

---

[120] Editor's title. From the French. Incomplete: parts of the letter on other topics have not been translated.
[121] order | of things, which embraces too much for us to understand in our present state | deleted.
[122] An allusion to Romans 8.28.
[123] 'divines et la justesse, justice et beauté accomplies' missing in Klopp.

in everything which is pleasing to God. If we were already sufficiently perceptive to see this wonderful beauty of things, it would be a knowledge which would constitute the pleasure of our blessedness; but as this beauty is currently hidden from our eyes, and we even sense a thousand things which disturb us (things which in the poorly educated cause the temptation to weaknesses and scandal), our love of God and our hope are still only based in faith, that is, in an assurance of reason which is not yet accompanied by anything obvious or verified by sense-experience. And in this, Madam, consists the three Christian virtues of faith, hope and love,[124] taken in their general sense. They constitute the essence of the piety Jesus Christ taught us admirably well, in accordance with supreme reason,[125] and to which our reason hardly reaches without divine grace, even though there is nothing so reasonable.

---

[124] love | or charity | *deleted*.
[125] reason | but which philosophers have (α) largely ignored (β) seen only through a cloud | *deleted*.

5

The Bible

1. Short commentary on the judge of controversies, or, The balance of reason and the textual norm (1669–71 (?))[1]

Manuscript:

M: LH I 3, 8a Bl. 1–8.

Transcription:

A: A VI 1, pp. 548–54.

This piece is reminiscent of the controversialist literature of the sixteenth and seventeenth centuries, and was influenced by Leibniz's reading of Adriaan and Pieter van Walenburch's *Tractatus generales*, 2 vols (Cologne, 1670).

Short commentary on the judge of controversies, or, The balance of reason and the textual norm (v. §. 58.)

(§1) The controversy of controversies is *the question of the judge of controversies*, upon which the decision, discussion, outcome and effects of other controversies depend.

---

[1] Author's title. From the Latin. Incomplete: the second half of the piece, which concerns controversies in the secular sphere, has not been translated.

(§2) This question has exercised the whole world for all time, but never more so than in our time, when agitated *religious* disputes have increased in intensity beyond anything known before.

(§3) Of course the *Roman Church* contends that some visible and infallible judge is needed to put an end to the controversies, and to offer at long last a solution to the disputes. This may seem to concern God's providence, lest he utterly abandon the cause of his people, that is, his Church.

(§4) Regarding Protestants, that is, those who have seceded from the Roman Church, some are *textualists*, others are *mixed* and others *rationalists*.

(§5) The *textualists* are therefore those who think that the judge of controversies is the text itself of Holy Scripture. Some people subject this to considerable criticism, yet it seems to me that they do so unfairly. For they claim that the text of Holy Scripture is not its own interpreter, and that it can no more be said to be the judge of religious controversies than it would be sufficient in a republic to have written laws unless interpreters or judges are appointed to apply them to individual cases.

(§6) The critics argue this way, but they do so fallaciously. For I agree that the text itself is not sufficient for precisely deciding questions about its meaning unless additional resources are consulted. And yet I say that the text itself is sufficient for all the matters of religion pertaining to faith. Is this not a contradiction? Not at all. For matters regarding faith, i.e. pertaining to the basis of salvation, should not be derived from the text through an inference but contained in it explicitly.

(§7) If the rule were upheld that *nothing should be admitted as known to be necessary for salvation unless it is expressly contained in Holy Scripture*, then all the problems about salvation through faith would be removed, and consequently Scripture would be the judge of all controversies about what is necessary for salvation.

(§9)[2] Yet this does not occur in other laws, for in a republic it is also necessary to decide those questions not contained in the law itself, whereas in questions of faith this is not necessary.[3]

(§10) But, you say, questions not explicitly decided in Scripture may occur to a theologian as well, e.g. the question about the marriage of first cousins, and the like; likewise the question of absolute divorce.

---

[2] I here follow Leibniz's numbering, which jumps (presumably by mistake) from §7 to §9.
[3] The text up to this point is strongly influenced by Adriaan and Pieter van Walenburch's *Tractatus generales*, 2 vols (Cologne, 1670), I: pp. 137–8, which is concerned with questions such as whether all that is necessary for salvation is to be found in Scripture, whether Scripture is an infallible judge of controversies and whether the Church is an infallible judge of the word of God.

(§11) I respond that these are not questions of faith but of customs; they are not theoretical questions but practical ones. In these cases we are commanded not to believe but to follow.

(§12) So what should we do in these cases? I respond that here Holy Scripture is not the judge of the controversies, and here we do not need to adhere to the Scriptures. It is otherwise with respect to questions remote from practice, such as about a God who is both one and three, about the nature and person of Christ, about the presence of Christ and the bread in the supper, about predestination and whatever else agitates humankind. In these issues, no proposition is to be accepted as pertaining to faith unless it is explicitly contained in Holy Scripture when translated literally from the sources.

(§13) But what if there is a question about the meaning of the original text because it is doubtful, as happens on account of Hebrew equivocations? I respond: even in such a case it will be easy, if only those things in which all versions agree are said to be about faith. For if I am not mistaken, the versions do not disagree in matters of great importance, and the original Greek text is not obscure at all. And although the Hebrew text is more obscure, key points of faith are hardly overturned on account of this.

(§14) Therefore it doesn't matter whether we use the old versions the adversaries themselves use when we dispute with them, or by common consent we translate the New Testament literally. This translation should be done with care like this: where all versions agree, it is appropriate to opt for that common *usage* of the word, and where they differ, to look for a word's origin or its etymological meaning, or when this is not apparent, which happens in the case of ambiguous words, the meanings of the ambiguous words (which are few and easily decidable) should be laid out.

(§15) And in truth, even when there is a question about the meaning of a passage, it is still usually the same translation. For example, the Evangelicals and the Reformed translate in entirely the same way the passages from Scripture about the Lord's Supper, and the same is true of other passages.

(§16) But, you say, Holy Scripture at any rate cannot be the judge of its own authenticity. And this is so, for it cannot be the judge of whether the text itself, for example 'there are three that bear witness',[4] is authentic. That,

---

[4] A slight misquoting of 1 John 5.7: 'there are three that testify'.

then, must be proved by reason and history, just like Holy Scripture's own divinity, which cannot be deduced from itself since in such cases its own testimony is not permitted; for although it calls itself the word of God, this must nevertheless be proved in another way.

(§17) But what can be skilfully woven into a single usage from the words stitched together in centos of Scripture,[5] where it is assumed they have many meanings? I answer: centos are composed from Holy Scripture in two ways: either to show those things regarding faith (wherein they extend to catechisms, the substance of faith, the instruction of religion, confession etc.), or to support, explain and illustrate the fundamental questions of theologians. Other centos stir people in speeches and writings, and adorn an oration just like tesserae of a mosaic.

(§18) In centos composed to represent the cause of the faith, a sentence should not be mutilated in any way, but used in its entirety, in order to give no opportunity for dispute. Hence, if a sentence begins with some conjunction or relative pronoun, or what follows it begins with one or other, then antecedents and consequents are to be used up to the point at which the sentence is complete.

(§19) Yet perhaps it is not necessary for us to be so scrupulous here as long as we just avoid that common bad habit of centos in which the practice is to divide one proposition into two parts and then to give only the predicate or the subject, or only the antecedent or the consequent, or – and there is nothing worse – just one of the disjuncts. For in these cases one thing is not affirmed *per se* and straightforwardly (it is different in conjunctions), and for this reason it should not be moved indiscriminately to any place whatsoever, otherwise anything can be constructed out of anything, as Tertullian rightly objects to the improper usage of 'Homerocentos' in his book of prescriptions for writings.[6] Therefore the entire proposition should be given somehow. And in controversial passages it is necessary that we be even more rigorous: we must give the full sentence, however long, and up to where it is complete.

(§20) But a not inconsiderable problem remains: because faith pertains to the meaning of words rather than the words themselves, it is not therefore sufficient for us to believe that he who asserted the proposition 'this is my

---

[5] A cento is traditionally a poem whose verses are lifted (either verbatim, or with minor modifications) from Virgil and Homer; a biblical cento followed the same procedure, but using the books of the Bible as source materials.
[6] See Tertullian, *De praescriptione haereticorum*, ch. XXXIX.

body' has spoken the truth unless we also know what he has said.[7] But we do not know what he has said if we possess only the words, being ignorant of their meaning and force. I prove it like this: faith is to believe something. To believe something is to think it true. Truth does not pertain to words but things, for whoever thinks something true, thinks that he considers the thing is such as the words signify; but nobody is able to do this unless he knows what the words signify, or at least unless he thinks about their meaning.

(§21) This is a very difficult problem, though a solvable one. For I respond that for faith we do always need to know which meaning of the words is true, provided that we understand a meaning and do not positively reject it but rather consider ourselves undecided about it even if we are inclined to another meaning. Indeed, sometimes this is sufficient insofar as we believe that whatever meaning is contained in those words is true, and this is especially the case regarding those mysteries wherein practice does not vary no matter what the meaning may ultimately turn out to be.

(§22) Yet it is necessary that the understanding not fall into simple repetitions of words, like a parrot, but that some meaning be apparent to it even if it is general and confused, and as it were disconnected, which is the sort of grasp a peasant or any common man generally has of all theoretical matters.

(§23) So if I hear Christ saying 'this is my body', it is necessary that under the sound 'this' I confusedly attend to everything that preceded it in the prior phrase, namely the bread and whatever is contained in it. So as not to determine in this confused sense whether the bread is made the body of Christ or whether something contained within it actually is the body of Christ, it would be sufficient to accept the 'this' as 'that which is the body of Christ'.

(§24) But what about the non-strict sense? In this case, I think that, when hearing the words of the text, Christians should take them as true in the strict sense, yet with the pious simplicity where one knows one may be mistaken, and that perhaps the proposition is true in a figurative sense; in this way one acts more safely. And thus such faith will be disjunctive, yet inclining to one side. And this, in truth, is what most Christians do in practice, if you look carefully.

---

[7] Leibniz is referring here to the Last Supper, when Jesus broke the bread and gave it to the apostles, saying 'this is my body', an event which is the foundation of the Eucharist. See Matthew 26.26, Mark 14.22 and Luke 22.19.

(§25) Therefore I am not denying that the mind should think of something other than words, but I do deny that any formula regarding faith should be prescribed besides the words contained in Holy Scripture. And yet, an explanation can be added separately for the sake of more uncultivated folk, an explanation which brings to mind this meaning that can be piously believed despite not having been prescribed or absolutely denied by God himself, so that through his own supreme wisdom he has perhaps brought about these effects in a way not otherwise than they imagine.

(§26) Doubtless, if you pay attention you will observe, as I said, that most mortals have only a confused and often equivocal understanding of the sense of the words in propositions concerning theoretical matters, that is, not those which prescribe what is good or what is to be done, but what is true.

(§27) For consider us mortals; all think often about truth and falsity, existence and essence, matter, cause, etc., but I ask: how many of them will have had these words explained to them at any time? Ask a peasant and you will discover that in his whole life he has only used these words casually, often without even knowing what they mean, a kind of thought I usually call 'blind'.

(§28) Indeed, and this is more important and more surprising: all Scholastics, led by Aristotle, use the term τῆς αἰτίας[8] for 'cause', and this goes both for material and formal causes, and efficient and final causes, and even those species they call causes.[9] And yet neither Aristotle, nor any of the Scholastics, nor anyone from the beginning of the world has explained what is meant by the word 'cause' when used so broadly. Indeed, all those who wanted to define the term 'cause' in this broad sense have used words that are even more obscure and for the most part metaphorical, wherein ambiguities are concealed. And thus it is evident that they never understood their own word which they so often employed. Suarez defines 'cause' as that which flows being into something, but what does it mean to flow being into something?[10]

(§29) Therefore, it would be sufficient for us to understand Christ's words 'this is my body' just as much as the Scholastics understand their axiom that there are four kinds of causes. If they have appropriately discoursed for so

---

[8] 'the cause'.
[9] See Aristotle, *Physics*, 194a16–195a3.
[10] See Francisco Suarez, *Disputationes metaphysicae* (Venice, 1619), p. 243 (XII.ii.4). Leibniz frequently complained that Suarez's notion of cause was obscure. See for example A VI 1, p. 229/L, p. 75 and A VI 2, p. 418/L, p. 126.

long about causes and relied on Aristotle, not knowing any meaning of the word that is more distinct, it will be possible for the faithful to believe in God's word even if there is to hand no more distinct understanding of the things that are to be believed.

(§30) Indeed, it can be shown that the actual faith of the majority of Christians today consists, and has always consisted, in the approval of propositions that are not understood. For consider: if you were to ask a peasant whether he believes that there is a God, he will be indignant at the thought that he doubts it. But if you ask him what it is that he calls God, he will also be surprised to be asked this, and will eventually admit that he has hardly ever troubled himself about what is meant by the word 'God', and that it has been enough for him to repeat that proposition with some confused meaning conceived in the words, wherein God is imagined inconsistently, sometimes as an old and wise man, and sometimes in a different way.

(§31) But what I say about peasants I say also of the most learned philosophers and theologians: they harp on so much about 'essence', 'person', 'nature' and 'suppositum', and propose among the articles of faith that God is one essence and three in persons, and yet the majority of them are perplexed, or at least have sometimes been perplexed, about what is meant by these words. Nevertheless, even while they deliberated about the meaning of these words, they would not tolerate anyone denying that they believed in the unity of essence and the trinity of persons. However, a common person who repeats the formulae of the catechism in imitation of pastors never reaches, through his own industry, a point where he even suspects that there is a degree of obscurity underlying those words. So he is content to repeat with untroubled tranquillity the inculcated words of another like him, than to appear diligent by inquiring into the meaning of the terms.

(§32) I therefore conclude: if anyone thinks that a distinct knowledge of the meaning of the mysteries of faith is necessary for salvation, I will demonstrate to him that scarcely one Christian in a thousand ever had it, and indeed even he who thinks in such a way generally doesn't have it. And consequently, the apprehension of the explicit formulae in Holy Scripture, along with the understanding's confused recognition of its meaning and some disjunctive assent or opinion, is sufficient for salvation. For even those who deny that faith is that fear of the contrary position being true, or an opinion, they – if they are speaking truly – should try to explain why faith is accepted in greater and lesser degrees. Yet that it is accepted is evident from the testimony of Christ.

(§33) So much for the textualists. The *rationalists* are either pure or mixed. Both sides at any rate make use of the text and both make use of reason, and they grant that what can be demonstrated by a necessary consequence of reason, and likewise what is explicitly contained in the text, is true. But sometimes it may be asked whether the greater probability lies with reason or with the words of the text; this is so when the meaning of the text is doubtful, likewise when reason can determine nothing, such as in matters of fact, and also when a conflict arises between text and reason. In the latter case, this is not an absolute conflict to be sure, but a conflict of probabilities, such as this: the real presence of Christ's body, and the Trinity in God, are probable according to the text (for from the text nothing whatsoever may be inferred except probabilistically), and improbable according to reason (although not impossible, for we do not concede this point to the Socinians and the Reformed). The Reformed (in practice) and the Socinians (in theory and practice) say that one should stand more on the side of reason and interpret the words in a contrived way rather than admit something that is improbable according to reason. On the other hand, the Evangelicals (in practice and theory) and the Reformed (in theory) say that one should stand on the side of the strict meaning of the words, even if it is improbable according to reason (provided it is not impossible), rather than interpret the words in a contrived or figurative way. And the state of the controversy between the 'Philosopher Interpreter of Scripture' and Wolzogen specifically consisted in this.[11] I say that the Reformed take this side in theory but not in practice because they deny that the presence of Christ's body in the supper is only improbable according to reason, claiming instead that it is in fact impossible. Improbability is proved only through induction from other examples, in such a way that when the Socinians assert that in the whole of nature there is to be found not one being of which there are three subsistences, it is not impossibility that is inferred, but only improbability. One infers improbability from an induction, and impossibility from a demonstration.

(§34) My view is that one should rather side with the strict meaning of the text, provided it is possible, even if it is improbable according to reason,

---

[11] Leibniz is here referring to a debate between Lodewijk Meyer (1629–81), who is the 'Philosopher Interpreter of Scripture', and Ludwig van Wolzogen (1633–90), a Reformed theologian. In his *Philosophia S. scripturae interpres; exercitatio paradoxa, in qua vera philosophiam infallibilem S. Literas interpretandi norma esse* (Amsterdam, 1666), Meyer argued that Scripture should be interpreted according to reason; in response, Wolzogen published *De scripturarum interprete adversus exercitatorem paradoxum* (Utrecht, 1668).

and this is on account of it being God's saying. For since he is wise he will not give us words which would deceive us. Yet he would have given such words if that meaning which is most in harmony with the text according to the rules of interpretation (leaving aside reasonings acquired from elsewhere) were false. And since he is powerful, he can accomplish whatever he has promised.

(§35) I shall prove this with an example. Suppose these two: Titius and Cajus. Titius is a rich man, and pious, while Cajus is poor and untrustworthy. Titius swears to me with these exact words: 'I will give you 1000 thalers'. Cajus says the same, merely promising. I say: if considered in itself, ignoring the promise, it is improbable that Titius will give me 1000 thalers, for the presumption is that no one will give money away, especially such a large amount. But that Cajus will give it away is not only improbable but also impossible, since by hypothesis he does not have nor is he going to have so much money. Therefore, either Cajus's words should not be taken on faith, or if they are taken on faith then they should be understood in a contrived and figurative way, for example as 'I will give you 1000 thalers, namely thalers written on paper'. But Titius would rightly resent his words being explained in that way, not only because he is rich and able, but also because he is wise and willing, especially since he made his declaration with an oath, and in an oath it is not, as a general rule, pious to deceive using an equivocation. Consequently, although it is improbable *per se* that Titius will in fact give me that sum of money, nevertheless when considering *the words* and especially the weight given to *that person's* words, it is probable that he will, and is to be held in practice.

(§35)[12] Let us apply this to God. God is that Titius eminently, for he is the richest or most powerful, and the wisest as well, and consequently all his words have greater weight than the oaths of others. This God promises that our bodies will be resurrected numerically the same as they are now. When considering this in itself, without the promise, it is certainly not impossible, by everyone's acknowledgement, but yet it is improbable that at some future time the parts of a thing dispersed in millions of places should be gathered together again. A Socinian concludes from this that resurrection is improbable, even when taken with the promise, and that the words of the promise should rather be interpreted differently, namely in a contrived, figurative or metaphorical way. On the other hand, a Catholic

---

[12] The duplication in the numbering is Leibniz's.

concludes that, considering the words of the promise, and combining those words with the circumstances of the person speaking, it is probable, and to be held in practice, that God wants his words to be understood in the strict sense and to fulfil them that way, and since he is able to do this he will do so.

2. Brief explanation of Revelation (January 1677)[13]

Manuscripts:

M1:   LH I 4, 4 Bl. 4 (version 1).
M2:   LH I 4, 4 Bl. 1–3 (version 2).

Transcriptions:

A1:   A VI 4, pp. 2473–4 (following M1).
A2:   A VI 4, pp. 2474–83 (following M2).

Leibniz rarely undertook detailed studies of books of the Bible. Only three are known: this piece, which focuses on the Revelation of St John the Divine (often referred to simply as Revelation, or sometimes as Apocalypse), another on the parts of the book of Numbers (see below, pp. 187–93) and another on parts of the gospel of Matthew.[14] In the following piece, Leibniz very closely follows the interpretation of Revelation that had been given by Hugo Grotius in his 'Annotationes ad Apocalypsin' (1650).[15]

---

[13] Author's title (from version 2). From the German (version 1) and Latin (version 2). Complete. The translation of the German piece was kindly made by Daniel J. Cook.

[14] LH I 6, 10 Bl. 9–10. Leibniz likely wrote his commentary on Matthew's gospel in the first decade of the eighteenth century. It consists of numerous statements expounding and interpreting selected verses from the first ten chapters.

[15] In Hugo Grotius, *Annotationum in Novum Testamentum pars tertia ac ultima. Cui subjuncti sunt ejusdem auctoris libri pro veritate religionis Christianae* (Paris, 1650). In what follows, I refer to a later edition, namely: *Annotationum in Novum Testamentum. Volumen VIII* (Groningen, 1830), pp. 234–469.

[Version 1]

I observe that many God-fearing and well-meaning people have been misled by false or quite dubious interpretations of the *Revelation* of John, so that all sorts of elaborate schemes as well as rebellions and mutinies arise from them. Some, under the colour of [it being] God's command, dare to dictate to kings and princes what they ought to do, and, in the case of refusal or whatever, incite the public against them. I therefore wish to propose – with little effort – a special interpretation of the *Revelation* that will cut off these dangerous thoughts once and for all. Not that I consider this interpretation to be the best or most correct, but [I offer it] so that one sees how easy it would be – if a man is well read and quick-witted – to devise something clever out of both the text and its history.

Whether the *Revelation* originates with John the Evangelist and apostle or with John the Presbyter had already been questioned in olden times, which is why even Luther did not want to discuss such a dispute.[16] Whoever the author is, this book is written in a grand and captivating style, specifically to comfort the Christians who were being persecuted by the pagans. As such it was doubtlessly a great incentive for strengthening them and enabling them to go gladly to martyrdom.

Therefore I take as fundamental whatever can be appropriately understood as being about John's own time, so as not to stretch it to things very far away from him. First of all, for Babylon, Rome is meant, and the number of the beast, i.e. 666 as has been added up already by Irenaeus (seen as the disciple of the apostle),[17] is

Λ	Α	Τ	Ε	Ι	Ν	Ο	Σ
30	1	300	5	10	50	70	200

which was the name of a certain king, as also Virgil reckoned, and from whom the Latins, i.e. the Romans, descended.[18] Thus it appears that the author of the *Revelation* had wanted to point to the Romans of that time as enemies or persecutors of the Christians – not seen in his own time but taken somewhat earlier.[19]

---

[16] See Martin Luther, *Biblia: das ist: Die gantze Heilige Schrifft: Deudsch auffs new zugericht* (Wittenberg, 1545), II: p. 395.
[17] Leibniz here follows Irenaeus, *Against Heresies*, V.30.3.
[18] The name whose Greek letters add up to 666 is that of Latinus. A King Latinus is mentioned in Virgil, *Aeneid*, VII, though it is a mythical figure.
[19] earlier. | Whether all the distinctive events of Christianity until the end of the world are recorded in *Revelation* | deleted.

Thus, what was prophesied here about the fall of Babylon has been understood by the early Christian as [referring to] the destruction of pagan Rome.

[Version 2]

Brief explanation of Revelation

January 1677

I

When I reflected upon the *Revelation* recently, I thought that this basis of interpretation should be supposed: *it is probable that all the events, as far as possible, should be understood of things contemporaneous with John.* For it is certain that the prophets, when they seem to speak of things which are remote and of wide relevance, have often described things which are near and quite specific, which should not surprise us, because this grandiloquence befits their majesty. Another reason is that the *Revelation is to be regarded as one of the most artistically accomplished writings which remain to us from all antiquity.* There is therein such simplicity of speech, such propriety of words, such majesty of thoughts and such insights of eloquence that one cannot read it attentively without some admiration and without being stirred in the depths of one's soul. In that regard it is similar to Plato, whose *Phaedo*, on the immortality of the soul, persuaded some to embrace a voluntary death;[20] and to Virgil, whose verses on the death of Marcellus could not be read by Livy without tears.[21] Thus I hold it as certain that many of those who, in this century and the last one, were carried away with a certain enthusiasm, considered by some as fanatics and by others as inspired prophets, were stirred up by their reading of and meditation on Revelation. Nor do I doubt that it had great influence over the first Christians, for whose consolation it was written. Since, therefore, so much artistry is manifest therein, we must be wary of every trivial, contrived and overtly detailed explanation. Next, I assume that it is well known to everyone that 'Babylon' is Rome. I say nothing about chapters 1, 2 and 3, for as they permit a literal sense, they are easy. It is both useless and unbecoming to search for an explanation of certain details, like how Grotius explains the four animals as meaning the four apostles, and

---

[20] See Seneca, Letter 24, to Lucilius. English translation: Seneca, *Dialogues and Letters*, trans. C. D. N. Costa (London: Penguin, 2005), p. 88.
[21] Virgil, *Aeneid*, VI.860–86.

the twenty-four priests as meaning certain living priests,[22] even though those who are introduced as standing permanently before the throne of God do not seem to be living men.[23] Therefore it is no more necessary that specific people be designated here than by the four animals of Ezekiel.[24] The twenty-four elders is double the number of patriarchs or apostles, so it seems that he has added both together. The passage in Irenaeus about the word Λατεῖνος,[25] which contains 666, is good.[26] The evangelist says this is the number of a man. Now Latinus is the name of a man. But it is obvious why the apostle would have preferred Λατεῖνος over *Roman*, because doubtless he would have been unwilling to express his thought too clearly. Grotius's explanation of the beast whose wound is healed is pleasing.[27] In chapter 6[28] Grotius seems to be speaking of the empire, troubled under Otho and Vitellius, and restored by Vespasian. And likewise, by 'another beast',[29] which serves the first one and causes idolatry, he understands, not inappropriately, the magic of Apollonius,[30] who was renowned throughout Asia at that time as a rival to Christ, and harmed many Christians. And these are important matters which closely concerned the apostle. But we should work through the structure of the whole work to some extent. Setting aside the letters to the churches and the preparations for the vision in chapter 5, the actual revelation seems to begin in chapter 6. It begins with the resurrection of the Lord, and describes the early state of Judea up to the overthrow of Jewish military campaigns under Hadrian. By the figure carried on a white horse, crowned and going forth to victory,[31] is meant the resurrection of the Lord, his ascension and triumph over his enemies. Moreover, the same horseman returns later with a few changed details in chapter 19.11-13. Other horsemen follow, representing events which have followed in Judea; the angels, that is, the executers, one of which indicates war, about which see Josephus 20.1,[32] and another, famine, followed, which Agabus had predicted (Acts 11.28). This famine begins in

---

[22] Grotius, *Annotationum in Novum Testamentum. Volumen VIII*, p. 280.
[23] Revelation 4.4.
[24] An allusion to Ezekiel 1.5 and 1.10.
[25] 'Latinus'.
[26] Leibniz is referring here to Irenaeus, *Against Heresies*, V.30.3.
[27] Grotius, *Annotationum in Novum Testamentum. Volumen VIII*, p. 357. An allusion to Revelation 13.3.
[28] Above this Leibniz wrote 'and indeed 7'.
[29] An allusion to Revelation 13.11.
[30] Grotius, *Annotationum in Novum Testamentum. Volumen VIII*, p. 362.
[31] An allusion to Revelation 6.2.
[32] Flavius Josephus, *Antiquitates Judicae*.

the rule of Claudius; see Josephus 20.2. By οἰκουμένην[33] is rightly understood Judea and the surrounding lands, for the apostle undoubtedly intended it this way. 6.9 seems to be talking about the first martyrs slain by the Jews, like Stephen and James. It is promised to them that their blood will be avenged after some delay. Besides, their vengeance is the destruction of Jerusalem. For even Christ said it thus (Matthew 23.37-38): 'Jerusalem, you who kill the prophets … Behold your house is left unto you desolate.' And he states a little after (24.2) 'not one stone will be left on another'. It is therefore obvious that here, in *Revelation* 6.10, by 'the Earth' is meant Judea, and by 'men' the Jews. For the slain say 'how long before you avenge us against those who inhabit the Earth?' And they show that this vengeance awaits the Jews. There follows in chapter 7 earthquakes and anguish: and the seal of those who will be saved from Israel. And verse 9 and onwards indicates that even the gentiles are called to salvation. Now follows chapter 8, the preparation for ruin which, as is usual with great events, is preceded by a silence in heaven of around half an hour. When it is said that the censer, having been hurled to the earth, caused thunder,[34] the sense is that God was touched by the prayers of the pious and bestirred himself for their vengeance. The four trumpets which follow the seals of the earth, the sea, the rivers and the stars, signify the blindness, the stubbornness, the fury and the errors in the plebs and the populace of the Jews (for the vulgar is ordinarily designated by the *earth*, and the multitude by the *sea*), in the colonies of Jews settled like streams throughout Asia, and finally in their stars, or their doctors. But to want to explain in minute detail this mountain of fire, for example, and the name of Wormwood, is useless and unbecoming, for they are the images of a vision. Chapter 9 follows. The first *woe* and the fifth trumpet seem to designate a certain sedition in Judea, and the conflicts with those who are not marked with the seal (verse 4). When it is said in 9.1 that a star has fallen from heaven, to whom was given the key to the abyss, I understand it of some great doctor, author of heresies, and Grotius explains it not inaptly with regard to Eleazar, and the turmoils with regard to the faction of zealots, of whom Josephus speaks, 2.3.[35] Moreover, it is called the first woe because for the first time evils have broken out over the Earth. Two other woes are said to follow (9.12), that is, two trumpets, for (8.13) there are as many woes as remain

---

[33] 'whole earthly dominion'.
[34] An allusion to Revelation 8.5.
[35] Grotius, *Annotationum in Novum Testamentum. Volumen VIII*, p. 315. The reference is to Flavius Josephus, *Bellum Judaicum*.

trumpets. 9.13: from the four corners of the altar, that is, from the four corners of the Earth, a voice said that the four angels at the Euphrates should be loosed. The Euphrates signifies the gentiles, and just as it once did the Chaldeans, so now it does the Romans in imitation of them, like Babylon for Rome; the four angels come from the four corners of the altar, that is, enemies will come to Judea from all parts of the empire. Many are killed, as in Jotapata,[36] chapter 10. The angel whose face is like the sun is undoubtedly Christ.[37] He cries out, there will be time no longer:[38] this is a prediction about what will follow the trumpet of the seventh angel, which will begin the kingdom of Christ on Earth (as we see in 12.1 together with 10.7). I cannot readily interpret the little book that is swallowed,[39] unless someone wants it to be a prophecy commanded of John, but about things which are perilous and ruinous to him, for he adds 'thou must prophecy again'.[40] At the beginning of chapter 11 or at the end of chapter 10, he adds that a reed was given to him to measure the temple, that is, to show the extent of the church, but he is ordered not to measure the interior of the temple, but to reject it,[41] which signifies that the Jewish nation, formerly the holy people, is rejected, and that the gentiles are called. It is said that the gentiles will tread underfoot the holy city: this is at the end of chapter 10 of Luther's edition, or at the beginning of chapter 11 of other editions. When it is said that they will tread upon the city for forty-two months, we should understand this to mean that it will be for a considerable time, just like Daniel, who used the same number.[42] I do not fully understand what is said about the two witnesses,[43] unless siding with Grotius in taking it to refer to the two kinds of Christians, the Jews and the pagans.[44] The beast rising from the abyss makes war with them and overcomes them,[45] and Grotius explains this as about bar Kokhba,[46] but I do not see how this is possible since the beast from the abyss is the Roman Empire (below, chapter 13; this is therefore said in anticipation).

---

[36] Leibniz is referring to the siege of Jotapata of 67 AD, in which many of the town's inhabitants were killed by Roman forces.
[37] Revelation 10.1.
[38] Revelation 10.6.
[39] Revelation 10.9-10.
[40] Revelation 10.11.
[41] An allusion to Revelation 11.1-2. However, Leibniz has it the wrong way around: the author of Revelation is instructed to measure inside the temple and to ignore that which lies outside.
[42] Daniel 7.25 refers to a period of three and a half years.
[43] Revelation 11.3.
[44] Grotius, *Annotationum in Novum Testamentum. Volumen VIII*, p. 333.
[45] Revelation 11.7.
[46] Grotius, *Annotationum in Novum Testamentum. Volumen VIII*, p. 335.

Therefore I understand that this double church is greatly afflicted: perhaps even these two witnesses are Peter and Paul, killed in Rome. And their reawakening is the continuation of Christians, who were thought to be crushed by the persecution of Nero. There follows in chapter 12 the seventh trumpet and it is predicted that the Roman Empire itself will be conquered. This is sketched out in few words, as in shorthand, in the parable of the woman and the dragon who produce a child.[47] The woman is the *Church*; the child is the *kingdom of Christ*. The Church is in the wilderness for 1260 days,[48] that is, the time of the oppression of the Church, because this is the same time as the prediction of the witnesses.[49] Hence by the name of the witnesses should no doubt be understood the Church itself. The same thing is expressed in two different visions. The casting out of the dragon, which was overcome by the blood of the lamb,[50] is the preservation of the Church and the observance of the faith, which cannot be destroyed when the dragon persecutes the woman,[51] that is, when it pursues the Church itself. Allusion is made at the same time to the Jewish tradition of the battle between the dragon and the good angels, according to what is said in the Gemara, and as a result Lucifer was cast out of heaven. Grotius's interpretation, which understands it of Simon the magician, is weaker.[52] It is too finely detailed. The dragon knows that it has a short time,[53] that is, that the kingdom of Christ will soon follow. The battle between the dragon and the woman and her seed (12.17, perhaps an allusion to Genesis) is touched upon here in a few words, and is explained in more detail in chapters 13 and 14. The seven-headed animal, which is doubtless Rome, rises up out of the sea,[54] that is, from the gentiles, for it seems to me that here the Earth means Judea, and the sea means the gentiles. The healed wound was the war under Otho, Vitellius and Vespasian, ended by the latter. The wound to the head signifies the burning of the Capitoline.[55] The forty-two months are the same as noted above at the beginning of chapter 11 or the end of chapter 10. It signifies the length of time of the alienation of the Roman Empire by Christians, and also the treading under foot of the holy land. For after the reign of Constantine, these

---

[47] Revelation 12.5.
[48] Revelation 12.6.
[49] Revelation 11.3.
[50] Revelation 12.9 and 12.11.
[51] Revelation 12.13.
[52] Grotius, *Annotationum in Novum Testamentum. Volumen VIII*, p. 346.
[53] Revelation 12.12.
[54] Revelation 13.1.
[55] Revelation 13.3.

things stopped. These forty-two months harmonize with the 1260 days. Moreover, the καιρόν, καιρούς, καί ἥμισυ καιρού[56] are a year, two years and half a year, and also forty-two months. The beast which comes on behalf of the first imitates a lamb:[57] this means false philosophy, magic, the Pythagoreans. On the number 666, see above. Grotius explains it well with regard to ΟΥΛΠΙΟΣ.[58]

O	Υ	Λ	Π	Ι	Ο	Ϛ
70	400	30	80	10	70	6

70
400
30
80
10
70
6

For Trajan was more commonly spelled by the Greeks 'ΟΥΛΠΙΟϚ'; Gruter's inscription says that *sigma* sometimes stood for six in ancient times.[59]

II

Revelation 13.17-18: 'The number of the name of the beast is the number of man: 666.' It is rightly noted that at one time instead of a name was used the number that formed the Greek letters of the name added together.[60] It is said that this is the number of a man, that is, the number of a name of man. Irenaeus says that it was accepted by some that this name is:

				30	1	300	5	10
	70	200						
50								
N	O	Σ	Λ	A	T	E	I[61]

---

[56] 'time, times, and half a time'. See Daniel 7.25 and 12.7; Revelation 12.14.
[57] Revelation 13.11.
[58] 'Trajan'. See Grotius, *Annotationum in Novum Testamentum. Volumen VIII*, pp. 368–9.
[59] Janus Gruter, *Inscriptiones antiquae totius orbis Romani, in corpus absolutissimum redactae* (Heidelberg 1602–3), p. 60 and p. 327. Leibniz is here following Grotius, *Annotationum in Novum Testamentum. Volumen VIII*, pp. 368–9.
[60] Ancient Greek had no separate symbols for numbers, and so for counting used the letters of their alphabet instead, with each letter standing for a particular number. In what follows, Leibniz (and Iranaeus) simply substitutes for each letter of a name the particular number for which that letter also stood.
[61] Irenaeus, *Against Heresies*, V.30.3.

Nor is that absurd, for it is the name of a man, as there was a King Latinus. Therefore the apostle has preferred to use Λατεινος[62] over Ῥωμαιος,[63] so that the sense would not be too clear, and not easily conspicuous to the Romans, which would endanger Christians. Some will object, in the first place, that this name does not seem to have been sufficiently known to the Greeks for it to be probable that John would have come across it, and much less that he got it from Virgil, in whose work there was a king of this name.[64] This is why others seem to have preferred Grotius's interpretation, which is the name of Trajan, ΟΥΛΠΙΟC.[65]

Ο	70	80
Υ	400	70
Λ	30	50
Π	80	300
Ι	10	10
Ο	70	70
C	6	6
	666	

For this truly is the name of a man, and of the man who, of all the emperors, was in fact the most harmful to Christians. Now the name of some Roman emperor hostile to Christians seems to be indicated by both Irenaeus himself and Aretha.[66] The name of Ulpian was better known to the Greeks than that of Trajan. This is evident from an inscription related in Gruter, p. 60.[67] It should be noted, however, that at the end he should have written not Σ, which means 200, but ς, as we write the letter sigma today, which signifies 6, or rather C, as it often appears in inscriptions. For C is used in place of 6 in an inscription in Gruter, p. 327, and in many others that Grotius says were shown to him by Isaac Vossius.[68] There are two beasts in Revelation chapter 13: one from the sea, which is the Roman Empire, the other from the Earth. But just as in the earlier passage the sea signifies the gentiles, in contrast with the Earth, that is, Judea, so here the Earth, from which arises the second beast, seems to signify a man of the lower classes.

---

[62] 'Latinus'.
[63] 'Roman'.
[64] Virgil, *Aeneid*, VII.
[65] Grotius, *Annotationum in Novum Testamentum. Volumen VIII*, pp. 368–9.
[66] Irenaeus, *Against Heresies*, V.30.3; Arethas, *Commentarius in Apocalypsin*, chapter 37.
[67] Gruter, *Inscriptiones antiquae totius orbis Romani*, p. 60.
[68] Grotius, *Annotationum in Novum Testamentum. Volumen VIII*, p. 369.

So the meaning is that the idolatrous philosophy, such as that of Apollonius of Tyana, is said to have had two horns, like a lamb.[69] That is, that these magicians have imitated Christ. What was said a little before, 'He who kills with the sword shall die by the sword' (13.10), will be aptly applied to Domitian, who persecuted Christians, and was cut to pieces by his own people. Perhaps, however, we shall more correctly say that the first beast is the Roman Empire, and the second is Caesar Trajan, who was from the Earth, that is, from the lower classes, and like a lamb, because he assumed probity, and 'he speaks as a dragon' means his bloodthirsty edicts against the Christians. 'He performed signs',[70] that is, does great things; 'he orders all to adore that beast whose wound was healed',[71] that is, Rome; 'he gives breath to the image of the first beast',[72] that is, he gives his vigour to the Roman Empire. And it seems that 'the number of the beast' could be understood as the number of the second beast, and in that case it would be the name of *Ulpian*, but if it is interpreted as being about the first beast, that is, Rome, the word Λατεινος[73] will prevail.

In chapter 14 the fall of pagan Rome is predicted, and the consolation of martyrs. Moreover, the harvest and the gathering of grapes from the vines mean only that the time has come for the gladdening of the faithful, propagated by the fruit of faith, and the punishment of the wicked under the press, as it were. Nor does it seem fitting to want to push this explanation down to the detail of the smallest circumstances. In chapter 15 there is the preparation of the seven angels who will pour the seven bowls on pagan Rome, whose ruin was predicted in the preceding chapter. In chapter 16 the bowls are poured upon the Earth, upon the sea, the fountains and the sun; these four bowls correspond exactly to the four trumpets from before. But it does not follow from this that the same thing should be understood in both cases, for these are the acts of the seventh trumpet, and therefore not a repetition of the previous consequences. They explain each other, and the sense is that men of every kind are the *earth*, and the sea, that is the populace subject to the Roman Empire; the fountains and the rivers are the allies; the sun and the stars, the leaders and rulers on whom God's wrath is poured. It brings to mind also the bowl which is poured upon the very seat of the beast, namely

---

[69] Revelation 13.11.
[70] Revelation 13.14.
[71] Revelation 13.14.
[72] Revelation 13.15.
[73] 'Latinus'.

Rome.⁷⁴ Another bowl is poured upon the Euphrates, so that, with it dried up, the way might be prepared for the kings of the East.⁷⁵ It seems that the Roman Empire was threatened by the Parthians, the Scythians and other barbarians from the Euphrates and the Rhine.

Chapter 17 concerns the ruin of pagan Rome more distinctly. It says 'The seven heads are seven mountains upon which the woman sits, and there are seven kings.'⁷⁶ No one can doubt that Rome is meant here, but as for the seven kings, Augustus, Tiberius, Caius, Claudius and Nero seem to be those five who have fallen.⁷⁷ (Nor do I think that Galba, Othon and Vitellius should be included, as they all reigned for a brief duration in which the empire was not peacefully possessed, although Grotius counts them.)⁷⁸ 'One is': might this be Vespasian? 'The other has not yet come to the kingdom': evidently this is Titus. 'And when he comes, he will continue for a short time': indeed, he died early. 'And the beast which was and is no longer' is the eighth king: this will be Domitian. Yet Grotius interprets it like this: Domitian had already claimed for himself the majesty of Caesar in the lifetime of his father and his brother, but having been brought to order he adopted the pretence of restraint until he had recovered the empire.⁷⁹ This explanation should therefore carry the day, because I do not see who else could be meant by this eighth king. The only problem is that it is not consistent with the name of *Ulpian* which was attributed to the beast, unless, as I said above, we take this first beast to be Domitian, and the second, which has risen from the Earth, to be *Ulpian*. But there is a difficulty here, because afterwards that beast, which has risen from the Earth, is called a false prophet (19.20). Hence it does not seem to be an emperor but some leader of a sect, which in turn favours the opinion about Apollonius. It is also obscure that it is said that the eighth king is 'of the seven'.⁸⁰ These conjectures almost convince me to believe that the beast itself is the Roman republic or the senate, which 'is and is not', since only a shadow of it remained; 'it is of the seven', because the senate has governed with them, and I do not see how the whole beast of seven heads and ten horns could be taken for one Caesar, since the heads

---

⁷⁴ Revelation 16.10.
⁷⁵ Revelation 16.12.
⁷⁶ Revelation 17.9-10.
⁷⁷ Revelation 17.10.
⁷⁸ See Grotius, *Annotationum in Novum Testamentum. Volumen VIII*, p. 398. For the five kings, Grotius has Claudius, Nero, Galba, Otho and Vitellius.
⁷⁹ Grotius, *Annotationum in Novum Testamentum. Volumen VIII*, p. 396.
⁸⁰ Revelation 17.11.

are said to be kings. Therefore I strongly believe that the republic or the senate is meant. But I do not really know what I should make of the ten kings which have received no empire as yet.[81] Perhaps it is talking about future emperors up to Constantine, which are summed up by the number ten like a round number. 'These [ten horns] shall hate the woman',[82] that is, the Roman republic, and will ravage it. Or might it be talking about foreign nations, about Parthinians and Germans, because it is said in 17.15 that they will hate the woman? But even this explanation is inapt because it is said that the same horns give their kingdom to the beast until the will of God should be fulfilled.[83] Perhaps it is possible to reconcile them in this way: that they give their own power to the beast until God's will is that they hate the woman. But all those things do not agree well with the words 'the ten horns are ten kings which have received no empire as yet, but which for some time will have power with the beast',[84] and therefore it will be more readily understood of future Caesars, and with respect to that their hatred of the woman should be understood as meaning not that they hate Rome particularly, but that they will do a great deal of harm to it, and will treat it tyrannically like Domitian and others.

The rest is clear. What is said in 19.7 about the marriage of the lamb and his wife should be understood in contrast with the Babylonian woman. Moreover, the wife of the lamb seems to be the Christian empire. It is said that the beast and the false prophet will be thrown into the lake of fire:[85] this is obvious with regard to the beast, but not equally so with regard to the false prophet, since there is no mention of him in the preceding chapters. Yet he seems to be called a false prophet for the same reason as that second beast, namely idolatrous magic, and in this way it cannot be explained of Ulpian. Besides, it is clear that it mixes the destruction of Rome and the overthrowing of idolatry, even though these did not happen at the same time or for the same reasons. For it seemed that this punishment was due to pagan Rome in order that afterwards it should be completely ruined, and at any rate idolatry ceased in Rome after its ruin, under Honorius, not before; for it was flourishing even under Theodosius. In chapter 20 the dragon is bound for a thousand years, and the saints judge the Earth

---

[81] Revelation 17.12.
[82] Revelation 17.16.
[83] Revelation 17.17.
[84] Revelation 17.12.
[85] Revelation 19.20.

and reign.[86] The souls of the slain reign with Christ for these thousand years, that is, their memory is publically venerated. Thus says Grotius.[87] But this is not consistent with what follows, where it is said that the other dead did not rise again.[88] Unless we say that it alludes to Jewish traditions about the double death and resurrection, about the thousand years between the two, about Gog and Magog. From Constantine's edict for the liberty of Christianity in 340 AD to the Ottoman Empire, there are a thousand years. But everyone knows that the Saracens had already inflicted many defeats on the Christians, and that therefore these thousand years were not especially happy years. Then it is said that the other dead will be resurrected a thousand years after the first (20.5). Then in verse 12 it is said that the same thing will happen after Gog and Magog are ruined. So there must be a thousand years between the beginning of the reign of saints, and the ruin of Gog and the day of judgement. And yet more than a thousand years had passed, and Gog is not ruined. It seems we should say that this allegory is alluding to old traditions where exactitude is not considered necessary. Grotius thinks that chapter 21, about the new heaven and Earth,[89] should be understood as referring to the time of the reign of the saints,[90] not to the time after judgement. But that conflicts with 22.5, where it is said that the New Jerusalem will be eternal, so it is not a thousand years.

3. On the Revelation of St John (30 June/10 July 1691)[91]

Manuscript:

M: LBr 366 Bl. 8–9.

Transcription:

---

[86] Revelation 20.2-4.
[87] Grotius, *Annotationum in Novum Testamentum. Volumen VIII*, p. 431.
[88] Revelation 20.5.
[89] Revelation 21.1.
[90] Grotius, *Annotationum in Novum Testamentum. Volumen VIII*, pp. 436–7.
[91] Editor's title. From the Latin. Incomplete: those parts of the letter on other topics have not been translated.

A: A I 6, p. 548.

This piece is part of a letter to Hermann von der Hardt (1660–1746), a professor of Oriental Studies and Church History at Helmstedt, with whom Leibniz enjoyed an extensive correspondence on theological topics from 1691 until his death in 1716.

If it could be shown that the Revelation of St John pertains more to the past than to the future then many turmoils of souls would cease. For there are those who draw great hopes from their own particular interpretations and raise them in others, hopes which develop into bold strategies among those who dream that they are instruments appointed by God to carry out the punishments of the wicked and to hasten the reign of Christ. And they want not just to believe or hope for promises but also to fulfil them, because they think, by what contrived calculations I have no idea, that the time (about which, Christ says, it is not fitting for us to be acquainted)[92] has already come. Consequently, Grotius's attempt was not unsatisfactory;[93] he tried to show that the Revelation can be construed fittingly enough as about the judgements of God against the old persecutors of the Christian name and especially about the fall of the Roman pagan state. But if the same arguments were to include the destruction of Jerusalem and the dispersion of the Jewish nation, I would not think that the idea is to be despised.

4. The Story of Bileam (early September 1706)[94]

Manuscripts and versions:

M1: LBr 366 Bl. 311–12 (draft, in Leibniz's hand).
M2: *Histoire de Bileam* ([no place], [no date]) (printed text without pagination, following M1, but containing numerous minor copyediting errors).

---

[92] See Matthew 24.36; Mark 13.32-3; Acts 1.7.
[93] Hugo Grotius, 'Annotationes ad Apocalypsin' in *Annotationum in Novum Testamentum pars tertia ac ultima*.
[94] Author's title. From the French, and translated by Daniel J. Cook, with revisions and annotations by Lloyd Strickland. Complete.

M3: Karlsruhe HLB Ms. 320, 4 (zw. Bl. 73–4) (same as M2, but with Leibniz's handwritten corrections of some of the copyediting errors).

M4: *Histoire de Bileam* ([no place], [no date], pp. 3–19 (printed text, following M3, with further corrections in Leibniz's hand).

Transcription:

B: G. W. Leibniz, *Verfasser der Histoire de Bileam*, ed. Wilhelm Brambach (Leipzig: Johann Ambrosius Barth, 1887), pp. 30–8 (following M3).

On 27 August 1706 Leibniz received from Hermann von der Hardt a lengthy Latin essay entitled 'Bileami Asinus' [The ass of Bileam], about a soothsayer who features in several chapters of the Old Testament book of Numbers.[95] This prompted Leibniz to write his own essay on Bileam (M1), which he sent to von der Hardt on 7 September 1706, noting that it had been produced from both his own reflections and those of his correspondent.[96] Within six weeks, von der Hardt had had Leibniz's essay printed, along with a title page indicating that it was to be the first piece in a compendium along with three other essays written by von der Hardt (one each on: the jawbone of an ass wielded by Sampson, the crows of Elijah and the Antichrist). The first printing (M2), entitled *Histoire de Bileam*, contained just Leibniz's essay, and no details were given of a printer, a place of printing or even a date. The pagination was unfinished also, with all pages numbered as p. 0. It was probably just a set of proofs. Despite not having given his permission for his essay to be printed, Leibniz was sufficiently relaxed about it that he corrected in his own hand a number of copyediting errors (M3), and in subsequent letters advised von der Hardt of the errors that he hoped would be corrected on subsequent printings.[97] The changes were made, and a corrected printing was sent to Leibniz; as before, the printing was entitled *Histoire de Bileam* and contained only Leibniz's essay, with no details of a printer, place of publication or date, though this time the essay was properly paginated. On this corrected copy Leibniz made further corrections in his own hand (M4), though whether these were forwarded to von der Hardt is uncertain. Two versions of the published book exist: the first contains Leibniz's essay and four others by von der Hardt, though only a very few copies

---

[95] The manuscript of von der Hardt's text is held in the Gottfried Wilhelm Leibniz Bibliothek, Hanover, under the shelfmark LBr 366 Bl. 297–310.
[96] See Leibniz, *Verfasser der Histoire de Bileam*, p. 18.
[97] See Leibniz, *Verfasser der Histoire de Bileam*, pp. 18, 19 and 22.

of this were printed;[98] the second version, published the following year, omits Leibniz's essay, and instead contains five essays authored by von der Hardt.[99]

[M1, Leibniz's handwritten draft]

The story of Bileam

The[100] Israelites, led by Moses, left Egypt, came to the border of the Edomites, and asked them for passage to enter into the Promised Land. However, the Edomites refused this request and opposed the Israelites with such great forces (Numbers, chapter 5) that Moses thought it best to go around their land.[101] This detour was lengthy, but it served to make the people stronger and more disciplined, for along the way they overthrew several minor kings, such as those of Arad, of Heshbon and of Bashan (chapter 21).

After this, they arrived at the frontiers of the Moabites. Balak, King of the Moabites, was alarmed by this, as were the neighbouring lords of the Midianites. The former induced the latter to send for Balaam, or Bileam, a noted soothsayer of the time, who lived *with the Ammonites*[102] (chapter 22 verse 5), and who had come from[103] the eastern mountains of Aram (chapter 23 verse 7) which some take to be Armenia. [Balak told him that] he should come and see the people of Israel from the heights of Moab in order to curse them and sing songs or imprecatory prayers capable (according to the view

---

[98] Some years later, an English broadsheet entitled *Memoirs of Literature* devoted several issues to English translations of the essays in this version of the book, Leibniz's included. See *Memoirs of Literature* IV (3 April 1710), pp. 13–15; VI (17 April 1710), pp. 23–4; VII (24 April 1710), pp. 25–6. The journal editor, Michel de la Roche, described the book thus: 'We have received from *Germany* Five Dissertations, Entitled, *Histoire de Bileam. Renards de Samson. Machoire d'ane. Corbeaus d'Elie. Antechrist.* That is, *The History of* Balaam. Samson's *Foxes. The Jaw-bone of an Ass.* Elijah's *Ravens. Antichrist.* The first is ascribed to a Gentleman of that Countrey, Famous for his Universal Knowledge; and the Others, to a Learned Member of the University of *Helmstad.* We are inform'd that some few Copies only have been printed in *French* at the desire of a great Princess.' *Memoirs of Literature* IV (3 April 1710), p. 13. The 'great Princess' may be Electress Sophie of Hanover; Leibniz certainly discussed with her some of the themes of the book, such as Elijah's ravens. See Leibniz, *Verfasser der Histoire de Bileam*, p. 16.
[99] This version was entitled *Renards de Samon. Machoire d'ane. Corbeaus d'Elie. Les quatre monarchies. L'antechrist* (Helmstadt, 1707). The book was published anonymously.
[100] The | Israelities, led by Moses, left Egypt, and having obeyed when he wanted to lead them by the straight path into the Promised Land, were obliged to make a great detour which lasted forty years, but which would make them stronger. | *deleted.*
[101] Leibniz's reference is wrong; it should be Numbers 20.14-22.
[102] *Ammonites* | and who was Armenian, according to some | *deleted.*
[103] '(chapter 22 verse 5), and who had come from' omitted in M2.

of that time) of rendering a whole people wretched. Bileam, accustomed to deciding matters according to his dreams, asked the messengers to wait to see what the night would reveal to him, and his dream was such that he thought that God forbade him from doing what Balak had requested.

The messengers having returned home, Balak sent higher-ranking lords to importune him with greater urgency. Bileam once again took counsel during the night, and God told him that he could go, but that he should take care to do only what was ordered of him. That is,[104] he had a dream which he interpreted in this fashion, following the rules of his art. Consequently, he departed the following day with the Moabite lords. But en route he had another vision, which was an omen of all that was going to occur. It was the vision of the adventure and of the dialogue with a she-ass and with an angel or messenger of God.

It is likely that this version was also a dream. For the journey doubtless lasted several days; thus Bileam, being in bed, at night dreamt (as is understandable) that he was on the road on his she-ass, and that she had trouble advancing, and so on. By day, he travelled in the company of the Moabite lords, but in this vision he was accompanied only by his she-ass and his two servants. Also, he continued on the road with the Moabites after his vision; this discrepancy implies that the road he was on alone was only in his mind. The text says nothing which denies this interpretation, and the circumstance I have just noted favours it. It is also worth noting that God had permitted him to go (verse 20) and yet it is said a little later (verse 21) that God was incensed with him.[105] This is because Bileam's intentions were not quite honest: he wanted to please Balak who had made him grand promises. This is why, in a troubled spirit, along with a bad conscience, this new menacing vision occurred of an angel or messenger of the Lord holding an unsheathed sword to kill him; in effect, his vision was an omen of all that was to come, and apparently this is why Moses recorded it and preserved it.[106] [107]

It appears that in this[108] allegorical vision, the she-ass represents[109] Bileam

---

[104] In M4, Leibniz deleted 'That is' and replaced it with 'At least'.
[105] Leibniz's first reference is correct (Numbers 22.20) but his second is slightly inaccurate (it should be Numbers 22.22, not 22.21). In the printed copy of this piece (M2), Leibniz's references were changed to 'verse 10' and 'verse 11' respectively; apparently he did not spot the mistake as he did not correct it.
[106] it. | And Bileam, having been tempted by Balak to give him advice which was harmful to the Israelites for want of impeccations, was then caught up in the Israelites' massacre of the Midianites, when the people of Israel put them to the sword. Chapter 31. | *deleted.*
[107] it | in the records. | M4.
[108] this | hieroglyphic vision | *deleted.*
[109] represents | the prophet Bileam | *deleted.*

himself, who is being urged on by Balak as the she-ass was urged forward by his master. The she-ass was like the prophet, for she saw the angel of the Lord[110] unlike he who urged her on; in this, the prophet [in the vision] represents King Balak, who did not know the design and will of God. The she-ass, seeing the obstacle, made efforts – as did the prophet – to do nothing against God's command, and she was mistreated and threatened by her master just as the prophet was scolded and threatened by the King of the Moabites (chapter 23). The evasions of the she-ass to get off the road, fearful of the sword of the angel, indicate that the prophet, fearing God's prohibition, would do what Balak had not asked, and would bless instead of curse. When the she-ass pressed the foot of her master against the wall of the narrow road to avoid the angel,[111] this indicated that the prophet, no longer able to avoid revealing his thoughts plainly to the king at the third sacrifice (which was hardly ever done, so as not to overly pressure the divinity),[112] greatly angered this Prince and made him incensed with him. Finally the she-ass spoke and the eyes of her master were opened so as to see the angel; this signifies that the prophet finally spoke plainly to the King and opened his eyes in order to make him understand the imprecations were futile, and that God had blessed the people he wanted to curse. Chapter 24.

However, God's anger at Bileam, and the threat of the angel who carried an unsheathed sword in this prophetic dream, also had its effect on the true course of events.[113] The angel represents a messenger of God: this messenger, carrying a sword, represents Phinehas, son of the great Israelite high priest, who kills Bileam (chapter 31 verse 8). For this prophet or soothsayer did not do enough this time and thought he had fulfilled God's command in changing the curses into solemn blessings. But at the same time, he thought that to gain the gifts and good graces of the King, he could forsake for a while the role of the prophet who spoke in the name of the Lord and take on that of an ordinary mortal and give advice to the King simply as a learned man, which was harmful to the Israelites and would undo them, had not Moses, impelled by a superior divine spirit, settled matters in conformity with the will of God.

The advice which Bileam gave Balak before leaving and which gave

---

[110] Lord | and the obstacle put in the way of what was asked | *deleted*.
[111] Numbers 22.25.
[112] In M4 Leibniz deleted the bracketed words and replaced them with 'which was ordinarily the limit'.
[113] In M4 Leibniz deleted the final clause and replaced it with 'was also in fact fulfilled'.

Balak hope (chapter 24 verse 14)[114] was, as one knows from chapter 31 verse 16, to make a grand celebration in honour of Baal-peor, God of the Midianites, to invite to it the Israelites who resided in the area; to attend to them and to entertain them well, and to seduce them with pleasing young women, who would be on display there. See chapter 25. Balak and Bileam thought that such transgressions and such idolatry would serve to estrange the Israelites from their own God who protected them, and subject them to the gods of their enemies. For it was the custom of gentiles to believe that there were differences[115] between the gods of each nation, as there were between the nations themselves. Beyond that, it would win over a part of the Israelites and divide them amongst themselves; it also would, through sensual pleasures, soften up the mettle of men hardened by rough journeys in the desert and by fighting against other peoples. But Moses, seeing where such confusion would lead, hanged some of the principals who had acted with abandon. He did this to expiate the people.[116] At the same time, he commanded the Judges to execute the guilty ones (chapter 25 verse 3).[117] And Phinehas, a courageous young man, grandson of Aaron and son of the High Priest Eleazar, knowing the intention of his great uncle, and motivated by a zeal worthy of his high birth and his hereditary priestly origins,[118] when he saw that one of the greatest Israelite leaders, chief of the tribe of Simeon, named Zimri, son of Salu, went to pay a visit to a Princess of Midianites named Cozbi, daughter of Prince Zur, followed him and, finding them lying together, pierced both of them as one in a fashion which marked their crime.[119] [120] In the end, *24,000 Israelites*[121] perished in this tumult, and God's anger towards his people[122] was appeased by this purification (verse 9).

However, the Midianites, instigators of this calamity, also had to feel God's anger (verses 17-18). This happened some time later (chapter 31) when Moses, taking his time in order to surprise his enemies, sent 12,000 well-trained soldiers into their land, led by this same Phinehas. This army

---

[114] In M2 this is changed to '(chapter 24 verse 4)', which would appear to be a typesetting mistake.
[115] In M4 Leibniz deleted 'there were differences' and replaced it with 'there was pure animosity'.
[116] In M4 Leibniz amended the final part of the sentence to read 'the sins of the people'.
[117] Leibniz's reference is wrong; it should be Numbers 25.5.
[118] origins, | went to kill one of the chief Lords | *deleted*.
[119] crime. | Whether that caused a tumult, or Phinehas pushed his zeal further | *deleted*.
[120] In M4, Leibniz amended the final clause to read 'pierced both of them, who were in a situation that as it were illustrated their crime'.
[121] M2 has instead 'several thousand Israelites', but Leibniz crossed it out and wrote 'many Israelites' in its place. However, 24,000, the number Leibniz wrote in M1, is correct, according to Numbers 25.9.
[122] In M4 Leibniz changed 'his people' to 'the rest of his people'.

destroyed five Midianite Princes and killed this very same Bileam, who apparently had been attracted once again to the land by the presents and honours of Balak and the Princes of Midian, who were satisfied with the success of the advice of this clever soothsayer, which had cost the people of Israel so dearly, but which would also cost the life of he who had given it, and had thus gone against that which he himself had believed conformable to God's will.

It appears that Moses, both a great statesman and a great prophet, considered Bileam a noted rival and antagonist and deemed him worthy of having his fate conveyed to posterity. On the other hand, he did not deign at all to name Jambres and Jannes, Egyptian soothsayers or wise men, whose fame was preserved by others and somehow known to the Greeks, as is apparent from a passage in Pliny.[123]

There is a fine passage at the close of the final prophecy of Bileam, which could lead us to believe that at times he had been seized by God's spirit. It is that he appears to have predicted the coming of Alexander the Great in the East, and the destruction of the Empire, which had been previously held by[124] the Assyrians and by the Persians. For he says, assuming that it is he who spoke, that one day vessels would come from Chittim, that is, from Greece, and not from Italy (as some have taken it to refer to the Romans) and that these newcomers would destroy Asshur and Heber. For Asshur signifies the Assyrians and Heber several other neighbouring peoples. That is why in Genesis chapter 10 verse 21, Shem is called the father of all the sons of Heber.[125] To show that it is Alexander that is meant, it is added that the leader of those from Chittim will himself perish soon after having conquered the East.

---

[123] See Pliny, *Natural History*, XXX.3. Pliny mentions only Jannes; the pairing of Jannes and Jambres can be found in 2 Timothy 3.8.
[124] by | the Mesopotamians | *deleted*.
[125] Heber | such that Heber seems to signify all the Semites | *deleted*.

6

Miracles and Mysteries

1. The devil cannot prophesize (3 March 1680)[1]

Manuscript:

M: LH 1, 3, 8c Bl. 9–10.

Transcription:

A: A I 3, p. 356.

From a letter to Christophe François de Bragelongne (1646–1721), a counsellor in the Parisian parliament, with whom Leibniz had a brief correspondence between 1680 and 1681:

It is true that the devil can mimic some miracles. But there is a kind of miracle that the devil could not imitate, all powerful and all enlightened as he is, which is prophecy. For if a person can tell me many particular truths about general affairs which are due to happen, for example in a year here, I will hold it as certain that it is God who enlightens him. For it is impossible for anyone bar God to see the general chain of causes which have to come together in the production of contingent things.

---

[1] Editor's title. From the French. Incomplete: parts of the letter on other topics have not been translated.

2. On the threefold God (1680–4 (?))[2]

Manuscript:

M: LH I 3, 4 Bl. 3.

Transcription:

A: A VI 4, pp. 2291–4 (following M).

One of a number of papers on Christian theology authored between 1680 and 1684 (for others, see also 'On the person of Christ', pp. 199–202, and 'On Scripture, the Church and the Trinity', pp. 227–32):

On the threefold God

There are three persons of the Godhead, and of these persons there is numerically one essence[3]

We are not demonstrating this mystery of faith through reason, instead we are merely illuminating it and defending it against objections. And the strongest of the objections is this: if three things differ from each other, every one of which is God, it also follows that there are three Gods. For if the Father is God, and the Son is God, and the Holy Spirit is God, and the Father is not the Son or the Holy Spirit, and the Son is not the Father or the Holy Spirit, and finally the Holy Spirit is not the Father or the Son,[4] then either it will have to be said that there are three gods, or that we do not know what 'one' and 'several' mean. Accordingly, one will be able to deny with equal right that a father, a son and a grandson are three men; alternatively, a reason will have to be given as to why we say that these are three men and deny that the former are three gods. We respond that even

---

[2] Author's title. From the Latin. Complete.
[3] *essence.* | ¶ This mystery of faith cannot be demonstrated through reason, but only illustrated and defended. | *deleted.*
[4] Son, | then of course either we have to acknowledge that there are three Gods, or we overturn the notions of words and do not know what we mean when we say 'one' or 'several'. | *deleted.*

if the Father is not the Son, the Father is nevertheless he who is the Son, that is, that God who is numerically one. This cannot be said of the two men who are father and son, and this is a genuine reason for the difference. Moreover, when it comes to how different persons may be understood in a case where they are numerically one, I don't know anything that illustrates this more appropriately than a mind understanding itself. For it is clear that there is some distinction between that which understands and that which is understood, of which the former has the power of perceiving, the latter the power of being exhibited, while each is one and the same mind numerically, and nevertheless it cannot be said absolutely and in all respects that the one is the other,[5] although they are correlated. Moreover, what happens in some way in a created mind, takes place in God in the most perfect manner. In truth, the Holy Fathers expressed the three persons of the Godhead elegantly through the three primary perfections of the mind: ability, knowledge and will. Hence the Father is the source of all things, the Son is called the Logos, that is, the Word of the mind or the wisdom of the Father, and the Holy Spirit is called love, or will. That is to say, the Father multiplies the person of the Godhead when he understands himself and loves himself. And so the Son springs from the Father, and the Holy Spirit proceeds from the Father and the Son,[6] because understanding presupposes the power to act, while will presupposes both the power to act and understanding,[7] although, on the other hand, to understand and to be understood, to love and be loved, are common to all three persons. Yet only the Son is produced through[8] the essential primitive act of understanding, and only the Holy Spirit proceeds through an essential primitive love, and through them the several persons of the one God reflected back upon himself arise, in precisely the same way as, when our mind understands itself, all things are common to that which understands and that which is understood (since they are one). However, there is some distinction arising from this very reflection of the mind back upon itself, to the point that the understanding of the person doing the understanding is expressed also in the person of the mind being exhibited or the person understood, but in a sort of derivative way. As for those who

---

[5] other, | or known that that which understands, insofar as it understands, is that which is understood, insofar as it is understood. | *deleted.*
[6] Son, | (or as the Greeks say, albeit less accurately, by the Father and through the Son) | *deleted.*
[7] understanding | . This catholic doctrine is consistent with the sentiments of Holy Scripture and the early Church. | *deleted.*
[8] through | essential love, through which the different persons of the one God reflected back upon himself arise | *deleted.*

think otherwise, the Anti-Trinitarians, aside from the fact that they are compelled to vandalize the words of Holy Scripture by an overly forced interpretation, and to depart from the ancient traditions of the Church, they accept completely intolerable consequences. For they have not dared to deny that Christ should be worshipped, with the exception of Franciscus David, who was already Judaizing, and whom Socinus himself refuted, along with a few others.[9] Therefore the Arians worship the first-born creature, and the Photinians worship a mere man whom they say received the name and honour of God through adoption. But how much better is it to side with the Catholics in bestowing divine honour upon nothing other than that one omnipotent and infinite substance? Those who conceive the persons of the most Holy Trinity as individuals of the same species, and their common essence as a universal, also make a very grave error. For it was demonstrated above that God is numerically one, and to remove the difficulties it is sufficient to keep in mind the likeness mentioned a little earlier, of persons multiplied in some way in one mind that understands itself. Nor is it less absurd to consider the Holy Spirit only as some attribute of God, for how then is he sent, or how are we bidden to baptize through him in the same way as through the Father and the Son? Finally, it is the height of absurdity to take choirs of angels for the Holy Spirit, as a certain Neo-Arian has done. If this were so, a sin against the angels would be more serious than one against the Son, whom we have nevertheless already shown to be the supreme God. Also, the Apostles who gathered in Jerusalem did not wish to say 'It seemed good to choirs of angels and to us',[10] evidently having forgotten God; and when the Angel Gabriel told Mary that she was going to conceive, that the Holy Spirit was going to come upon her, and that the power of the Most High was going to overshadow her,[11] he did not indicate himself or other angels. But if that was meant, one will have to say that the Virgin Mary was conceived by the Holy Spirit, that is, by angels, and that Christ is not the Son of God. And Peter will have spoken wrongly in saying to Ananias: 'when you lied to the Holy Spirit, you lied not to men but to God'.[12] Finally who does not

---

[9] See Franciscus David, *Defensio Francisci Davidis in negotio de non invocando Jesu Christo in precibus* (Kraków, 1582); Faustus Socinus, *Disputatio de adoratione Christi, habita inter Faustum Socinum & Christianum Francken, nec non Fragmenta Responsionis fusioris, quam F. Socinus parabat, ad Francisci Davidis de Christo non invocando scriptum: alioq nonnulla ad hoc argumentum pertinentia* (Kraków, 1618).
[10] See Acts 15.28.
[11] See Luke 1.31 and 1.35.
[12] See Acts 5.3-4.

see that in the formula of baptism a third person, the Holy Spirit, is added to the Father and the Son, not a crowd of Holy Spirits, who of course have never intervened in any matter except as messengers and as ministers to the mystery of salvation? One may judge from this how pitiably men stumble when they stray from the Catholic path.

3. On the person of Christ (1680–4 (?))[13]

Manuscript:

M: LH I 3, 4 Bl. 3.

Transcription:

A: A VI 4, pp. 2294–7 (following M).

Leibniz wrote this piece on the same sheet as 'On the threefold God' (see pp. 196–9 of this volume) and apparently after that piece was finished, since he begins this one by alluding to what he had shown 'A little earlier' in the companion piece.

On the person of Christ

In Christ there is one person, but two natures, the divine and the human

A little earlier it was shown that the Word, that is, the Son, is the second person of the Godhead;[14] the same Son is the man who is called Christ. Hence the person of Christ is itself the second person of the Godhead, which assumed flesh in time. Therefore there is one person which is both man and God, but two natures, the divine being eternal, and the human being assumed, which subsists in the personality or the subsistence of the word as an arm does in the subsistence of the body. And just as in the Trinity there are three persons, but one nature, so in the Incarnation there are three natures (deity, soul and flesh) with one person. From these considerations it is clear

---

[13] Author's title. From the Latin. Complete.
[14] Godhead; | and therefore is one and the same person. Accordingly, the second person of the Godhead is a man, and is called Christ, | *deleted*.

how beautifully all things are in agreement in the Catholic faith – things which are said on the one hand about the Trinity, and on the other about the Incarnation – and how wisely conceived are the formulae which the Church uses; nor do I see how[15] we could speak more soberly and more in accordance with the intention of Scripture and with the analogy of faith and with ὑποτύπωσιν τῶν ὑγιαινόντων λόγων,[16] and with the force of expression too, I would add, than by using[17] the words 'nature' and 'person' in the way that has been said. For those who acknowledge two persons, or who make from Christ a being by aggregation like a society, composed of a man, or rather God living within a man as a demon lives in those he has possessed, or at any rate make two Christs, or Sons, one of man and one of God: those people have to deny one or other of the propositions that 'Christ is man' or that 'Christ is God'. On the other hand, those who acknowledge one nature either have to deny one of these propositions or say that the divinity is humanity.

The mystery of the Incarnation is most beautiful

The apostle insinuates that this mystery, hidden for eternity, struck the angels themselves as wondrous. Certainly there appears to be contained within the mystery the consummation of the works of God, in that a created being was raised to the greatest possible height, and God, in accordance with his supreme benevolence, sent himself down and shared himself as far as is possible, and established a kind of kingdom, adapted to the capacity of created minds, and satisfied his own justice with the most precious sacrifice. Moreover, just as the mystery of the Trinity is best illustrated by its likeness to a mind reflected back on itself, so the mystery of the Incarnation is best illustrated by the union of mind and body, which was also recognized by the Holy Fathers Justin Martyr, Athanasius and Augustine. For mind and body remain two natures, and one person is made from them, and perhaps it may also be said, not inappropriately, that the body is sustained by the subsistence of the soul, or that matter is sustained by the subsistence of form, in such a way that the subsistence of the composite is nothing other than the subsistence of the form. Some Scholastics seem not to be averse to this view. And it seems we should say that the person of man and the person of the separated soul are the same.

---

[15] how | the Trinity and the Incarnation can be more appropriately expressed than by the distinctions drawn between 'nature' and 'person'. | *deleted*.
[16] 'the pattern of sound words'. From 2 Timothy 1.13.
[17] Reading 'utendo' in place of 'utendi'.

The attributes and operations of the one nature are not to be ascribed to the other nature

Therefore it should be said against the Theopaschites that the Godhead did not suffer, and against the Ubiquitarians that humanity is not omnipresent, and against the Monothelites that there is not a single operation or will of the Godhead and humanity. Otherwise what is the advantage of distinguishing the natures, and at any rate it seems contradictory to ascribe to a second nature things that are peculiar to the first one. But it may be said that God was born, that a virgin gave birth to God and that a man is everywhere, just as it may be said that a poet cures illnesses, if the poet is a doctor too, provided of course it is understood in the right way that he who is man is everywhere, although not by virtue of being man but by virtue of being God, and that he who is God was born of a virgin, but not by virtue of being God. For we call this very thing the divine or human nature in Christ, in accordance with which divine or human attributes are ascribed to Christ. Therefore the union of natures does not consist in the sharing of individual properties, but in one subsistence. And so to its humanity the Word attributed its subsistence, not its essence or essential properties, which are of course common to the remaining persons of the Godhead. And certainly if the hypostatic union consisted in the sharing of attributes then even the Father would be hypostatically united to the Son, with whom he shared his attributes.

It seems that all the perfections of which a created being is capable should be attributed to the human nature of Christ, except for those which conflicted with the duty of the redeemer

And so his soul was from birth full of all wisdom and grace, and we should not approve those Agnoites who thought that Christ was ignorant of some things. Yet he refused to reveal those perfections in their entirety while on earth, but had to make himself like his brethren in all except sin, as the *Letter to the Hebrews* says.[18] And indeed, at the time of the passion he wished to offer prayers in the human fashion, which he knew would not be answered, so that he might bear witness to his sorrow and to the inclination of his human nature which abhorred death, yet with the addition of a resignation to the will of the Father.[19] And so he suffered in mind and body, in order to expiate the sins of men. For the rest, it is not necessary that Christ

---

[18] See Hebrews 2.17 and 4.15.
[19] See Matthew 26.37-44; Mark 14.32-9.

should, when acting, reflect upon all the things the Godhead had poured into his soul. Hence among the doctors of the school too, Bonaventura and Gabriel say that he knew all things through habitual knowledge but not through actual knowledge.[20] So he was able to make progress in the human fashion by actual knowledge, and he was not tempted by the actuality of supernatural knowledge except when there was need, and so it may be said that he did not know the Day of Judgement, because of course he was most unwilling to draw out this actuality when the apostles asked him. Unless I am mistaken, this explanation is more appropriate than the recourse of those who say that he denied that he himself knew simply so that the apostles would say that he did not know.[21] Some might abuse this in order to excuse their mental reservations.

4. On the Trinity (autumn 1685 (?))[22]

Manuscript:

M: LH I 20 Bl. 342.

Transcription:

A: A VI 4, p. 2346.

This short piece appears to be one of the many texts on Christian and Catholic doctrines that Leibniz wrote in preparation for the so-called *Examen religionis christianae*.

This principle, *that things which are the same as a single third thing are the same as one another*, if taken with the greatest rigour, entails that identity

---

[20] Leibniz is referring to Bonaventure, *Breviloquium Theologiae sancti*, IV.6, and Gabriel Biel, *Epitome et collectorium ex Occamo super quatuor libros sententiarum* (Tübingen, 1512), 14, l. 3. The categories of 'habitual knowledge' and 'actual knowledge' were commonly invoked in medieval writings. Habitual knowledge is innate and intellectual, whereas actual knowledge is that which arises through action in the world (such as perceiving). The categories were even appropriated, albeit in a slightly different form, by some early moderns; see for example Locke, *An Essay concerning Human Understanding*, IV.1.8.
[21] See Mark 13.32, Matthew 24.36 and Acts 1.7.
[22] Editor's title. From the Latin. Complete.

holds good in the divine sphere no less than in the natural. When we say *the Father is God*, and *the Son is God*, and *God is one*, so is the Father and so is the Son, then the Father and Son would be the same, unless 'God' were taken in the two preceding propositions for a person of the Godhead and in the last for the divine nature, i.e. a single absolute substance that we call God. Hence we say that the three persons of the Godhead are nevertheless not three Gods, and in this sense we make some distinction between God and a person of the Godhead, for if there is a distinction between two words articulated in the plural, in such a way that one cannot be substituted for the other, there will also be some distinction between the same words in the singular, since the plural is a repetition of the singular. When it is said *that the same one who is the Father is also the Son*, the meaning is that in the same absolute substance of God there are two relative substances numerically different from each another. So those expressions should be properly explained lest they imply a manifest contradiction. However each expression is literal, since there is no reason why we should say that one is more literal than another, for in human matters there is no example of such a manner of speaking. Let us thus argue about the proper signification from the use. Can we say that *the Father is that one God*? I do not think so, but we can say the Father participates in the divine nature which is one in number.

5. Some thoughts on the Trinity, occasioned by the reading of Stephen Nye's *Considerations on the Explications of the Doctrine of the Trinity* (1693–end 1695)[23]

Manuscript:

M: LH I 6, 3b Bl. 1–2.

Transcription:

A: A IV 5, pp. 513–18.

---

[23] Editor's title. From the French. Complete.

In the early 1690s, a debate on the doctrine of the Trinity erupted in England, eliciting heated contributions from various churchmen such as John Wallis, William Sherlock and Robert South (the latter publishing anonymously). Stephen Nye's *Considerations on the Explications of the Doctrine of the Trinity by Dr Wallis, Dr Sherlock, Dr S-th, D. Cudworth and Mr Hooker* (London, 1693) was an anonymously-published compilation of some of the contributions to this debate, as well as a response to them. Leibniz's reading of Nye's book (which, by his own admission, was the only contribution to the debate that he had seen) prompted him to put down his own thoughts in the following piece. It could not have been written earlier than 1693 (which was when Nye's book was published), nor could it have been written later than the end of 1695 (which is when Leibniz learned that the man he knew at the time of writing only as 'Dr S-th' was in fact Robert South).[24]

Remarks on the book by an Antitrinitarian Englishman, which contains considerations of several explanations of the Trinity, and which was published in 1693 in quarto[25]

As I have not seen what Mr Wallis,[26] Mr Sherlock[27] and Dr S-th[28] have written on the Trinity,[29] and as I do not currently have to hand *The Intellectual System* by the late Dr Cudworth,[30] which I once read and found to have been written by a very able man,[31] I do not want to enter into the discussion of their opinions,[32] and I will speak of the matter in itself.

---

[24] When writing this piece, Leibniz refers to South as 'Mr S-th, whoever he may be' (p. 208), suggesting he did not know who the figure was. Thomas Burnett revealed the identity of Robert South in his letter to Electress Sophie of 14/24 November 1695. Leibniz was aware of this letter, as he made a French copy of it, from the original English. See A I 12, p. 367.
[25] Leibniz is referring to [Stephen Nye], *Considerations on the Explications of the Doctrine of the Trinity by Dr Wallis, Dr Sherlock, Dr S-th, D. Cudworth and Mr Hooker* (London, 1693). Leibniz wrote out extracts of this book for himself; these are printed in A IV 5, pp. 504–11.
[26] John Wallis (1616–1703), a mathematician who wrote also on logic, grammar and theology. He became one of Leibniz's correspondents in 1695, their correspondence continuing until 1701.
[27] William Sherlock (1641–1707), a high-ranking Anglican theologian who became Dean of St Pauls in 1691.
[28] Robert South (1634–1716), churchman and polemicist.
[29] John Wallis, *Theological Discourses; Containing VIII Letters and III Sermons Concerning the Blessed Trinity* (London, 1692); William Sherlock, *A Vindication of the Doctrine of the Holy and Ever Blessed Trinity, and the Incarnation of the Son of God, occasioned by the Brief Notes on the Creed of St. Athanasius, and the Brief History of the Unitarians or Socinians and containing an Answer to Both* (London, 1690); [Robert South], *Animadversions upon Dr. Sherlock's book, entitled A Vindication of the ... Holy ... Trinity* (London, 1693). South's book was published anonymously.
[30] Ralph Cudworth, *The True Intellectual System of the Universe* (London, 1678).
[31] Leibniz read the book in 1689, during his stay in Italy. He wrote out many pages of extracts from the book; see A VI 4, pp. 1943–55.
[32] Leibniz's reluctance to discuss the opinions of Wallis, Sherlock, South et al. is likely due to his

Firstly, I agree that the Commandment of the supreme worship of a single God is the most important of all,[33] and should be considered as utterly inviolable. This is why I do not think we should accept three absolute substances, each being infinite, all-powerful, eternal and supremely perfect.

It also seems a very dangerous thing, to say the least, to conceive the Word and the Holy Spirit as intellectual substances inferior to almighty God, and nevertheless[34] worthy of a divine worship, since this worship should only be made to one single individual substance, absolute, supreme and infinite.

However the Sabellian view, which considers the Father, the Son and the Holy Spirit as merely three names, or as three aspects of one and the same being,[35] could not be consistent with the passages of Holy Scripture without vandalizing them in a strange way, which would be no more approvable than the radical explanations the Socinians give to passages of Scripture.

The difficulty is that when it is said that the Father is God, the Son is God and the Holy Spirit is God, and each one of these three is not the other, and in spite of all that there are not three Gods but one alone, it seems that there is an obvious contradiction, since according to common sense it is precisely in this that the notion of plurality consists. For if John is a man, and if Peter is a man, and if John is not Peter and Peter is not John, there will be two men. Or else we have to admit that we do not know what 'two' is. So when in the symbol [of faith] attributed to St Athanasius it is said that the Father is God, that the Son is God, that the Holy Spirit is God and that there is nevertheless only one God,[36] we have to admit that if this word or term 'God' were always taken in the same sense, both in naming three beings, each of which is God, and in saying that there is only one God, it would be

---

belief that Nye's book was insufficiently detailed for him to obtain a good understanding of them. Nye's book was short, at just 35 pages, and he devoted only a handful of pages to each of the thinkers discussed. Later in this text Leibniz claims that there must be more to Wallis's opinion than what is given by Nye.

[33] Namely, the commandment found in Exodus 20.2-3 that 'I am the Lord your God … you shall have no other gods before me.'

[34] nevertheless | worthy of a worship that approaches the worship the pagans gave to their gods | deleted.

[35] Sabellianism, named after the third-century theologian Sabellius, is the view that the Father, Son and Holy Spirit are not distinct persons within a single Godhead, but rather different modes or faces of God. So for Sabellianism, there is no inherent trinity within God.

[36] Leibniz is referring to the Athanasian creed, which contains the following statement: 'So the Father is God, the Son is God, and the Holy Ghost is God. And yet they are not Three Gods, but One God.' Although attributed to Athanasius, it is questionable whether he was the author of this creed.

an untenable contradiction. We should therefore say that in the first case it is taken for one person of the divinity, of which there are three persons, and in the second case for an absolute substance which is unique.[37]

I know there are Scholastic authors who believe that this principle of logic or metaphysics – *quae sunt eadem uni tertio sunt eadem inter se*[38] – does not hold good in the Trinity. But I am not of their opinion, which I think would involve handing victory to the Socinians by overturning one of the basic principles of human reasoning, without which we could no longer reason about anything or be certain of anything. This is why I have been very surprised to see that able people among Scholastic theologians have admitted that what is said of the Trinity would be a formal contradiction in creatures, as I think that what is a contradiction in terms is a contradiction everywhere.

One could doubtless content oneself with leaving it at that, and saying only that one recognizes and adores only a single and unique all-powerful God, *unum numero*,[39] one single absolute individual, in whom there are nevertheless three substantial and individual beings, but relative beings that Holy Scripture calls Father, Son or Word, and Holy Spirit,[40] and that the Church calls 'persons', like a father and son are actually called persons; and just as much should be concluded of the Holy Spirit. That these three persons have this relation between themselves, that the Father is the principle of the other two, that the eternal production of the Son is called birth in Scripture and that of the Holy Spirit is called procession. But their outward actions are common, excepting the function of the Incarnation along with what depends on it, which is peculiar to the Son, and that of sanctification, which is peculiar to the Holy Spirit.

However the objections of opponents have meant that people have gone much further, and that they have wanted to explain what a person is. It has been all the more difficult to succeed in this since explanations depend on definitions. Now those who give us sciences are used to giving us definitions as well. But this is not the case with legislators, and even less with religion. So Holy Scripture as well as tradition provides us with certain terms, and at the same time they do not give us precise definitions of them, which

---

[37] unique. | But the great difficulty is to say what a 'person' is in this conjuncture. | *deleted*.
[38] 'things that are the same as a single third thing are the same as one another'.
[39] 'one in number'.
[40] Probably a reference to the *Comma Johanneum*, that is, 1 John 5.7: 'For there are three that bear record in heaven, the Father, the Word, and the Holy Ghost: and these three are one.'

means that when we want to explain things we are reduced to making possible hypotheses, in much the same way as is done in astronomy. And often jurisconsults are obliged to do a great deal of research to give a word a sense which is able to satisfy at the same time all the passages of the law as well as reason. The difference is that the explanation of the mysteries of religion is not in any way necessary, whereas the explanation of law is necessary in order to judge disagreements. So the best thing with regard to mystery would be to stick precisely to the revealed terms as much as is possible.

I do not know enough about how Mr Cudworth and Mr Sherlock explain themselves. But their erudition, which is so well known, means that I have no doubt that they have given a good sense to what they put forward. However, I would venture to say that if three infinite minds are postulated as absolute substances, there would be three Gods; notwithstanding perfect intelligence, which would mean that each one would understand everything that happens in the other. There has to be something more for a numerical unity, otherwise God, who perfectly understands our thoughts, would be essentially united with us to the point of making one and same individual. Moreover, this would be a union of several natures if each person has his own, namely if each person has his own infinity, his own knowledge, his own omnipotence. And this would by no means be the union of three persons who would have one and the same individual nature, which nevertheless should be the case.

Neither have I seen what Mr Wallis and Dr S-th (cited here) have written on this subject, and I have no doubt that they explained themselves in a manner in accordance with orthodoxy, since I know the penetration of Mr Wallis, who is one of the greatest geometers of the century, and who will always do himself justice no matter what direction his mind may turn itself. Leaving aside the fact that the author of the booklet acknowledges Mr Wallis's explanation has had public approval,[41] I venture to say, however, that a personality similar to the one whom Cicero heard speak, when he said *tres personas unus sustineo*,[42] is not sufficient.[43] I am therefore certain that Mr

---

[41] See Nye, *Considerations on the Explications of the Doctrine of the Trinity*, p. 8, where he explains that Wallis claimed to have received many letters from learned Trinitarians complementing him on his views.

[42] 'I am one man, but bear three persons', Cicero, *De oratore* II.XXIV.

[43] In the short extract of Wallis's work printed by Nye, Wallis berates those who do not accept the *tres personas unus sustineo* formula found in Cicero. See Nye, *Considerations on the Explications of the Doctrine of the Trinity*, pp. 7–8.

Wallis will also have added something else. Nor is it sufficient to say that the Father, the Son and the Holy Spirit differ by means of relations similar to modes, such as are positions, presences and absences.[44] These kinds of relations attributed to one and the same substance will never make three different persons existent at the same time. So I imagine that this Dr S-th, whoever he may be, will not have contented himself with that.

Therefore we should say that there are relations in the divine substance which distinguish the persons from each other, since these persons could not be absolute substances. But we should also say that these relations have to be substantial, which is not sufficiently explained by simple modalities. Moreover, we should say that the divine persons are not the same concrete thing under different designations or relations – as would be one and the same man who is a poet and orator – but three different concrete relative beings in one single absolute concrete being. We should also say that the three persons are not parts of the unique absolute divine substance, since the parts are themselves substances as absolute as the whole.

It has to be admitted that there is no example in nature which fully corresponds to this notion of divine persons. But it is not necessary that we be able to find one, and it is sufficient that what has just been said does not imply any contradiction or absurdity. The divine substance doubtless has privileges which surpass all the other substances. However, as we do not know all creatures well enough, we cannot be certain that there is not and cannot be outside of God any absolute substance which contains several relative ones in itself.

Our mind itself gives us some image of that, and to make these notions easier through something similar, I find in creatures nothing more suitable to clarify this subject than the reflection of minds, when one and the same mind is its own immediate object, and acts on itself while thinking about itself and what it is doing. For this[45] redoubling gives us an image or shadow of two relative substances in one and the same absolute substance, namely of the one which understands, and of the one which is understood. Both of these beings are substantial, both are concrete individuals, and they differ through mutual relations, but they compose only one single and self-same absolute individual substance. Yet I do not dare to take this comparison too far, and I do not undertake to put forward the view that the difference

---

[44] Wallis claimed that each divine person was a mode in the extract printed in Nye, *Considerations on the Explications of the Doctrine of the Trinity*, p. 7.
[45] this | gives an image of God | *deleted*.

that exists between the three divine persons is not greater than the one that exists between that which understands and that which is understood when a finite mind thinks about itself; all the more since what is modal, accidental, imperfect and mutable in us, is real, essential, complete and immutable in God. It is enough that this redoubling is as it were a vestige of divine personalities. Nevertheless, in calling the Son the Word,[46] or Logos, that is, the mental word, Holy Scripture seems to lead us to suppose that, for us, nothing is more suitable than these things, and nothing is easier to conceive than the analogy of mental operations. It is also for this reason that the Fathers have related the will to the Holy Spirit, just as they have related the understanding to the Son and power to the Father, when distinguishing power, knowledge and will, or else the Father, the Word and Love.

The verses by Hugo Grotius deserve to be added.[47]

6. On miracles and mysteries (August–September (?) 1697)[48]

Manuscript:

M: LH 1, 11 Bl. 365.

Transcription:

A: A I 14, pp. 433–4.

From a letter to Thomas Burnett:

I have read with pleasure and profit Mr Bentley's fine sermon on Revelation and the Messiah.[49] He could not put his opponents in their place in a better way than by beginning with a confession and the establishment

---

[46] John 1.1-18.
[47] Possibly a reference to parts of Hugo Grotius's poem 'Eucharistia', from his *Poemata omnia* (Amsterdam, 1670), pp. 20–6. Certain passages of this poem are concerned with the Trinity.
[48] Editor's title. From the French. Incomplete: those parts of the letter on other topics have not been translated.
[49] Richard Bentley, *Of Revelation and the Messias. A Sermon Preached at the Publick Commencement at Cambridge July 5th 1696* (London, 1696).

of the true rights of reason, for, very far from our religion being contrary to them, it is rather the case that it is grounded in reasons. I agree that the union of the soul and the body is a kind of natural miracle, as Mr Bentley very shrewdly says on page 9,[50] but that does not prevent me from thinking that in one of *Journaux des Sçavans* I have explained how it could be and how it should be,[51] and given a reason for their commerce which seems to solve the difficulty entirely: it is somewhat as the incommensurability of the side of the square and its diagonal is a natural miracle, even though it has been fully explained by geometers. But with regard to the mysteries of religion, men will never go so far. It is sufficient, however, that we are assured of their reality, and that the objections can be resolved, by showing that there is nothing in these mysteries that implies any absurdity.

7. Hasty comments on the book *Christianity not Mysterious*, written 8 August 1701[52]

Manuscript:

M: LH I, VI, 19 Bl. 1–4.

Transcription:

JT: *A Collection of Several Pieces of Mr John Toland* (London, 1726), II: appendix, pp. 60–76.

In 1696, John Toland caused a stir with the publication of his *Christianity not Mysterious*, which denied that there were any true mysteries in the Christian

---

[50] 'That the human soul is vitally united to the body by a reciprocal commerce of action and passion, this we all consciously feel and know, and our adversaries will affirm it; let them tell us, then, what is the chain, the cement, the magnetism, what they will call it, the invisible tie of that union, whereby matter and an incorporeal mind, things that have no similitude nor alliance to each other, can so sympathise by a mutual league of motion and sensation? No, they will not pretend to that; for they can frame no conceptions of it. They are sure there is such a union, from the operations and effects, but the cause and the manner of it are too subtle and secret to be discovered by the eye of reason; 'tis mystery, 'tis divine magic, 'tis natural miracle.' Bentley, *Of Revelation and the Messias*, p. 9.
[51] Leibniz is referring here to his essay 'Système nouveau de la nature et de la communication des substances', G IV, pp. 477–87/SLT, pp. 68–77.
[52] Author's title. From the Latin. Complete.

religion. The following piece contains Leibniz's comments on the book (the overly descriptive title of the piece is Leibniz's own). As Leibniz indicates, he obtained a copy of the book only five years after its publication. In fact, he probably obtained it from Toland himself, who arrived in Hanover in early August 1701 ahead of an official English delegation sent to present Electress Sophie with a copy of the Act of Settlement. After making his comments on the book, Leibniz apparently passed them on to Toland, as he tells a correspondent: 'I have taken the liberty to pass on in writing my reflections on his *Christianity not Mysterious*, which he took well'.[53]

Hasty comments on the book Christianity not Mysterious, *written 8 August 1701*

I had often heard about but not seen a book written in the English tongue, entitled *Christianity not Mysterious*, and when it came into my hands recently I could not stop myself reading through it straightaway, and while I was reading I put down in my own way some brief comments on paper, which I quite often do when the books are noteworthy. It is right to acknowledge that this book is very cleverly written, and since charity is not suspicious I am willingly persuaded that the goal of the author – who shows uncommon erudition and genius, and I think is well-disposed – was to bring men back from theoretical theology to practical theology, and from disputes about the person of Christ to the desire to imitate his life, although the route he has taken to arrive at this goal does not seem to be everywhere straight or uniform enough. For my part, it is evident that a truly Christian theology is practical, and that the principal aim of Christ was to inspire sanctity of will rather than to plant notions of secret truths into the intellect.

Yet one should not for that reason deny[54] that Christ has revealed to us some divine doctrines which reason cannot discern. And the sorts of things to be avoided seem to me to be not only those which could stir up the sectarian views of theologians, but also, and much more, those which can make the reformed clergy odious to people or can inspire people to contempt. This kind of sect would be the most dangerous of all, for it could give rise to troubles, the fuelling of which is, I think, the furthest thing

---

[53] Leibniz to Thomas Burnett (27 February 1702), A I 20, p. 809.
[54] deny | that Christ taught us mysteries hidden for many centuries (α) by which our piety (β) thus obtaining for us the economy of salvation | *deleted*.

from the mind of the author, who, as befits an honourable man, professes to want to direct his thoughts towards the public good. Certainly the errors and abuses which have crept into the Church should often be attributed not so much to the wiles of the clergy as to the fault of the times; and it is evident that the excessive authority of the Pope has gradually arisen due to circumstances which favoured it, and the intervention of chance, as is often the case. Besides, in those times in which the clergy alone were wise, all the other nobles were military men; it was not absurd that a military empire of the wise (that is, the clergy) be combined with authority.[55]

The very title of the book seems to me to be longer than it should be, for it goes like this: *Christianity not Mysterious, or, A Treatise Shewing, That there is nothing in the Gospel Contrary to Reason, Nor Above it: And that no Christian Doctrine can be properly call'd a Mystery*. Indeed, all people acknowledge that there should be nothing in Christian theology that is contrary to reason, that is, absurd. But I do not see that it can be said with any probability that there is nothing in it that is contrary to reason, that is, nothing that our reason cannot comprehend, since the divine nature itself, which is infinite, is necessarily incomprehensible. In the same way, there is something of infinity in all substances too, which is why we can perfectly understand only incomplete notions, like those of numbers, shapes and other such modes that are abstracted from things by the mind. I admit that we have, as the author quite rightly observes, some distinct notion of the infinite (namely the infinite in itself, or absolute infinite), but through the finite intellect given to us there is no distinct consideration of infinite varieties, yet this would very often be needed in the comprehension of divine matters. Consequently I am surprised that at the very beginning of the book, in the preliminary formation of the state of the controversy, he criticizes those who say that 'we must adore what we cannot comprehend'.[56] Yet nothing seems more certain to me than this proposition, unless of course we should interpret 'comprehension' as meaning nothing other than 'knowledge', as he does elsewhere (section III chapter 2). But this meaning is not the usual one, and hence should not be readily employed in popular use.

---

[55] authority. | ¶ For the sake of brevity I set aside the preface, but I cannot | *deleted*.
[56] See John Toland, *Christianity not Mysterious* (London, 1696), p. 1.

On section I

I come to the principal contents of the book, and indeed to the *first section*, on reason. In *chapter 1* the ingenious author says that there are in us faculties of forming ideas and perceptions of things, and of affirming or denying according as we perceive the ideas to agree or disagree with each other, and hence of loving and desiring the good, or of hating and avoiding evil. And he says that the proper use of these faculties is the *common sense*, or *reason in general*.[57] I shall gladly grant him this definition because it permits a good meaning, although something in it is lacking inasmuch as he does not explain in what that proper use consists. But this can be more readily excused here, because the aim of the author is not to treat these things specifically. The author defines 'idea' as the immediate object of thought,[58] which likewise does not differ from the meaning others give to it.

He treats in *chapter 2* of that wherein reason consists. He says that 'knowledge' is the perception of the agreement or disagreement of ideas,[59] wherein I find some difficulty. For it seems to me that this is indeed true with regard to our rational knowledge, namely knowledge deduced from ideas or definitions, which we call *a priori*, but not true with regard to knowledge obtained *a posteriori*, or from experience, where often we do not have distinct ideas, and consequently we do not perceive their agreement or disagreement.[60] So, to give an example, we know from experience that the syrup acid of violets stains things with a red colour, but we do not perceive any agreement of the ideas; the ideas we have of acid, of red and of a violet are not yet distinct. It is for God alone to deduce all things from the ideas of his own mind.[61] I commend the points made about twofold knowledge (rational knowledge, that is), immediate and mediate,[62] although I think

---

[57] 'Every one experiences in himself a Power or Faculty of forming various Ideas or Perceptions of Things: Of affirming or denying, according as he sees them to agree or disagree: And so of loving and desiring what seems good unto him; and of hating and avoiding what he thinks evil. The right Use of all these Faculties is what we call Common Sense, or *Reason* in general.' Toland, *Christianity not Mysterious*, p. 9.

[58] 'By the word IDEA ... I understand *the immediate Object of the Mind when it thinks.*' Toland, *Christianity not Mysterious*, p. 11.

[59] 'all our Knowledg is, in effect, nothing else but *the Perception of the Agreement or Disagreement of our Ideas*'. Toland, *Christianity not Mysterious*, p. 12.

[60] disagreement. | (α) For example, how the colour red is connected by a kind of refraction (β) It pertains to God alone, who intuits all things *a priori*, to have no other knowledge than that arising from ideas | *deleted*.

[61] mind. | And in this I think consists, if it is permitted to put it this way, πρῶτον ψεῦδος [the first mistake], or the source of the error here admitted. | *deleted*.

[62] See Toland, *Christianity not Mysterious*, pp. 13f.

it should be entered into more deeply, so that the matter is sufficiently explained, which I admit is not done here.

I seem to be able to pass over *chapter 3* without comment.

In *chapter 4*, I can grant that the basis of persuasion is evidence,[63] as long as this doctrine is not abused. For although that of which we are persuaded is not always evident, it must nevertheless be that the evidence presents itself in a way that persuades us. For example, the authority of those on whose testimony we believe that something happened must be evident to us, though we may not always perceive how this something happened. Thus there are those who do not know how a water-drinker, within a very short space of time, could emit from his mouth a great quantity of milk, ink, beer, wine from the Valtelline, alcoholic spirit and other liquids, in the presence of observant men who were watching closely; yet they can believe that it happened, not so much on my account, although I have seen it twice in Hanover, as on that of so many others who were eyewitnesses like me.[64] And they may put aside the error rashly asserted by some writers, on account of which they are persuaded that those were not the true liquids but only fake ones, and in accordance with appearance just some unknown essences of dye. And this evidence in matters of divine faith is encountered in those proofs that many theologians generally call (less elegantly for sure) motives of credibility.[65] But the criterion of evidence needed to be explained, for I have seen that many people have challenged the evidence where there was no such criterion. Therefore I placed in the *Acta Eruditorum* of Leipzig an outline 'De cognitione, veritate, et ideis',[66] the aim of which was in part to put right this common defect in writers.

On section II

The most illustrious author acknowledges that none of the theologians known to him teaches that one should believe something that one admits to be contrary to reason, although it is taught by many that it can indeed

---

[63] See Toland, *Christianity not Mysterious*, p. 18.
[64] Leibniz believed he knew how the trick worked: see G. W. Leibniz, *Leibnizens nachgelassene Schriften physikalischen, mechanischen und technischen Inhalts*, ed. Ernst Gerland (Leipzig: B. G. Teubner, 1906), p. 248 n.6.
[65] credibility. | I do not wish to dispute here whether it is correctly said that cold is real in things. | deleted. Leibniz has in mind here Toland, *Christianity not Mysterious*, p. 19: '*some Ideas are but the Result of certain Powers in the Particles of Bodies to OCCASION particular Sensations in us*; as the *Sweetness* of Sugar and the *Cold* of Ice, are no more inherent in them than *Pain* in the Knife that cuts me, or *Sickness* in the Fruit that surfeits me'.
[66] G. W. Leibniz, 'Meditationes de cognitione, veritate, et ideis', *Acta Eruditorum* (November 1684), pp. 537–42. English translation: L, pp. 291–4.

happen that a dogma of faith may at least seem contrary to reason.[67] This is what he attacks in *chapter 1*, in which I note in passing he incorrectly ascribes to the Evangelicals whom he calls Lutherans (though some of the most distinguished of them reject the name) the dogma of impanation;[68] and ubiquity, or rather the omnipresence of the body of Christ, is not recognized by all their theologians either. But he justly criticizes the Socinians for admitting a kind of created God capable of receiving divine honours.[69] With regard to the common notions with which divine truths agree or do not agree, prudent theologians have for a long time distinguished between truths which are of metaphysical necessity, where the contrary implies contradiction, and with which no divine truth can disagree, and physical truths which are drawn from experience and, so to speak, from the custom of the world; nothing prevents God from withdrawing from this custom, since we often see such a thing happen even in natural matters, as the most illustrious author himself acknowledges further on. Such is the truth that a mass of iron will sink in water by its own nature; yet this does not happen as long as it is crafted into a hollow kettle. And who doubts that God has to hand many more ways of producing the same effect,[70] while making use of the secrets of nature in some method? But leaving this aside, let us examine whether a genuine contradiction and an apparent contradiction amount to the same thing, as the author says.[71] I cannot be persuaded of this. For my part, I admit that as a general rule we should follow appearances and that they serve as the truth; but when there are a number of mutually opposed appearances, the rule is necessarily void, and we have to make a judgement about which probability should be followed. Here, one must consider not only which opinion is the more probable, but also which is safer to hold. For example, if an option were proposed to me

---

[67] 'no *Christian* I know of now (for we shall not disturb the Ashes of the Dead) expressly says Reason and the Gospel are contrary to one another. But, which returns to the same, very many affirm, that tho the Doctrines of the latter cannot in themselves be contradictory to the Principles of the former, as proceeding both from God; yet, that according to our Conceptions of them, *they may seem directly to clash*'. Toland, *Christianity not Mysterious*, pp. 25–6.

[68] See Toland, *Christianity not Mysterious*, p. 27. Toland was not the only English writer to claim that the Lutherans endorsed impanation; see also Anthony Collins, *A Discourse of Free-Thinking* (London, 1713), pp. 24–5.

[69] Leibniz is referring here to Toland's claim that 'Nor should we be ever banter'd with the *Lutheran Impanation*, or the *Ubiquity* it has produc'd, as one Monster ordinarily begets another. And tho the *Socinians* disown this Practice, I am mistaken if either they or the *Arians* can make their notions of a *dignifi'd and Creature-God capable of Divine Worship*, appear more reasonable than the Extravagancies of other Sects touching the Article of the *Trinity*.' Toland, *Christianity not Mysterious*, p. 27.

[70] effect | by some invisible method | deleted.

[71] 'A *seeming* Contradiction is to us as much as a *real* one.' Toland, *Christianity not Mysterious*, p. 35.

where the probability of gaining is greater than the probability of losing, but the gain will be modest and the loss considerable, and the ratio of loss to gain is much greater than that of hope to fear, I should more justly abstain from the option proposed. Likewise, if the words of a master favour one view, and the appearance of things another view, and the word of the master should create no extra danger for the master's affairs, but departing from the words exposes me to danger, surely I shall more justly stick to the words and not withdraw ἀπὸ του ρητου[72] under the pretext της διανοίας.[73] And this is all the more true to the extent that the master is more prudent and more powerful, since even in a military setting one does not leave unpunished a soldier who abandons, without a very important reason, the words of the order given by his own general. Moreover, I understand here 'apparent contradiction' to be the contradiction that is present before the matter has been sufficiently investigated; for example, if someone should glance in passing at records of accounts passed on by his agent of affairs, and seems to spot an error either in the calculation or in the numbers of the calculation, he should not have confidence in this judgement unless it is absolutely confirmed by a second, fuller examination and discussion, since there is nothing more dangerous in complicated matters than a hasty judgement. However, what is said here, that one can believe only what is conceived by the soul,[74] is true, so long as it is not taken too far. It befits words to have some sense, but experiences (of the kind I mentioned above) show that distinct concepts are not always necessary, still less adequate ones; we trust these experiences even though we do not have distinct concepts of many immediate objects of the senses (like colours and odours). Even in metaphysics, our illustrious author, like many others, speaks about substance as a support, about cause and many other things, even though it may be that sufficiently distinct notions of these things are lacking among common folk. And indeed, I have shown elsewhere that there are certain things in the first notions of geometry which have not been sufficiently explained thus far by geometers. And the more someone turns to meditations, the more he recognizes our faults, and he disposes his soul to the self-restraint that neither demands nor promises too much, especially in sacred matters.

---

[72] 'from the saying'.
[73] 'of the intention'.
[74] 'A Man may give his verbal Assent to he knows not what, out of *Fear, Superstition, Indifference, Interest*, and the like feeble and unfair Motives: but as long as he conceives not what he believes, he cannot sincerely acquiesce in it, and remains depriv'd of all solid Satisfaction.' Toland, *Christianity not Mysterious*, p. 36.

In *chapter 2* it is claimed that revelation is only a means of information, and not a proof which forces assent.[75] If the sense of this claim is that revelation has no more authority than a teacher whom we should believe only because he offers proof, or because he explains a matter by means of distinct concepts, then it cannot stand. For once it is clear that it is God himself who does the revealing, the revelator not only has the character of a teacher or instructor, but also of a witness or, more correctly, an indisputable judge. Even[76] in human affairs, *evidence in things* (which the most illustrious author requires) is not always needed, so long as there is *evidence in persons*, as is plain from our trust in them. It is otherwise in the doctrines based on reasoning, like if a teacher instructs me in geometry; for here, what the illustrious author seems to claim in a slightly over-general way in fact holds good, namely that the basis of my persuasion is not the authority of the teacher, but the clarity of the conceptions. At any rate it is very true that there is nothing in divine revelation which is unworthy of God, who is reason supreme. But yet we also know that, in the economy of nature, many things have seemed to us to be absurd on account of our ignorance, because we are not situated in the true centre, from where the beauty of things should be considered. Thus King Alphonse, renowned for his study of astronomy, absurdly believed that he could have given the creator the idea for a better system had the creator invited his counsel.[77] Yet since we have now learned to transport ourselves mentally into the sun (which has been discovered to be the centre of this system), it is evident that this system is the most beautiful constitution of things.

In *chapter 3*, the author accepts, as he should, that miracles were wrought by Christ. But in this very fact, if I am any judge, he also allows there to be in the Christian religion something we should believe that is above our reason. For what else are miracles[78] than operations that cannot be derived from

---

[75] 'There I said REVELATION was not a necessitating Motive of Assent, but *a Mean of Information.*' Toland, *Christianity not Mysterious*, p. 38.

[76] Reading 'Etiam' (M) in place of 'Itaque' (JT).

[77] After receiving an account of the Ptolemaic world-system with all its epicycles, the thirteenth-century King Alphonse of Castille is said to have claimed that God ought to have consulted him before embarking on creation as he would have advised something simpler. The story may be apocryphal, though is reported in Bayle's *Dictionnaire historique et critique* (Rotterdam, 1702, 2nd edn), I: p. 852 (article 'Castille (Alfonse X du nom roi de)', note H). Leibniz was fond of repeating the story; see for example LTS, pp. 235–6.

[78] miracles | ? The same is to be said about the creation of the world, which he grants in the following chapter, although it cannot of course be understood by reason, but there is more about these things below, section 3 chapter 5. | *deleted.*

the laws of created nature that a created intellect can perceive, whatever its capacity? For the rest, he argues well against those who think that the evangelists and apostles wrote badly and obscurely about matters necessary for us to know.

In *chapter* 4 he responds to those who object that our reason is corrupt. Here again it seems to me that he argues well when he distinguishes between reason itself and the bad use of a good faculty,[79] just as we distinguish between art and artist. However, I would not be prepared to say, as the author does in §31, that all our thoughts are entirely free,[80] for I think that we are liable to servitude to the extent that our nature is weak or corrupt. And when he then argues for all kinds of free will, I am afraid that he goes on longer than the matter may bear, or rather longer than may be necessary. But here is not the place for this subject.

On section III

In *chapter 1*, the author shows that, among the pagans, 'mysteries' signified secret rites from which the profane or the uninitiated were to be excluded.[81] So a mystery was a thing that at one time was not understood, but yet was perfectly intelligible if it were revealed. I shall gladly accept this, for the religion of gentiles did not consist in dogmas so much as in ceremonies, which each interpreted as he pleased; from which it also happened that they did not dispute amongst themselves about religious matters.

In *chapter 2* he observes straightaway that mysteries are not those things of which we do not have adequate ideas or know of all their properties at once.[82] I too willingly accept this point, for otherwise even circles and other shapes would be mysteries. But now the question is whether there are any mysteries in nature, about which I say that if one means by 'mystery' whatever surpasses our present reason, then there are countless mysteries in physical nature. So if it were asked whether the knowledge of the innermost parts of water is above our reason, my response is that it is above our present reason, for I do not believe that anyone has yet satisfactorily explained the structure of these parts, but I have not lost hope that an explanation which satisfies the phenomena may be given at some point. There are also many

---

[79] Toland, *Christianity not Mysterious*, pp. 62ff.
[80] 'We are perswaded that *all our Thoughts are entirely free.*' Toland, *Christianity not Mysterious*, p. 60.
[81] Toland, *Christianity not Mysterious*, pp. 71f.
[82] 'And, first, I affirm, That *nothing can be said to be a Mystery, because we have not an adequate Idea of it, or a distinct View of all its Properties at once; for then every thing would be a Mystery.*' Toland, *Christianity not Mysterious*, p. 74.

things placed above human reason, not only our reason, but also that of future generations, that is, not only such as exists today, but also such as will ever exist in this life we spend on the Earth; although it can indeed happen that these things may be understood by another, nobler creature, and that in the future they may be intelligible to us as well, when we are raised to a nobler state. But if someone should call 'mystery' whatever is above all created reason, I venture to say that there are in fact no natural phenomena above reason, but that comprehensions of individual substances are impossible for the created intellect because they involve infinity. This is why it is not possible to give a perfect explanation of the things of the universe. And nothing prevents there also being such dogmas revealed by God[83] such that they cannot be sufficiently explained by any power of reason although they should affect a soul in some way, and can also be duly vindicated against the charge of contradiction. Moreover, I call 'comprehension' not only when distinct ideas are present, but also when the ideas are adequate, that is, not only when one has the definition or resolution of the term proposed, but also when one has resolved in turn every term which enters into that, all the way down to the primitive ones, as we experience in the case of numbers.

In *chapter 3* he attempts to show that in Holy Scripture and in books of the earliest antiquity the term 'mystery' is unknown in the usual sense theologians give it. He himself nevertheless cites a passage from Paul's 1 Corinthians II.9-10, where it is said that 'the eye has not seen, nor ear heard, neither have entered into the heart of man the things God has prepared for those who love him'.[84] Here, Paul seems to indicate something which is unknown to us, not only because we have not been told of it, but also because even were we to be told of it we could not perceive it, unless our senses were made more discerning and we should come upon it by some kind of higher experience. It is rather like a blind man who, unless his sight should be restored to him, cannot make a judgement about colours, even if the doctrine of colours were explained to him. Moreover, our

---

[83] God | . What the most learned author says in §20 of this chapter, that nothing about things is known to us except what is necessary and useful for us to know, I think is said somewhat loosely (α), unless we extend usefulness in such a way that (β) . For how many things do we know about numbers and shapes, how many in anatomy and botanics? Clearly more than just what is useful. However, I admit on the basis of another consideration that a certain curiosity, even about useless things, is useful, and it can happen that what is now useless may at some point become useful. | *deleted*. Leibniz has in mind here Toland, *Christianity not Mysterious*, p. 86: 'I remark'd in the Beginning of this Chapter, that we knew nothing of things, but such of their Properties as were *necessary* and *useful*.'

[84] Toland, *Christianity not Mysterious*, p. 90.

author rightly observes that many things were unknown to philosophers and could not be obtained by reason alone, not because they were incomprehensible but because they depended on a matter of fact known only through a divine revelation.[85] He gives as an example the doctrine of the Fall of Adam, which removed the difficulties that had vexed philosophers about the origin of sin.[86] However, I do not think it is always correct to say, as he does in §30, that nothing of importance is manifested if an incomprehensible truth should be revealed.[87] Thus in natural things, the discovery of the magnetic needle is and will be a great matter, even if the workings of the needle should remain forever unknown to us. In the same way, in theology a truth which cannot be explained nevertheless can be of great importance for the economy of salvation. In 1 Timothy 3.16 it seems that 'mystery' also signifies something more than a thing that was unknown beforehand but then made easy to understand by a revelation.[88] For when it is said that God was manifested in the flesh, seen by angels and received into glory, it seems to refer to things which transcend created nature and the powers of reason.[89] I note in passing what the author says in §39, that the ancients lived in the infancy of the world, and we live in a more mature stage of it, and therefore it should be said that the present generation are rather the ancients;[90] that is indeed very true, and diminishes the authority of the ancients with respect to matters of science and experience, but not with respect to matters of history and tradition. For it is obvious that the stories that have been preserved, whether oral or written, become more imperfect by the day the more remote they are from the source.

In *chapter 4* he responds to objections drawn from passages of Scripture,

---

[85] See Toland, *Christianity not Mysterious*, pp. 89ff.
[86] See Toland, *Christianity not Mysterious*, p. 92.
[87] See Toland, *Christianity not Mysterious*, pp. 95f.
[88] Toland mentions this passage in *Christianity not Mysterious*, p. 98. The entire verse reads (in the new King James version): 'And without controversy great is the mystery of godliness:
　God was manifested in the flesh,
　Justified in the Spirit,
　Seen by angels,
　Preached among the Gentiles,
　Believed on in the world,
　Received up in glory.'
[89] The only claim Toland made about 1 Timothy 3.16 was that it was one of eight passages in which '*Mystery* is read for the *Gospel* or Christianity in general.' Toland, *Christianity not Mysterious*, p. 95. Leibniz's remark does not obviously address this claim.
[90] See Toland, *Christianity not Mysterious*, p. 112. Note, however, that this is not Toland's own description; instead, Toland quotes (with approval) the words of Charles Perrault, *Paralleles des Anciens et des Modernes* (Paris, 1693), p. 34.

likewise from the nature of faith. I do not think it necessary for me to dwell on these at this point. I note only what is said in §54, that faith is from hearing, but if we do not understand the things we hear then faith would be weak and even non-existent.[91] This is indeed most true, but it is evident even in natural things that the understanding of words differs greatly from the comprehension of a thing. For often either the ideas we have, or the method we have of reasoning according to ideas, are not sufficient for understanding the connection between the subject and predicate, even if they offer some notion of the subject and the predicate. Even in geometry, who can demonstrate the theorems of figures that are known distinctly, even though these theorems have already been discovered and communicated by others?

In *chapter 5*, the most illustrious author wisely considers the same objection I made above, namely that miracles are above reason. The definition of 'miracle' he thus gives is, unless I am deceived, in keeping with the common teaching of theologians, such that miracles are beyond the laws of nature and their ordinary operations.[92] Yet he rightly acknowledges that they are possible and intelligible. But in the same way, even the mysteries are possible and intelligible to theologians. For who doubts that, with regard to the mysteries, there is no contradiction, and we understand the words used to express them, even if the manner of explaining both of these things transcends the power of our reason? And so the illustrious gentleman seems to me not to have done enough to meet the objection. It is of no consequence that mysteries are doctrines and miracles are histories, for miracles are so to speak transitory mysteries, and some mysteries have in some way the nature of an enduring miracle.

For the sake of brevity I am not following up the things said in *chapter 6* about the introduction of mysteries and the origin of ceremonies, being content that he has done enough on this matter. For the things which pertain to church history are spread out too broadly to be able to be treated in brief remarks, and are not necessary for our scope.

In the *conclusion*, the illustrious author indicates that he desires to hope for an intelligible explanation of the doctrine of the New Testament.[93] I

---

[91] '*Faith* is likewise said *to come by hearing*; but without Understanding 'tis plain this Hearing would signify nothing.' Toland, *Christianity not Mysterious*, p. 129. The expression 'faith by hearing' or 'faith from hearing' is from Romans 10.17.
[92] 'A MIRACLE then *is some Action exceeding all humane Power, and which the Laws of NATURE cannot perform by their ordinary Operations.*' Toland, *Christianity not Mysterious*, p. 144.
[93] 'And tho by convincing People that *all the Parts of their RELIGION must not only be in themselves, but to them also must appear, sound and intelligible*, I might justly leave every one to discover to

too think that such an explanation can be given, and in fact is to be had now (although perhaps not all in one place), should we be content with a lower degree of intelligibility. But since that work has not appeared, there is no reason for me to dwell on it here. Therefore I and he come to the end, and I add only that many eminent philosophers of our time recognize in nature powers above our reason. Some distinguished Cartesians take the union of soul and body for something miraculous; others deny that we can comprehend the composition of the continuum, or the reconciliation of free will with divine preordination. Locke, the English philosopher of great renown, whose opinion our author everywhere approves, had once taught that all the phenomena of bodies could be explained from solidity and extension and their modes; now, in a response to Stillingfleet, who was the most learned Bishop of Worcester until recently, he retracts this opinion with a great display of candour and, persuaded by the arguments of the most insightful Newton, he admits in nature an original attraction between any given part of matter and any other;[94] this attraction is not derived from mechanism, and accordingly is not explicable by reason.[95] I admit to hoping for some explanation of the things discussed here, and I have even given an account of the union of soul and body,[96] but I nevertheless recognize the greater incomprehensibility of the interior of nature which arises from an influx of infinity. This infinity is the source of ideas

---

himself the Reasonableness or Unreasonableness of his Religion ... My next Task therefore is (God willing) to prove the Doctrines of the *New Testament* perspicuous, possible, and most worthy of God, as well as all calculated for the highest Benefits of Man.' Toland, *Christianity not Mysterious*, pp. 171–2.

[94] Reading 'Attractionem cujusvis materiae partis a quavis in natura admittit originariam' (M) in place of 'Attractionem cujusvis materiae partis admittit originarium' (JT).

[95] 'Tis true, I say, "That Bodies operate by impulse and nothing else". And so I thought when I writ it and yet can conceive no other way of their operation. But I am since convinced by the Judicious Mr. Newton's incomparable Book, that 'tis too bold a Presumption to limit God's Power in this Point, by my narrow Conceptions. The gravitation of Matter towards Matter, by ways unconceivable to me, is not only a Demonstration that God can, if he pleases, put into Bodies, Powers, and ways of Operation, above what can be derived from our Idea of Body, or can be explained by what we know of Matter, but also an unquestionable and every where visible Instance, that he has done so. And therefore in the next Edition of my Book, I shall take care to have that Passage rectified.' John Locke, *Mr. Locke's Reply to the Right Reverend the Lord Bishop of Worcester's Answer to his Second Letter* (London, 1699), p. 408. Locke did indeed change the passage; from the fourth edition of *An Essay Concerning Human Understanding* onwards, II.8.11 read: 'The next thing to be considered is, how bodies produce ideas in us; and that is manifestly by impulse, the only way which we can conceive bodies operate in.' For this change of view Locke was indebted to Isaac Newton's *Philosophiae Naturalis Principia Mathematica* (London, 1687).

[96] Leibniz is referring to his 'Système nouveau de la nature et de la communication des substances, aussi bien que de l'union qu'il y a entre l'âme et le corps', *Journal des sçavans* 25 (27 June 1695), pp. 294–300, and 26 (4 July 1695), pp. 301–6. English translation: SLT, pp. 68–77.

that are clear and yet confused at the same time (such as the ideas we have of some sensible qualities). I do not think these ideas, which cannot be thoroughly penetrated by any creature, were sufficiently distinguished from other ones in the controversy between the illustrious gentlemen Stillingfleet and Locke. And all these reflections doubtless show that it is much less surprising if in divine matters there should occur things which far transcend the powers of reason. But if, therefore, there are some difficult and awkward questions in the writings of theologians, I do not think they should be reviled for that, or that we should cast aside theological systems (that is, the ordered exposition of doctrine) any more than we should cast aside philosophical or medical systems. But we should only beware (likewise in medicine) that in disputing too much we neglect practice and salvation.

7

The Churches and their Doctrines

1. On the host (October 1677)[1]

Manuscript:

M: LH I 2, 4 Bl. 1.

Transcription:

A: A VI 4, pp. 2202–4.

The provenance of the text is unknown, though Leibniz's interest in Catholic doctrines at the time was no doubt fuelled by the fact that his new employer, Duke Johann Friedrich, was a Catholic convert.

October 1677

The host of the Roman Church is either the creator or a created thing. If it is the creator then it follows that the creator, i.e. God, is a thing which is white and round, since it is undeniable that a host is a thing which is white, round etc., and indeed, theologians maintain that the whiteness we see is not apparent but real. Therefore if a host is God, God will be a thing of such kind too.

Likewise, a host in Rome is not a host in Paris, i.e. there are many hosts, but because there are not many gods, God is therefore not a host, or, a host is not God.

---

[1] Editor's title. From the Latin. Complete.

Now let us assume that a host is a created thing – it will either be a created thing assumed by God, for instance the body of Christ, or it will be a purely created thing. That it is not the body of Christ is proved by the same argument which proved that the host is not God. For the body of Christ is not round, yet a host is round, and the body of Christ is one, yet there are many hosts.

It is necessary, then, that a host be a purely created thing. From this, however, it plainly follows that a host cannot be adored, i.e. that it is not an object of *cultus latriae*.

Suppositions

1) It is a widespread custom of the Roman mass that many thousands of consecrated hosts are used, not just in Europe, but in other parts of the world too.

2) A purely created thing (that is, one not assumed by God) should not be adored in itself, and especially not with *cultus latriae*.

Proposition I

A host is not God.

There are many consecrated hosts, *by supposition 1*. God is unique. Therefore a host is not God.

Proposition II

A host is not the body of Christ.

There are many consecrated hosts, *by supposition 1*. The body of Christ is unique. Therefore a host is not the body of Christ.

Proposition III

A host should not be adored or honoured with *cultus latriae*.

A host is not God (*by proposition 1*). Therefore it is a created thing. If it is a created thing, it will either be a created thing assumed by God, or a purely created thing. It is not a created thing assumed by God, because it is not the body of Christ (*by proposition 2*), while it is conceded that it is not the soul of Christ. Therefore it is a purely created thing. But (*by supposition 2*), a purely created thing should not be adored with *cultus latriae*. Therefore nor should a host. Which was to be demonstrated.

I suppose with the theologians that in the Sacrament of the Eucharist there is no deception of the senses but that the whiteness, roundness and other accidents are no less real in a host than in other things.

There is genuine whiteness and roundness in this place.
That which is white is also round.
Therefore there is a subject of whiteness and roundness.
Therefore it is demonstrated that a host is not to be adored, but that adoration is to be restricted to Christ.

2. On Scripture, the Church and the Trinity (1680–4 (?))[2]

Manuscript:

M: LH I 3, 4 Bl. 1–2.

Transcription:

A: A VI 4, pp. 2286–91.

This text appears to have been inspired by reading Robert Bellarmine's *De controversiis Christianae fidei* (1586-91), and in fact follows it in a number of places. Leibniz made notes on Bellarmine's book at some point between 1680 and 1684,[3] so it is reasonable to suppose that the following text was written at around the same time.

It is safer to hold that Holy Scripture contains nothing except the word of God, and that the authors of the books, even with regard to those which do not pertain to salvation, have not asserted a falsehood insofar as they are philosophical, chronological and geographical. If there are errors, however, they have crept in because of the failings of copyists, or have arisen from words that have been poorly understood.[4]

---

[2] Editor's title. From the Latin. Complete.
[3] See A VI 4, pp. 2556–77.
[4] Marginal note: 'Whenever I consider which doctrines I myself would put forward if I were granted the supreme power of deciding, I would by all accounts be inclined to preserve the doctrines of the Roman Church, and I would only correct certain practices condemned a little while ago by pious and prudent men of that side, which hitherto have been tolerated far and wide in the Roman Church on account of the failings of times and men.

There is nothing contained in the books of Judith, Tobit, Wisdom and Maccabees which prohibits them from being considered canonical. But although it should be acknowledged that St Jerome did not attribute to the majority of them that supreme authority appropriate for canonical books, nevertheless the more common opinion of the old Church seems to have been quite the opposite, and hence the Catholic Church, aware of tradition, has been able to establish that they should be considered canonical. Certainly no sufficiently weighty arguments for doubting can be adduced against these books, and the majority of the arguments which are put forward can be wielded against certain books accepted by all.[5]

Protestants also grant that these books, which they call apocryphal, are holy, but they deny that the books are suitable for confirming the doctrines of faith. But since there is no doctrine of faith at all which requires these books, it seems pointless to argue about the canonicity of these books, nor is there any cause to depart from the common opinion of the Church.

Sometimes books are not written by those to whom they are attributed, but collected together by others from their opinions or records. Thus Bellarmine, in *de verbo Dei*, book I chapter 14, says that it may be the case that even Sirach may have brought together the opinions of David and collected them in one volume.

The third and fourth books of Maccabees and the third and fourth of Esdra are apocryphal, since they have not been assigned to the Canon by any Council.[6]

Since the books of Moses and the prophets are written in the pure Hebrew tongue, and (Daniel aside) have no admixture of Chaldean, it is likely that they were not written after the Babylonian captivity but only revised then.[7]

The Hebrew text is occasionally doubtful, though at any rate there is

---

If I had been born in the Roman Church I would certainly not have abandoned it, even if I were to believe all the things I now believe.

The authority of the pope, which deters many people the most, does not deter me in the least, for I believe that nothing can be understood as being more to the Church's advantage than its proper use. By all accounts it seems very likely to me that the union of the Western Churches will be restored at some point, in particular when in the Roman Church reform is applied not to doctrines of faith, but to certain practices which have been wrongly received and not approved by the Church itself.

[5] This paragraph incorporates claims from Robert Bellarmine's *De controversiis Christianae fidei* (1586-91), controversy I ('de verbo Dei'), chapters 10 and 12.

[6] This follows Bellarmine's *De controversiis Christianae fidei*, controvesy I, book I, chapter 20.

[7] This follows Bellarmine's *De controversiis Christianae fidei*, controvesy I, book II, chapter 3.

no doubt that its exposition is supported by the version of the seventy translators.[8]

Those who think the Vulgate authentic do not deny that there are still certain things which can perhaps be corrected in it. For an authentic document is one which is officially considered capable of being safely read by the faithful, and contains no error from which danger may be able to arise to those who read it. Accordingly it is sufficient that there is nothing in it from which danger may be able to arise to those who read it.

With regard to the vernacular translations, it is thought only that they should not be permitted or recited indiscriminately.[9] For it is undeniable that it is sometimes dangerous for them to be in the hands of common folk, although it has to be admitted that sometimes such a thing happens without any danger, like now in France and Germany, and so there should be regard for times and men. And where the reading of Scripture is denied to the common folk, the core of it at least should be offered …[10]

Luther, in the preface to the Psalms, says 'I know him to be a person of the most imprudent temerity who ventures to declare that he has, by himself, understood any book of Scripture in all its parts.'

Luther, in book 1 against Zwingali and Oecolampadius, says 'if the world should stand any longer it would again be necessary, because of the different interpretations of Holy Scripture which now exist, for us to receive the decrees of the Councils and have recourse to them in order to preserve the unity of faith'.

Brenz, in the prolegomena against Peter of Soto, admits that at least this tradition concerning Holy Scripture should be received.[11]

Catholics think that the soul of Christ had, from the time of conception, all the qualities which it had afterwards.

It is a great question whether all the things in which it is not possible to err without endangering one's salvation are held to be defined in Holy Scripture. It seems to me that the first undisputed point is that the very authority of the Holy Books is received through the tradition of the Church, hence I am afraid that we cannot satisfactorily evince the Most Holy Trinity from Scriptures, without appeal to tradition, yet it is divulged far more

---

[8] This follows Bellarmine's *De controversiis Christianae fidei*, controvesy I, book II, chapter 6.
[9] This follows Bellarmine's *De controversiis Christianae fidei*, controvesy I, book II, chapter 15.
[10] There follows an additional sentence, most of which is illegible in the manuscript.
[11] This paragraph, along with the two preceding ones, follows Bellarmine's *De controversiis Christianae fidei*, controvesy I, book III, chapter 1. Leibniz appears to have taken the quotations and references from Bellarmine rather than from the original sources.

clearly by joining Scripture with tradition. It is nonetheless certain that Holy Scripture much more favours the Trinity, and that it is sometimes violently twisted by the Anti-Trinitarians.

As far as an interpreter of Scripture is concerned, with regard to the doubts which can arise it will undoubtedly be better for him to consult the Church, if it is agreed that God so guides it by his own Spirit that one can safely have confidence in its interpretations. And so Trent rightly requires that the unanimous consent of the fathers be respected,[12] and accordingly St Augustine says that he who decides to dispute with the whole Church is suffering from the most arrogant madness.[13] Nor do I think that there is any example of a doctrine received in the Church which is associated with a danger to one's salvation. Yet it does not follow from this that the Church is infallible in all things, for example, if it were to lay down something about those matters not pertaining to salvation such as factual matters and philosophical matters, like about the antipodes, the motion of the earth etc. Until now, as far as I know, the Church has not supposed that any such thing should be laid down, and it is likely that it will also observe the same position in the future. And by what other authority than that of the Church has the washing of feet been abandoned, which according to certain people was instituted by Christ and should be regarded as the 8th Sacrament? Here belongs the change of the Sabbath day to Sunday,[14] and the abrogation of the teaching with regard to abstaining from blood and from the meat of strangled animals.[15] When disputing with the Socinians and the Anabaptists, refuge should be taken in the traditions and authority of the Church.

It should be regarded as certain that God is one in number, and that there are not three Gods but three persons of the Godhead;[16] accordingly we do not say that the Father, the Son and the Holy Spirit are Gods, but persons

---

[12] Asserted in the 'Decree concerning the edition and the use of the sacred books', Council of Trent, Fourth Session (8 April 1546).
[13] Leibniz appears to be here following Bellarmine's *De controversiis Christianae fidei*, controvesy I, book III, chapter 6, which locates this claim in Augustine's Epistle 118. However the claim is actually to be found in chapter 5 of Epistle 54.
[14] Early Christians are thought to have kept various Jewish customs including observation of the Sabbath, which covered the period from Friday sunset to Saturday sunset. Sunday gradually became the accepted Holy Day for Christians.
[15] An allusion to Acts 15.29, which states: 'You are to abstain from food sacrificed to idols, from blood, from the meat of strangled animals and from sexual immorality.' By the time of Augustine this teaching was rarely observed; see Augustine, *Contra Faustum*, XXXII.13.
[16] This follows Bellarmine's *De controversiis Christianae fidei*, controversy II ('de Christo'), book I, chapter 3.

of the Godhead. Moreover, a person of the Godhead is a sort of uncreated singular substance subsisting through itself, but which involves an essential relation, such that it implies that it alone exists. In created things there is nothing that better illustrates this plurality in unity than what we experience in ourselves when our mind perceives itself. In this example there is some difference between the person perceiving and the person perceived, which are nevertheless one individual.[17]

The Catholic opinion of the Trinity and Incarnation is more suitable than the Arian or Socinian by far. For the Arians insist on a certain supremely distinguished creature prior to the world, whereas the Socinians admit a pure man, and yet both hold that this creature is the Son of God, the former hold that he is God's natural son, the latter that he is God's adoptive son, and they claim that he should be worshipped. But the Catholics would not worship Christ unless they thought that there is in him that supreme divinity, creator of all things. And I do not see that what they say – that God has suffered with regard to human nature – is against God's honour, since it is understood in such a way that every imperfection is furthest removed from God. Conversely, however, it is evident from Conrad Vorst and the metaphysics of the Socinians that Anti-Trinitarians think things unworthy of God.[18]

Yet it should be acknowledged that, among Catholics and Protestants alike, in worshipping God the multitude of men often conceives Christ's humanity more than his divinity, which should be the other way around. Consequently, I think it is the duty of ministers to correct this abuse, and to rouse minds to the divinity itself, which is to be loved and worshipped above all things, especially since contrition is justly said by the Catholics to consist in that, contrition which I have discovered in practice is a necessary admonition no less among Protestants than among Catholics.

As for the person of Christ, the union of natures cannot be better explained than Holy Fathers have done, by the union of soul and body.

It will be said more correctly that the deity did not suffer, and that his

---

[17] Marginal note: 'The Word, i.e. that which is comprehended, is the image of the father, since the father perceiving the Word perceives that which he is himself, namely, that mind which comprehends itself. The perception itself, or love, is the Holy Spirit, since for God to perceive himself is the same as for him to love himself. Moreover, the Holy Spirit proceeds from the Father and the Son, because the lover and the beloved are prior to love, not in time, however, but in the nature of the thing. (α) Moreover, it should be understood that in the whole of nature I know of no real, abstract being aside from perception. For elsewhere it is shown that motion is only a mode. (β) The Greeks admit that the Spirit proceeds from the Father through the Son.'

[18] Leibniz is probably thinking here of Vorst's *Tractatus theologicus de Deo*.

humanity is not everywhere. Nor I do not see what benefit ubiquity brings, since Christ is not present in the supper in the same way in which he is everywhere, but in a special way. So it is sufficient for us to believe that through the Incarnation all perfections that fall under human nature were communicated to humanity, and that the divine perfections were in Christ the man, by the very fact that he is God, i.e. that the fullness of divinity dwelled in humanity by a true union. Just as certainly neither does the soul communicate, by union with the body, its force of willing or understanding to the body itself, nor does it take extension and other attributes of that kind from the body. Nevertheless there are some operations that can only be understood by the union of both. Add Morlinus, *Disputatio de communicatione idiomatum*.[19]

3. On God and the Church (autumn 1685–spring 1686 (?))[20]

Manuscript:

M: LH I 20 Bl. 227–8.

Transcription:

A: A VI 4, pp. 2347–50.

This piece appears to be another of the many texts on Christian and Catholic doctrines that Leibniz wrote in preparation for the so-called *Examen religionis christianae*.

It is evident by the natural light that there exists some most perfect substance, which we call God, and evident in the same way that he is unique, necessary, i.e. eternal, and the author and conserver of all the perfections in other things, whereas whatever imperfection exists anywhere originates from the particular limitation of creatures. It also follows that God is an

---

[19] Joachim Morlinus, *Disputatio de communicatione idiomatum* (Giesen, 1571).
[20] Editor's title. From the Latin. Complete.

omnipotent and omniscient mind, and that all things are arranged by him in the best way, such that it cannot be better.[21] In short, God possesses the greatest power of reason in the universe of minds, the society of which composes the best commonwealth under this most just monarch. It would be evident to us that all things are beyond the wishes of the wisest men in this commonwealth if only we were to become acquainted with the secrets of providence.

Moreover, from these things it is concluded that minds in turn owe him supreme love and worship, and that all should strive with the utmost effort to satisfy his presumed will, and that each person should adorn his own Sparta[22] and the circumstances in which he is placed in a way that, insofar as he can judge from the things known to him, will be consistent with the divine will. But if the effort does not meet with success, yet so great is God's goodness that he is satisfied with our best will as well as affection towards him, as long as it is serious and sincere.

Although these things are such that nothing appears easier to one reasoning aright than to love and worship God, yet it is apparent from experience that humankind has deviated from the perfection of natural reason to such an extent that nothing appears more difficult and more uncommon. And philosophy, that is, reason practised with skill, has not produced an adequate remedy, both because a demonstration is difficult in the case of matters remote from the senses, and because men are insufficiently stirred by reasons alone without some greater force and impression.

And so it was in accordance with divine goodness and wisdom that humankind be corrected by revealed religion, and that minds be stirred to embrace better things, both that we might learn what reason cannot teach, and that a greater authority might be added to our arguments.

Moreover, the religion sent by God is undoubtedly the Christian religion, which has so many and such great marks of the truth that we are compelled to recognize the plan of divine providence in establishing it, unless we imagine that God himself wished to deceive us by so many proofs that are presented to us (which is absurd).

Moreover, there exist holy books; that these books are genuine, at least for the most part (to put aside for now the remaining ones which have been

---

[21] better. | But in particular that he is King and Lord of all other minds (that is, of the substances which are able to become acquainted with him and themselves), and that God possesses the foremost power of reason in the universe of minds | *deleted*.

[22] An allusion to Euripides' 'Telephus' (fragment 73).

subject to even the slightest doubt), and that they should be attributed to the first preachers of our religion, to the disciples of Christ to whom they are ascribed, is as certain among experts as it is that the chief books read under the names of Cicero and Virgil were actually written by those authors.

But since it is evident that, for almost fourteen centuries from that time, opinions have predominated in the Christian Church which cannot be entirely, adequately and clearly proved from the holy books alone, and which, if they were false, would surely be most dangerous, it seems that one or other of the following must be asserted. First, that the Christian religion, if these doctrines are false, was horribly corrupted shortly after its inception, and that divine providence failed in its plan, and that even the promises of Christ, about safeguarding his church and leading it towards every truth with the help of the divine spirit, were ineffective against the prevailing gates of hell; yet although it is clear that even false religions have preserved their purity for a longer time, I think it likely that false doctrines would overthrow the Christian religion and would lead to some kind of bare deism, if not to atheism. Alternatively, one will have to acknowledge that the authority of the Church is sufficient to safeguard these doctrines, and will have to depend on the safe judgement of the Church, fortified by divine promises and acts of assistance, with regard to salvific truths. And it cannot be doubted that what Christ chiefly commended to his followers before departing is entirely suitable for preserving the faith of simple folk and also for preserving the bond of charity among Christians.

Furthermore, in order to avoid schisms, it is not only consistent with reason that the Church be bound together by some common government and hierarchy, but it is also consistent with the tradition of the Church itself and the words of Christ in Scripture, in which he gave the instruction 'Tell it unto the Church',[23] and granted it the power of binding and releasing,[24] and with the practice of the apostles who held the first Council in Jerusalem.

In fact, though, universal councils cannot always be held, and yet it is fitting that some system of common government should survive even in the time between councils, and that the Christian commonwealth is never readily without some head and leader. Since the time of the apostles, however, no college has existed to which such leadership can be attributed, and no man except the Bishop of Rome alone has claimed so great a right for himself. But as a Roman, the pastor of what was once the foremost city

---

[23] An allusion to Matthew 18.17.
[24] An allusion to Matthew 18.18.

in the entire world, has the precedents as well as the authority and long possession of this leadership bestowed by antiquity, and – which is truly remarkable – is unambiguously supported by certain sayings of Scripture, it seems it has to be admitted that heaven has granted him as much power as is required to govern the Church as well as is possible.

But it should be considered as certain that those who, through their own fault, destroy the unity of the Church or foster schism commit the gravest sin and expose their souls to the greatest danger. For the world has learned by bitter experience how great are the evils of schism. And those who do not do as much as is in their power to restore Catholic unity from schism rashly deprive themselves of certain ordinary acts of assistance of divine grace which God has bound to the sacraments of the Church in order that the souls of the faithful might be joined together with a stronger bond.

For it is received in the Church and, so I believe, divinely established to such an extent that neither the Sacrament of the body of the Lord, in the partaking of which the body of the Church also recognizes its members, can be performed, nor the supreme power of the keys exercised, except by a duly ordained pastor. Moreover, ordination itself is the responsibility of bishops, who are considered the successors of the apostles. And even if we were to grant that, out of necessity, exceptions can be made in some cases whereby a part of this power would either be shared with others or supplied by divine benevolence, especially if God has such regard for a person that he is inflamed with a true love of God, this still cannot furnish a defence for the contempt of others. For it is clear that he who loves God above all things with all his heart cannot spurn the remedies prescribed by him for our weakness.

The Church has also established a canon of holy books which can be safely trusted, even if sometimes doubts have been raised about some of them. Nor, in fact, are we guilty of a circular argument, as though the Church were proved through Scripture, and Scripture in turn through the Church. For it is evident that the better part of the holy books is acknowledged on the same grounds ordinarily applied to other ancient authors, even if it were not supplemented by any decree from the Church, and these authors can in turn support the authority of the Church with their testimonies. However the canon and the remaining sacred volumes and indeed the entire body of Scripture provides a gesture of acknowledgement towards the Church. However the authority of the Church is laid down in a clear light to so great an extent that it can be established by those arguments we mentioned above, even without Scripture.

4. Suppositions (autumn 1685–spring 1686 (?))[25]

Manuscript:

M: LH I 20 Bl. 260–1.

Transcription:

A: A VI 4, pp. 2351–4.

As with the previous text, this piece is possibly a preliminary study for the so-called *Examen religionis christianae*.

Suppositions

God (that is, a substance which is infinite, eternal, omnipotent, omniscient, good in the utmost degree and unique) exists.

Every perfection creatures have is from God, every imperfection from the particular limitation of creatures.

God does everything so well that nothing better can even be wished for by a wise man.

Every mind (that is, a substance which is conscious of itself, and is able to become acquainted with God) is immortal, and not only is it not destroyed, but also it never entirely loses its established personality, i.e. its memory and consciousness of itself.

God demands nothing else from men than the best will, as long as it is serious and sincere, or what amounts to the same thing, a true love of God above all things, from which there follows charity towards others too.

It is consistent with the laws of the best commonwealth, of which God is the monarch, that there be no good deed without reward, and no sin without punishment.[26]

---

[25] Author's title. From the Latin. Complete.
[26] punishment. | There was a need for revelation not only in order that we might acquire knowledge of those things which reason cannot teach, but also in order that men who are insufficiently influenced by arguments alone might be moved by religion. | *deleted*

Experience has shown that the corruption of men is so great that reason alone cannot be enough for them, and so there was a need for particular grace and divine revelation, both that souls might be moved to a greater extent by the authority of religion, and that we might acquire knowledge of the divine will concerning our correction and the means of salvation.

Divine providence will not permit a lie to adopt all the marks and, so to speak, the cloaks of truth. Therefore, since the Christian religion is fortified by such a great number of such great arguments, and has brought together the holiest teachings and a remarkable origin, which has shown the divine touch everywhere, it has to be admitted that either it is true, or that God has led us into error, which is absurd.

It is as certain that there are some books of Holy Scripture which are genuine and written by the first teachers of the Christian religion, to whom they are attributed, as it is that a good many records of the writings of the secular ancients are genuine.

It is consistent both with the plan of providence and the divine promises recorded in the indisputable holy books that the gates of hell prevail not against God's Church, but against Christ, who will always assist it until the consummation of the world, and against the divine spirit, which will lead the Church towards every truth.

Yet it would be most unbecoming for a religion divinely instituted and authorized by so many promises if it was seized by a monstrous corruption barely after it had arisen and for fourteen centuries and more thereafter, since we see that false religions have preserved their purity for a longer time.

Those who believe otherwise should beware lest they destroy the whole of revealed religion, indeed even providence, and are led not only to deism, but also to atheism.

We see, however, that there are doctrines in the Church that have been received for so many centuries, especially with regard to the Trinity and Incarnation, which would be most dangerous if they were false, and yet they cannot be adequately evinced from the holy books, nor are they more strongly confirmed by any other argument than that they are approved by the judgement of the Church and even of providence, which will not permit so much corruption to prevail.

From this it is now inferred that so much authority is owed to the Catholic Church that one can safely adhere to its judgement regarding truths about salvation.

A legitimate and ecumenical council represents the character of the Church, for its judgement cannot be better known by another method.

On occasion an extra-conciliar judgement is needed for the general guidance of the Church.

No college and no man has claimed, without the support of a council, the power of governing the universal Church, aside from the bishop of ancient Rome, which was the most cultivated part of the world and had the majority of Christians under its rule.

The authority of the Roman Pontiff in governing the universal Church is favoured by very longstanding examples and testimonies, very long possession and – which is significant – by certain notable passages of Holy Scripture.

And so, since the government of the Church should be bestowed upon someone, and there is no one aside from the Roman Pontiff to whom it should be ascribed, it follows that it is to be bestowed upon him.

It is to be said that the concession of power to the great pontiff is divinely inspired inasmuch as it is beneficial for the Church to be ruled well.

By divine law (ordinary divine law at least), certain Sacraments can only be administered in the Church, and only by persons duly ordained for this purpose. Thus the Sacrament of the Lord's body is performed only by a priest, only a priest exercises the power of the keys in absolving penitents and only a bishop ordains a priest. And this line of ordination is to be considered as a sort of mark and duty of the governing body of the Church.

The schism is among the greatest evils of the world and the Church, and whoever caused it is guilty of the greatest sin; however, whoever keeps the schism open, sins most gravely through his own fault.[27]

Indeed, he who lives without fault in himself, just like a person who is unjustly excommunicated, does not enjoy certain benefits of God in the same way as those who make use of the actual communion of the Church. And he lives with a greater danger to his salvation, and to that extent has need of greater devotion and endeavour, not only that he may be reconciled, but also, if that cannot be obtained, that he may obtain from God through Christ a superabundance of good will by his prayers for ordinary assistance.

I fully believe that one should stand firm in the judgement concerning the canon of sacred books of the Catholic Church, even concerning those

---

[27] fault | and exposes his soul to great danger. | *deleted*

whose authority is susceptible of greater doubt; we know that these are the ones about which the ancients did not speak consistently enough.

No circular argument is committed in saying that Scripture is proved by the Church and the Church by Scripture. For the chief part of those books which are attributed to the evangelists and the apostles is undoubtedly genuine, nor does it have need of any decree from experts; indeed, its testimonies rather confirm the authority of the Church, which is also proved by the very counsel of Providence. Moreover, there is no need for the remaining part, which lacks canonicity, to prove the authority of the Church.

5. On the certainty of salvation (17/27 March 1695)[28]

Manuscript:

M: Hannover HStA Dep. 84 A 180 Bl. 137–8r.

Transcription:

A: A I 11, pp. 349–50.

For many years Leibniz had a sporadic correspondence with Duchess Benedicta Henrietta (1652–1730), wife of Leibniz's former employer, Johann Friedrich, Duke of Brunswick-Lüneberg. The correspondence generally focused on matters of Catholic doctrine, which Leibniz knew to be of great interest to Benedicta. The following piece was written for the Duchess at her own request; Leibniz explains the circumstances of the request at the start of his letter to her of 17/27 March 1695: 'As Madam de Brinon[29] seems to have taken the question of the certainty of salvation in a completely different way from how the Protestants understand it, and as Your Serene Highness has indicated that she would like me to explain their meaning clearly, I have not failed to obey her orders.'[30] The following text was enclosed with the aforementioned letter.

---

[28] Editor's title. From the French. Complete.
[29] Marie de Brinon (1631–1701), secretary to Electress Sophie's sister, Louise Hollandine, the Abbess of Maubisson.
[30] A I 11, p. 347.

A much discussed question among gentlemen of the Roman Church and the Protestants is about whether we can be assured of being fully reconciled with God, and consequently of being in a state of salvation. The former seem to say no, and the Protestants protest loudly about that, saying that this doctrine gives rise to insurmountable perplexities and anxieties, which are capable of making a dying man despair, and are completely contrary to the internal joy of God's children as well as to the tranquillity of their conscience.

In my opinion, the two sides agree upon what Holy Scripture says: that we should work for our salvation with fear,[31] that is, that we should not have any presumption of our powers, and that we should labour diligently in that which concerns our salvation,[32] since it is very true that the path is narrow,[33] and that we would not be able to walk it without the assistance of grace.

It is also agreed that we are not assured of the future, or of our final perseverance. For although one may be in a state of salvation at the present time, one may yet commit a new sin, and die unrepentant. This is why he who is upstanding should take care not to fall.[34] Thus we do not know if we are among the elect, and consequently if we are an object of love or hatred.[35]

Therefore, there remains only the question that can be asked about our present state: whether, when we are reconciled with God, we can be assured that we are so, and whether we are thus assured of our conversion, of our true repentance and consequently of our justification; so that we could have grounds to believe that we would be saved if we were to die at this moment of time. For this is what is called being in a state of salvation. The Protestants are in favour of it, and they have grounds to be surprised that some on the opposite side throw into doubt a doctrine that is so clear and so salutary, throwing consciences into strange turmoils and anxieties, without any grounds, and removing every possible way of having the mind at rest, which can only serve to keep superstition alive and to frighten feeble minds, which helps to stir them into action though it can bring about despair at the point

---

[31] An allusion to Philippians 2.12: 'So then, my beloved, even as you have always obeyed, not only in my presence, but now much more in my absence, work out your own salvation with fear and trembling.'

[32] An allusion to 2 Peter 1.10: 'Therefore, brethren, be even more diligent to make your call and election sure.'

[33] An allusion to Matthew 7.14: 'Because strait is the gate, and narrow is the way, which leadeth unto life'.

[34] An allusion to 1 Corinthians 10.12: 'Therefore, whoever thinks he is standing secure should take care not to fall.'

[35] hatred | because we do not know if we will have the gift of perseverance. | *deleted*.

of death. The unshakeable foundation of the Protestants is that we are in the state of salvation when we have faith which is deep or accompanied by charity, that is, faith together with a love of God. Now each man can know if he has, at the present time, this deep faith or not. For as faith and charity are internal acts of our understanding and of our will and, in a word, consist in our thoughts, we cannot fail to know whether we have these thoughts, and we cannot fail to feel them when we have them. Consequently, since we are able to know whether we have deep faith, we will also be able to know if we are in a state of salvation at the present time.

Perhaps the Council of Trent is not so averse to this doctrine as is thought. For it speaks very cautiously and denies only that we should believe with a certainty of divine faith that we are in a state of salvation: that is, it denies that this reflection on ourselves, or rather this knowledge of our own state, is a point of faith.[36] I believe that one can agree with the Council about that, since the articles of faith specifically concern universal doctrines and not our particular circumstances. It is therefore sufficient to have here the same degree of human certainty which is considered sufficient in the ordinary actions of life. And even if a person were not to make this express reflection on his state, he would not cease to be justified, provided that he truly had a sincere faith and love of God.

I will not mention the passages from Holy Scripture which the Protestants employ in this matter, like for example the one by St Paul, who notes that the spirit of God testifies to our spirit that we are God's children,[37] and many other passages, for they are familiar enough. And the reason I have given, based on Scripture, is sufficient to resolve the question.

6. On the authority of the Pope (1705)[38]

Manuscripts:

M1:   LH 1, 7, 6 Bl. 13 (draft).
M2:   LH 1, 7, 6 Bl. 14–15 (fair copy).

---

[36] Leibniz is referring to chapter IX ('Against the vain confidence of heretics') of the sixth session of the Council of Trent, held on 13 January 1547.
[37] An allusion to Romans 8.16: 'The Spirit himself testifies with our spirit that we are God's children.'
[38] Editor's title. From the French. Complete.

This piece was written on the occasion of the engagement of the Princess Elisabeth Christine (1691–1750), the granddaughter of Duke Anton Ulrich, to the future Emperor of the Holy Roman Empire, Charles VI (1685–1740). She converted to Catholicism in 1707 to enable the union to go ahead, and they were married in 1708.

[M2, fair copy]

Upon departing this earth, the divine saviour left to his disciples his doctrine, his commandments and a certain government and power in order to maintain them and to preserve order and union among the faithful. This government constitutes a sort of state that the sacred books of the New Testament already called the *Church*.[39]

And in order that this State be separate from worldly states and powers, he gave to it purely spiritual arms, the power of which extends over souls. This is the power to absolve sins, to retain them[40] and to excommunicate the disobedient by depriving them of the assistance of heavenly graces and the use of sacraments to which these graces are joined, over which the Church has dispensation.[41] And one of these sacraments, that of the Eucharist, is the symbol of the union and of the mutual charity of Christians.

The apostles exercised this cardinal power, as is apparent from the assembly of Jerusalem where they ruled on important matters.[42] But the others exercised it in a way dependent on them. For in various passages the apostles created bishops, priests and other ecclesiastical officers,[43] retaining supreme direction by virtue of the Holy Spirit, who assisted them. This is why they say in their Council: *it seemed good to the Holy Spirit and to us.*[44]

It is even apparent from the passages of Holy Scripture and from those of Fathers who lived close to the apostolic age that St Peter, as the first of the apostles, had some authority and direction, just as indeed order requires that there be moderators in meetings. Jesus Christ commended his flock to him in a very special way,[45] and charged him in particular with this power of the keys given to the whole Church.[46]

---

[39] See Matthew 16.18; Acts 9.31.
[40] See John 20.22.
[41] See Matthew 18.17.
[42] See Acts 15.
[43] See for example Acts 14.23 and Titus 1.5.
[44] Acts 15.28.
[45] See John 21.15-17.
[46] See Matthew 16.19.

And as all the ancients agree that he was martyred in Rome under Nero,[47] this firm belief that he had governed the Church in this city, capital of the Roman Empire and the most important of the known Earth, and that the bishops of this capital had to have the same direction in the universal Church, is found deep-rooted in minds from the outset, and consequently must have had some basis in fact. So this cardinal direction that the Bishop of Rome has exercised from all time in the Christian Church seems to be of apostolic institution, and even divine, since the apostles were inspired and did nothing except what is in accordance with the divine order.

This truth has been acknowledged by wise and moderate Protestants. And those who have been engaged in a negotiation started by a bishop by order of the Pope and the Emperor have access to an authentic – yet still secret – declaration, given by Protestant theologians who acknowledge this divine authority of the Bishop of Rome, or Pope.[48]

These same theologians have decided that, in accordance with certain declarations of the bishop negotiator and some conditions that they added to those, communion with Rome could be re-established, and the authority of the ancient, universal government of the Catholic Church recognized even in Protestant lands.

But it is a separate question whether well-informed persons can, with good conscience, and before these conditions to restore the union are settled, be in the Roman Church.[49] And this question requires a special discussion, in which it is necessary to consider carefully what the Roman Church requires of those who recognize it.

---

[47] See for example Gaius/Caius, *Disputation with Proclus*, in Eusebius, *History of the Church* 2.25.5, and Lactantius, *On the Deaths of the Persecutors*, 2.5.

[48] In M1 this sentence reads 'And as I have been engaged in a negotiation started by a bishop by order of the Pope and the Emperor, I have access to an authentic – yet still secret – declaration, given by Protestant theologians who acknowledge this divine authority of the Bishop of Rome, or Pope.' M2 was originally written this way also, but Leibniz subsequently replaced references to 'I' with 'those'.

[49] Church |, or even enter it. | *deleted* (M1).

7. Exposition of the doctrines and practices authorized by the Roman Church (1705 (?))[50]

Manuscript:

M: LH 1, 7, 5 Bl. 117–20.

This piece is not, as its title might suggest, a simple exposition of Roman Catholic doctrines and practices, but rather Leibniz's examination of them, in which he indicates points of agreement and disagreement. It is likely a companion piece to the previous text, 'On the authority of the Pope' (pp. 241–3).

To the doctrines and practices of Rome it is important to give a sense which is true and in keeping with the great principles of piety and reason, since there are well-intentioned persons in the Roman Church whose conscience one should endeavour to ease.

Firstly, it should be recognized, along with the most learned men of this Church, that faith must be grounded in reason, that is, that there are rational motives which lead us to believe that the revelation on which the articles of our faith are founded comes from God, and in particular that Holy Scripture is a divine book.

(2) There are doctrines that one is obliged to believe although they are not in Holy Scripture, or not there explicitly enough, for example the perpetual virginity of the Holy Mother of our saviour. So the *tradition* of the Universal Church, preserved for all time, is an auxiliary principle, which helps to clarify Holy Scripture in the important articles, and to supplement it in points of lesser importance. The *councils* together with the *Fathers* are witnesses of this tradition, and the *Ecumenical Councils* should be recognized as the voice of the Universal Church, to which God has promised his Holy Spirit in matters concerning salvation.

---

[50] Author's title. From the French. Complete. A proposed title is given on one side of the first sheet, but is deleted: 'Exposition of the doctrines and practices authorized by the Roman Church, for those who seek to fulfil the duty of their conscience and'. Underneath that Leibniz wrote: 'It is important to see whether or not there is a way to give a reasonable sense to the doctrines and practices' and deleted that too, before starting again on the other side of the sheet.

(3) Now the councils considered universal by the Roman Church expressly recommend the antiquity and the universality of doctrine, and the unanimous consent of Churches and principal doctors,[51] and even in the profession of the faith one is obliged to uphold this. But the superstition of common folk, and the self-interest and ambition of some priests and individual doctors, have introduced abuses and new and suspect doctrines and practices, which the Protestants rightly criticize. Consequently, wise persons of the Roman Church itself have the right and the obligation to reject them too, without it being possible to criticize them for that; and people in Rome itself do seem quite inclined to reject them, as has been apparent in many a meeting with them.

It should also be acknowledged that in a certain way we hold the books of Holy Scripture as the actual testimony of the Church. And just as a constant tradition in the Republic of Letters has preserved and guaranteed for us the books of Cicero or Virgil, it may likewise be said that the tradition of the Church has distinguished the books of Holy Scripture from all others.

It should also be acknowledged that the visible Universal Church, that is, united[52] by a common government to the particular Churches of which the one of Rome has always been the foremost, has to have great advantages and signs in its favour. So there is no need, or should be no need, to depart from the communion of the Church without an extreme necessity. For unity and charity have been highly recommended to us not only by the ancient Church but also by Our Saviour, particularly when at his last supper he instituted the Sacrament of the Eucharist as a bond of the communion of faithful,[53] and so ordained that those who would not listen to the Church would be considered heathens. He has appointed authorized persons in the Church, that is, firstly the apostles and the disciples, who have left after them bishops and priests, who were ordained by the apostles and by those who had been ordained according to a propagation of the laying on of hands, accompanied by the grace of the Holy Spirit which is called the Sacrament of Holy Orders. He has given to them the Key to Heaven, that is, the power to absolve sins and to retain them, and he has even given the power of excommunication

---

[51] doctors, | and so it is right to avoid certain new opinions that particular doctors introduce into the Roman Church despite their not being grounded in reason, in Scripture or in tradition. And in this way, a number of doctrines and explanations that the Protestants reject in the doctors of this Church must be rejected even by wise persons of this very communion. And I find that even in Rome itself people are quite inclined to this | *deleted.*

[52] united | by the communion of faithful recommended in the symbol of apostles | *deleted.*

[53] See Matthew 26.17-30; Mark 14.12-26; Luke 22.7-38; John 13-17.

to those who govern Churches, so that one cannot disregard their authority with impunity. It is true that they can be mistaken in the exercise of the keys (*clave errante*),[54] and that they can excommunicate unjustly, something which cannot be harmful to the salvation of innocent persons or those who are only material heretics or schismatics, that is, those without bad will, whom it is unjust to persecute and to want to force to change. Nevertheless, it is always true that those who govern have the presumption in their favour; that they should be listened to and obeyed as far as possible, as long as error or evil is not discernible. The order as practised in the Church, for which there are grounds to consider apostolic, has distinguished the bishops from priests just as Jesus Christ distinguished the apostles from seventy chosen disciples.[55] And it has always been believed that, according to the ordinary rules, priests must be ordained by bishops, and bishops by other bishops, just as the apostles ordained another apostle in place of Judas Iscariot.[56]

It may even be said that, with God being a God of order, good order demands a direction in the Church, and there are some traces in Holy Scripture and in the words of Jesus Christ that St Peter, to whom in particular Christ entrusted his flock,[57] had the foremost authority among the apostles. Moreover, the whole of ecclesiastical history seems to acknowledge that this power, so useful to the Universal Church, was passed to the bishops of the metropolitan city of Christianity, that is, Rome. Therefore this direction afforded by bishops of Rome is by divine law, but the Churches have granted these bishops more or less power at certain times regarding what human law they can make. And learned Protestants have recognized that the authority of popes has often served to keep in check secular princes who gratified their passions without local bishops being able to muster sufficient resistance to them.[58]

Until now we have spoken of the principles of authority that should be followed[59] in the doctrines and in the practices as much as the nature of things may allow. Now we must come to the doctrines and practices individually. The principal doctrine of Christianity which brings the natural light to its perfection consists in the precept to love God above

---

[54] An unjust or incorrect sentence pronounced through a mistake of the Church.
[55] The seventy disciples are described in Luke 10, but not in any of the other gospels.
[56] See Acts 1.20-6.
[57] See John 21.15-17.
[58] them. | The infallibility of the Universal Church is clearly detectible in the councils | *deleted*.
[59] followed | and obeyed | *deleted*.

all things;[60] the love of one's neighbour is merely a consequence of this. This divine love which fills our will arises from the light that divine grace has illuminated in our understanding, which represents God to us as supremely perfect, and consequently as lovable above all else. This grace was obtained for man by the mediation of Jesus Christ. Now the grandeur and goodness of God, together with his other perfections, are particularly apparent in the mystery of the Redemption which faith teaches us is above reason. Thus the divine Word – only son of the eternal Father and consubstantial with him – took on human nature in order to be able to sacrifice himself for our sins, to reconcile us with God and to lead us to the happiness of eternal life by following his commandments. And to sanctify our souls he sent to us his Holy Spirit, third person of the Holy Trinity, along with the Father and the Son; this does not destroy the unity of the divine substance, just as, according to the comparison of the Holy Fathers, power, knowledge and will do not destroy the unity of our substance.

It is true that one should presume God's mercy, such that persons of good will who were lacking the proper knowledge, the history of Jesus Christ and therefore the revelations that he shared with us have nevertheless been able to be enlightened by an internal grace[61] and led to love God above all and to know his eternal Son in the Spirit as much as is needed to be saved. And it may even happen that God gives to such persons before they die an actual revelation of Jesus Christ in the flesh, and in a word the light that is necessary for them, without this coming to our attention. In a word, one should presume that persons who do what is incumbent upon them will be saved by the love of God above all and by any other extraordinary acts of assistance required. Yet we should do our utmost to stick to the ordinary ways [of salvation], leaving everything else to the impenetrable wisdom of God.

The true faith in Jesus Christ therefore leads us to the love of God, so when we gain it by the internal and living grace which binds us to the divine saviour, who has redeemed us and delivered us from the[62] punishment of hell by his passion and his satisfaction for our sins, we are justified before God and enter into a state to do works agreeable to him, which he desires

---

[60] See for example Mark 12.29-30; Matthew 22.37-9.
[61] grace | and purified without meditation on the Gospel | *deleted*.
[62] the | eternal | *deleted*.

to reward by bestowing his own gifts on us even in eternal life.[63] This is sufficient to have a good idea of the ground of our conversion, justification and regeneration.[64]

Now Jesus Christ desired that, in accordance with the ordinary ways, regeneration in children as well as in adults is obtained through the Sacrament of Water Baptism, in the name of the Father, the Son and the Holy Spirit. But it is true nonetheless that there is a baptism of the Holy Spirit which can take place when there is no water, namely when the divine love touches our hearts; and the baptism of blood approaches this when the sacrifice that martyrs make of their life makes up for their other failings. There was also a laying on of hands for all the faithful along with the invocation of the Holy Spirit in order to attract an effusion of its grace into our souls, and this is what was later called *the Sacrament of Confirmation*.

And when, after regeneration, one falls again into a mortal sin, however grievous it might be, the door to salvation is[65] still open, and there are two ways to reach it: the first is through the Sacrament of Absolution and the ministry of the priest who exercises the power of the keys when one sincerely repents of his sins with a genuine and serious intention to mend his ways, which at least is an attrition; the second way to the door of salvation is through a contrition grounded in the love of God above all things, which is sufficient even without the Sacrament and the ministry of the Church provided that it is not treated lightly, which would be a new sin, and one incompatible with this contrition. And it may be that through the grace of the Sacrament of Absolution, God excites in the hearts of those who feel only attrition some movements similar to those of divine love, of which they are unaware, just as children too are unaware of movements aroused in their hearts by the Sacrament of Baptism. Yet one must always do what one can to obtain them in oneself in a perceptible way.

This remission of sins that delivers us from the pains of hell by virtue of the blood of Jesus Christ does not, however, prevent there still being some punishment in this life or in the other, and the one which is in store for us in the other life, and which serves to purge souls, is called *purgatory*. Holy Scripture insinuates it, and reason endorses it on the grounds that according

---

[63] us. | And this is all that should be understood by meritorious works. | *deleted*.

[64] regeneration. | And when we have again fallen into a mortal sin, such as are those which are against conscience and which destroy the love of God in us, we can be received in grace and reconciled by the | *deleted*.

[65] is | opened by the penitence that one can obtain both by contrition | *deleted*.

to the rules of perfect government, which is God's government, no sin should be left entirely unpunished. It is true that blessed souls shall suffer it with joy, just as we willingly suffer a surgical operation that restores us to health. Yet it is still reasonable to think that God has so desired it that the prayers of the faithful, which have a great power over him, serve to diminish these pains; and upon these prayers of the whole Church are founded the *indulgences* granted to them, and the more plenary these indulgences are, the better the soul is purged here and now by the fire of the divine love.[66] But no one, under this pretext of prayers for the dead and of these indulgences, should take advantage of the credulity of good souls[67] by holding them to ransom and imposing on them an unbearable burden through doctrines and practices that distance them from true piety, which should be[68] enlightened and directed towards the essentials.

Christians who are regenerated, confirmed and reconciled must offer God the supreme worship due to the supreme substance, the pleasure from which constitutes all our happiness. This worship requires that we love him with a disinterested love as much as is possible, and that we relate everything to his glory, and to the execution of his commandments, the goal of which inclines towards our own good and[69] salvation. This is why we must praise God while considering and admiring his wonders in nature and in grace, imitating his perfections and the life of the saviour, and so instructing the youth in it; and above all we must be united as brothers, and practise charity amongst ourselves. And just as God loved us through his Son[70] – who loved us enough to sacrifice his blood for us – he wanted us to love, establishing the Holy Communion of the faithful in the Sacrament of the Eucharist in order to spark our charity.

This Holy Sacrament should not be neglected; and although the Churches of the east have retrenched the cup to the faithful, learned Protestants have judged that this would not be a sufficient reason for separation since in effect nothing is lost by it.[71] After all, one cannot participate in

---

[66] An indulgence is a remission of one's temporal punishment in purgatory. Indulgences can be partial and plenary; as the names suggest, a partial indulgence involves a partial remission of one's purgatorial punishment, while a plenary indulgence is a full remission, such that no further punishment is required.
[67] souls | and the fear of the dying | *deleted*.
[68] be | directed towards God | *deleted*.
[69] and | perfection | *deleted*.
[70] Son | and Jesus Christ | *deleted*.
[71] The general trend of restricting the communion wine to priests, with the laity receiving only the bread, was challenged in the fifteenth century by Bohemian Reformers who argued that salvation

the body of Jesus Christ without having participation in his blood.[72] And as for the commandment, it does not appear to be entirely absolute; a number of fathers believed that Jesus Christ had celebrated communion in Emmaus.[73] Communion under one kind was often practised in the ancient Church,[74] by carrying the host into the deserts during the persecution, and by sending it as a symbol of the union even to faraway persons. Those who cannot take the wine can commune under one kind according to the decision of learned Protestants; a moral obstacle, which cannot be remedied without greater risks, takes the place of a physical obstacle. And ultimately, in these sorts of arbitrary precepts, which are considered to be ceremonial, the Church has always been granted a dispensatory power. It is by using this that it has transferred the celebration of the Sabbath to Sunday; that for several centuries Passover was celebrated at times which were not in keeping with God's institution; that the faithful were permitted to eat blood and the meat of animals that had not been bled to death, contrary to what the apostles speaking on behalf of the Holy Spirit deemed necessary; and that baptism, which means 'immersion', was changed into 'aspersion',[75] contrary to the view of a number of Eastern Christians and Muscovites[76] who consider our baptism as useless. Yet the Protestants themselves do not believe that they are thereby obliged to separate from Churches in which these changes have taken place. The Church had a good intention in the retrenchment of the cup, namely to prevent irreverences and aversions. These could be remedied in a different way, however. Great princes and entire nations have demanded the restitution of the cup in a very insistent manner, for good reasons, and it would be wished that they could have obtained it, as could still doubtless happen, and there are even examples of these concessions.

---

required one to receive both the bread and cup. In 1431 the Council of Basle, while insisting that one's salvation was not harmed by receiving communion under one kind, that is, either through the bread or the cup, nevertheless permitted the Bohemians to receive both, a concession that was subsequently revoked in 1462 by Pope Pius II; this revocation is sometimes referred to as the retrenchment of the cup. The custom of receiving communion under one kind was subsequently made law in session 21, chapter 2 of The Council of Trent (1562).

[72] An oft-made point in the debate about the Eucharist was that there is no need to partake of communion wine, which would be converted into Christ's blood, because the bread (the host) was converted into Christ's body, which would itself contain his blood. Hence the wine is superfluous.

[73] See Luke 24.30.

[74] 'Communion under one kind' is the practice of receiving only the wine or (more commonly) only the bread.

[75] 'Aspersion' is a sprinkling of water, whereas 'immersion' requires one to be submerged in water.

[76] Muscovites | from the Greek Church | *deleted*.

The Roman Church holds that the body and blood of Jesus Christ is present with the species after the consecration of visible symbols. But worship does not extend to the thing which is white or round, and which is seen and touched and carried. It extends only to Jesus Christ, because of his divinity, since the supreme worship, which is called Latria, has as its object only the eternal and supreme good. The body of Jesus Christ is not enclosed within this morsel called the host; the roundness, the whiteness, the taste and the other visible qualities of this host are not qualities, attributes or accidents of the body of Jesus Christ, for it has been declared that they are without any substantial subject to which these qualities may belong now that the substance of the body and blood of Jesus Christ has succeeded the presence of the substance of the bread and the wine. It is also in this way that the unfitting things that can happen with regard to the symbols and visible species do not dishonour the body of Jesus, since the presence alone with the species (which are not in him, as has just been said) do not affect him any more than God, who is everywhere and in all things, is affected by the pollution and impurities of material things. This is why, to speak wisely and with precision, there are no grounds to say that the flesh of our saviour is broken and torn in the mouths of those taking communion, nor that the sister who eats the host participates in the body of Jesus Christ; for this participation requires more than a simple presence next to species.

It is the obligation of those who are enlightened on this point to enlighten the ignorant, to prevent them from falling into idolatry by taking as the object of their adoration an object other than the supreme good. And we should not do less with regard to the honour given to the images of Jesus Christ and the cross, as well as to the saints. It is through a figure of speech, or else often through misuse, that one speaks of the adoration of a crucifix, since the wood and the stone can serve only to put us in mind to adore the divinity, and to remember the goodness it showed to us in Jesus Christ. As for the Holy Virgin and other saints that are honoured as well as God's angels, this worship should be infinitely inferior to that which should be given to God, and it should have it in sight to honour God through those things too. One must make use of all reasonable opportunities to emphasize the difference between the Latria that must be given to God, and worship of dulia, that is, the veneration given to created beings which participate in his holiness, and to relics of saints. One should avoid all superstition, levity, avarice and other indecent practices which scandalize not only the Protestants but also enlightened persons among the Roman Catholics, and which contribute greatly to irreligion and atheism, by giving grounds to many persons of substance, albeit ones wearing their faith lightly, to believe that everything is a fable and a legend in our religion, as happens only too often when such things are authorized among the common folk. Those who are able to do so are obliged to oppose this with all their strength. As for the invocation of saints, it commits one only to asking for their intercession, and when one desires the assistance of the saint it should always be inferred that the assistance is only in the form of them praying for us. And the safest thing is to indicate this often, specifically to avoid misunderstandings. Nothing has been decided in the Church about the detail of the saints' knowledge. Yet it is certain that they pray to God on our behalf, that their prayers in the Church triumphant are more precious before God than those of men in the Church militant, to the extent that their holiness is more confirmed, and that often the Church addresses itself to God to pray to him to have regard for the prayers and vows of these blessed spirits who are so dear to him. But confidence in the saints, and affection for them, should always be infinitely inferior to the confidence and affection that we have in an unmediated way with God, and that we have for them only on account of God, as has already been pointed out about worship. And by restricting it in this way, one avoids all risk of idolatry, which is nothing other than giving to created beings what is owed only to God.

8

Grace and Predestination

1. On freedom, fate and God's grace (spring–winter 1686/7 (?))[1]

Manuscript:

M: LH I 6, 2 Bl. 3–6.

Transcription:

A: A VI 4, pp. 1595–614.

The circumstances surrounding the writing of this piece are unknown. However it is one of a clutch of texts dealing with the themes of freedom, predestination and grace that were written in the mid-1680s,[2] suggesting that these issues were ones of great interest or concern to Leibniz at that time. The piece is dated by its watermark.

Of all the questions that are considered after providence has been established, none is more widespread in religions and nations, or has more influence on human life, than that which concerns freedom, fate and God's grace, as well as associated matters: it is debated back and forth everywhere, often with stirred emotions and displays of piety. And it can be treated in two ways: first by starting from first principles and thence deriving conclusions whenever they present themselves, or second, by proposing to oneself the

---

[1] Editor's title. From the Latin. Complete.
[2] See also A VI 4, pp. 1514–24 and 1590–4.

conclusions that religion and practical philosophy command us to hold, and then reconciling them with each other and with the principles of speculative philosophy. Although these methods lead to the same place, the former is more sublime, while the latter is easier and also safer in light of our feebleness.

Therefore, pious and prudent men insist that the *propositions* that follow are to be held and upheld, so far as this is possible.[3]

God is omniscient, and as such no intelligible proposition can be formed of which he does not know for certain whether it is true or false. Accordingly, he knows not only past and present contingents, but also future ones, and not only conditioned ones but also absolute ones, such that it comes as a surprise that Christians and philosophers could have defended or even suspected the contrary about future conditionals.[4]

God preordains all things. For his is not an idle knowledge, nor does anything present itself to his intellect without being an object of his will; he cannot suspend judgement either, because suspension of judgement can arise only from ignorance.

God is the creator of all things. That is to say, there is no real being that is not from God, whether it is produced from nothing or from some preceding thing. Accordingly, whenever some new reality begins to exist in nature, whether it be a substance or an accident, so long as it is really distinct from other things, it should be held that it was produced by God.

God is the conserver of all things. That is to say, not only are things produced by God when they begin to exist, but also they would not continue to exist unless some continuous action of God's towards them were ended, whereby if it ceases, they themselves also cease. Hence creation is in fact nothing other than the beginning of this action. I know that certain learned men call this proposition into doubt, because they think that, if it is granted, divine justice and holiness are endangered. However, I think they will acknowledge that, if this threat could be removed, it is more worthy of God that creatures depend upon the divine operation for their existence not only in the beginning, but continuously. Consequently, I am right to place this proposition among those to be upheld, if possible.

---

[3] possible. | God is omniscient, and cannot form any question or proposition | *deleted*.
[4] conditionals. | *God is omnipotent.* That is to say, God is able to do anything that does not imply contradiction, for in general the notion of possible and impossible consists in this. Consequently, God's power not only extends to those things that have been or will be, but also to those things that can be conceived, at any rate those that can be conceived distinctly and adequately. And in this sense Holy Scripture says that no word is impossible for God, with 'word' obviously meaning 'that which can be perfectly understood'. | *deleted*. Leibniz is referring here to Luke 1.37.

God is supremely just. I understand this not in the same way as those who say that just is what pleases the more powerful, and that omnipotence makes the law for all things; rather I understand it in such a way that, if we were to imagine that God, having laid aside his power, desired to submit himself to the judgement of the most wise (as is said of Mars, who pleaded his cause in the Areopagus)[5] – if indeed it were possible for others besides God to be supremely wise – the pronouncement that would be made by all is that the Lord is just, as are his judgements. Or, to speak of more possible things, if we were to have a sufficient understanding of the divine government, we would acknowledge not only that it is within God's power to make one vessel unto honour and another unto dishonour,[6] but also that he uses each one in the wisest and most fitting way, so that no one who understood the entire harmony of things would have grounds to complain, except perhaps about himself.

God is not the cause of evil or sin. This should be understood in such a way that evil can in no way be attributed to the divine will, even though the physical reality in evil, like all other entities, cannot fail to depend upon God. But this will be explained more distinctly later.

God wills all men to be saved,[7] *and bestows sufficient grace on all.* I know this proposition is denied by certain Christians because they think it cannot be consistent with that divine supereminence and efficacy. But I think they will be unable to deny that their view seems overly harsh and offends many people; consequently, if our position can be defended without detriment to the greatness of God, then of course it is preferable that we uphold it. Effort should be made so that we understand that God is no less the best than the greatest.

In acting, men have freedom not only from coercion, but also from necessity. Consequently, none of God's precepts are ever impossible for a man to observe, nor is the grace whereby the precepts are rendered possible ever lacking.

These are the most important propositions, and it greatly concerns virtue and piety that they be reconciled with each other and with right reason.

---

[5] In Greek mythology, Neptune's son, Halirrhothius, was slain by the god Mars for dishonouring Alcippe, Mars' daughter; at the place where the killing occurred Neptune made Mars stand in judgement before twelve gods. Mars pleaded his case, and was acquitted. The hill where this took place was thereafter known as Areapagus, which literally means 'Mars Hill'. See for example Pausanias, *The Description of Greece*, I.

[6] An allusion to Romans 9.21: 'Hath not the potter power over the clay to make from the same lump one vessel unto honor and another unto dishonor?'

[7] An allusion to 1 Timothy 2.4, in which it is stated that God 'will have all men to be saved'.

Yet upon a closer inspection it seems first of all that 'God is omniscient' is incompatible with 'there are free actions'. For if God infallibly knew in advance that Peter was going to deny Jesus, it was infallible that Peter was going to deny him. But if it was infallible, then assuredly it was necessary. The response to this is that infallibility does not bring about necessity. For Peter was not going to deny because God knew it in advance; instead, God knew it in advance because Peter was going to deny. And since (even leaving aside God's foreknowledge) the truth of future contingents is determinate in itself, to such an extent that it will have been true from eternity that Peter was going to deny, then foreknowledge must leave the truth as it was, namely contingent.

However, someone will retort that a future thing, i.e. one not yet existing, which must be infallibly in conformity with an eternal pre-existing thing, should not be called the cause of that eternal thing, but rather its effect, and on account of the fact that this truth was already determined from eternity it cannot at any rate be contingent. And let us assume the certainty of the truth; now, since at the beginning no Peter yet exists, nor therefore his denial, evidently something already exists beforehand in things outside Peter, from which his denial infallibly follows. This something may be God's foreknowledge or its objective reality, namely that eternal truth itself; the truth certainly is something real, wherever it ultimately subsists, whether in causes, or in the divine intellect, or in the divine will. But whatever infallibly follows from these things which exist long before, that at any rate is necessary.

[The following paragraph was written in small lettering and not deleted, although it looks to be superseded by the two subsequent paragraphs.]

But this should be the response: it is indeed conceded that something exists before the existence of Peter, from which it infallibly follows that Peter is going to deny, and this something is his perfect possible idea or concept, consisting of the objective realities of all the truths about Peter, whether they are necessary ones, flowing from the essence of Peter, or contingent; and that reality of the possible notion of Peter subsists in God from eternity. But it is not for that reason conceded that Peter's denial is necessary; for we define 'necessary' as that of which the opposite implies contradiction. But now, something following infallibly from what has been posited, and hence being hypothetically necessary, is entirely different from demonstrating something – without any supposition of existing things – solely from the necessity of essences or from terms or ideas, such that its contrary implies contradiction. But you will insist that Peter's denial, or another such thing, follows from the divine essence, for God foresees all future things by the power of his own essence, and knowledge (whether called knowledge of vision or middle knowledge) seems to be essential to God, not only knowledge in general, but also knowledge of any foreseen truth in particular. My response is that it is indeed essential to God that he foresee any truth whatsoever, or that he be able to resolve any question, but it is not essential to him that he resolve it by affirming or denying; it is indeed essential to him that he resolve it truthfully, but since the truth itself is not essential here, for that reason neither will the resolution be essential to him. But you will further insist, since that objective truth to which the resolution conforms can have no other foundation of its reality than God himself, seeing that no other substance aside from God exists from eternity, what ultimately is the source of that resolution of the question if not the divine essence? Here, it seems to many learned and pious men that one must necessarily have recourse to that one thing that is not essential in God but free, namely a decree of the will, in which alone the principle of contingency in things can be sought.[8]

Here one of two things must be said, either that the objective reality of divine knowledge or of the truth of future contingents (absolute or conditional) is essential to God, or that this reality depends upon some free decree of God. For since this reality is nowhere else than in God, I think there cannot be a third alternative. For example, the eternal objective reality of the truth that the inhabitants of Keilah were, if besieged, going to hand David over to Saul,[9] either depends or does not depend upon the hypothesis, i.e. upon the truth (that is likewise conditional) of some antecedent or of a divine decree implicit in that reality, a decree regarding what must be concurred with proximately or remotely, i.e. a decree regarding other things that must be presupposed for this choice to be made by Keilah's inhabitants. If the reality of the truth does not depend upon such a hypothesis

---

[8] sought. | (α) For I do not see in God anything else concerning the matter except intellect and will, but if from the divine intellect alone this truth should follow, that Peter is going to deny, but the objects of the divine intellect are not existing (β) Consequently it should be said that contingent truths result from a certain combination of God's intellect and will, and hence are not rendered necessary; | *deleted.*
[9] Leibniz is referring here to events recorded in 1 Samuel 23.7-13: after having helped to save the city of Keilah from the Philistines, David asked God if the inhabitants of Keilah would deliver him and his men into the hands of Saul, who was planning to besiege the city, if he chose to stay there. God replied to David that the inhabitants would indeed do so, and to avoid this fate David left the city.

of a decree, or if it does indeed depend upon it but that decree ultimately supposes another future conditional contingent that does not depend upon any further decree, it must be said that the reality of this truth is indeed essential to God, and yet that the contingent object itself remains free, i.e. that the contingency of some truth can be essential to God. That is, unless someone prefers to appeal to a progression to infinity, by always founding other decrees in other conditional truths, and these in turn in decrees. But if it is not possible to say such things, and a progression to infinity in these suppositions seems absurd, then it is not possible to maintain that contingency is essential either, and it does not seem possible to establish in creatures anything positive, even hypothetically, that does not involve some supposition of a free divine choice and action. Consequently, having put these things out of our mind, what remains is to appeal to that one thing that is not essential in God, but free, namely a decree of the will, in which alone a principle of contingency in things can be sought. Moreover, it would have to be said that contingent truths result from a certain combination of power, understanding and divine will, and hence are not rendered necessary even though they subsist constantly from eternity and do not have any other foundation of their reality besides God.

But here I seem to discern some subtle philosopher pushing further like this: God decrees nothing without an accurate knowledge, and knows most perfectly, even before he decrees that this Peter (who later denied) should exist, what is going to become of Peter if he exists; or – what is the same thing – since God has in his understanding a most perfect concept or idea of Peter as a possible thing; and since this concept or idea contains all the truths about Peter, and the objective reality of these truths constitutes the whole nature or essence of Peter, therefore it is essential to Peter to deny and to God to foreknow this. The response to this should be that in this complete concept of possible Peter that appears to God, there are contained – I admit – not only essential or necessary truths (which of course flow from incomplete or specific concepts, and as such are demonstrated from terms, in such a way that the contrary implies a contradiction), but also so to speak existential or contingent truths. This is because it is of the nature of an individual substance that its concept is perfect and complete, and contains all the individual and contingent circumstances down to the most trifling, otherwise, it would not be complete, nor would it be distinguished from any other; for those things differing even in the smallest detail would be distinct individuals, and a concept that is still indeterminate in the smallest details will not be complete, but could be common to two different individuals. Yet these individuals are not for that reason necessary, nor do they depend upon the divine intellect alone, but also upon decrees of the divine will insofar as the decrees themselves, considered as possible, are contemplated by the divine understanding. For different possible individuals belong to different possible orders or series of things, and any series of possible individuals depends not only upon the specific concepts that enter into it, but also upon certain free decrees, by which the fundamental order and, so to speak, laws of that series are constituted. And so there remains what I have said, namely that, according to this explanation, contingent things depend not only upon essences but also upon God's free decrees, and as such there is no necessity in them except, in a certain way, hypothetical necessity.

But here, by the very fact that the matter is referred back to the divine will, we become entangled in another difficulty, which concerns *divine preordination or fate*. And when human freedom is defended, divine holiness seems to be abandoned. For certainly God determines all questions, even those that are absolutely necessary, merely by understanding them, i.e. by contemplating the ideas of his intellect; but with contingent things, he seems always to exercise his will by joining it to the contemplation itself, so that one or the other of opposed contingent things can prevail, and he never considers them idly. Consequently, no contingent actuality is presented to his will about which he does not decree whether it should or should not exist. For this reason he will even decree that sin should exist, and doubtless he makes the sort of decrees from which – if coupled with the essences of things – actuality infallibly follows.[10]

---

[10] follows. | And as such – and this rightly shakes us – God will be the author of sin, not man, who does not yet exist and cannot at any time fail to follow an eternal decree of God. These are difficult matters, I admit, though with God's help we do not despair of overcoming them. It should be acknowledged, then, that the eternal truth of some contingent thing can have no other reality than that which flows partly from the divine intellect and partly from the divine will; likewise, that God makes decrees about all future contingents, even the sinful ones, and although he does not want or decree that sin exist, he does decree that sin be permitted, and as such he is not the author of sin. However, you will say, since the whole series of future things proceeds from the divine decrees, and no man yet exists, and yet from these things that God now decrees it follows by an infallible consequence that a man will choose something bad, why do we ascribe the action to the man rather than to God? It is possible to respond, first, from the things granted and those defined a little earlier, that human freedom is not destroyed by foreknowledge, nor therefore by a decree. But you will insist that even if human freedom is not destroyed, what is destroyed is divine justice, which makes us use our freedom badly. Authors respond to this in various ways. Most are content to say that God is purely permissive concerning the act of sin. This is correct, but it does not seem sufficient to opponents, seeing that the act follows infallibly from God's permission, from which it seems just the same, in truth, whether God is said to permit sin or to will it. I answer that it does amount to the same thing insofar as it concerns the certainty of a future sin, but not insofar as it concerns

From which, it seems, two things can be inferred: first, that men are not free when all their acts are predefined either by the essence or by the will of another, and second, that God wills evils and is the author of sin. The response to the first is easy given what has been said above, for freedom is no more destroyed by a decree than by foreknowledge, for while it is foreseen, nevertheless it is also foreseen together with a choice, or it is decreed that the man is going to choose freely, i.e. in such a way that indifference is preserved, or, if you will, that no absolute necessity is imposed. And although prevision is in turn grounded in God's essence or will, nevertheless it was explained earlier how it must be said that contingency – i.e. the possibility of the contrary – remains, so there is no new difficulty here. The second inference is more difficult. For even if man were free and therefore blameworthy, God is no less blameworthy, and in fact he is more so since he makes us use our freedom badly, and as such he would be a voluntary cause of evil. At any rate it seems that that hypothetical necessity is sufficient to excuse man; for it may be supposed that what a man is going to do follows from divine decrees, or from the realities (pre-existing from eternity) of future contingents, or from the essence of some man, or God, or the universe (just as the properties of a circle follow from its nature); but in each case it seems to make no difference in practice, and mortal beings seem likewise bound fast to sin. However the response to this second difficulty will be given below, when we come to the sophism called 'lazy' by the ancients. Now as for the causality of God, it should be said that God does not bring about evils, or will them, but that he only permits them; this will be more clearly understood from what follows. Now it will be worthwhile to maintain that God does not decree that Peter sin, but rather that from an infinite number of possible creatures he chooses Peter, on account of secret causes of his wisdom. There is contained in the possible concept of Peter, i.e. in the most perfect knowledge God has of him before he decrees Peter's existence, the truth that if he should exist, he will freely sin; in other

---

God's blame. You will insist: why, then, does he permit what he can prevent? Here I do not see a better response than the one given by St Augustine, that God would not permit evil unless he could also make a good out of evil. Therefore, you will say, God wills my sin so that he can elicit a greater good from it. I answer that this is not to will but to permit, or, if you prefer, to will to permit. For God does not will to sin, he does not will to produce sin, but he wills that you exist, i.e. you whom he knows will sin, because he knows how to transform your sin into something better. Therefore what we should say is what Hugo of St Victor already observed, that strictly speaking, God does not decree | *deleted*. Leibniz is thinking here of St Augustine's *Enchiridion ad Laurentium liber unus*, I.100: 'But a good being would not permit evil to be done, unless in its omnipotence it can make a good from the evil.'

words, out of an infinite number of ways of creating the world, i.e. from an infinite number of his own possible decrees, God chooses those connected with that series of possible things containing the Peter-who-is-freely-going-to-sin. Consequently, in the actual decree, God really only bestows existence on the possible Peter-who-is-going-to-sin, and as such he does not decree that Peter sin, but only that possible Peter be admitted to existence, despite the fact that he is going to sin. But he who is not going to sin (albeit freely) would not even be this Peter; in the same way, when Hugo of St Victor asked 'why would God have loved Jacob but hated Esau?', he responded that no answer can be given for this other than: 'why is Jacob not Esau?'[11] And that is most true.

But here in turn a third difficulty arises. For suppose that freedom is not destroyed by foreknowledge or even by the determinate truth of contingents; likewise, suppose that, from the fact that God decrees the existence of that series of things containing sin, it does not follow that he directly wills or decrees sin. Now even if we grant these things, having assumed *God's concurrence with creatures in all of their actions*, it follows that God acts in the sin no less – and indeed more – than does the man who sins, and hence, sin should be imputed to God no less than to man. I know that some learned men inveigh most solemnly against the doctrine of God's proximate and immediate concurrence with all the actions of creatures, claiming that it is very dangerous and contrary to divine holiness. But in turn they are overwhelmed by the strongest arguments taken from the dependency of creatures, for in action, motion and thought there is not a simple modality or relation; rather, some new reality is superadded, for there is a real difference between a thing that acts and a thing that doesn't. The question is: where does this new reality come from? Certainly it was not present beforehand, and for that reason obviously it was produced, but for new real beings to be produced without God's concurrence does not seem to be fitting for creatures, or worthy of God. And in any case, who believes that while substances cannot be produced except by God, accidents can be produced without God's concurrence and as such are more independent? And to say that this new accident is produced from a preceding one is to

---

[11] 'The question is: why was Jacob not younger and Esau older, so that in this way Esau would be chosen? The solution: this is to ask why Jacob is not Esau, and vice versa, and therefore it is a meaningless question.' Hugo of St Victor, *Quaestiones et decisiones in epistolas divini Pauli*, in *Patrologia Latina*, ed. J. P. Migne (Paris, 1862–5), 175: p. 490B (qu. 237). The question is based on Malachi 1.2-3, in which God states that he loves Jacob but hates Esau.

say nothing, for in fact the prior accident no longer exists, and a new one exists in its place; the rest is just words, like the eduction of forms from the potency of matter. And with equal justification someone may say that even new substances are produced from other substances without God's concurrence, and ultimately the point will be reached where, once creatures have been granted the means of acting, it can be said that God does not now act at all (except perhaps by performing miracles). And with those who suppose that a world existing from eternity does not imply contradiction, it will follow that God's not existing doesn't imply contradiction either; accordingly I fear that this opinion conflicts with the nature of the first being, since it may even be inferred from it that the world can subsist for however many thousands of years hereafter without needing anything further from God. And with this, most of the stronger arguments for God's existence collapse. For if the world now has no real dependence upon God, it cannot be demonstrated that the world is in God unless it were first demonstrated that the world had a beginning, which even many Christian philosophers doubt can be demonstrated from the light of reason. Moreover, from the beauty of things alone it is indeed very probable that the world was constructed by a most wise architect, though one cannot infer this with necessity, for metaphysically speaking it would be possible for there to be an infinite number of worlds or systems of things in infinite time and space, and it would not be surprising if, among an infinite number that were assembled by chance, some turned out beautiful and well-ordered, of which one by chance has fallen to our lot. Of course this means of escape was used by the Epicureans a long time ago. But in truth, the argument drawn from the nature of the primitive being, upon which derivative beings continuously depend, requires neither the rejection of a progression to infinity (which many think possible), nor the beauty of things, which produces a moral faith more than certain knowledge.

But how shall we respond to that great difficulty, that God is at any rate a concomitant cause of sin no less than man – and indeed more so – if he concurs with all that is real in sin? For it seems like a joke to say that God concurs with the material aspect of sin but not with the formal aspect, which is a privation, i.e. ἀνομία.[12] But it should be noted that this response is more solid than it seems at first sight, for all depravity is in the imperfection, all imperfection in the limitation. Therefore, with God and man

---

[12] 'absence of righteousness'.

coacting,[13] the action is perfect in God and limited or imperfect in man, and this imperfection is sometimes so great that it constitutes the reason for sin; consequently, it is obvious why the formal aspect of sin belongs only to the action of man. We shall be able to clarify the matter with an example. Suppose I throw a little feather with great force, and that my action is very perfect; even so, the action of the little feather that arose from the throwing will be very much imperfect and weak, because the limitation proceeds from its own nature, which is not capable of rapid motion. In the same way, then, the essential limitation of creatures diminishes the effect of the divine concurrence that extends to the perfection of the act, and sometimes corrupts its effect, but with God nonetheless obtaining the perfection of the whole from imperfect parts, in accordance with his supreme wisdom. On account of this, it is no longer surprising that sin arises without any blame attaching to God. The foundations of this admirable thought are found to have been established already by St Augustine. In the end, we should bear in mind that for God, who sees the consequences of all things, it is the same (morally speaking) whether he assists sin by a remote concurrence or a proximate one, since he bestows faculties and coordinates all circumstances in such a way that sin will infallibly follow. Therefore we gain nothing by denying the immediate concurrence of God, and in making such a denial we side with the imagination of the common man more than inner reason. For a difficulty always remains, that either sins are absolutely necessary or at any rate that they follow necessarily, whether from certain eternal realities independent of the divine will (if indeed it is possible for contingency to have a place in such realities) or from the decrees of the divine will that are added to necessary truths. In each case men are freed from blame, and the second seems also to accuse God.

The preceding difficulties, then, were metaphysical, and now at last we turn to the moral difficulties, which will occupy us in what follows. For from the fact that God preordains sins, or at least foreknows them, and assists their performance by means of a remote or proximate concurrence, it seems to follow that man, whether he is free or not, is either not culpable or, if he is culpable, is certainly not to be punished by God, who is himself much more culpable. Let us imagine that there can be some poison of such a nature that, when a man drinks it, it corrupts his will and inclines it (all the while with it remaining free) to evil, in such a way that it can be foreseen

---

[13] That is, acting together. In Leibniz's view, this is the case with every action performed by man, since all require God's concurrence.

that very often the man will choose evil even though he deliberates freely. Let us concede that this man nevertheless deserves punishment. But what shall we say is deserved by the one who mixed up the poison and gave it to the man to drink? Especially if he is a legislator, and has become so tyrannical that he desires to torment the wretch in the cruellest way on account of his evil will, as though the man were disobeying him? Now this seems to be how things look with regard to human nature, for what better comparison can there be than to a poison for that corrupt disposition we call original sin? And since souls are actually produced by God as soon as they begin to exist (whether someone calls this creation or traduction), who does not see that God either produces the soul with the corrupt disposition, or plunges it, as it were, into the abyss of a corrupt disposition? (It does not much matter which of the two we assert.) And there is no less a difficulty with regard to Adam himself, for no matter what is said about original justice, it seems that a corrupt disposition was created in him, which would ensure that he would be presented with a specific temptation, that he would succumb to it and thereafter be wickedly inclined. Now let us imagine that the same someone who gave him the poison now offers up an antidote (just like sufficient grace), but by virtue of the very disposition of the poison he knows that no one will even try to make use of it unless their soul has been prepared by him first pouring a few drops of some potent liquid (or virtuous inclination) into their mouths while they are sleeping. He also knows that, of those who will use it, there may be no one who will be restored to health unless they have some specific natural constitution, or he has poured into them a sufficient quantity of some third liquid, which is the most potent of all and infallibly potent if it is added to the curative mixture (or efficacious grace). He knows too that those who are cured very often suffer a relapse and need the same rites in order to be cured once again; and that few are considered worthy of an absolutely final curing (grace of perseverance). And finally, he knows that when men were chosen, account was taken either of some absolute pleasure or of very unusual distinctions: like for example, grace is rather given to those who seem that they will cooperate by their own nature once they are aroused, as if to spare the cure and expense as much as possible; or sometimes, conversely, grace is rather given to those who are most weak in themselves, as if to show the efficacy of the cure, and sometimes grace is given in other ways, so that either no specific rule is observed or, if there is a rule, it seems scarcely equitable. This is because it would be more fitting that he who has bestowed evil upon all either restore all (since that can indeed happen), or certainly that those who are not freed from the corruption of the soul at least not be punished; certainly it is not possible to think of anything harsher than their being thrown to the most cruel tormentors for all eternity. What, then, shall we say of such a poisoner, doctor and legislator?

When I consider this comparison carefully, it straightway seems that the initial part of it should be denied, namely that the legislator took the trouble to make that poison which has corrupted souls, for the first origin of imperfection is not from the will of God, but from an essential limitation of creatures before all sin. It should also be denied that the doctor and the same legislator have only unusual reasons for distinguishing those who will be cured from those who will not; instead, it is to be said that he conducts himself so that he cannot do better without violating his own wisdom. Consequently, I have thought of a more suitable analogy, which shows at the same time the justice of the legislator, the wisdom of the doctor and the guilt of the sick. Let us imagine, then, a story of this kind: when Deucalion and Pyrrha threw stones behind their backs by order of the oracle, what immediately arose as a result was not men, as the poets tell us,[14] but rather statues with human form. And when Deucalion consulted the oracle again, the response was that the gods had given him the power to bring to life which of the statues he wished, though he could only choose those ones which together were affected by the same mode of song. Consequently it was for him to decide which chorus of statues he wanted to be granted human life. Deucalion commanded the Lydian mode be sung. And immediately a number of statues stirred themselves, and when Deucalion's lyre fell silent again, they danced to music of their own making, and through song they described everything they would do if it befell them to be made human, so as to encourage Deucalion to choose them. The Phrygian mode came next, and other statues danced and similarly related their own future lives if it were granted them to live. Soon a third chorus followed, and a fourth, and a good many others, until all the statues had danced, for no statue belonged to more than one chorus.[15]

---

[14] Leibniz now proceeds to reimagine a story concerning the repopulation of the world by Deucalion and his wife Pyrrha, who in Greek mythology were held to be the only two human survivors of the great flood. After the waters receded, they were told by the goddess Themis to throw stones behind their backs; when they did so, the stones changed into human form, and thus the world was repopulated. The original story is to be found in Ovid, *Metamorpheses*, I.324–431.

[15] chorus. | But it was memorable that as each chorus danced there appeared to Deucalion a sort of musical tablet (a different one always appeared when the chorus changed), which served as a director of its chorus; it was partly inscribed with diamond notes by the hand of the Fates and partly inscribed with notes of gold by the very finger of Jupiter. And from the Fates indeed there were certain necessary and immutable properties of harmonic numbers, but Jupiter seemed to have

One chorus was promising a most innocent world, but dull in its simplicity; some choruses were going to give great examples of strength, others great examples of genius and still others great examples of other virtues. But in any chorus whatsoever there was always something you would find lacking, and which you would desire to supply from other choruses, if the oracle had given permission for that. There was one of these choruses in which great evils were foretold: a corruption of this whole human race by a certain poisonous food, and from that the dinner of Thyestes,[16] the sexual transgression of Oedipus,[17] the punishments of Ixion and Tantalus in the underworld.[18] But these were compensated by much greater goods, namely the descent to Earth of supreme Jupiter himself out of mercy for human affairs, and his life in human form, all mortal sins expiated by him, from which would come a golden age and eternal peace, and the greatest assimilation of the blessed with the gods as is possible.[19]

So after much deliberation the two spouses unanimously chose this chorus, which was promising such things, chiefly because mortals were seen to be enjoying the fellowship of the gods. Suddenly all the remaining statues, as if indignant, burst apart into stones again similar to their earlier form. But those that had been chosen out of the whole number, those who had been victorious in that vote, straightaway they had human nature. Thereafter the race of mortals was propagated over the entire Earth and the losses of the flood put right. And Deucalion, having discharged his duty so admirably, was indeed seen as the restorer of our race, and he lived a happy life on Earth until he and his wife, worn out by the years, were freed on the same final day. And they had already crossed the inexorable Styx in Charon's skiff, had gone straight ahead and then turned to those Elysian

---

chosen the key and other (albeit few) arbitrary principles of the song. But from the noble gold of Jupiter and the invincible gems of the fates there suddenly appeared a wonderful splendour, in which, as if in a mirror, were represented the future of that chorus and the entire outline of human affairs that would be produced if that chorus were chosen. These things that were seen and heard no less terrified Deucalion and his wife than made them confused regarding their choice, on account of the variety of outcomes that had been so wonderfully arranged. | *deleted*.

[16] In Greek mythology, Thyestes unwittingly ate his own sons after they were killed and served at a banquet by his brother, Atreus. See, for instance, Seneca, *Thyestes*, 703–1034.

[17] In Greek mythology, Oedipus unwittingly married his mother, and so committed incest. See Sophocles, *Oedipus the King*.

[18] Tantalus was condemned by Zeus to eternal hunger and thirst; he was stood up to his chin in a lake which receded whenever he tried to take a drink; above him were the branches of fruit trees, which were blown out of his reach by the wind every time he tried to take a fruit. See for example Homer, *Odyssey*, XI.794–805.

[19] Leibniz is here of course treating Jupiter as an analogue of Jesus, who in Christian tradition is said to have been sent to expiate the sins of all mankind.

gardens in which blessed souls get a foretaste of heavenly goods, when there was a great uproar in the whole court of the underworld. You would think that the ground had been opened up with cracks by the tremors of Enceladus,[20] and ruinous daylight admitted into the underworld; or that he again was present who leads Proserpina to the bedchamber of Dis, and drags away Cerberus shackled in chains.[21] The vulture of Tityos stops;[22] and the wheel of Ixion for a while ceases spinning.[23] Eventually, when there was silence, it was understood that the wretched souls were complaining of Pyrrha and Deucalion as the authors of all their ills, and demanding their punishment. They were saying that, by a cruel favour, these two transformed them from a stony nature to a human nature in order to torture them forever, and it seemed that only the punishment of this pair would calm them. Pluto referred so great a question to the triumvirate responsible for capital crimes, namely Aeacus, Minos and Rhadamanthus. The couple, dismayed by so great and so unexpected a danger, looked at each other with tears, and called as witnesses the authors of the oracle, the gods, and especially holy Themis, whose orders they had followed, and in this matter they cited the testimony of Ovid and I know not which Greek writer of the *Metamorphoses*. Deucalion could scarcely be heard saying these few things over and over and was immediately drowned out by the confused shouts of all when he threw back his own crime onto the gods, who indeed had given him the power of choosing, though they had not prescribed his choice.

With the judges in an awkward situation, and wanting to adjourn the trial, if it were possible, there arrived as legates Lycurgus and Solon (the former renowned for his justice, the latter for his wisdom), who had been sent by the souls of Elysium.[24] For as news of the trial had been conveyed

---

[20] After having been injured by a spear in his side, Enceladus was said to be buried underneath Mount Etna. And when he shifts onto his wounded side, his groaning causes a tremor throughout the whole of Sicily. See Virgil, *Aeneid*, III, 750–7.
[21] In Greek mythology Proserpina's abductor was Pluto, the god of the underworld; Dis was his Roman equivalent. See Claudian, *De raptu Proserpinae*.
[22] The giant Tityos was cast into the underworld for assaulting a goddess, and condemned to have two vultures feeding upon his ever-regenerating liver for all eternity. See for example Homer, *Odyssey*, XI.705ff.
[23] Ixion attempted to seduce Zeus's wife, and as punishment was bound to a fiery wheel which rolled forever through the underworld. See for example Pindar, *Pythian Odes*, 2.22ff.
[24] In the Homeric tradition, Elysium (also known as the Elysian Fields) was the abode of the heroic and virtuous. It was situated in the distant west, at the edge of the world. In later tradition, as well as in Virgil, the Elysium was considered to be part of the underworld and a pleasant resting place for the righteous dead.

to the blessed, it seemed unworthy that the memory of evil things should be livelier than the gratitude for good ones. Here there arose a new and extraordinary battle between the pious and impious, between vices and virtues, some part of which our Prudentius described in his *Psychomachia*,[25] though where he got it from I do not know. But at any rate the entire question before the judges turned on this point, whether it was better that the wicked and wretched not exist, or indeed that the blessed exist, and whether it was of greater consequence that evils be avoided or goods be procured. How many things were said by men of the utmost eloquence and prudence on behalf of each side cannot be expressed in a few words, and perhaps others will explain it more successfully. At last, following a request from Pluto via Mercury, Jupiter sent from the Zodiac itself Themis's starry scales, on which was placed the fates of each side, for the judges themselves, although leaning towards the blessed, were afraid to pronounce in case they might be seen to have favoured them. And it is the wonderful nature of these scales, wherein not corporeal weights but the weight of cases is assessed, in such a way that words take the place of matter, and just through the arguments that are given the scales incline according to the force of each. And with everyone frozen in an incredible state of suspense, the clerk read out the arguments of each side, the scales tipping now this way, then that, as though trembling. On one side it was said that if pleasure is equal to pain, it is better not to feel pain than to feel pleasure; the other side responded that in a musical piece it is better to have dissonances that are artfully corrected and compensated than an insipid uniformity of sound. To this it was replied that a mixture of disorder and restoration could be excused in one and the same person, but not scattered around so that good things fell to some and bad things to others. To compound the point, it was said that both wretchedness and blessedness could not have been mixed in one and the same person. While thirdly, it was said that there could have been enough variety[26] even if one had not gone to these extremes of goods and evils. And thus did the argument go back and forth in many different ways, until at last it was urged that the happiness of the elect was not just any kind of happiness, but the one where gods were united with mortals, in light of which the amount of suffering of each person is of no importance. And it was after having been moved by this argument that Deucalion gave

---

[25] Prudentius's poem *Psychomachia* (fifth century CE) described a battle between seven virtues and seven vices, with the virtues victorious in each.
[26] Leibniz wrote in the margin here: 'it is ridiculous that there could'.

preference to this series for humankind. Hardly had these things been proclaimed when suddenly the scales began to descend on one side, as though a great weight had been placed in that pan, nor was it moved even in the least by any of the things that were said after that. Thus acquitted by the indubitable vote of Themis, Deucalion and Pyrrha fulfilled vows to the gods. But there arose in the whole of the underworld a roar of the wretched souls, as though they were being damned now for the first time, and it was impossible to hear the dark blasphemies made against the gods, for whose greatness and pleasure or glory the eternal misfortune of the wretched was sacrificed, whereby the gods' blessedness would become more conspicuous to them and be more keenly felt by the existence of its opposite. For besides those series of men – from which, it will have to be admitted that Deucalion chose the best – the gods had it in their power to present to him other series in which mortals were made no less happy, and in fact were made more happy, without the wretchedness of anyone polluting the joys of the blessed. So with these complaints directed at the gods, the rage of the impious burned more strongly, but in Elysium an astonishing and novel spectacle presented itself to those who were delighted by these goods and astounded by the magnitude of the question raised, as the images of all the statues that had danced before Deucalion appeared again. But hanging above each chorus was a golden tablet on which the laws written in the eternal adamant of the fates were preserved. These laws, which were few in number where the greatest of the gods had fastened a golden key with his own hand, were determining in advance all the future motions and actions of the chorus; and the wonderful power of the connection and consequence of so many of a song's events with so few musical notes (in which the whole lay concealed, impenetrable to mortals while they pass their lives on Earth) was manifestly apparent to those purified souls. At last, to the minds carried off into the depths of the divinity, the very Archive of Eternal Reason presented itself in the place they had been admitted, and there appeared the infinite (albeit complete) number of tablets, or all the choruses that could be thought about, that is, of possible worlds, and finally the light of the unapproachable dwelling illuminated the ultramundane.[27] At this point, the indescribable harmony (not only of those things which had been and are going to be, but also of all the things that could be) was understood in such a way that, with the infinite worlds weighed, as it were, in scales, now at last

---

[27] Leibniz is probably alluding here to 1 Timothy 6.16, which describes God as dwelling in unapproachable light.

it would be recognized that the eternal and infinite wisdom itself could not have found anything better than what was done. And for that reason, once the best and most choiceworthy series of things had been posited, the evil and the wretched are not chosen but rather permitted, because they follow from its laws. Nor in the deliberation of providence was it asked whether Busiris should sacrifice his visitors,[28] but whether this series of possible things should be preferred even though the murderer Busiris would be contained in it. And once the happy souls had been admitted to these secrets, having understood the heights of things, and with the beauty and justice of their author acknowledged to be near at hand, now at last they confessed themselves clearly blessed. And for us it is remarkable enough to acknowledge from faraway in this life what in that place will appear before our own eyes, among the highest benefits of eternity.

---

[28] Busiris, a king of Egypt, was advised by an oracle to sacrifice visitors to the country to Zeus. He was eventually slain by Hercules. See Apollodorus, *The Library*, V.2, and Ovid, *Metamorphoses*, IX.205–6.

9

Sin, Evil and Theodicy

1. The author of sin (1673 (?))[1]

Manuscript:

M: LH I 3, 5 Bl. 25.

Transcription:

A: A VI 3, pp. 150–1.

This piece takes up a topic (whether God can be considered the author of sin) that Leibniz discussed in two of his early writings, namely 'Von der Allmacht und Allwissenheit Gottes und der Freiheit des Menschen' (1670–1 (?))[2] and 'Confessio philosophi' (autumn 1672–winter 1672/3).[3] This piece is therefore likely to be from the same period. Leibniz indicates on the manuscript that it is part of a larger work, but this has not been discovered.

Regarding this great question *of the author of sin*, it is commonly believed that one can sidestep the difficulty by saying that sin, in its essence, is merely a pure privation without any reality, and that God is not the author of privations.[4] For indeed, people have introduced that famous distinction between the physical and moral aspects of sin, which is misused somewhat although it is good in itself.

---

[1] Editor's title. From the French. Complete.
[2] A VI 1, pp. 537–46/CP, pp. 5–27.
[3] A VI 3, pp. 116–49/CP, pp. 27–109.
[4] See for example Aquinas, *Summa Theologiae*, Ia–IIae Q79, art. 2, ad 2.

The physical or real aspect of theft, for example, is the object or booty that arouses the thief's feeling of need, the visual rays that strike his eyes and go into the depths of his soul; the imaginings, the anxieties and the deliberations that occur there, and which ultimately terminate in the resolution, which is to take advantage of the opportunity and commit the crime.

One would not be able to deny that all this is reality, and one would even have to acknowledge that the final determination of the will, after having been in balance for a long time, and after it has examined all the circumstances, is a real act, which is in the category of action, as is thought and movement: and nevertheless this final determination is that which makes us criminals.

Therefore where is the moral part of the sin about which people speak so much? It will perhaps be said that it consists in anomie, as Holy Scripture calls it,[5] i.e. in the lack of accord between the act and the law, which is a pure privation. I agree with that, but I do not see what it contributes to the clarification of our question. For to say that God can be called the author of all that is real and positive in the sin, and yet is not the author of sin because he is not the author of a privation, is a manifest illusion; it is a remnant of the visionary philosophy of times past; it is an equivocation which no reasonable man would allow himself to accept. I shall make this clear with an example. An artist produces two paintings, one of which is large in order to serve as a model for a tapestry, while the other is only a miniature. Let us take the miniature one and say that there are two things to consider in it: firstly, its positive and real aspect, which consists of the board, the background, the colours and the brush-strokes; and secondly, its privative aspect, which is the disproportion to the large painting, or its smallness. It would therefore be absurd to say that the artist is the author of all that is real in the two paintings, without also being the author of the privative, or of the disproportion between the large one and the small one. For by the same reason, or rather by a stronger reason, one could say that an artist can be the author of a copy, or of a portrait, without being the author of the disproportion between the copy and the original, i.e. without being the author of this flaw. For in fact the privative is nothing other than a simple result or infallible consequence of the positive, and does not require a separate author. I am surprised that these people do not go any further and try to persuade us that man himself is not the author of sin, because he is

---

[5] 'ἀνομία', that is, anomia: literally 'without law' but usually translated as 'iniquity' or 'unrighteousness'. See for example 1 John 3.4, and Hebrews 8.12.

only the author of the physical or real aspect, the privation being something for which there is no author.

I conclude from what I have just said that those who say that God is the author of all that is real or positive in the sin, and who admit that God is the author of the law, and who nevertheless deny that God is the author of what results from those two things, that is, the lack of accord between the law and the positive aspect of sin, are not far from Calvin in the way they speak, and that they make God the author of the sin without saying it, although they protest that they do the opposite.

2. On the goodness of God's works (autumn 1684 (?))[6]

Manuscript:

M: LH IV 8 Bl. 90.

Transcription:

A: A VI 4, p. 1514.

The provenance of this piece is unknown. Its dating is based on the watermark of the paper.

This great being who thinks about everything so perfectly, his thoughts being unobstructed, and who also produces everything according to his thought, makes things as he wants, that is, according to whether he finds them good.

It will be objected to me that he made what he found good for himself, but not perhaps for us. I respond that he would hardly be perfect or able if he did not also produce all the good for his works. And I believe that without that they could not be good for him, or, what is the same thing, they would not be good enough. For what would also be good for them, would be best, absolutely speaking.

---

[6] Editor's title. From the French. Complete.

3. Genuine dialogue (25 January 1695)[7]

Manuscript:

M: LBr 208 Bl. 1–4

Transcription:

A: A II 3, pp. 9–17

The following piece is Leibniz's record of an actual discussion he had with Baron Friedrich Boguslaus Dobrzensky (?–1704), counsellor of state and war in Brandenburg. On 26 January 1695, a day after the discussion took place, Leibniz sent a copy of the dialogue to Dobrzensky along with a covering letter which reads: 'I told you yesterday, Sir, that according to the ancients every sin punishes itself. Do you want a proof of this? Well your curiosity is punished by my incommensurables, which follow you to your doorstep since I got it into my head to put our discussion into writing. However, you have the advantage of being able to free yourself from this inconvenience, since you are the absolute master of it, and it is up to you not to read it or to have it read, and it will be as if it hadn't happened.'[8] In the following dialogue, the 'A' character represents Dobrzensky, the 'B' character Leibniz.

Genuine dialogue   25 January 1695

A.   – I am often burdened by the thought that sin seems to me to be necessary and inevitable. Fine things are said on this matter, to which I could not reply very well, though ultimately they do not satisfy me, and afterwards soon fade away.
B.   – These things require deep meditation, and if one does not give the necessary attention to them, one cannot be sufficiently content with them.
A.   – Father Sperandio in Munich advised me not to apply myself to the matter at all. One day I put forward my doubts to him, and he replied

---

[7] Author's title. From the French. Complete.
[8] A II 3, p. 18.

very eloquently and in a very plausible way which reduced me to silence. After he finished, he asked me if what he had said seemed right to me or not. I said Yes, and he replied 'Well Sir, content yourself with this for now, and to have peace of mind do not think about this matter any more.' It is true that I have not been able to heed his advice.

B. – It would be very easy for a mediocre mind to follow this Father's advice, but not a person of your penetration. I admit that one does not need to burden oneself with these subtle questions, and I do not advise anyone to get involved with them. I say only that when someone has had enough application to raise these difficulties, he must also have enough to go deeper into their solutions. And as for Father Sperandio's advice, I do not agree with it. Good and solid answers are of such a nature that, the more they are thought about, the more solid they should appear; and it is characteristic of evasions that one should consider them as little as possible if one wants to be content with them.

A. – Then I will tell you what bothers me. We all agree that God knows all things and that the future is present to him just like the past. Right now I cannot move my arm without his having foreseen it from all eternity. He knows whether I will commit a murder, a crime or some other sin. And consequently, as his foresight is infallible, it is inevitable that I will commit the sin he has foreseen. It is therefore necessary that I will sin, and it is not within my power to refrain from it. Thus I am not free.

B. – It must be admitted, Sir, that we are not absolutely free; only God is, since he alone is independent. Our freedom is limited in many ways: I am not free to fly like an eagle or to swim like a dolphin, because my body lacks the necessary means. Something similar can be said about our mind. Sometimes we admit that we have not had a free mind. And strictly speaking we never have a perfect freedom of mind. But that does not prevent us from having a certain degree of freedom that beasts lack, since we have the faculty for reasoning and for choosing according to how things appear to us. And as for divine foreknowledge, God foresees things as they are, and does not change their nature. Events that are fortuitous and contingent in themselves remain so, notwithstanding the fact that God has foreseen them. Thus they are assured, but they are not necessary.

A. – Assured or inevitable – aren't they more or less the same thing?

B. – There is a difference: it is necessary that three times three is nine, and this does not depend upon any condition. God himself cannot prevent it. But a future sin can be prevented, if the man does his duty, even though God foresees that he will not. This sin is necessary because God has foreseen it, and if God has foreseen it only because it will happen, it follows that it is tantamount to saying that it will necessarily happen, assuming that it will happen. This is what is called a conditional necessity.

A. – [9] These distinctions do not remove the difficulty.

B. – I confess I don't see any difficulty. Is there something wrong with granting that God foresees everything? On the contrary, since that is the case, it would be of no use to be upset about it, and it would even be[10] to not love God.

A. – I am very satisfied with divine foreknowledge, and it only displeases me that I cannot reply to the unfortunate consequences which seem to me to arise from the certainty or necessity which results from it, whether it is taken as conditional or as absolute necessity. For if my sin is necessary, or at least if it is foreseen and inevitable that I will sin, then even if I take good care to avoid committing the sin it will happen anyway.

B. – These 'unfortunate consequences' do not hold. Among ancient philosophers there was a similar sophism which was called the sloth's syllogism because it concluded that we should do nothing on the grounds that, if something is foreseen and inevitable, it will happen without my effort, and if it is not foreseen, it will not happen, irrespective of whether I am able to do it. I respond to this by denying what has been put forward without any proof, namely that the foreseen thing will happen whatever I do. If it is foreseen that I will do it, it is also foreseen that I will do what is needed for that, and if it will not happen because of my laziness, my laziness itself will also have been foreseen. What a German proverb says about death, that it needs to have a cause, can also be said about eternal death or damnation, and about sin or anything else. So as we know nothing about what is foreseen, we should do our thing without focusing on the useless question of whether success is foreseen or not, all the more since God is content with our good will when it is sincere and ardent.

A. – This is very good advice, and it is absolutely in line with my view. However, there still remains the great difficulty of the origin of evil. I

---

[9] A. – | These distinctions do not destroy the unfortunate consequences of this necessity, whether it is conditional or absolute. | *deleted.*

[10] be | a great crime | *deleted.*

am asking about the origin of origins, and I am not easily fobbed off with the ordinary evasions. It is said that man sins because his nature is corrupted by Adam's sin, but we come back to the same question with regard to Adam himself, for how is it that he sinned? Or, to speak more generally, how did sin come into the world, since God, the world's creator, is infinitely good and infinitely powerful? To explain sin there would have to be another infinite cause capable of counterbalancing the influence of divine goodness.

B. – I can name you such a thing.
A. – You will therefore be a Manichean, since you will acknowledge two principles, one of good and the other of evil.
B. – You yourself will release me from this charge of Manicheanism when I name this other principle.
A. – Then please name it now, Sir.
B. – It is nothingness.
A. – Nothingness? But is nothingness infinite?
B. – Undoubtedly so: it is infinite, it is eternal and it has many attributes in common with God. It includes an infinity of things, for all those things that do not exist are included in nothingness, and those that no longer exist have returned into nothingness.
A. – You are joking, no doubt. Rather like a learned man whose book about nothing I remember having seen. (Passentius, *de Nihilo.*)[11]
B. – I'm not joking at all. The Platonists and St Augustine himself have already shown that the cause of good is positive, but that evil is a defect, that is, a privation or negation, and consequently, comes from nothingness or non-being.
A. – I do not really see how nothingness, which is nothing, can enter into the composition of things.
B. – Yet you know how in arithmetic zeros joined to ones make different numbers, like 10, 100, 1000, and a witty man, having written several zeros in succession, wrote above them 'unum autem necessarium'.[12] But, without going so far, you will admit to me that all creatures are limited, and that their limits, or if you like their *non plus ultra*,[13] constitute something negative. For example, a circle is limited because

---

[11] Jean Passerat, *Nihil* (Paris, 1588).
[12] 'but a one is needed'. This recalls Luke 10.42, where Jesus says 'porro unum est necessarium' ['one thing is needed'].
[13] 'nothing further beyond'.

the opening of the arms of the compass used to draw it was not wider. So the limits or the *non plus ultra* of this opening determine the circle, and it is likewise with all other things, for they are limited or imperfect by the principle of negation or of the nothingness they contain, by the lack of an infinity of perfections which are only a nothingness with respect to them.

A. –[14] Yet you will admit to me that everything was created good, and in such a way that God had reason to be pleased with it, as Holy Scripture reveals. Original sin arose afterwards. And this is what surprises me – how original sin could arise from things which were wholly good.

B. – Before all sin there was an original imperfection in all creatures, which comes from their limitation. Just as it is impossible for there to be an infinite circle, since every circle is delimited by its circumference, it is also impossible for there to be an absolutely perfect creature; this is why it is believed that Holy Scripture meant to speak of angels themselves when it insinuated that among the ministers of God there are none without defects. There was no positive evil in creatures in the beginning, but they always lacked many perfections. So through lack of attention the first man was able to turn away from the sovereign good and be content with some created thing, and he thereby fell into sin, that is, from an imperfection that was only privative in the beginning, he fell into a positive evil.

A. – But what is the source of this original imperfection, which is prior to original sin?

B. – It can be said that it comes from the actual essences or natures of creatures, since the essences of things are eternal even if things are not. It has always been true that three times three is nine, and will always be so. Things like this do not depend on God's will, but on his understanding. For example, the essences or properties of numbers are eternal and immutable, and nine is a square number, not because God wanted it that way, but because its definition entails it, for it is three times three, and being a square number comes about in this way, through the multiplication of a number by itself. God's understanding is the source of creatures' essences, such as they are in him, that is, limited. If they are imperfect, only their limitation or limits should be blamed, that is, the fact that they participate in nothingness.

---

[14] A – | But how can these limits give rise to sin? | *deleted*.

A. – I admit, after what you have just said, that creatures are limited out of necessity, rather like the circle we spoke about earlier. But it seems that it was up to God to create them at least perfect enough in order not to fall.

B. – I believe that God did create things in the highest perfection, though it does not seem so to us when looking at the parts of the universe. It's rather like in music and painting where shadows and dissonances do so much to reveal the rest, and the learned author of such works derives such a great benefit for the total perfection of the work from these particular imperfections that it is much better to include them than to attempt to do without them. So it should be believed that God would have neither permitted sin nor created creatures which he knew would sin unless he knew the way to derive from them a good which is incomparably greater than the evil which results from them.

A. – I would like to know what this great good is.

B. – I can assure you that it exists, but cannot explain it in detail. For that, one would have to know the general harmony of the universe, whereas we know only a very small part of it. Paul's exclamation – 'Oh depths of riches'[15] – holds good here. He made it when speaking with rapture about the depths of divine wisdom, while explaining this very same matter.

A. – It is a strange thing, though, that there are creatures who have fallen and others who have sustained themselves. So where does this difference come from?

B. – The difference between created things originally comes from their essence, as I believe I have already shown, and the order of things (from which the divine wisdom did not wish to distance itself) required this variety. I will even give you an example drawn from geometry, which is not unknown to you.

A. – It is true that this science demonstrates things, and shows what the human mind is capable of, if it is conducted in an orderly way. But as I do not see how one can find something there relevant to our subject, I will be all the more pleased to hear it.

B. – Geometers draw a great distinction between commensurable and incommensurable lines. They call 'commensurable' the ones that can be expressed by numbers, that is, by measures or by parts of a measure. But when neither a whole number nor a fraction of a number can be found to express them, they are incommensurable. For example, if there were

---

[15] Romans 11.33.

two lines, one of which was nine feet and the other ten feet, they would be commensurable, since there is a common measure, which is the foot. And if one was ten feet and the other nine feet and a fifth, they would still be commensurable, since the fifth of a foot would be the common measure, being contained fifty times in the ten feet line and forty six times in the line that is nine feet and a fifth.

A. – That's easy to understand, but incommensurables are a little more difficult.

B. – Here's an example of one: the square root of two is incommensurable with one. This number is called a surd number because it cannot be exactly expressed either by whole numbers or by fractions. And you will never find a number, whole or fraction, or half a whole number or half a fraction, which multiplied by itself produces the number two, as will be easily understood when beginning to look for such a number.

A. – But I expected incommensurable lines rather than numbers.

B. – Here is one, which corresponds to the square root of two: the diagonal of the perfect square. For it is a very ancient observation that this line is incommensurable with the side of the square. Let ABCD be a perfect square, whose sides are all equal and whose angles are so too, namely right angles; I say that the diagonal AC is incommensurable with the side, for example with AB.

A. – Let's see the proof of this.

B. – It's easy. Make another perfect square whose side is the diagonal of the first square. This new square will be ACEF. It is obvious that the second square is exactly twice the first square, ABCD, for square ABCD contains two triangles, ABC and ADC, whereas square ACEF contains four of these triangles, namely ADC, CDE, EDF and FDA, and all these triangles are equal. And that which contains the same magnitude four times is doubtless twice that which contains it only twice.

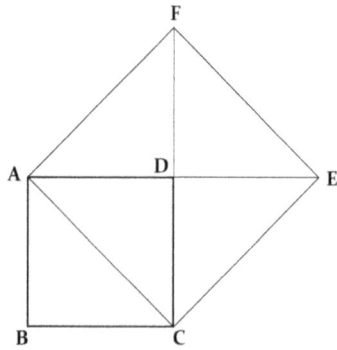

A. – That's obvious enough, but what do you conclude from it, Sir?
B. – It follows that if a side of the small square ABCD, namely the line AB, is one foot, the side of the large square ACEF, namely AC, will be the square root of two. For its square has the value of two square feet, and to find its side, we must derive the square root of the area, which is two, as all arithmeticians know. Now we have already shown that the square root of two is incommensurable with one, and totally inexpressible in rational numbers.
A. – Yes, that is surprising. Could God not find a number suitable for exactly expressing the square root of two or the length of the diagonal of a square?
B. – God could not find absurd things. It is as if we asked God to teach us the way to divide three coins into two equal parts with no fraction, that is, without saying one and a half, or something similar.
A. – You are right – it is to ask for absurdities unworthy of God, or rather it is to ask for nothing, not to know what it is that one is asking for. I see the necessity of what you are saying about incommensurables, although it goes beyond our imagination. This should enable us to understand our inadequacy and our adequacy at the same time. About many things we know *that* they are, but we should not claim to know perfectly *how* they are. Nevertheless, what do you draw from this fine meditation of geometers that can be applied to our question?
B. – Here it is: isn't it true that if the order of things or divine wisdom required God to produce perfect squares, then God, having resolved to fulfil this requirement, could not avoid producing incommensurable lines, even though they have the imperfection of not being able to be expressed exactly?[16] For there could not be a square without a diagonal, which is the distance between its opposite angles. Let us push the comparison further, and compare commensurable lines with minds which sustain themselves in their purity, and incommensurables with less disciplined minds which then fall into sin. It is obvious that the irregularity of incommensurable lines comes from the very essence of shapes, and should not be imputed to God; it is likewise obvious that this incommensurability is not an evil that God is able not to produce. It is also quite true that God would have been able to avoid it by creating only numbers or discrete quantities, not shapes or continuous quantities. But this imperfection of incommensurables has been compensated by

---

[16] exactly | nor known exactly by any finite mind? | *deleted*.

much greater advantages, such that it was better to permit incommensurables in order not to deprive the universe of all shapes. It is the same with minds less firm in sustaining themselves, whose original imperfection comes from their essence, which is limited according to their degree. Their sin, which is only an accidental or contingent thing (although it has its basis in their essence, albeit without resulting from it by a necessary consequence), comes from their will; and the incommensurably greater good that God knows how to derive from this evil comes from his infinite wisdom, and led him not to exclude them from existence, nor to prevent them from sinning, as he could have done by using his absolute power, albeit by simultaneously overturning the order of things that his infinite wisdom made him choose.

A. – These are quite remarkable meditations which throw new light on this matter.

B. – Although I think it could have been explained by expressions and comparisons very different from mine, I hold that ultimately my explanation cannot be denied, so long as one thinks deeply about it. It is in accordance with St Paul, St Augustine and, in part, with Luther's excellent work on the servitude of the will,[17] which in my opinion is extremely good, provided that one tones down some extravagant expressions, and which has always seemed to me, from my youth, to be the finest and most solid book he left to us.

4. Can the bad outcomes of wicked actions be ascribed to wickedness? (after 1695 (?))[18]

Manuscript:

M: LH 1, 1, 4 Bl. 100.

Transcription:

GR: Grua I, pp. 372–4.

---

[17] Martin Luther, *De servo arbitrio* (1525).
[18] Author's title. From the Latin. Complete.

At some point between 1695 and 1697 Leibniz wrote a short plan for a work that would seek to defend God's justice in the face of objections drawn from the existence, character and prevalence of evil in the world.[19] He gave this project the title of 'Theodicy', a term he coined from the Greek words *theos* [God] and *dike* [justice]. A theodicy thus involved one arguing 'on behalf of divine justice'.[20] The following piece was most likely written after that plan, since it begins with Leibniz referring to his theodicy, and takes up a question at the heart of it. Leibniz would later write a lengthy book with that title, publishing it in 1710.[21]

Can the bad outcomes of wicked actions be ascribed to wickedness?

The question pertains to my theodicy whether unfortunate outcomes really and truly are due to sins, as they are thought to be by historians, preachers, good men and common people, irrespective of whether they are pious or superstitious. In this matter there is truly a certain confusion of views. In his unpublished notes on the *Annales* of Baronius,[22] I remember that Tassoni, although bound in good faith to the Roman Church, nevertheless rebuked and ridiculed that bad habit of certain historians who assign to providence their own dispositions, implying that misfortunes happen to certain leaders because they have thought and acted, I shall not say wickedly, but scarcely according to the custom of the Roman curia.[23] Nevertheless it is worth asking whether unfortunate events may be ascribed not so much to men's imprudence (which no one denies), but rather to sin and wickedness in cases where men have not failed in themselves but have been overthrown by a greater power (although even imprudence can sometimes – especially in extreme cases – be considered as a kind of blinding inflicted from on high). There are examples of this when someone who has broken a treaty and then lost the resultant war seems to declare to himself and to others that he will learn justice; for example, as Vladislaus, King of Hungary and Poland, said:

Like the Romans at Carrhae,[24] I have made Varna famous for defeat
For mortals to learn not to violate trust;

---

[19] See Grua I, pp. 370–1.
[20] Grua I, p. 370.
[21] [G. W. Leibniz], *Essais de Theodicée sur la bonté de Dieu, la liberté de l'homme, et l'origine du mal* (Amsterdam, 1710).
[22] Caesar Baronius, *Annales ecclesiastici a Christo nato ad annum 1198*, 12 vols (Rome, 1588–1607).
[23] Alessandro Tassoni, *Annali Ecclesiastici*.
[24] The Romans engaged the Parthians at Carrhae in 53 BCE, and were routed despite having superior numbers.

If popes had not ordered me to break the treaty,
The Scythian yoke would not have come to Pannonia.[25]

For my part, where justice is doubtful and controversial, I say that an outcome should not be considered as a sentence pronounced by God; and I think that those who once said that disputes should be decided by a trial by combat, which is entrusted to divine judgement itself, were putting God to the test, although they were acting imprudently rather than wickedly. But where the depravity of a deed is indisputable, and it is followed by a bad outcome, what shall we say then? Certainly it is often said against this that the wicked are happy, such that if one were to undertake an induction from known cases and carry out a census of histories, as it were, one would not so boldly claim that the wicked have been punished more often than (I will not say the unconvicted) the happy. But the question is not to be decided by the atheist and the subverter of providence, but by a man convinced of God's supreme wisdom and power and the most just administration of things. For it is evident that far too often punishments are deferred to another life, and so it rather seems that there is a law in favour of wickedness in these times, and it prevails, so to speak, in the kingdom of this world. So just as a certain wise man was afraid he had spoken badly when he was applauded by a crowd, in the same way success could be seen as a sign of an evil cause.

So shall we order those preachers or moralist historians to get out of our sight, even though they are talking about genuine sins rather than imaginary ones? Or shall we tolerate them by a kind of pious fraud that will be useful to men and for that reason gets our vote? And shall we decide to say that sin really has been the cause of misfortune or one of its causes?

It seems to me that this final opinion is the truest, since it is certain that God, and not an evil genius, is the director of things, and he doesn't do anything rashly; instead, all things are traced back to some infallible calculation and are adjusted to each other by eternal decrees. Someone will urge, not implausibly, that this statement is made truthfully but in vain. For on

---

[25] This poem emerged in the late sixteenth century, purporting to be the epitaph of Vladislaus I (1424–44). It refers to the battle of Varna in 1444, which began after the papal envoy had urged Vladislaus to violate the truce with the Turks ('Scythians'). In the battle, the Turks defeated the Hungarians, killing Vladislaus, and took over Central Europe (Pannonia). Leibniz's quotation of the poem is slightly inaccurate, and incomplete (omitting lines 2 and 4); for the complete poem, see Szentmártoni Szabó Géza, '"Romulidae Cannas", avagy egy ál-Janus Pannonius-vers utóélete, eredeti szövege és valódi szerzője', in *Convivium Pajorin Klára 70. Szletésnapjára* (Budapest: Debrecen, 2012), p. 184. Géza identifies the poem's author as Christophorus Manlius (1546–75), a poet and historian.

account of the universal connection of all things, even virtues are among the causes of future unhappiness, not so much because anyone suffers on account of justice (or where there is a similar cause, by the reward being postponed to the future), but in general, i.e. adverse events arise that are no more due to sin than to virtue. But to meet this deeper objection we must understand that all things work together, but for a very different reason. And when it concerns a moral matter, and the actions of the wise, we should consider as causes those things that influence the effect through the reasons of wisdom and the will, and not those that influence the effect through the principle of individuation or contingency (which some call material necessity, although that is somewhat improper talk), i.e. have effect through the general conspiring of things. Eternal wisdom constructs this very thing also, but this wisdom transcends the grasp of the finite[26] intellect and we cannot nor should not trace it back into its reasons. In the present circumstances, causes should be put forward that act through themselves, that is because few people distinguish this from the laws of universal principles (if not the necessary or essential laws then at least the presumptive or natural laws, just as jurisconsults distinguish essential and natural laws too). Of course when God produces bodies naturally he makes them regular, uniform, suitable for their function whether as animals or planets in the sky, except when he has to act otherwise because one thing impedes another; although even then the beauty of the whole is evident, as my demonstrations about the laws of motion show.[27] Therefore God punishes evils and metes out rewards naturally, that is, according to reasons of wisdom, or according to certain universal principles (which perform the same role in moral matters as laws of motion in physics), and he does so immediately, at least if this is permitted by the greater reasons that should be pursued as a result of the concourse of other moral matters: moral, I say, not natural. For in this matter the most excellent Malebranche has not been sufficiently discerning, because he thought that moral matters are disturbed by natural ones,[28] when in fact the laws of any kingdom are perfect in

---

[26] Leibniz here wrote 'infiniti' [infinite] though this is presumably a mistake. Transcription G has 'finiti'.
[27] See for example Leibniz's paper 'Brevis demonstratio erroris memorabilis Cartesii & aliorum circa legem naturae, secundum quam volunt a Deo eandem semper quantitem motus conservari; qua & in re mechanica abutuntur', *Acta Eruditorum* (March 1686), pp. 161–3; English translation: L, pp. 296–301.
[28] Malebranche believed that although the natural world usually operates in accordance with the natural laws that God established, God occasionally overrides these laws when greater (moral) reasons demand. Thus on such occasions, which involve God working a miracle (such as the

themselves and have inviolate success. But if it is not possible immediately then God will surely punish as soon as conveniently possible, and thus a person will be brought to punishment by a natural impetus: that very thing is what Holy Scripture insinuates when it says that God hates sin.[29] Indeed, this was so from the very beginning, when from the infinity of possible worlds he chose the order of things in which the fewest possible sins would happen, and in which the sins would be punished by penalty and correction as early as possible. And so it should be considered most certain that misfortune after wickedness is to be ascribed to that wickedness as it is that death following malignant fever is to be ascribed to that fever,[30] even if the knowledge of doctors was so great that most of them could cure fevers of this kind.

5. On God and man (December 1705 (?))[31]

Manuscript:

M: LH IV 2, 2c.

Transcription:

G: G III, pp. 28–38.

In late 1705, as part of his efforts to reunite the Protestant Churches, Leibniz wrote a commentary on article XVII of Gilbert Burnet's *An Exposition of the Thirty Nine Articles of the Church of England* (London, 1699),[32] and also prepared a detailed index to his commentary, entitled (by one of his later editors) 'Synopsis'.[33] Although ostensibly just an index, the 'Synopsis' is arranged thematically (and at times logically) and gives the impression of being a plan for a different and much

---

sending of the great flood to punish mankind), the moral sphere imposes on the natural, as Leibniz notes. See Nicolas Malebranche, *Meditations chrestiennes* (Cologne, 1683), pp. 116–17.
[29] See for example Psalms 5.4 and 45.7.
[30] Transcription G omits 'febris tribuenda esset'.
[31] Editor's title. From the Latin. Complete.
[32] One of the drafts of Leibniz's commentary has been published as *Dissertation on Predestination and Grace*, trans. Michael Murray (New Haven: Yale University Press, 2011).
[33] See Grua II, pp. 473–7.

more ambitious project. The following piece follows the structure of the first half of the 'Synopsis', and appears to be developed from it. Leibniz revisited the piece some years later, redrafting and expanding it under the title *Causa Dei*, which was published as an appendix to the *Theodicy* (1710).

When the writings of the most renowned *Bayle* were considered and read by persons of the highest rank, on account of the elegance and erudition these writings offer, my opinion was repeatedly sought, and I was often forced to make clear my disagreement, especially in those matters concerning religion and piety. For he asserted everywhere that there is so much conflict between faith and the reason we apply to Holy Scriptures that there is no place for harmony of the two. And he said that the dogmas of theology we call 'revealed' are not only above reason but also against it, and not only[34] can we not understand these dogmas in the slightest, but they cannot in any way be defended against objections either: and he even seemed to regard this as praise and greatness, or as he calls it the triumph of faith, when it is rather a matter of its defeat and subversion. For what qualifies as absurd if not[35] a dogma that can be overturned by invincible arguments? Besides, when coming to the crux of this very important issue, he tried to demonstrate in detail what he had previously stated in general terms, and in particular seemed to act in such a way that he recommended Manicheanism, that is, the doctrine of two principles, one good, the other evil, saying that without it the origin of evil is impossible to conceive; although the author professes that in saying this he has no interest in the ruin of the Christian Church, many consider his protestation to be contrary to fact.[36]

Therefore since I would often take part in these debates in which Bayle's arguments were bandied about, and I would frankly explain just how far from right reason are his arguments, which he explains more shrewdly and cleverly than correctly, it was suggested to me more than once by a prince of the highest rank among mortals that I should put down in writing the things I was saying, and this I have done gladly and without difficulty, because I have carefully treated this matter from my youth, when I applied

---

[34] only | can we not prove the articles of faith with reason | *deleted*. None of the deletions or marginal notes are recorded in G.
[35] not | something where there is nothing that can be brought against opponents | *deleted*.
[36] fact. | ¶ Therefore since I have treated the same argument most attentively from my youth, when I applied myself to philosophy and also revealed the sources of right; | *deleted*.

myself to philosophy and revealed the sources of eternal right. Thus when from time to time I had treated different questions in a short paper, I was then encouraged by friends, some of whom are renowned for their study of religion and expertise in theology, to organize them all into one little work, whereby they might prove useful to more people.

But since my aim in this subject is to uphold piety and religion, and since the dogmas of the Churches of the Augsburg confession always seemed to me the safest and most suitable for this purpose,[37] I have written a sort of very brief synopsis of my views which I thought could be used in this cause, so that it could be subjected to the scrutiny and judgement of some of our distinguished theologians.

The discussion has two parts, one about *God*, the other about *man*. In the part on God, I consider greatness and goodness and the characteristics of each, while in the part on man, I consider[38] both his nature and grace.[39]

Divine greatness is to be assiduously asserted especially against the Socinians, and Conrad Vorst, and other semi-Socinians. It consists in three things in particular: primordiality, omnipotence and omniscience.

Primordiality has two parts: God's independence from other things, and the dependence of all things upon God.

God's *independence* means that he is necessary and eternal in existing, which is called *ens a se*,[40] and that he has a perfect freedom in acting, and is determined in his actions only by himself.

But this independence does not mean that he acts tyrannically, i.e. where his will stands in place of reason, or that he founded right itself by his own choice, in the manner of a positive law. For such things conflict with his wisdom and goodness, which we shall discuss shortly.

In the same way, *the dependence of things upon God* is apparent both in

---

[37] purpose, | I wanted a sort of synopsis of my doctrines for some eminent theologians to examine | *deleted*.
[38] consider | his status before the Fall and status after the Fall, and then not only the reason for his corrupted nature but also the reason for the grace that is intended for his restoration | *deleted*.
[39] Marginal note: 'It is possible to boil down divine magnitude into omnipotence and omniscience. Omnipotence involves God's independence from other things (his independence is not only physical, as he does not have his origin in another, but also moral, as he has no superior, ἀνυπευθυνία [unaccountability]), and the dependence of other things upon him (the dependence of essences upon his intellect and existences upon his will, whereby he not only conserves created things in their existing, but also concurs in their acting.'
[40] 'being from itself'.

their existing and in their acting. *In existing*, inasmuch as all things are not only created by God but also conserved by God, nor is his conservation inappropriately called continuous creation.

In acting, inasmuch as God concurs with the actions of things, and directs them, even the evil actions, because even in those there is some degree of perfection that must flow from God.

And *concurrence* is immediate and specific, contrary to what Durand thinks.[41] It is *immediate* since the effect not only depends upon God (because the cause of it derived from God), but since God concurs in producing the effect no less than in producing its cause.

The concurrence is[42] *specific*, because God directs his action not only at the existence of the thing, but also at the mode of existing and the thing's qualities and actions, insofar as there is some perfection in them.

And it will be shown below how God is not for that reason the cause of sin, and does not impose necessity on free creatures, and how his will does not concur with culpable evil except by permitting it.

God's omnipotence[43] is so broad in extent that it has for its object everything that is possible, or does not imply contradiction, and he has such power that those things he wills completely, or decisively, unquestionably come to pass.

Moreover, those things he does not will by a decree but by an inclination, and by what is called the antecedent will, obtain their effect as much as they can through the conflict of other antecedent wills.

Even those things God does not make or will, namely the bad ones, he still governs by his providence.

To God's omnipotence also pertains ἀνυπευθυνία,[44] such that no one can compel him to give reasons, but his justice does not consist in this, and those who draw out God's right from his omnipotence are in error.

Since *God's omniscience* is most perfect, his knowledge thus embraces all truths and undergoes no progress and increase. And his knowledge covers both possible things and actual things.

Knowledge of possible things is called *knowledge of simple intelligence*,

---

[41] Durand of Saint-Pourçain (1275–1334), renowned Scholastic philosopher and theologian. In the *Theodicy*, Leibniz complains that Durand, along with various others, acknowledged only God's general concurrence. See G VI, p. 341/H, p. 353.
[42] Reading 'est' (M) in place of 'et' (G).
[43] *omnipotence* | consists in the fact that those things he wills completely, or decisively, come to pass | *deleted*.
[44] 'unaccountability'.

and it encompasses the connections of these things with each other, and therefore all necessary truths.[45]

And it also encompasses contingent possibles and their connections, and therefore future conditionals as well, i.e. what is going to follow from some given contingent event, even though there is also contingency rather than necessity in this connection, so for this reason what some call *middle knowledge* is rightly included under the knowledge of simple intelligence.

Moreover, God knows possible things, not only individually, but also as arranged together into innumerable possible worlds, from which he chose one in accordance with his supremely wise judgement.

God's simple knowledge of this world he has chosen, added to his knowledge of the decree of the choice, becomes *knowledge of vision*, which embraces all actual things, past, present and future. Nor is there need for any other foundation for God's foreknowledge of future contingents.[46] [47]

We now turn from God's greatness to his *goodness*. And just as truth is related to the intellect, so goodness is related to his will. God's will is divided into the antecedent and the consequent.

An *antecedent will* is that by which God (and every wise man, according to the object of its will) inclines to produce every good and remove every evil.

Accordingly, with an antecedent will God wills that all men be enlightened, sanctified and saved.

The antecedent will is to be distinguished from velleity, which does not occur in God, and should also be distinguished from the conditional will which, although it does occur in God (as does knowledge of conditionals) is never alone, but is always combined with knowledge and a will of the absolute. Sometimes God does not will the action but only the attempt to perform it, like when he commanded Abraham to sacrifice Isaac he wanted Abraham to obey his command, not carry it out.[48] But when he commands virtuous actions and prohibits vicious ones, he really does will the obedience as well as the thing he commands.[49]

---

[45] Marginal note: 'Knowledge of possible things extends to necessary truths and contingent truths.'
[46] Marginal note: 'Just as truth is the perfection of the intellect, so goodness is the perfection of the will. Every will has as its object the apparent good, but the divine will has only the genuine good. Therefore what is to be done according to both the will and goodness involves either an antecedent or a consequent will. The antecedent is serious and sometimes efficacious. The consequent is fully efficacious, or decretory.'
[47] contingents. | ¶ Just as truth pertains to the intellect, so goodness pertains to the will. | *deleted*.
[48] See Genesis 22.1-12.
[49] commands. | Every one of God's antecedent wills would have effect if certain things did not

If all the effects of the antecedent wills could occur at the same time then every one of God's antecedent wills would have its full effect. But since God wills every good according to the measure of[50] goodness possessed by the object of his will, it thus happens (since not all goods[51] can exist at the same time) that from the conflict of all the antecedent wills there arises the *consequent* or decretory will, which is in conformity with the highest degree of wisdom, and through it there arises as much good as possible. And so God's antecedent will does indeed tend to the good, but the consequent will tends to the best.

It also follows that the consequent will, which you may call the final will and the entirely absolute will, and we may generally call the decree, is immutable and always has effect, since in forming this decree all things have already been taken into consideration, and no new argument against it can be given.[52]

Yet this will is free because it results from antecedent wills that are assuredly free, and it is spontaneous because it arises from an internal principle, namely God's wisdom and goodness.

And although God's will is in this way determined to the best, this nevertheless happens by a moral necessity rather than a metaphysical one; ultimately there would be a metaphysical necessity if that object of the divine will chosen by God were the only possible one, in which case there would not have been any choice among many alternatives, contrary to the hypothesis.

Three kinds of good or evil are usually recognized: metaphysical, physical and moral. Metaphysical good or evil is perfection or imperfection in general, but it especially applies to those goods and evils which happen to non-intelligent creatures, or creatures considered as non-intelligent.

Physical good or evil usually applies to the conveniences and inconveniences of intelligent creatures, insofar as they have agreeable or disagreeable experiences. The evil of punishment is an example of this.

---

prevent it. | *deleted.*
[50] of | its own goodness, and wills against every evil according to the measure of its own badness | *deleted.*
[51] goods | are mutually compatible | *deleted.*
[52] Marginal note: 'Accordingly, those who think that the use of prayers and the usefulness of human studies are destroyed by an eternal decree about future things, and who revive the old lazy sophism, should consider that the prayers and other things which now occasion God to act influenced him in his decision a long time ago, since he took heed of them before the existence of things.'

Lastly, moral good and evil is virtuous or vicious action, and culpable evil is an example here.[53]

From this it should now be said that God wills[54] the best as his ultimate end, good of whatever kind (under which I include the removal of evil) as a subordinate end, and indifferent matters and sometimes even metaphysical and physical evil as indirect goods, or as evils for an end; but moral evil is not even considered as a means.[55]

So the question is, what ultimately is the reason for the existence of culpable evil,[56] and why do we say that God in no way wills sin, but only permits it?

We should note that although evil exists, it is nevertheless not the object of God's antecedent will, and therefore it emerges in his consequent will only by concomitance, because God would not permit evil unless he could bring about a greater good from evil, as Augustine has already observed.[57]

But sin, that is, culpable evil (which is more difficult than the other evils), is permitted, and although it would be useful for some good, i.e. could serve as means to an end, this would nevertheless not be sufficient for the object to be permitted by the will; this is the very thing the apostle warned about, that one should not commit evil in order that good may come.[58]

Therefore the only legitimate reason for permitting sin is when it cannot be prevented without a breach of duty. For example, suppose there is someone who (especially in a time of danger) had been placed on guard at a post he must not abandon without the order of a captain or officer and that he were to hear that two of his other soldier friends want to fight in a duel: doubtless he would not be permitted to run over to them to prevent the evil. In the same way, it could one day happen that a prince would be unable to prevent the sin of a subordinate with sinning himself, in which case the permission for the other to sin would indeed be necessary.

---

[53] The distinction between culpable evil (*malum culpae*) and the evil of punishment (*malum poenae*) was made by Augustine, who believed that all evil is ultimately of one kind or the other. See his *De Genesi ad Litteram Imperfectus Liber*, and *De Libero Arbitrio* I, i.
[54] wills | (α) the evil of punishment only as a subsidiary good, but he does not will culpable evil except | (β) the good as an end, the evil of punishment and other physical or metaphysical imperfections as a subsidiary good, that is, as a means to an end; | *deleted*.
[55] means |, nor does God in any way will sin | *deleted*.
[56] evil, | which God's antecedent will rejects before other evils | *deleted*.
[57] See St Augustine, *Enchiridion ad Laurentium liber unus*, I.100.
[58] An allusion to Romans 3.8: 'And not *rather*, (as we be slanderously reported, and as some affirm that we say,) Let us do evil, that good may come? whose damnation is just.'

God cannot sin; he is obliged by a sort of moral necessity of his own wisdom and goodness to do and choose the best, and his failure to do this would be worse than any creaturely sin because it would conflict with divine perfection. For a lesser good has the character of evil.

Consequently, for the fact that God has permitted sin there can be no other reason than that he was unable not to permit it without undermining his own wisdom, since evidently he has chosen the best from innumerable possible worlds, and some culpable evil was included in this, as we can judge *a posteriori*, i.e. from the outcome, or from the fact that he has permitted it.

And hence we ought to conclude that even if worlds without sin were possible, they would in the end, and with all things considered, still be inferior in perfection to our world, in which the picture is enhanced by shadows and the harmony by dissonances, these things being permitted quite appropriately.

Therefore sin is the object of the permissive divine will, not as an end, and in fact not as a means either, but only as a condition without which it was impossible to obtain the best, i.e. as something which, had God not admitted it, would have left unsatisfied his supreme wisdom and goodness.

From this it is clear that the[59] ultimate origin of evil should be sought not in the divine will but in the original imperfection of creatures (which is contained in ideal form in the eternal truths that constitute the internal object of the divine intellect), and that therefore evil could not be excluded from the best possible system of things.

Moreover, God permits sin so that there be culpability, not for its own sake, but for the sake of those doing the sinning. He does not determine any one to sin but only decrees never to prevent someone who is going to sin; nor for that reason should he be held as an accomplice to the sin, since on account of the laws of supreme wisdom he ought not to have prevented it.

But if, then, there is a single legitimate reason for permitting sin, as we have shown, it is readily apparent when sin should not be not permitted, as can be proved by the arguments of certain superlapsarians, who think that God permitted the Fall only so that there might be justice in his punishment of some, or that he might show mercy in the indulgence of others. For unless God was moved by greater reasons, he would better demonstrate his justice by preventing sin and better demonstrate his goodness by preventing wretchedness.

---

[59] the | origin of evil is the eternal truths | *deleted*.

Thus in the preceding we have preserved God's *justice* (the highest degree of which is *holiness*), although it originates not from goodness alone but from goodness and wisdom combined, namely when goodness is directed towards other intelligent substances. And so it pertains to the *common features of greatness and goodness*, about which we shall now speak.

God's justice, then, is not something arbitrary, but flows from the eternal rules of wisdom. Nor is God exempted from any law, in such a way that he could (say) punish the innocent. For although he has none above him, he nevertheless satisfies himself.

Here also belong those things that simultaneously concern God's concurrence and his goodness, and so especially his concurrence with sin, which is something that cannot be denied unless the reality of sin is said to be independent of God. And this same thing seems to conflict with divine holiness, to which there is nothing more contrary than sin. But Augustine has already aptly observed that the formal element of sin consists in privation.[60] And privation arises from the limitation of creatures, which means that their knowledge does not extend to all things, and that their will, which should be directed at the highest good, i.e. God, instead remains fixed on inferior goods.

I have illustrated the matter with a comparison of a boat travelling down a river, such that the more laden it is, the more slowly it will be carried along. Therefore just as the river is the cause of motion and the load is the cause of the arrestment, so God is the cause of the perfection, virtue, vigour and goodness in things, while the contrary flows from receptivity, that is, from the original limitation of creatures, which often ultimately materializes in sin, when the soul is attached to things with a misdirected love, neglecting God, and harmful ignorance weakens the impetus that has been divinely impressed in us by resisting it.

Moreover, when Scripture says that God hardens the heart,[61] and attributes to him similar influences toward sin, it is only insinuated that man is, with divine permission, thrown into the circumstances included in the series of things, in which the opportunity arises for him to sin or else to persevere in sin or even to make progress, but divine providence has not allowed these circumstances to be changed: for it was not reasonable for God to abandon his own wisdom in order that men be released from sins as though by force; in fact, his judgement on them was just, and he has

---

[60] See Augustine, *Enchiridion* I.XI.
[61] See for example Exodus 4.21 and 7.3; Isaiah 63.17.

governed evils so that he would obtain the greatest goods. Thus it is ascribed to God by a certain manner of speaking what should be of the series God has chosen with his most just decree.

Now the choice of the best series of things originates from the combination of wisdom and goodness, and thus there proceeds that wonderful harmony and περιχώρησις[62] of all things which makes all things most fittingly connected together. Nor is there even an order among God's antecedent wills, according to the degree of goodness in the object, but as there is in fact no order among God's decrees, or rather as there is in fact only a single decree of God, if you consider the matter carefully, namely the one whereby he decreed that out of infinite possible systems the best of all should exist, i.e. this very one that does exist. For a wise agent decides nothing unless all things have been considered.

And doubtless the strongest reason for favouring the best series of the universe (i.e. this one) was Christ, the noblest part of this universe, God's eternal son incarnated, in whom should be found the key to all human salvation.

Accordingly, the old Church called Adam's sin 'happy', because it merited such a redeemer,[63] that is, his momentous evil was the occasion for a much greater good.

Thus far we have been concerned with God; it remains for us to turn now to the subject of man, considering in him both nature and grace: nature not only as it is in itself, but also as it has been corrupted.

The nature of man, if you consider it in itself, consists in a soul and a body, which on a metaphysical account constitute one person when united,[64] although on a physical account each substance follows its own laws, which conspire in accordance with the harmony pre-established by God from the outset.

Many people think that souls are created by God every day, while others after Augustine lean towards traduction;[65] and if this is properly explained it does not seem worthy of scorn.

---

[62] 'coinherence'.
[63] Leibniz is alluding here to the Exsultet, the Easter proclamation of the Catholic Church, which includes the lines 'O truly necessary sin of Adam, which was erased by the death of Christ! O happy fault, that merited so great a Redeemer!'
[64] united, | yet physical things do not mutually influence one another, nor does the soul disturb the laws of body or the body the laws of the soul. However, the soul is the essential representation of the body, and the body the essential instrument of the soul. | *deleted.*
[65] See Augustine, *De Genesi ad litteram libri duodecim*, X.18–19.

Indeed, some men very clearly versed in the examination of nature today think, on the basis of evidence, that it is not contemptible to think that animals were already in some way preformed in seeds since the origin of things, and even then these very same seeds were organic and animated. In this way, two great difficulties are removed, one about the origin of souls, which are all created in the beginning, the other about the formation of the foetus, which for the most part is due to divine preformation.

On this account it is credible that the soul – which is only a sensitive soul when in the seeds – eventually receives, at the time of conception, the superior degree of being human, that is, it receives the power of reason. On this way of explaining things, there is no recourse to the pre-existence of the rational soul, nor is a soul thrust into a corrupted body; instead, the sensitive soul that exists beforehand and is infected with the physical root of the original evil already in Adam, is raised to a new perfection and endowed with reason.

Man's nature was corrupted by Adam's fall, and God permitted the Fall since an Adam who sins freely was contained in the best series of things chosen by God, as has already been explained sufficiently.

All of Adam's descendents are involved in the Fall, since their souls – although not yet rational – contracted a defect in Adam, a defect which in the rational soul is then called original sin, on account of which human powers, especially in matters pertaining to God, are quite considerably corrupted.

And it can be said that all souls corrupted by original sin are equally bad, albeit not in a similar way, with some inclining more to a different kind of vice. Accordingly, no one has a reason to boast that he has been preferred to another.

Yet I would not venture to assert that original sin without an accompanying actual sin (in other words, in those who die before they attain the use of reason) is sufficient for damnation, which some have thought.

We should now see what remains in a nature corrupted in its powers, i.e. what are the vestiges of the image of God. These consist in two things: in the light of the understanding and the freedom of the will.

The light of the intellect is composed of simple innate ideas and complex items of innate knowledge, by means of which we are given – as long as we are attentive – the ability to reason correctly. For although the ideas and truths latent in us are not immediately to hand, they can nevertheless be drawn out from the innermost parts of our mind by meditation. Here belongs necessary truths that are independent of the evidence of the senses.

But even though this natural light contains God's eternal law inscribed in our minds, it is nevertheless not sufficient to reconcile us with God.

Freedom of the will consists in that wherein we act not only spontaneously but also in a deliberated way; nor are we necessitated to what we decide, but only inclined to it.

Now, although future contingents and therefore also man's free actions are of determinate truth, not only as a result of one's own nature but also as a result of divine foresight, nevertheless certainty is one thing, necessity another. And although it is necessary that what God foresees will happen, this necessity, since it is only hypothetical, nevertheless does not destroy contingency and freedom.

Neither does divine preordination conflict with freedom, for if God should see among possible things a man acting freely, and then grant him existence, he does not change the nature of the thing and therefore the freedom of the action.

Now every effect is determined by its causes and their predispositions, such that there is always some reason why it exists rather than not, and as a result there is no instance of indifference of equilibrium where all the things on both sides are the same; nevertheless the reasons that determine a free cause are never necessitating but only inclining,[66] and to that extent the indifference or contingency in them is preserved.

Accordingly, neither original sin nor our other bad dispositions make the act of sin necessary, although our inclination to sin is such that it is certain we will not avoid sinning unless prevented from doing so by a divine grace.

On the other hand, God's grace does not in any way undermine our freedom, or impose a necessity of good action upon us, since it must be said that God acts freely, as do angels and blessed souls also, even though they are very much inclined to the good.

It was explained above how man's actual sin was not only permitted but also governed by God, and how God concurs with its reality.

So much for our nature; we now turn to grace, which is useful inasmuch as it assists our good actions and reins in our bad ones.

The aids afforded by grace are twofold: external and internal. The external aids are circumstances, and just as for some people circumstances are aids to sin, so for others they are aids to virtue. They consist in the lottery of one's birth, education, conversation and events of life, which make

---

[66] Transcription G here omits 'sed tantum inclinantes'.

some act in one way and others in another, and this leads to greater fortune for some not only in human affairs but also in spiritual and divine ones. Our theologians recognize in these dispensations what Paul called τὸ βάθος.[67]

And although it is credible that often those left wretched by external obstacles are those who would have made bad use of favourable circumstances, yet generally such a thing cannot be pronounced for certain. For who would affirm that all those in remote countries who died without knowledge of Christ should have been damned, and that none of them would have achieved a true conversion if the light of the gospel had been kindled there in the same way as among other peoples?

Internal grace consists in the illumination of the mind and the direction of the will; each is perfected by the mind's attention on its own functions, which is the greatest gift of divine grace. For generally men do not sin out of ignorance, but because they do not sufficiently call to mind at the right time the things they know.[68]

Grace in turn is divided into that which is sufficient for willing, i.e. sufficient so long as someone wills, and that which is efficient for willing.

And in this matter it is very probable that sufficient grace is given to all, even if God's ways are not always evident to us, for just as our theologians recognize faith given to infants in baptism even though there are no traces of it occurring, so nothing prevents God from sometimes bestowing a certain grace upon the dying, in such a way that no one can complain of being neglected.

On the other hand, grace can be divided into grace of conversion and grace of perseverance, and the latter into any kind of perseverance and final perseverance, the latter coinciding with the grace of election.

The grace of conversion is so necessary that we cannot have any good spiritual emotions unless God has aroused them, since in spiritual matters we are like the dead.

But in the converted the grace of persevering – which consists in the exercise of faith, hope and charity – does not do all the work, but receives our co-operation, once we are granted a new life.

Regarding the grace of election by merit, some think that there is no grace of conversion except in the elect, and that τοὺς προσκαίρους[69] were

---

[67] 'the depth'. An allusion to Romans 11.33: 'O the depth of the riches both of the wisdom and knowledge of God! how unsearchable *are* his judgments, and his ways past finding out!' See also Romans 8.39.

[68] know. | ¶ Grace in turn is divided into sufficient and efficient. Grace is sufficient to make us act if only our will agrees with it; efficient is for the express purpose that we so will. | *deleted*.

[69] 'those who believe for a season'.

not truly justified either: their view is to be rejected. This doctrine is prone to dangerous consequences.[70]

For even if no pious man should call his own election into doubt, there is still no absolute certainty of final perseverance in the future, in fact no more than there is of our present conversion. And if the truth of justification were to depend upon the truth of election, we would also be less certain about our justification unless we were to assume a perfect certainty of our election at the same time. But belief in this would readily give rise to a dangerous feeling of security, just as doubt about our justification would readily give rise to desperation. Therefore we can be entirely sure about our justification, and should maintain a great and pious hope about our election since we cannot perish once the right of salvation has been obtained except through our own culpability.

6. On the composition of a stirring theological poem, 'Uranius' (3 September 1711)[71]

Manuscript:

M: Kopenhagen KB Thott 4° 1230.

Transcription:

D: Dutens V, pp. 293–4.

The following piece is an extract from a letter to one of Leibniz's long-time correspondents, Johann Fabricius (1644–1729), who had been Professor of Theology at the University of Helmstadt from 1701 to 1709. It concerns a stirring theological-cosmological poem that Leibniz wanted to be written by Johann Wilhelm Petersen (1649–1727), a theologian and mystic.

---

[70] consequences. | For since there is no absolute certainty of election | *deleted*.
[71] Editor's title. From the Latin. Incomplete: remarks unconnected on the 'Uranius' poem have not been translated.

I have often thought to myself that no one is more able than Petersen to compose a poem with the title 'Uranius', or rather, 'Uraniados', which would, with due intensity and in Virgilian measure, celebrate the city of God and eternal life.[72] It would have to begin with cosmogony and paradise, which would be the subject of the first book, or even the first and second. The third, fourth and fifth, if it were thought fit, would relate the Fall of Adam and redemption of mankind through Christ, and touch on the history of the Church. Then I would readily allow the poet to give in the sixth book a description of the millennial reign,[73] and to depict in the seventh the anti-Christ invading with Gog and Magog, and finally overthrown by a breath from the divine mouth. In the eighth we would have the day of judgement and the punishments of the damned; in the ninth, tenth and eleventh, the happiness of the blessed, the grandeur and beauty of the City of God and of the abode of the blessed, and excursions through the immense spaces of the universe to illuminate the wonderful works of God; one would also add a description of the heavenly palace itself. The twelfth would end everything with the restitution of all things, that is, with the evil themselves reformed and restored to happiness and to God, with God henceforth operating all in

---

[72] It seems that Leibniz had been toying with the idea of asking Petersen to write such a poem for around five years at least. On the back of a letter from Petersen written in October 1706, Leibniz drafted (but never did send) the following reply: 'I, who am often accustomed to think about how the talents of great men might be put to the best use, have seen that you are able to accomplish what I have often wished for – a fit work about heavenly things in the form of an epic poem. For although theology shines forth in prose, it would be even more sublime if clothed in Virgilian majesty, which you alone, out of everyone, could do best. The substance of such a work would be thus: first, God, sufficient in his secret and perpetual eternity, then cosmogony, then the economy of providence in the government of things. But the second part of the work should be about future matters, whether they pertain to bodies or souls or any other things, and here it should be about the purification of souls and the restitution of things, or rather their gradual improvement and elevation. I would like that the last but not least part of the work be devoted to the grandeur of the celestial kingdom, or, as I shall call it, the divine court. There the extraordinary virtues of the angels should be depicted in vivid colours, and the happiness of blessed souls celebrated: to them, innumerable worlds are exhibited, not just the world under our feet; and as they see for all time the different scenes of divine wisdom and goodness, their love and veneration for the supreme mind grows more and more. Here is the holy place for the most elegant fictions, although the truth surpasses anything we can imagine, no matter how beautiful. But aside from you, with your divinely inspired power of expression, and your insight into the inner recesses of divine matters, I know of no one from whom such a work could be hoped for.' G. W. Leibniz, *De l'horizon de la doctrine humaine*, ed. Michael Fichant (Paris: Vrin, 1991), p. 25.
[73] The inclusion of the millennial reign of Christ in the poem may well be a concession to Petersen, who was a committed millenarian. In 1692 he had been dismissed from his post as superintendent of the churches of Lüneburg for teaching millenarian doctrines. Leibniz did not share Petersen's millenarian beliefs, but still thought that Petersen's dismissal was harsh; see A I 7, p. 37/LTS, p. 80. For Leibniz's attitude towards millenarianism, see Daniel J. Cook and Lloyd Strickland, 'Leibniz And Millenarianism', in F. Beiderbeck and S. Waldhoff (eds), *Pluralität der Perspektiven und Einheit der Wahrheit im Werk von G. W. Leibniz* (Berlin: Akademie Verlag, 2011), pp. 77–90.

all without exception. Here and there one might engage in a more sublime philosophy mixed with mystical theology, where the origin of things would be treated in the manner of Lucretius,[74] Vida and Fracastor.[75] A poet would be forgiven for things which would be harder to tolerate from a dogmatic theologian. Such a work would make its author immortal and could be wonderfully useful for moving the souls of men to hope for a better state, and for lighting the sparks of a more genuine piety.

---

[74] Lucretius (first century BCE), Roman poet and philosopher who authored *De rerum natura*.
[75] Marco Girolamo Vida (1485–1566), Bishop of Alba and humanist scholar; Girolamo Fracastoro (1478–1553), a physician and scholar.

10

The Afterlife

A. RESURRECTION AND PURGATORY

1. On the resurrection of bodies (21 May 1671)[1]

Manuscript:

M: LH I 3, 4 Bl. 4–5.

Transcription:

A: A II 1 (2nd edn), pp. 183–6.

Leibniz wrote this piece for Duke Johann Friedrich, and sent it as one of two appendices to his letter to the Duke of 21 May 1671.[2]

Appendix
On the resurrection of bodies

(1) Many see the resurrection as difficult to explain, for instance because it would seem impossible to recover bodies which various accidents had

---

[1] Editor's title (taken from Leibniz's description of the piece, in the accompanying letter to Johann Friedrich, as 'An appendix on the resurrection of bodies'. From the Latin. Complete.
[2] See A II 1 (2nd edn), pp. 170–7. The second appendix concerned the immortality of the soul. See A II 1 (2nd edn), pp. 177–83.

dispersed throughout all corners of the world. This is especially so for the ancient semi-Christian followers of Aristotle, who have invented a difficulty of their own. For since they think that the essence of each thing consists in matter and a certain substantial form which is extinguished by the corruption of the thing, and since they assume as an axiom that there is no return from privation to possession,[3] they have been unable to grasp how the same flesh can return.

(2) On the other hand, the Democritean philosophy explains every essence of bodies by means of size, shape and motion, and no matter how the body is corrupted, nothing of the matter or the mass is destroyed; consequently there is nothing which will prevent the same shape being reintroduced into the same mass of a given size; and hence a body can be remade numerically the same in the way that a clock is remade if the cogs that have been removed are put back together in precisely the same way.

(3) Let that be so, you will say, since God can recover all those atoms. But what if another man claims them for himself with an equal right? For instance, suppose a man has been devoured by another man, or even by beasts, which have passed into the latter man in his food; or suppose that he has rotted, which gives rise to grass which is turned into food; a part evaporated into the air which is taken in by another by respiration and converted into nourishment: to whom will God assign it? To its first owner. But what if some later usurper is left completely destitute of any body and 'should provoke laughter like the daw stripped of his stolen colours'?[4] For assume a man has been raised solely on human flesh from infancy. What will be left for him? Augustine, in chapter 20 of book 22 of *City of God*, thinks it should be returned to him whose flesh it was first, which he drew from the womb of his mother along with her flesh; that other supplementary matter is added from the elements, just as they who die as children will be resurrected in a mature size.[5] For, as Paul said in Ephesians 4, all will meet unto a

---

[3] The principle referred to here, namely that there is no return from privation to possession, derives from Aristotle's belief that the numerical identity of a thing or disposition of a thing cannot be restored in the event that the thing or disposition undergoes corruption (that is, destruction). Leibniz is correct in assuming that this principle was inherited by Scholastic thinkers, though he overlooks the fact that some, such as Aquinas, held that the principle holds good in the case of every natural thing bar that of human beings (such that the numerical identity of human bodies which are corrupted or destroyed *can* be restored). See Aquinas, *Summa contra Gentiles*, trans. Charles J. O'Neil (New York: Image Books, 1957), IV.81.
[4] Horace, *Epistolae* 1.3.19f.
[5] Augustine, *City of God* XXII.20: 'That flesh, therefore, shall be restored to the man in whom it first became human flesh. For it must be looked upon as borrowed by the other person, and, like a

perfect man, unto the measure of the age of the fullness of Christ.⁶ Therefore this seed and as it were yeast of the original body, will readily swell up to the right size by the addition of supplementary matter, just as fungi spread themselves in a single night, and loaves multiplied in the hands of Christ.

(4) And that is shrewdly observed. But what if the mother was likewise fed on human flesh? For what a child has drawn from the mother is either the very thing which the mother drew from her mother, or has been added through nourishment. If the former, then at the time of the resurrection it is to be claimed by the mother, not by the child; if the latter, it is to be claimed by neither the mother nor the child, but by those whose flesh was eaten, so either way the child will be deprived of a body. I admit that these cases can be imagined even though they have never happened. For who has ever lived on human flesh alone? But I don't want to avail myself of this extreme solution.

(5) So let us grant that it happened as has been posited: there will still be no reason why we should despair of solving the problem. And firstly, if we shall speak the truth of the matter about this flesh and these bones, it seems that the point scarcely needs to be laboured, since the mind and memory of things done and done to us makes us the same, not the flesh or bones; even if not a single atom (aside from that point in which the mind is implanted) now remains in my body, or in the last judgement there was flesh left over, which I have drawn from my mother, it will make no difference, nor will the loss be felt, since bodies insensibly change by a continual flux and renewal. Physicians debate about whether the blood is part of the body, and it can of course be drawn out of a healthy body by the cutting of a vein, and replenished by transfusion. Therefore neither the membranes, nor the flesh, nor the entrails will be in our possession, for they are renewed by a continuous transpiration drawn off from the blood.

(6) Passages from Holy Scripture do not prove this identity of the flesh. Even Job 19, when he says 'I know that my redeemer liveth,'⁷ I suspect he is talking of his restoration and elevation from dust rather than the

---

pecuniary loan, must be returned to the lender. His own flesh, however, which he lost by famine, shall be restored to him by Him who can recover even what has evaporated. And though it had been absolutely annihilated, so that no part of its substance remained in any secret spot of nature, the Almighty could restore it by such means as He saw fit ... From all that we have thus considered, and discussed with such poor ability as we can command, we gather this conclusion, that in the resurrection of the flesh the body shall be of that size which it either had attained or should have attained in the flower of its youth.'
⁶ Ephesians 4.13.
⁷ Job 19.25.

resurrection of the dead. When bones are clothed with flesh in Ezekiel 37,[8] leaving aside the parable, the event is not thought to be controversial, for if the members survive they will undoubtedly be restored. If they do not survive, there will be no more need for the bones and flesh of this life in the next one than there is for the flesh of an infant in old age. Even Alfenus has recognized in *Digest* 1.76 that we consist of certain particles, and that our bodies are in perpetual flux.[9]

(7) But it is not necessary to go to such extremes here. Let us instead maintain that the flesh and bones remain. But how are they constituted? Are they clothed in a mass of filth? Certainly not, if a spiritual body should rise again. For it is known that in each thing there is a certain seminal centre which diffuses itself, and contains as it were the tincture and preserves the specific motion of the thing. This is established from the regeneration of plants from seeds (this at least is uncontroversial), from the plastic power of the seed in the womb and from the essences of chemicals. Therefore it is likewise in the bones: in our flesh, besides that *terra damnata*, *phlegm* or *caput mortuum*,[10] as chemists call it, a subtler part lies hidden in the spirits. When a member is cut off or rots away, this subtler part returns to the fountain of life, to which the soul itself is implanted. This is evident, for

---

[8] Ezekiel 37.1-14.
[9] The Alfenus in question is Publius Alfenus Varus. Leibniz is referring to Justinian's *Digest* V.1.1.76, which reads: 'ALFENUS, *Digest*, book 6: The case was put that several of the judges appointed for the same trial had been excused after the case had had a hearing, and others had been put in their place. The question was whether the replacement of individual judges had resulted in the same case or a different court. I replied that not merely if one or two but even if all had been changed, the case and the court both still remained the same as they had been before. And this was not the only example of a thing being considered the same after its parts had been changed, but there were many others too. For a legion too was held to be the same although many of its members had been killed and others had been put in their place. A people too was thought to be the same at the present time as it had been a hundred years ago, although no one was now alive from that period. Likewise, if a ship had been repaired so often that no plank remained the same as the old had been, it was nevertheless considered to be the same ship. For if anyone thought that a thing became a different one when its parts were changed, it would follow from this reasoning that we ourselves would not be the same as we were a year ago, because, as the philosophers said, the extremely tiny particles of which we were made up daily left our bodies and others came from outside to take their place. Therefore, a thing whose appearance remained the same was considered also to be the same thing.' Justinian, *The Digest of Justinian*, trans. Alan Watson (University of Pennsylvania Press: Philadelphia, 1985), vol. I: V.1.1.76.
[10] According to a lexicon of technical terms prevalent in Leibniz's day, *terra damnata* [accursed earth] is 'the last of the five Chymical Principles, and is that which remains after all the other Principles are extracted by Distillation, Calcination, &c.' *Phlegm* is 'the Fourth of the Five Chymical Principles' and is 'The Insipid Water that comes first in the Distillation of Acid Spirits.' *Caput mortuum*, meanwhile, is 'that thick dry Matter that remains after Distillation of any thing, but of Minerals especially.' John Harris, *Lexicon Technicum: or, an Universal English Dictionary of Arts and Sciences* (London, 1708, 2nd edn), vol. 1 [no page numbers given in the text].

instance, in the experience of those who have had a hand or a foot cut off: they often feel these members as though they were still present; they seem to be pinched, tickled and hurt, for no other reason than that this subtle spirit, in which the substance of the member was contained, as it were, is still present and exercises the same movements even now.

(8) So let Thyestes devour his sons,[11] and let him, if you please, swallow the entire living being, and let it be digested somehow in his stomach; nevertheless the seminal part, victorious over all violence, will gather itself into its own centre, the subtlety of which cannot be diminished by teeth, or dissolved by the acid of the stomach, nor likewise can it be converted into nourishment, since it is evident from the example of plants that the seminal part is even resistant to fire and survives in the ashes.[12] It will restore the coarse part, or rather its own coarse part, purged of filth to the extent it deserves, for when the world is liquefied by fires and heat joins homogenous things together,[13] kindred things which retain the traces of similar motions will also come together again at that time. Or rather, since it does not matter which coarse part is most alike, the fires will create by fermentation one and the same body by means of the flower of substance, the mass and impurities having been corrected by transformation. Indeed, the Jews say that in a certain little bone, which they call Luz, the soul with the flower of substance survives, unconquered by all eventualities.

---

[11] See p. 266 n.16.
[12] The alchemists' example of plants which grow again after having been burned to ashes was often used to establish the existence of an indestructible (or at least incombustible) seed or core not just in plants, but in humans too, and consequently was often cited in connection with the resurrection. See, for instance, Joseph Du Chesne, *The Practise of Chymicall, and Hermeticall Physicke, for the Preservation of Health*, trans. Thomas Timme (London, 1605), X; Kenelm Digby, *A Discourse Concerning the Vegetation of Plants* (London, 1661), pp. 73–5; Thomas Browne, *Religio Medici* (London, 1682, 8th edn), p. 109.
[13] Leibniz is probably thinking here of the Apocalypse as described in Revelation 8.5-12, where the Earth is destroyed by fire.

2. On purgatory (January 1677)[14]

Manuscript:

M: LH I 3, 4 Bl. 6–11.

Transcription:

A: A VI 4, pp. 2123–5.

The following text was written at around the same time Leibniz conducted an investigation into the various passages from Scripture and the Church Fathers that were often adduced in favour of the doctrine of purgatory. The investigation itself consisted of quoting the relevant passages and then interpreting them, the results of which are summarized here.[15]

January 1677

I have examined the many passages of the ancients which are deemed by writers of the Roman Church to prove purgatory, and having rejected those which seem to have no great force, I have at least considered those which can give some indication of the prevailing opinion of the Roman Church today.

And from that examination I have at any rate learned this – that nearly all the Holy Fathers thought that some fire of purification, i.e. some temporary punishment after death, and more painful according to the weight of the sins, is to be inflicted even on the majority of the faithful. Yet there is a distinction between them. The doctors of the Greek Church have announced that there is in fact a transition to that fire, which it will be necessary for all to experience at the time of the resurrection, when they are brought before the Lord, though they also seem to have conceded that there is some delay to this fire. Meanwhile, the Western Church ever since Tertullian and Cyprian seems to have inclined to the view that the soul is immediately subjected to certain punishments after death, and that it is

---

[14] Editor's title. From the Latin. Complete.
[15] This investigation itself is printed in full in A VI 4, pp. 2126–44. Two other minor texts related to this investigation can be found in A VI 4, pp. 2145–7 and p. 2153.

freed from them and granted beatitude once it is purified. Therefore the Western Church's opinion, which flourishes today in the Roman Church, cannot be denied, as there are traces of it expressed well enough even in the old Latin Church. But in the Greek Church, neither formerly nor today, as I observe, is a purgatory of this sort accepted.

Of all the passages of the ancients which are invoked to prove purgatory, very few pertain to the matter itself. The Roman Church teaches today that *purgatory* is either a place or a state of the souls of the faithful in which for some time after death they suffer the gravest punishment for their sins, and they are helped by the prayers and sacrifices of the living until divine justice is placated and they, now purged, are granted beatitude.

But *some* passages from the holy Fathers which are invoked to prove this prove only that we should pray for the dead, while *others* show only that there is some such thing as purgatory. But in fact many ancient and more recent authors accept this purgatory at the time of the resurrection, when they think all men should be tried by fire, and therefore they do not acknowledge the purgatory of the Roman Church.

I believe *that the purgatory of the Roman Church does not follow from an oration on behalf of the dead* by the force of such an argument like this one: if we should pray for the dead, it follows that the dead are helped by prayers; if the dead are helped by prayers, it follows that they are neither entirely damned nor entirely saved, but are still subject to punishment; if the faithful dead are subject to punishment, it follows that purgatory exists; therefore if we should pray for the dead we should admit that purgatory exists.

To this argument we can respond, *first, by denying that it is necessary that the dead are helped by prayers*. But, you will say, prayers are therefore useless. I believe they will be useless to the dead themselves, but not entirely to all others. For there will be prayers on behalf of the dead, or at least certain votive offerings. But votive offerings can be, and usually are, made even when a matter is no longer undecided, and at any rate they are useful in that we demonstrate our feelings, and trace all things back to the will of God, whom we implore, by some kind of honour and worship. Thus we are accustomed to utter votive offerings, and not merely prayers, concerning past events. Suppose I was notified of a great battle in which my brother or my friend had taken part. I immediately turn to God and to votive offerings: I wish with all my heart that nothing bad has happened to him; although I will readily understand afterwards, when the matter has subtly sunk in, that what is done cannot be undone, and, if he is killed, he will not therefore be not-killed, and that if he has escaped unharmed, he will not therefore be killed today in yesterday's battle. I do not know what others do, but certainly with me votive offerings of this sort have often slipped out with the first mental impulse. Perhaps there is no shortage of people who have also expressed such offerings in a similar case and, having been bound, have paid their obligation. Therefore it is hardly surprising that the living break out in votive offerings on behalf of the dead, aroused by charity, because it concerns the most important matter, namely the happiness of the deceased's soul. For things which are uncertain and unknown to us are usually considered as not yet done, which is the real reason why we utter prayers concerning matters which are past and finished. It is the same with regard to future things that are certain and determined. No one doubts that the beatitude or the damnation of the dead is certain and cannot be changed by any prayers or good deeds, since even according to the opinion of the Roman Church, if they are damned, they will certainly not be saved from hell; if they are conveyed to heaven, they will not fall from happiness; and if they are in purgatory, they are secure in their future happiness. So the beatitude and damnation of the dead is not subject to any change. Therefore the votive offerings with which we demand from God their eternal salvation will be useless to them. However, no one will deny that this conforms to usage and a certain natural instinct.

Secondly, *we deny that it follows from the fact that the dead are helped by prayers that they are under punishment*, for they are able to obtain greater glory by our prayers.

Thirdly, *we deny that the purgatory of the Roman Church follows from the fact that the faithful dead are punished*, for the ancient Greeks understood it with regard to one's own purgatory, which they thought everyone undergoes on the day of the resurrection.

And all this is said with regard to the passages in which mention is made of prayers for the dead. I come to the passages in which mention is made of actual temporary punishment after death, of fire, of purification – such are the passages that say every soul is saved by fire, that those whose work has been burned will be saved, so to speak, by fire and that (by an argument from the contrary sense) certain sins will be forgiven in a future world. All these can be very neatly explained by the purgatory of the resurrection.[16]

---

[16] 'purgatory of the resurrection…is said to apply to all men after the resurrection, although it will not be equally severe and long-lasting for everyone. And it is not [a purgatory] of the separated soul, but of the whole man after the reunion of body and soul. Conversely, the purgatory of the Roman Church is peculiar and particular to each person, although it happens in one common place and it

3. St Augustine's opinion on purgatory (6/16 December 1694)[17]

Manuscript:

M: Hannover HStA Dep. 84 A 180 Bl. 122–3.

Transcription:

A: A I 10, pp. 90–3.

The following text was written for Duchess Benedicta Henrietta, and sent to her via Leibniz's patroness, Electress Sophie of Hanover. In the accompanying letter to Sophie, Leibniz wrote 'As for purgatory, I wanted to verify what I said recently to Your Electoral Highness. I have accurately represented St Augustine's opinion, drawn from his own words. From those words it is obvious that he speaks about purgatory with uncertainty, and that therefore it was not an article of faith in his time. And that therefore the Roman Church has changed in a matter of faith.'[18]

(6 December 1694)

St Augustine's opinion on purgatory[19]

It is very certain that St Augustine talked about purgatory as an uncertain thing. And after having read his passages attentively, one cannot doubt this unless one rejects his sincerity. And he wrote in that way when he was already old, and he never retracted it. He effectively leaned towards a kind of purgatory, and he believed it *probable* that those who are too attached[20] to worldly things will suffer pain in the other life by the detachment from

---

begins immediately after the death of each person, and immediately finishes when divine justice is placated, even before the resurrection.' A VI 4, pp. 2126–7.
[17] Author's title. From the French. Complete. In the left upper corner of the first page, Leibniz wrote: 'Taken from the paper for Madam the Duchess dowager of Hanover, 6 December 1694, in order to show to Her Highness that, in this instance, the Roman Church has changed, and that what today is an article of faith has not always been so.'
[18] A I 10, pp. 89–90.
[19] The title is in Leibniz's hand, and was added after his amanuensis had written out the copy.
[20] attached | in this life | *deleted*, M; this deletion is not recorded in transcription A.

what they loved, before they attain perfect beatitude. But more than once he declares that this is only *probable*, and he speaks about it in a doubtful way, specifically using 'perhaps', and saying that it will not seem 'unbelievable', just as if he said that it is not impossible. Which clearly shows that he did not hold it to be an article of faith.

Here is the passage from his *Enchiridion* chapters 67, 68 and 69, in which he attempts to clarify St Paul's 1 Corinthians 7.32,[21] which says that those who have built wood and straw on the foundation of rock will see their work consumed and will nonetheless be saved as by fire. First he explains it of this life, and says that when one renounces worldly things for the love of God one thereby suffers a bitter pain and is saved as by fire. Then he adds that 'it is not unbelievable' that something similar happens even after this life, and that there is a certain purgative fire that consists in the pain of detachment, and which brings it about that the soul is saved through this fire with more or less rapidity.[22] But it is better to give this Father's own words, faithfully translated, from chapter 68:

> This fire (that is, the one of which St Paul speaks)[23] nevertheless does in this life what the apostle has said of it, when two believers are exposed to it, of which one thinks about that which is of God, and how he may please God, and (thus) builds on the foundation which is Jesus Christ with gold, silver and precious stones; but the other thinks about worldly things, (for example) how he may please his wife, and (thus) builds wood, hay, and stubble on the same foundation. The work of the first is not consumed at all, since he has not loved those things whose loss[24] can grieve him. But the work of the second is consumed by fire, because one could not lose without pain what one has possessed with love. However, if in this choice he prefers to be deprived of these things than of Jesus Christ, and if he does not give up (his saviour) out of the fear of losing these things, or out of apprehension regarding the pain he has to suffer by losing them, he is saved, but as by fire. For the bitter pain of things loved and lost burns him, but without

---

[21] Leibniz's reference is wrong; 1 Corinthians 7.32 says 'He that is unmarried careth for the things that belong to the Lord.' The passage he is thinking of is in fact from 1 Corinthians 3.11-15: 'For no one can lay any foundation other than the one already laid, which is Jesus Christ. If any man builds on this foundation using gold, silver, costly stones, wood, hay or straw, his work will be shown for what it is, because the Day will bring it to light. It will be revealed with fire, and the fire will test the quality of each man's work. If what he has built survives, he will receive his reward. If it is burned up, he will suffer loss; he himself will be saved, but only as one escaping through the flames.'
[22] Leibniz is here summarizing part of Augustine's *Enchiridion ad Laurentium de fide, spe, et caritate*, 18.69. Later in this text he returns to the same passage, quoting it rather than paraphrasing it.
[23] The bracketed words are Leibniz's own interpolations in the quoted passage.
[24] Reading 'omission' in place of 'amission'.

subverting or destroying him, because he is fortified by the solidity of the foundation.²⁵

So far St Augustine speaks only of this corporeal life, but in chapter 69 he moves on to something similar that he thinks may happen in the other. Here again are his words:

> It is not *unbelievable* (he says) that something of this nature happens even after this life; and *it is a matter that can be enquired into, and discovered or left unknown*, namely whether some believers are saved sooner or later through a certain purgatorial fire, in proportion as they have more or less loved perishable goods.²⁶

Thus it is clear that by the purgatorial or purgative fire, St Augustine means nothing other than the bitter pain of detachment from the worldly things that one has loved too much. It is even true that everything that can be thought about this²⁷ fire, whatever it might be, seemed uncertain to him and – to tell the truth – worthy of being looked into, but of a nature that could be left unknown.

It is also very remarkable that St Augustine, far from having retracted this, repeated it word for word in another work, *On the Eight Questions addressed to Dulcitus*.²⁸ He gave the same interpretation to the same passage from St Paul in chapter 16 of his book *On Faith and Works*,²⁹ and what he says there is repeated again in the book to Dulcitius. This shows that it was his preferred opinion. But also in order to make it known that it is only an opinion, he even adds signs of doubt which are very deliberate and very

---

²⁵ 'This fire nevertheless does in this life exactly what the apostle has said when it comes into contact with two believers, with one thinking of things which are of God, how he may please God, that is, building upon Christ the foundation, gold, silver, and precious stones, and the other thinking of things which are of the world, how he may please his wife, that is, building upon the same foundation wood, hay, and stubble. For the work of the former is not burned, because he has not loved those things whose loss can cause him grief; but the work of the latter is burned, because things which are possessed with love are not lost without pain. But since, by our supposition, he would prefer to lose these things rather than to lose Christ, and since he does not desert Christ out of fear of losing them, although he is grieved when he does lose them, he is indeed saved, but it is so as if by fire, because the grief for the lost things he had loved burns him. But it does not subvert nor consume him because he is fortified by the stability and incorruptibility of the foundation.' Augustine, *Enchiridion*, 18.68.
²⁶ 'It is not unbelievable that something of this kind happens even after this life. And it is a matter that may be inquired into, and either ascertained or remain unknown, whether some believers are saved quicker or slower in proportion as they have loved perishable goods.' Augustine *Enchiridion*, 18.69.
²⁷ this | purgatorial | *deleted*, M; this deletion is not recorded in transcription A.
²⁸ Augustine *De octo Dulcitii quaestionibus liber unus*, I.3.
²⁹ Augustine, *De fide et operibus*, 16.29.

clear, mentioning as uncertain the question of whether this purgative fire should be understood of the tribulations of this life, or of the pains of the other. Here is the translation of his own words: 'Whether' (he says) 'that only takes place in this life or whether there are some judgements' (or punishments) 'that will follow it, the explanation I have given' (in the sense of St Paul) 'does not seem far removed from reason and from the truth.'[30]

Even in his book *The City of God*, book 21 chapter 26, he repeats this interpretation, but always while expressing uncertainty. For after having said that 'one could not lose, without a bitter pain, what one has cherished with an attractive love, here is' (he adds) 'the discovery of this fire which does not damn anyone, but which enriches some' (whose gold and precious stones become more brilliant), 'causes loss to others' (whose wood and stubble it consumes), 'and proves both.'[31] This shows again that, according to St Augustine, even the good pass through the fire of purgatory, but without being damaged by it.

Then he adds, still with uncertainty, that this fire could be understood not only of the tribulations of this life, but also of certain pains in the other. Here are his quite remarkable words:

> With regards to what should happen after the death of this body, until one comes to the last day of damnation and of remuneration following the resurrection of bodies – if it is said that in this interval of time the spirits of the deceased suffer such a fire which is not suffered by those whose manners and loves in the life of this body have not furnished wood, hay or combustible stubble, and if those that brought such works will suffer only there, or here as well as there, or for that matter just here, in order not to suffer there[32] according to the nature of this fire of passing tribulation, which must burn the earthly things that are venial and exempt [these people] from damnation: this is what I do not contest, for *perhaps it is true.*[33]

---

[30] 'Whether men suffer these [afflictions] in this life only, or whether some such judgements follow after this life as well, the interpretation of this opinion is not, I think, inconsistent with the principles of truth,' Augustine *De fide et operibus*, 16.29.

[31] 'one does not lose without a burning pain what one has possessed with an alluring love. Here, it seems to me, we have discovered a fire which destroys neither, but enriches the one, brings loss to the other, and proves both', St Augustine, *City of God*, 21.26.

[32] there | (if they will suffer, I thus say) | *deleted*. This deletion is not recorded in transcription A.

[33] 'But if it be said that, in the interval of time after the death of this body until the last day of damnation and remuneration which shall follow the resurrection of bodies, the spirits of the dead shall endure a fire of such a kind that shall not be felt by those who have not in this life of this body had such manners and desires as shall be consumed like wood, hay and stubble, but that it shall be felt by others who have carried with them structures of that kind, whether there only, or here as well as there, or just here so that there they do not come upon the fire of transitory tribulation

It is clear again from this passage of St Augustine, as well as from chapter 109 of his *Enchiridion* and other passages, that his ideas on the state of souls were quite different from those of today,[34] since he believed, with other ancient authors, that the spirits which are due to be saved remain in certain closed places, where the imperfect ones suffer from pain which consists in the regret caused by the deprivation of earthly goods, which continues for some time, until they are perfectly detached from these goods, and then afterwards they await at rest the great day of the final judgement, which will give them true beatitude.

4. On the time of purification (not later than spring 1698)[35]

Manuscript:

M   The manuscript was lost following its initial publication in *Otium Hanoveranum*, ed. J. F. Feller (Leipzig, 1718), p. 179.

Transcription:

A: A IV 7, p. 666.

The provenance of this piece is unknown. It found its way into the possession of Joachim Friedrich Feller (1673–1726), who worked as Leibniz's secretary from August 1696 until the spring of 1698. In 1718, two years after Leibniz's death, Feller published this text and a number of others, which are otherwise no longer extant. Since Feller did not have access to Leibniz's manuscripts after the spring of 1698, this piece – and the others published by him – must have been written before then.

The time of purification lasts as long as is needed for a soul to turn over in its contemplations the wickedness of its former sin, and therefore this pain

---

which burns away worldliness which is venial and exempts them from damnation – this I do not contradict, because perhaps it is true', St Augustine, *City of God*, 21.26.

[34] today, | and that he, and the majority of the ancients, believed that the souls of those who are due to be saved | *deleted*; this deletion is not recorded in transcription A.

[35] Editor's title. From the Latin. Complete.

consists in a vision of sin, evil and the devil, just as heavenly joy consists in the vision of God and the good. But those who die in enmity towards God, their evil is infinite since a will to harm is an infinite evil. For he who wills to harm has not just willed [to harm] that which he has harmed, but also all those things which, since he cannot harm them, he has neglected, and these are infinite. However the act of harming without the will to do so does not have a definite nature.

5. Whether purgatory is an article of faith (4/14 January and 2/12 February 1700)[36]

Manuscripts:

M1:   LBr 251 Bl. 79 (letter 1).
M2:   Warsaw, Biblioteka Narodowa III. 4879 Bl. 145 (letter 2).

Transcriptions:

A1:   A I 18, p. 244 (letter 1).
A2:   A I 18, p. 390 (letter 2).

These two pieces come from two letters to Johann Fabricius. The discussion about purgatory was prompted by the following remark Fabricius made in his letter to Leibniz of 27 December 1699: 'The requisite "unanimous consent of the fathers" is certainly associated with a great difficulty. If in its place was substituted "significant majority of the fathers", things would be easier. Nevertheless, purgatory has great support, even a consensus, among the most ancient Fathers, which the most learned William Forbes does not dare deny.'[37]

---

[36] Editor's title. From the Latin. Incomplete: the material in the letters on other topics has not been translated.
[37] A I 18, p. 218. Fabricius is referring to Forbes' *Considerationes modestae et pacificae controversiarum, de justificatione, purgatorio, invocatione Sanctorum et Christo Mediatore, Eucharistia* (London, 1658).

[Letter 1, 4/14 January 1700]

I once examined the majority of the passages written by the ancients on purgatory,[38] and discovered that opinions have varied greatly, as they would on an exceedingly problematic issue; even Augustine recognized that it was a problem. A great number [of the ancients] think that, except for martyrs and other privileged persons, neither blessedness nor damnation takes place before the day of judgement. The Origenists considered hell itself as purgatory, and some approved authors seem to have thought this too, at least with respect to Christians. Some ancient Greeks taught an unusual kind of purgatory, which I customarily call 'the purgatory of the resurrection', namely that those carried off to meet Christ pass through fire, and then cast aside their dross. But a purgatory similar to that of today seems to have flourished chiefly among the Latins. At any rate, it is absolutely certain that it is not possible to demonstrate any apostolic tradition (which the articles of faith require) in favour of the purgatory of the Roman Church. The actual profession of faith of the Roman Church requires *the unanimous agreement of the fathers* in interpreting Scripture, and on that point, unless I am mistaken, it disagrees with itself.

[Letter 2, 2/12 February 1700]

In the articles of faith there is a great presumption against anything which cannot be proved; nor is it necessary that our side should uphold negative articles, like 'purgatory is false'. It is enough to deny that purgatory is an article of faith, and for that purpose the belief in purgatory is to be considered as equivalent to false until it is proved. For the rest, I myself would not dare to swear that there is nothing analogous to purgatory, for the status of intermediate souls is an obscure matter, and one not sufficiently revealed by God. And it is absolutely certain that it is not possible to have the unanimous agreement of the fathers about purgatory, of the kind demanded by the monk Vincent of Lerins.[39] Moreover, I am afraid that this

---

[38] In January and February 1677. See A VI 4, pp. 2126–44, 2145–7 and 2153.
[39] Leibniz is alluding here to Chapter 28 of St Vincent of Lerins' *Commonitorium primum*: 'when the corruption of each wicked error begins to emerge, and to steal certain words of holy law in defence of itself, and to expound these words falsely and fraudulently, the opinions of the ancients in the interpretation of the canon are to be collected at once. From these opinions, any novel and therefore profane view that arises may be exposed without any quibbling, and condemned without any hesitation. But we should only collect the opinions of those fathers who, living holily, teaching

demand for negative articles may result in a less profitable disputation. It would be more for the good of the Catholics that they not be held as articles of faith, so why do they force them on us?

6. On the valley of Jehoshaphat (1715 (?))[40]

Manuscript:

M: LBr 705 Bl. 119r.

This short piece concerns the problem of how all of the human beings who have ever lived could simultaneously fit into the Valley of Jehoshaphat, which was traditionally believed to be the site of the Last Judgement, following Joel 3.2 and 3.12. The problem had been considered by numerous medieval and early modern thinkers.[41] Leibniz had previously considered it in a letter written in 1711, in which he indicated that there would likely be room for all (and if it turned out there was not, he thought the problem could still be resolved, for '[w]hen people are a little too crowded around a table, all they have to do to have more elbow room is everywhere move away from it a little, from the center toward the circumference, and so it is here: the good Lord would only have to pull men a little into the air to meet with him, and in this way there would be room for them, even if there were a lot more of them').[42] In the following piece, Leibniz attempts to show that the Valley of Jehoshaphat is sufficient to accommodate all.

Let us suppose that on the Earth now there are one hundred million souls, and that the men are replaced every fifty years.[43] If we grant that the

---

wisely, and remaining steadfastly in the Catholic faith and communion, were deemed worthy either to die faithfully in Christ, or to be happily killed for Christ. Whereby it should be thought, on this condition, that whatever is supported manifestly, frequently, persistently, and in one and the same sense by all or the majority – who form as it were a sort of council of teachers receiving, holding and bequeathing the same doctrine – should be considered as indubitable, certain and established.'

[40] Editor's title. From the French. Complete.

[41] For details, see Lloyd Strickland, 'Taking scripture seriously: Leibniz and the Jehoshaphat problem', *The Heythrop Journal* 52 (2011): 40–51.

[42] Klopp IX, p. 342/LTS, pp. 407–8.

[43] years |, in 6,000 years there will be 120 renewals. Let us suppose, with the usual chronology, that

world has existed for 6,000 years, in accordance with the usual chronology, there will be 120 renewals. But as the number of men was smaller in the beginning, let us content ourselves with 100 renewals of 100 million men, so all the men together would make ten thousand million.

Now a German league being 4,000 paces and a pace being 5 feet, it will be 20,000 feet, and such a league squared will be 400,000,000 square feet, that is, four hundred million square feet. Let us grant a square foot to each man, for although a man can be wider, as a rule he is smaller. So if the valley of Jehoshaphat were taken in such a way that it included the whole course of the stream which makes the region around Jerusalem fertile, and around a length of 12½ leagues with a width of 2 leagues, on average, this valley would contain 25 square leagues, and consequently ten thousand million square feet, without counting the fact that there is an enormous number of small children who will have no need at all for so much space.

B. SALVATION AND DAMNATION

1. On the damnation of the innocent (4/14 September 1690)[44]

Manuscript:

M: LBr F20 Bl. 941 and 945.

Transcription:

A: A II 2, pp. 340–1.

From a letter to Landgrave Ernst von Hessen-Rheinfels (1623–93), prompted by Antoine Arnauld's *Seconde dénonciation de la nouvelle hérésie du péché philosophique, enseignée par les jésuites de Dijon* (Cologne, 1690):

---

the world was created 5650 years ago. | *deleted*.
[44] Editor's title. From the French. Incomplete: the parts of the letter on a different topic have not been translated.

I do not think that the doctrine of the eternal damnation of so many almost-innocent people is as edifying and as useful for preventing sin as is imagined. It inspires thoughts scarcely compatible with the love of God, and serves to bolster libertinism by undermining the credence to religion in some minds. It is claimed that the fear this doctrine inspires in men is capable of restraining them, but instead it produces a bad effect, for they doubt everything when things are exaggerated. Mr Arnauld has very aptly shown elsewhere that those who only abstain from sins out of this fear of hell are not among the true friends of God, and in his view they will be damned. I cannot believe that all those who have not known Jesus Christ after the Gospel had been preached in the world will be lost without hope no matter how they have lived. One cannot stop oneself thinking that unjust, and one cannot get around that by saying with Mr Arnauld that we should not judge God by the ideas we have of justice. For one has to have a general idea or notion of justice when one says that God is just, otherwise it would be to attribute to him just a word. For my part, I think that just as God's arithmetic and geometry is the same as that of men (except that God's is infinitely more extensive), so too natural jurisprudence and every other truth is the same in heaven as on Earth. We must not imagine that God is capable of doing what would be tyranny in men.

2. On the imagination of the future life (not later than spring 1698)[45]

Manuscript:

M: The manuscript was lost following its initial publication in *Otium Hanoveranum*, ed. J. F. Feller (Leipzig, 1718), pp. 169–71.

Transcription:

A: A IV 7, pp. 661–2.

This piece treats a subject also dealt with in a short work from 1685,[46] and may date

---

[45] Editor's title. From the Latin. Complete.
[46] Namely 'De salute animae curanda' (February–October 1685 (?)), A VI 4, pp. 2328–9.

from around the same time. It cannot have been written later than spring 1698 for the same reason given for 'On the time of purification' (see pp. 315–16).

It is well known that *martyrs have endured the most excruciating tortures* for no other reason than that they had a vivid imagination of future pleasure, for it is impossible for us to resist pain or pleasure except by means of their opposites. It will be the case in general that the wise firmly impress upon themselves the beauty of the future life, that is, of God, in which also consists the love of God, i.e. of the harmony of things. If a man has impressed this strongly enough upon himself, if from this he grasps perpetual pleasure and if he always has recourse to this, two things follow: that he will always consider the end for which he acts, and that he cannot be separated from his love of God by any tortures; so much so that he will think solely of beatitude while in Phalaris' bull,[47] just as Stephen imagined heaven opened up to him while being stoned.[48] He who can do this will be superior to any human violence, and he will not need the trick of putting oneself into a stupor when being tortured. This imagination in the best state should, by every apparatus of art, be continuously impressed upon men from infancy, and without distinction, upon the wise no less than upon the common man. Nor will it hurt the wise man to make use of poems and allegories, and fables and sketches, and variegations; because all means are proper to what is in itself the best end, and no one needs these means more than the wise, who otherwise, out of all peoples, are least accustomed to be prone to emotions, and hence unaccustomed to be strengthened by a powerful imagination, and because of that they are scarcely accustomed to resist pains. As a result, I fully believe that a Japanese girl, who is by chance inspired by certain foolish ideas of the future life, will easily surpass in perseverance every one of the most profound European doctors of theology. Further, this imagination together with assent, in which in [matters of] faith St Thomas calls a pious affection,[49] also includes the love of God above all things, along with contrition, and hence certain salvation. Moreover, *the imagination is strengthened either by pictures or by sounds*, for things

---

[47] According to legend, the tyrant Phalaris ordered a well-known bronze-worker, Perilaus of Athens, to make a life-size, hollow bull out of bronze, for use as a torture and execution device. Victims were placed inside the bull through a door in the side, and a fire was then lit underneath it, thereby heating the metal and roasting the victim alive. See Cicero, *In Verrem*, IV.73.
[48] See Acts 7.58-59.
[49] See Aquinas, *De septem sacramentis ecclesiae*, II.

are not expressed so well to the other, less cultivated, senses. Pictures are clearer, sounds stronger, because in the former there is rest, in the latter motion. Words are sounds, which chiefly arouse a memory of pictures or of things previously seen. Hence the words in poems rendered into *songs* have an incredible power to affect us, because at the same time they both excite pictures and exhibit sounds. Nor do I doubt that a man can be driven into a frenzy by songs, and be calmed, excited and irritated, and be provoked to laughter, to tears and to every kind of emotion. And I see that the latest restorers of religion have made use of this art in order to entice the common man in every part of Germany and France to a more genuine worship through *songs*. Those who know what incredible power this has had, know that the common man is even now imbued with the gentlest pleasure by continuous repetitions of these songs, and that there is scarcely a workman or weaver whose labours are not made agreeable by this cheerfulness, which drives away tedium. *On the basis of that, I think that poets can serve Christendom in no better way than by using all their resources to depict eternal happiness in every shade of colour, and to impress it on minds.* And indeed, crimes are celebrated both in songs and in plays, and it is now the prejudice of the common man that songs of love typically be more tasteful. But if *comedies* were employed to represent the beauty of eternal life, and to depict the terrible punishments of evil deeds, it would fare better with human kind. If songs are already able to excite the greatest joy in souls, if soldiers are inspired to scorn death by military trumpets and if, lastly, all emotions are stirred by the musical art, then a memory which is lively and expressed in music will also be able, insofar as is possible, to impress any emotions whatsoever, and the pleasure of some emotions. The Sybarites decreed rewards to anyone who should discover new kinds of pleasure;[50] *I think that the Christian commonwealth would be greatly indebted to anyone who showed that the greatest enjoyment lies in piety.*

---

[50] The inhabitants of Sybaris were renowned for their love of luxury and pleasure.

3. On the salvation of pagans (not later than spring 1698)[51]

Manuscript:

M: The manuscript was lost following its initial publication in *Otium Hanoveranum*, ed. J. F. Feller (Leipzig, 1718), pp. 181–3.

Transcription:

A: A IV 7, pp. 666–7.

For the same reason as 'On the time of purification' (pp. 315–16), this piece cannot have been written later than spring 1698. Its provenance is unknown.

It is credible that *pagans* not dying in mortal sin, that is, not in a state of enmity towards God, or with the will to harm the whole world, are destined neither for heaven nor hell, but are granted pure grace through Christ in order that from enemies they may become not only non-enemies but also friends and allies. Therefore it is not Pelagian to suppose that pagans can avoid hell by their own natural powers, but to suppose that they can attain heaven that way – that is Pelagian. And thus the difficulties about pagans urged by certain good men are removed; for even the Jesuit Vasquez believed that, by an act of loving God above all things in pagans, some can be saved without Christ, which is false.[52] Indeed, there is no love of God above all things without Christ, because no one is able to love God above all things except he who understands that this is the greatest good to him, but no one understands this except a Christian. But if we imagine that there has been a love of God above all things in any of the pagans (which I do not believe): has he been saved? I think so, but I deny that this can happen by the natural powers in a man, powers which are, so to speak, hypothetical, not absolute. He who fears God above all things avoids hell; he who loves God obtains heaven. Anyone is able to fear God by his natural powers, but no one can

---

[51] Editor's title. From the Latin. Complete.
[52] Gabriel Vasquez, *Commentariorum, ac disputationum in primam partem S. Thomae, tom. 1* (Venice, 1609), p. 724.

love him except by grace through Christ. Moreover, it is credible regarding those who recover from mortal sin through their own nature that this is indeed sufficient to avoid eternal punishment, but not to avoid the greatest temporal punishment, which they will bring upon themselves since they lack the consolation of Christ. But even if this is probable, there is still the greatest doubt over whether there can be any cessation of enmity without Christ.

4. Blessedness and punishment (21 February 1705)[53]

Manuscript:

M: LBr 1010 Bl. 3a–3b.

Transcription:

GW: GW, p. 18.

From a letter to the mathematician and philosopher Christian Wolff, with whom Leibniz corresponded regularly from 1704 until his death in 1716. At the time Leibniz wrote this letter, Wolff was teaching at the University of Leipzig.

I do not think that a blessedness, which is entirely the fruit of prayers, can exist in a creature, but rather the true blessedness of a created mind consists in being free to progress to greater goods. It is not enough to enjoy a contented and tranquil mind, for that is also what happens with the stupid.

That God directs everything towards his own glory is also the same as saying that he directs everything according to the greatest perfection of things, for true glory consists in that, to act in the best way. Those who are punished are not the ones who impede the perfection of things, for, to put it briefly, that is impossible; but the ones who do not prevent the perfection of things from being impeded, these people by their own punishment contribute to the perfection of things.

---

[53] Editor's title. From the Latin. Incomplete: the parts of the letter on other topics have not been translated.

5. Preface to Ernst Soner's book on eternal punishment (1708)[54]

Manuscripts:

M1:   LH 1, 20 Bl. 194 (draft).
M2:   Wolfenbüttel, no catalogue number (final copy).

Transcription:

GELW: Gotthold Ephraim Lessing, *Werke* (Munich: Carl Hanser Verlag, 1976), pp. 175–6 (following M2).

In 1708 Leibniz planned to reprint a book by the Socinian-inspired philosopher Ernst Soner (1572–1612) entitled *Demonstratio Theologica et Philosophica, quod aeterna impiorum supplicia non arguant Dei justitiam, sed injustitiam* [A Theological and Philosophical Demonstration that the Eternal Punishments of the Impious do not Prove the Justice of God but His Injustice] (1603). The following piece was written by Leibniz to serve as a preface to the reprinted version of Soner's book, though ultimately the plan to reprint the book was not carried out. Leibniz's preface was first published more than 50 years after his death, in an essay by Gotthold Lessing entitled 'Leibniz von den Ewigen Strafen' [Leibniz on eternal punishment] (1773).[55]

[M2, final copy]

This demonstration by Ernst Soner, once a very distinguished philosopher in Altdorf, which he called a theological etc. demonstration of the injustice of eternal punishments, is praised by some as irrefutable. And it is all the more harmful because few have seen it, for people are generally accustomed to put a high value on that which they do not know. I therefore think that it is often useful to publish such things, as just reading them is sufficient to refute and overthrow this opinion which has been received among

---

[54] Editor's title. From the Latin. Complete.
[55] See Gotthold Ephraim Lessing, *Philosophical and Theological Writings*, trans. H. B. Nisbet (Cambridge: Cambridge University Press, 2005), pp. 37–60.

people for a long time. It certainly cannot be denied that Soner wrote in a subtle and ingenious way, but his demonstration still suffers from a major omission which is worthwhile pointing out lest an incautious reader should be deceived by the speciousness of his argument, the essence of which comes down to this:[56] sins are finite, there is no proportion between the finite and the infinite, therefore punishments must also be finite. Moreover, he attempts to show that sins are finite by rejecting the senses in which they can be understood as infinite, which he enumerates in these words: 'If the sins of the impious are infinite or are able to be considered as such, then they obtain this infinite degree either from themselves or from the one who commits them, or from the one against whom they are committed, or from some of these reasons or from all of them simultaneously. But they cannot be infinite, or be considered as such, in any of these senses. And yet apart from these, there is no other sense in which they can actually be or be said to be infinite. Therefore they are not infinite at all.'

What the theologians usually say in response to this argument, which they attack on the basis of the proportion between sins and punishments, may be read with profit in their own works. At this point, however, I would prefer to expose another flaw in Soner's argument, namely his incomplete list of the senses in which something can be called infinite. For sins can be called infinite not only with regard to the object against which they are committed, namely God, or with regard to the kind of sin or its degree of intensity, and the other senses mentioned by the author, but also with regard to their number.[57] So even if we should concede that no sin is infinite in itself, it can still be said that the sins of the damned are infinite in number, because they persist in sin throughout all eternity. Therefore if sins are eternal, it is just that the punishments should be eternal too. Of course evil men damn themselves, as the wise rightly say, since they are forever impenitent and turn away from God.[58] Given this, God cannot be deemed severe, as if his punishment was disproportionate to the sin.

---

[56] this: | sins are finite, there is no proportion between the finite and the infinite, but there must be proportion between sins and punishments, therefore punishments must also be finite. | M1.
[57] number. | So even if we should concede that no sin is infinite in itself, the sins of a damned man or angel are still in fact infinite, not indeed in magnitude, but in number. | M1.
[58] God. | And so neither the divine goodness nor the divine justice can be injured by such an eternity of punishment. | M1.

11

Non-Christian Religions

1. On a small book entitled *Seder Olam* (1694)[1]

Manuscript:

M: LH I, V 2 Bl. 22.

Transcription:

FC: A. Foucher de Careil, *La philosophie juive et la cabale avec les manuscrits inedits de Leibniz* (Paris: Auguste Durand, 1861), pp. 49–54.[2]

The following are Leibniz's private notes on the anonymously-published *Seder Olam, sive Ordo Seculorum* ([Amsterdam], 1693), often attributed to Francis Mercury van Helmont. Leibniz, however, believed the book to be of different authorship, advising one correspondent that 'The book itself was written not by Francis Mercury van Helmont, ... but by one of his doctor friends.'[3] The book itself is a work of Kabbalist-inspired metaphysics and chronology; Leibniz's notes are concerned exclusively with the former of the two themes.

---

[1] Author's title. From the French. Complete.
[2] There are numerous faults with this transcription, such as entire passages omitted, words misread, deletions not recorded etc. The faults are too numerous to record individually.
[3] A I 11, p. 22.

On a small book entitled Seder Olam, *published around 1693 or 1694*

The opinion of the ancient Kabbalists seems to have been that the Messiah, according to his humanity, or inasmuch as he is creature, was always the oldest of creatures. This is what the late Mr Knorr von Rosenroth has shown in his *Kabbala denudata*,[4] and the author [of the *Seder Olam*] sometimes follows the same principles. These are quite nice thoughts, but there is no certain proof of them at all.

The author speaks quite strangely when he says in §28 that all created spirits are corporeal.[5] If he had said that all created spirits are embodied he would have been more accurate. That was also the opinion of the ancient Platonic philosophers, and the majority of the Church Fathers believed that angels themselves had subtle bodies.[6] According to this opinion, souls would never be separated from all body, but only from this gross body.[7] If this is the author's opinion, there is nothing reprehensible in it.

It also seems quite probable that there is no corporeal substance in nature that is not endowed with some life, soul or perception, or at least with some entelechy or force of acting, which is the lowest degree of forms, and if it does not have the entire nature of the soul, it does at least have something analogous, which corresponds to perception and appetite. I say this of every corporeal substance and not of all bodies. So we are not supposing that a mountain, or even a heap of stones, is an animal or living body, for this is only a mass of many substances to which life belongs only inasmuch as it consists of living substances. Just as it is not actually the army which is rational, but the men which compose it, and the corpse is not alive but rather the worms which give it colour.

If the author had been content with these well-understood generalities, one could be pleased with him, but he moves on to particularities that cannot be known[8] either by reason or revelation. He lets himself get carried away with this, however, and comes up with some quite amusing ideas; he supposes a world of creation[9] from which comes the world of formation, which is twofold: superior for the souls which have remained in the purity of creation, the seat of which is paradise, and inferior for those which have

---

[4] Christian Knorr von Rosenroth, *Kabbala denudata* (vol. 1: 1677, vol. 2: 1684).
[5] *Seder Olam* §28.
[6] See for example Justin Martyr, *Second Apology*, 5, and Augustine, *On the Trinity*, III.10.21.
[7] body. | This opinion is not completely improbable. | *deleted*.
[8] known | by reason, and about which revelation says nothing further. | *deleted*.
[9] creation | which is that of souls (α) which have never fallen (β) which have retained their original piety. After that comes the world of formation, which seems to be, in his view | *deleted*.

fallen through sin and which remain outside of paradise in invisible places.[10] Finally, from this inferior world of formation came our world, which he calls the world of action, in which there is a stupidity or kind of death, as it were, which prevails over souls, so that there they act mechanically rather than through a vital principle.[11] Yet this should only be understood comparatively, since there is life and corporeity everywhere. He claims that this visible world was not created but made from other pre-existing things, and that the souls of this world were not created any more than our body with its life (which is called *nephesh*) belongs properly in the world of action, and that our spirit (which the Hebrews call *ruah*), which is midway between the body and the soul, is from the world of formation, and that lastly *neshama*, or the soul, alone remains to us from the world of creation. Finally, that the grossest is the vehicle for the others, *nephesh* for *ruah* and *ruah* for *neshama*, and that, vice versa, the subtlest penetrates and illuminates the other by its rays.[12]

These thoughts are not entirely correct in the rigour of true philosophy, for in truth[13] there is only one world that God still continually creates, and this world is animated everywhere and extended everywhere. But two kingdoms can be considered in it: one of minds, which God governs like a[14] prince, just as one person governs other people: and one of bodies, which he governs like an architect or a mechanic, just as an able master controls his machines. These kingdoms interpenetrate and perfectly correspond to each other, without one disturbing the laws of the other, with both carrying out what is in the ideal world of the divine word. It is true, however, that there is some difference between minds (or intelligences) and souls, and that one could perhaps join to them forms or entelechies inferior to souls. But all that only composes one world which continues and contains all these different beings endowed with organized bodies according to their capacity. Whether all these entelechies are of one and the same kind, as our author claims, so that the lowest could reach the state of the noblest – this is what I do not dare to determine. The difference between visible and invisible bodies is only so according to us, and does not change the kind. So if *ruah* is nothing other than a subtle body, it should not be distinguished from other bodies

---

[10] *Seder Olam* §38.
[11] *Seder Olam* §39.
[12] rays. | He even adds (in q24 which is on the Apocalypse) a fourth life called Chaja | *deleted*.
[13] truth | one may say that there are three worlds, the ideal world | *deleted*.
[14] a | King or father | *deleted*.

in any way than as small specks of dust which flutter about in the rays of the Sun are distinguished from pebbles.

Be that as it may, the author, following the cabalists, calls the world of creation *briah*, that of formation *jezirah* and that of action *asiah*, words that are all found in Isaiah 43.7. He climbs even higher and conceives a world of emanation that the Hebrews call *aziluth*, which signifies that which is closest to God, or to the best and supreme Being. But this world only belongs to the middle being between God and creatures, which is the Messiah. And the author says further on (question 24, on the *Apocalypse*) that, besides *psyché* or *nephesch*, drawn from the asiatic world, *ruah* from the *jeziratic* and *neshama* from the *briatic*, there is a fourth life called *chaja*, which comes from the *azilutic* world,[15] and which consequently has to be the internal dwelling place for the spirit of Jesus Christ. Thus the *azilutic* world is that of the Messiah, the *briatic* of souls, the *jeziratic* of the non-consummated angels and the *asiatic* of men clothed in visible bodies. It is true that the Hebrews conceived twelve emanations in the *azilutic* world, but their difference is only modal. This world lasts forever, but there is an infinity of briatics, or worlds that God creates from time to time, from which continually arise new jeziratic and aziratic worlds. This is why Solomon said that one could not find out the principle of God's works.[16] If by the *azilutic* world the author understands the intelligible world which is in[17] God's thought, it can be permitted, but then it should not be said that it holds the middle ground between God and creatures, since it belongs to God himself. As for the other worlds, I have already said what should be thought about them. One would even be able to distinguish two further spheres, or, if you like, two intelligible worlds in God, namely the one of[18] simple ideas, which is the world of the divine understanding, and the one of decrees, that is, of resolved or projected ideas, which is the world of the divine will. And this executed world is the universe of creatures, composed of[19] two kingdoms which are that of minds, the laws of which are moral and tend towards the best, and that of bodies, the laws of which are mathematical and tend towards the greatest, and this combination constitutes the

---

[15] *Seder Olam*, p. 131.
[16] An allusion to Ecclesiastes 3.11: 'He has made everything beautiful in its time. Also He has put eternity in their hearts, except that no one can find out the work that God does from beginning to end.'
[17] in | the intellect | *deleted*.
[18] of | possible ideas | *deleted*.
[19] of | (α) minds and bodies (β) substances | *deleted*.

perfection of things to such a degree that what is brought about is always the greatest good possible.

The author should not deny the present creation of souls under the pretext that nothing is created here: it is entirely the opposite, and he should say instead that everything is continually created and that conservation is a continual creation. Thus it is useless to argue about the pre-existence of souls since it is always true that God presently creates them irrespective of whether they existed before or not. To say that souls descend from a superior world into an inferior world – these are metaphorical expressions, and the only thing true about them is that a soul can change its state and increase or decrease in perfection without anyone being able to determine the detail since revelation does not explain it to us. For according to reason, if the different degrees of creatures form different worlds, there would be nothing that would oblige us to restrict ourselves to the author's three worlds. And if, beyond the *jeziratic* world there is an *asiatic* one, why would there not be yet another beyond that, and so on to infinity? So it is more reasonable to recognize an infinity of degrees in the perfections of creatures in the same world than to make different worlds from them, which serves only to astound people by the novelty of expression.[20] If the author wishes to call 'different worlds' the different kingdoms which interpenetrate, he will only find two real kingdoms in creatures, the moral kingdom of minds and the mechanical kingdom of bodies. It is true that subtle bodies pass through gross bodies, but they only penetrate the pure ones, whereas[21] subtle or gross bodies are likewise penetrated by the souls and entelechies which are intimately present in them.

---

[20] expression. | And if, in place of worlds, kingdoms of created nature were recognized, only two will be found: the kingdom of reason and minds | *deleted.*
[21] whereas | minds, souls and entelechies, or primitive forces, penetrate | *deleted.*

2. On the Jesuit mission in China (18 January 1700)[22]

Manuscript:

M: LBr 954 Bl. 30–1.

Transcription:

A: A I 18, pp. 272–3.

From a letter to Antoine Verjus (1632–1706), the Director of the French Missions of the Jesuits to the Orient, with whom Leibniz corresponded sporadically between 1695 and 1705. With this letter Leibniz enclosed a short paper entitled 'De cultu Confucii civili' [On the civil cult of Confucius],[23] in which he argued that Chinese ritual practices towards Confucius and deceased family members were likely to be civil in basis rather than religious.

Some of my friends have criticized the favourable view I have of your Mission in China, which makes me think that an injustice has been done to your Neophytes in accusing them of idolatry. I was delighted to see at last the collection of writings produced in Rome and recently published in Cologne, if we believe the title page,[24] in which I have nevertheless still not found anything that obliges me to change my view. And I am always of the opinion that a good interpretation should be given to the practices and doctrines of the Chinese, as far as that is possible, as did St Paul when he saw in Athens an altar erected in honour of an unknown divinity.[25] Otherwise, damage will be done to a Mission which seems to me very important for the good of Christianity and of all mankind. This is what obliges me to respond

---

[22] Editor's title. From the French. Incomplete: parts of the letter unconnected with the China mission have not been translated.

[23] See G. W. Leibniz, *Leibniz korrespondiert mit China. Der Briefwechsel mit den Jesuitenmissionaren (1689–1714)*, ed. Rita Widmaier (Frankfurt: Vittorio Klostermann, 1990), pp. 112–16. English translation: WOC, pp. 61–5.

[24] *Historia cultus sinensium, seu Varia scripta de cultibus Sinarum, inter vicarios apostolicos gallos aliosque missionarios, & Patres Societatis Jesu controversis, oblata Innocentio XII* (Cologne, 1700).

[25] See Acts 17.23.

to a friend in accordance with the extract that I take the liberty to send to Your Reverence. And as I take an interest in it, I would desire to learn what course the affair has taken in Rome.

I believe I have asked Reverend Father Gobien to find out (by writing to China) whether it is possible to see the Old Testament of the Jews in China in order to compare it with the Hebrew text of Europe.[26] For according to Father Semedo's account of China (part I, chapter 30),[27] and what Mr Bernier says about his letters from a father of your company (*Voyage de Cachemire*, p. 140 of the edition published in The Hague, 1672),[28] insight might be found there. Because it appears that for a long time these Jews in China have had no communication with those of Europe, and because one might thus find in their possession books or passages that the Jews of Europe may have changed or suppressed out of hatred for Christians, it would be important to make a copy at least of their beginning of Genesis to see if their genealogy of patriarchs agrees with that of the Septuagint, or at least with the text of the Samaritans.

---

[26] The letter in which Leibniz made this request appears to be no longer extant. However, Gobien's reply (of 10 May 1700) is; there he explained to Leibniz that 'Our Missionaries in China are not informed about what you desired to know concerning the Old Testament; they have not been able to discover anything till now, but perhaps will be more fortunate in the future.' A I 18, p. 625.

[27] See Alvarez Semedo, *Histoire universelle de la Chine* (Lyon, 1667), pp. 220–4, especially p. 223: 'Father Matteo Ricci has given his assurance that the Bible of the Jews of Peking is similar to ours. They have no knowledge of the Son of God, on account of which it is conjectured that their entry into China occurred before his birth, else that they have lost the memory of him. It would be a very desirable thing to see their Bible; perhaps they have not corrupted it, unlike some other Jews, who did it in order to obscure the glory of our Redeemer.'

[28] See François Bernier, *Suite des Memoires du Sr Bernier, sur l'Empire du Grand Mogol. Tome 2* (Paris, 1672). The 'father of your company' is identified as Adam Schall in Eusèbe Renaudot, *Anciennes relations des Indes et de la Chine* (Paris, 1718), p. 326.

3. On an intellectual exchange with the Chinese (18 August 1705)[29]

Manuscript:

M: LBr 954 Bl. 34–5.

Transcription:

W: Gottfried Wilhelm Leibniz, *Der Briefwechsel mit den Jesuiten in China (1689-1714)*, ed. Rita Widmaier (Hamburg: Felix Meiner Verlag, 2006), pp. 476–83.

A further letter to Antoine Verjus:

To Reverend Father Verjus

My Very Reverend Father   Hanover, 18 August 1705

As you look after the foreign Missions, and have been kind enough to look favourably upon my correspondence with your Missionary fathers, from which I have benefited now and again, I am desirous that Europe may benefit a little more, given the opportunity these fathers have to make discoveries in China. For I fear that, when the Chinese have learned our sciences, they will one day drive the Europeans out.[30] So it seems to me that we should not lose the opportunities to be compensated, by making an exchange of their knowledge for ours. For although I see most of our missionaries rather inclined to speak disdainfully about the knowledge of the Chinese, nevertheless their language and alphabet, their ways of living, their inventions and manufactured goods, even their games differ from ours almost as much as they would if they had been developed by people from a different planet. It is impossible that even a simple but accurate description of what is practised there could fail to give us insights of great significance, and ones that would be much more useful (to my mind) than the knowledge of Greek and Roman rites and furniture, to which so many learned people

---

[29] Editor's title. From the French. Complete.
[30] Leibniz often aired his concerns about the possible change of heart by the Chinese towards the Europeans. See for example his letter to Joachim Bouvet of 17 April 1703, A I 22, p. 348.

devote themselves. It is true that the chief task of missionaries is to work for the propagation of the religion, but it is for this very task that their investigations – into the language and the hieroglyphics and the critique of ancient books, and the ancient history of China, and even of Chinese sciences and their origin – will be very important, by confirming the history of Holy Scripture, by making our theology more acceptable to the Chinese and by making the Chinese return to the spirit of their ancestors (which I think is very similar to the spirit of the ancient Hebrews and others not yet corrupted by idolatry, as is shown by the example of Job, although some doctors of the Sorbonne may say otherwise).[31] And as it has been discovered that my new binary arithmetic (which uses dyadic progression in place of the decadic, and has no other symbols but '0' and '1', and consequently shows right from the outset a great order of periods, and a wonderful connection in every sort of number-sequences) is perfectly expressed by the ancient characters of Fu Xi,[32] the meaning of which had already been lost by the Chinese from the time of Confucius. It seems to me that this discovery, a minor one to be sure, but surprising, must contribute to awaken us both in Europe and in China, because it will be able to make a great impression on the Emperor of China,[33] and on intelligent persons of that country, to reawaken their curiosity as regards the investigation into the origins and theology and philosophy of the ancient Chinese, who are revealed through this report of Fu Xi's characters to have not always been as superficial as some might have thought. I think that in Rome itself the knowledge of this discovery will be able to make a positive impact, to promote a better opinion of the remote antiquity of these distant peoples. And with the Chinese themselves,

---

[31] See for example Noël Alexandre, *Apologie des dominicains missionnaires de la Chine* (Cologne, 1700, 2nd edn).

[32] Following an exchange of letters with Joachim Bouvet (1656–1730), a French Jesuit missionary who spent most of his adult life in China, Leibniz came to believe that his discovery of the binary system was in fact a rediscovery, and that it had originally been discovered by Fu Xi, a Chinese philosopher (probably mythological) said to have lived in the third millennium BCE. Leibniz initially informed Bouvet of his binary system in a letter of 15 February 1701 (see A I 19, pp. 412-15), and in his reply of 4 November 1701, Bouvet drew Leibniz's attention to the similarity between the binary system and the 'system of small lines' developed by Fu Xi (see A I 20, pp. 533-55). Leibniz received Bouvet's letter only in April 1703, and was so excited by its contents that within a week he had written a paper for the *Memoires de l'Academie Royale des Sciences*, making public the binary system; the second half of the paper repeated and developed Bouvet's claim that Fu Xi had anticipated Leibniz's discovery. See G. W. Leibniz, 'Explication de l'arithmétique binaire, qui se sert des seuls caracteres 0 & 1; avec des remarques sur son utilité, & sur ce qu'elle donne le sens des anciens figues Chinoises de Fohy', *Memoires de l'Academie Royale des Sciences* (1703), pp. 85–9. English translation: http://www.leibniz-translations.com/binary.htm (accessed 16 July 2015).

[33] At the time the Emperor was Kangxi (1656–1722).

it may serve to make more acceptable to them one of the great articles – and not the easiest – of our religion and our metaphysics, which holds that God and nothingness constitute the origin of all things, that God created everything from nothing and still makes everything, conservation being only a continuous creation. For this origin of things from God and nothing is greatly clarified by its analogy with the origin of all numbers from unity and zero, since all numbers may be and even must be expressed most scientifically by the two symbols '1' and '0', and consequently by a unique and continuous relation to these two first elements of numbers.

So given that the investigation into the antiquities, languages, alphabets, history, philosophy and sciences of China has to be so useful for the propagation of religion, and further, that it is so much in the interests of Europeans to take something useful from China in exchange for our sciences, it seems important and reasonable that a number of missionaries be principally tasked to undertake these investigations, which are no less included in the apostolic functions than other investigations. And as many able people in all sorts of professions from Europe have been sent into China, these persons would be well-placed to compare Chinese practices with those here. And to my mind, there would even be a way to pique the interest of the Emperor himself, and to induce him to contribute to it, because being Tartarian, yet from a nation other than the Chinese, he will be delighted that collections and descriptions of all Chinese knowledge are made in order to inform the Tartars of it; as indeed he has already got work started on a large Tartar-Chinese dictionary, which will be no small step, for when the dictionary is complete, and there is an explanation of all the Chinese characters in Tartar, it will be possible to examine all Chinese knowledge in detail, especially if the Emperor ensures that not only the ordinary characters are explained, but also the technical ones appropriate for all sorts of professions, and ensures that they are clarified by illustrations, for which our Europeans will be able to be very helpful to him. So it is only a question of making the right kind of insinuations.

Finally, the renowned Kepler once wrote a letter or dissertation on the occasion of a report by Father Terentius, coming from China,[34] in which Kepler took the opportunity to say that he desired that observations about Chinese astronomy be made.[35] I once mentioned this to Reverend Father

---

[34] See Leibniz's letter to Bouvet of 2 December 1697, in A I 14, p. 835.
[35] Johann Schreck [Latinized name: Joannes Terentius], *Epistolium ex regno Sinarum ad mathematicos Europaeos missum: Cum commentatiuncula Joannis Keppleri, mathematici* (Sagan – Silesia, 1630).

Bouvet, who has asked me for this piece by Kepler,[36] but as I have not found it in this country, and imagine that it will be found instead in Paris, I beg you, my Very Reverend Father, to give the order to have it copied to send on to this Father, and that he also be sent other books that can help explain hieroglyphics, to which he applies himself to good purpose, having the aim of rendering service to religion. But I urge you especially (if I dare to take this liberty) to bring order to the investigations into – and collections of – Chinese knowledge in physics, in mechanics, in history and in geography, which would give us insights. This goal should be first in our sights after the propagation of the faith.

4. On the Mohammedans and Socinians (2 December 1706)[37]

Manuscripts:

M1: LBr 517 Bl. 103–4 (draft).
M2: BBAW Hschr. 3, 2a Bl. 77–80 (final copy).

Transcription:

D: Mathurin Veyssière de La Croze, *Dissertations historiques sur divers sujets* (Rotterdam, 1707), pp. 164–81 (following M2).

This piece is a letter to Maturinus Veyssière La Croze (1661–1739), a French Benedictine historian and orientalist, later a Protestant convert. It was written in response to an essay La Croze had composed, 'Reflexions historiques et critiques sur le Mahometisme, & sur le Socinianisme on Mahometism and Socinianism'. La Croze subsequently published that essay,[38] along with Leibniz's letter (without his permission), in a book entitled *Dissertations historiques sur divers sujets* (1707).[39]

---

[36] See Bouvet's letter to Leibniz of 8 November 1702, in A I 21, p. 618.
[37] Editor's title. From the French. Complete.
[38] La Croze's essay was printed in his anonymously-published *Dissertations historiques et critiques sur divers sujets* (Rotterdam, 1707), pp. 1–163.
[39] Leibniz's letter was printed as 'Lettre de Monsieur de Leibniz à l'Auteur des Reflexions sur l'origine du Mahometisme' in La Croze's *Dissertations historiques et critiques sur divers sujets*, pp. 164–81. An English translation of the book appeared shortly afterwards, and included Leibniz's letter to

[M2, final copy]

Sir,

I have read with pleasure and profit your treatise which draws a parallel between Mohammedans and Socinians, wherein you have shown a great deal of erudition and zeal.[40] I am not at all surprised by the great progress of Mohammedanism; it is a kind of deism joined to the belief in some facts, and to the observation of some practices which *Mohammed* and his followers have added, sometimes quite inappropriately, to natural religion, but which have nonetheless been to the liking of several nations. We are obliged to that sect for the destruction of paganism in many parts of the world, and that would be one step to lead people towards the more sublime religion of Christianity if ours was preached as it ought to be, and if the ill-founded prejudices of the Mohammedans did not put a great obstacle in the way.

One can say of the liberty of the Arabians, the originators of that religion, what is known of the liberty of the Germans and Scythians, of whom the Romans said:

Libertas ultra Tanaim Rhenumque recessit,
Germanum Scythicumque bonum.[41]

It was the same with all populations which were not sufficiently policed, and into which it was difficult to penetrate. It seems that the worship of the planets formed a good part of the religion of the ancient Chaldeans and Arabs, whom *Maimonides* calls Sabeans,[42] though Judaism and Christianity have since made inroads there. I don't doubt that there were many Christians, but the conversion of the Kingdom of Himyarites, which must

---

La Croze. See [Anon.], *Historical and critical reflections upon Mahometanism and Socinianism* (London, 1712), pp. 245–54.

[40] Leibniz is referring here to La Croze's essay 'Reflexions historiques et critiques sur le Mahometisme & sur le Socinianisme'.

[41] An incomplete quotation of Lucan, *Pharsalia* 7.432-6:
  'Liberty, in flight from the crime of civil warfare, has withdrawn
  beyond Tigris and Thine, never to return,
  and wanders on, after our so many murderous attacks,
  a blessing on Germany and Scythia, no longer mindful
  of Ausonia – how I wish our people had never known her!'
The translation is from Lucan, *Civil War*, trans. and ed. Susan H. Braund (Oxford: Oxford University Press, 1992), p. 140.

[42] 'The Sabeans, in their ignorance of the existence of God, believed that the spheres with their stars were beings without beginning and without end', Maimonides, *The Guide for the Perplexed*, trans. M. Friedländer (New York: Dover, 1956), III.XLV, p. 366.

have been procured by *Gregentius*, has all the air of a pious fable.⁴³ However I remember reading that a King of the Himyarites, having exercised great cruelties upon the Christians of his country, was overcome by a Christian king of the Axumites, whom we call Abyssinians, who crossed the Red Sea with an army to make war upon him.⁴⁴ I am afraid that what you say, Sir, is only too true, namely that the horrible persecutions of Christians in the Roman Empire, committed under the pretext of Nestorianism and Eutychianism, have greatly contributed to populating Arabia and even more to weakening Christianity and to making it odious in the Eastern countries. Further, Christianity was already burdened with many superstitions and made itself vulnerable in many ways when *Mohammed* arose to establish a religion which⁴⁵ was fairly similar to the Jewish and not entirely different from some Christian sects, which soon gave him a great number of followers. You also very rightly remark that Christianity had perhaps not put down sufficient roots in Arabia in those times because there was not then apparently any translation of the Holy Scripture into Arabic. And you are right to think that even today missionaries would enjoy more success if they were to apply themselves to the translation of the holy writings into people's native languages. Missionaries propose some catechisms to them, and sometimes take the liberty of producing a new history of the gospel of *Jesus Christ* mixed with fables, as Father Jerome Xavier did, but these apocryphal books are far from having the power to inspire and preserve religion that the canonical books have.

What you say afterwards, Sir, about the articles of the Mohammedan doctrine, is very reasonable, and it is to be hoped that they do not surpass us in certain points of piety. As for usury, condemned by the Mohammedans, it may be said that if it is permitted to share the profits with those to whom we lend for their gain, it is not fair to overburden poor people who borrow

---

⁴³ The conversion of the Himyarites followed a four-day disputation between Herbanus, a Jewish Himyarite, and Gregentius, Bishop of Tephra (Dhafar). The disputation ended when Jesus Christ appeared in the clouds and miraculously struck the unbelieving Jews with blindness, though their sight was later restored when they were baptized. This event is said to have resulted in five and a half million Jews converting to Christianity. For more information see *S. Patris nostri Gregentii Tephrensis Archiepiscopi Disputatio cum Herbano Judaeo* (Paris, 1586), which is sometimes attributed to Gregentius.

⁴⁴ Leibniz is referring here to an event in sixth century Yemen in which, following his conversion to Judaism, King Dhū-Nuwas of the Himyarite kingdom engaged in a persecution of the local Christian population, which prompted King Caleb/Kaleb of the Axumites to invade from Ethiopia via the Red Sea.

⁴⁵ which | differs from the Jewish only through external observations | *deleted*, M1.

in order to live. I am, Sir, on your side against those who give themselves free reign to ill-treat the Fathers on every occasion, and particularly when it comes to their invectives against usury. The contempt of the Fathers, carried to excess, rebounds on the Christian religion, for if it has never had any truly pious and enlightened propagators, what opinion are we to form of it?

Moreover, Father *Michael Nau*, who was in the Levant, and endeavoured to instruct those who have to convert the Mohammedans, has related good things drawn from their books which can be used to recommend Christianity to them.[46] But the main thing is to remove the opinion they have of us that we multiply the divinity. And it would be hoped that poorly educated Christians, and sometimes even able men somewhat inclined to poor understanding, do not fall into a kind of tritheism seen in passages of some Remonstrants and in the Abbé Faydit's book against the Scholastics (which seems to me incomparably more confused than the Scholastics themselves) who endeavour to preserve the important point of God's unity.[47] Not to mention the controversy that arose some years ago in England, in which learned men showed their zeal against certain doctrines which smacked of tritheism somewhat.[48]

As for the Socinians, it must be admitted that they are very similar to the Mohammedans, and although the Socinians do not accept that Mohammed is the envoy of God, they nevertheless follow and develop the core of his doctrine, inasmuch as he contests the Trinity and Incarnation. On this score, I remember having read a while back in a book by *Comenius* against *Zwicker* that a Turk, upon hearing what a Polish Socinian said to him, was surprised that he did not get himself circumcised.[49] It is true that

---

[46] Michel Nau (1633–83), a Jesuit missionary best known for his travels around the Holy Land which resulted in an oft-reprinted book *Voyage nouveau de la Terre-Sainte, enrichi de plusieurs remarques particulieres qui servent à l'intelligence de la Sainte Ecriture. Et de diverses reflexions Chrétiennes qui intruisent les Ames devotes dans la conoissance & l'amour de J.C.* (Paris, 1674). Leibniz is referring to Nau's *L'Estat present de la Religion Mahometane avec les choses les plus curieuses qui regardent Mahomet & l'etablissemnt de la Secte, qui n'ont pas encore été imprimées. Avec des Conférences sur la Religion Chrétienne, & sur l'Alcoran* (Paris, 1688). The second part of this book contained six dialogues in which Christianity is defended against the Koran through passages of the Koran itself.

[47] Leibniz is referring to Pierre Faydit (1640–1709) and his book *Altération du dogme théologique par la philosophie d'Aristote, ou fausses idées des scolastiques sur les matières de religion* (Paris, 1696), in which Faydit defended a form of tritheism, and argued that the doctrine of the unity of God was a Scholastic invention.

[48] Leibniz probably has in mind the heated debate from the early 1690s involving John Wallis, William Sherlock, Robert South and Stephen Nye. See 'Some thoughts on the Trinity, occasioned by the reading of Stephen Nye's *Considerations on the Explications of the Doctrine of the Trinity*' (pp. 203–9).

[49] John Amos Komensky (1592–1671), who is often referred to by his Latinized name, Comenius,

the Socinians worship *Jesus Christ*, which the Mohammedans refuse to do, but it seems that the latter act more consistently than the Socinians, for why worship a mere creature? *Francis David* was right on this matter to declare himself against Blandrata and Socinus;[50] only the eternal and infinite God do we adore formally and precisely, and the union of the creator with the creature, no matter how important, ought not to alter this worship. If some ill-informed learned people, or some inadequately-educated people among Christians, depart from this great principle of true worship, we should zealously take issue with them and set them right. But we should not therefore destroy either the union of the Word with human nature, which is as close as is possible, or the diversity of three personalities and two productions, which Holy Scripture teaches us exists in God without multiplying God himself. There is something profound and incomprehensible in the divinity, of which Holy Scripture has given us some insight through words borrowed from what is found analogically among creatures, but by excluding the imperfection found to be joined with it in creatures.

The Socinians push their audacity further than the Mohammedans in points of doctrine, for not content with contesting that mystery and avoiding very strong passages, they go so far as to weaken natural theology when they deny God the foreknowledge of contingent things and when they contest the immortality of man's soul. And in desiring to distance themselves from Scholastic theologians, they overthrow everything great and sublime in theology, even down to making God limited, whereas we know there are Mohammedan doctors who have ideas of God worthy of his greatness. *Conrad Vorst*, too much carried away by his aversion to everything coming from the School, fell into extreme views incompatible with the supreme and immense perfection of God; but the Socinians had showed him the way, and the event has shown *King James* was not wrong to write so passionately against this doctor.[51] I am not familiar with this *William Henry*

---

wrote three books against Daniel Zwicker (1612–78), namely: *De Irenico Irenicorum hoc est Conditionibus pacis a Socini Secta reliquis Christiano orbi oblatis ad omnes Christianos facta admonitio* (Amsterdam, 1660); *J. A. Comenii de iterato Sociniani Irenico iterata ad Christianos admonitio* (Amsterdam, 1661); *Admonitio tertia ad D. Zwickerum* (Amsterdam, 1662).

[50] Francis David (sometimes known as Ferenc Dávid, 1510–79), popularizer of Unitarianism and court preacher to John II Sigismund, King of Hungary, was sentenced to life imprisonment in the dungeon of the castle of Deva for refusing to abandon his belief that Christ should not be adored or worshipped. He died there in November 1579. At his trial, his former Unitarian ally George Blandrata (c. 1515–88) acted as chief prosecutor and chief witness.

[51] In 1612 King James I of England (1566–1625) wrote a pamphlet against Conrad Vorst (1569–1622), namely *His Maiesties Declaration concerning His Proceedings with the States generall of the*

Vorst, son of Conrad, of whom you speak, Sir, and some of whose views you relate. One has to be very reckless and extravagant to treat as spurious those passages of the Koran which speak honourably of *Jesus Christ*, and those of *Pliny*, *Tacitus* and *Suetonius* which speak of Christians.

It seems that the Council of Nicaea did no more than establish by its decisions a doctrine which already held sway in the Church. It is true that there are passages in earlier writers whose expressions were not quite right, but this is because the phrases had not been fixed then, and often these authors are not properly understood. It seems that some Fathers, especially the Platonists, conceived two filiations in the Messiah before he was born of the holy virgin Mary, namely the one which makes him the only son inasmuch as he is eternal in the divinity, and the one which makes him the eldest of creatures, distinguishing and separating τὸν μονογενῆ ἀπὸ τοῦ πρωτοτόκος τῆς κτίσεως,[52] and conceiving that from the beginning of things the eternal Word was endowed with a created nature, the noblest of all, which made him the instrument of the divinity in the production and direction of other natures. This seems in keeping with the doctrine of the pre-existence of souls, taught by *Origen* and some other Fathers, where the soul of the Messiah must hold the first place; it also seems that this was the idea the ancient Jewish Cabalists had of their *Adam Kadmon*. The Arians have only retained this second filiation, and have forgotten the first, and some of the Fathers seem to have favoured them, in opposing the son to the Eternal, inasmuch as they considered the son in relation to this primogeniture among creatures, as they imagined. But they did not thereby deny him that which he had before creation, inasmuch as [he was God's] only and consubstantial son. As for the dialogue *Philopatris*, which talks so distinctly of the Trinity, although it does not seem to be by Lucian there are grounds to think that it is by a very ancient pagan who had had knowledge of Christianity.[53] As for *Theodisculus*, Greek Archbishop of Seville but deserter of Christianity when Mohammedanism began to spread,[54] it seems

---

United Provinces of the Low Countreys, In the cause of D. Conradus Vorstius (1612). In the same year Vorst was removed from his position at the university of Leiden, where he had held the chair in Theology. For further details of James I's opposition to Vorst, see Frederick Shriver 'Orthodoxy and diplomacy: James I and the Vorstius affair', *The English Historical Review*, 85 (1970): 449–74.

[52] 'his only begotten from the firstborn of creation'.

[53] *Philopatris* is a work of Greek Literature, a dialogue that was at one time attributed to Lucian (c. 125–80). Its authorship and date of composition is uncertain (scholars have dated it variously to the third, seventh and tenth centuries CE). The doctrine of the Trinity is raised in §12, and immediately derided by the character Critias.

[54] Leibniz is referring here to Oppa (or Oppas), Archbishop of Seville early in the eighth century CE.

that his audacity to treat *Jesus Christ* as the simple adoptive son of God did a disservice to later Spaniards, contemporaries of *Charlemagne* like *Elipandus* and *Felix*, who called Jesus Christ 'adoptive' only according to his human nature.[55] But they were treated harshly, although they erred only in their expressions, and they alleged ancient forms of prayers found in their churches where the same ways of speaking – which this *Theodisculus* had perhaps abused – were apparent.

The history of the modern Anti-Trinitarians is quite curious. It seems that the Italians and the Spanish, who were the originators of this sect, wanted to out-refine the Germans and French as regards reformation, but instead of purifying our religion they almost annihilated it. It is true that the severity to which they – and particularly Servetus – were subjected is inexcusable,[56] since only a perverse will may be punished, not error in itself: *Errantis poena doceri*.[57] A person is allowed to take measures to prevent the propagation of a pernicious error, but also this is all that anyone has the right to do, and these measures ought to be the mildest possible. I have all the more sympathy for Servetus's misfortune since he must have been of extraordinary merit, because it has been discovered in our time that he understood the circulation of blood, which surpasses everything discovered about this before him. It is a blessing for Christianity that the Turks were not minded to take advantage of the advice of men like *Adam Neuser*,[58] Minister of the Palatinate, who wanted to establish an understanding between them and the Anti-Trinitarian Christians, whereby they would have had a camp among us. It would be wrong to count Adam Neuser among the Reformed. There have been renegades from all of Christianity's camps, and if there are fewer from the Confession of Augsburg this is because they had less commerce with the Turks; and if *Neuser* had broader views than others, that has nothing to do with the Reformation.

I would not attribute the unfortunate end of some Anti-Trinitarians to their error of understanding, but rather to the irregularity of their heart, or

---

He is said to have defected to the side of Muslim invaders following a battle in 711.

[55] Leibniz is referring here to the 'adoptionist' debate which began in Spain in the 780s. Both Elipandus (c. 717–808), Archbishop of Toledo, and Felix (?–818), Bishop of Urgel, argued that Christ, as man, is the Son of God only by adoption and grace, not by nature.

[56] Michael Servetus (1511–53), a Spanish theologian who rejected the doctrine of the Trinity. He was charged with heresy and executed.

[57] 'The punishment for those in error is to be taught.' Cf. Plato, *Republic*, 337d1–6; Grotius, *De jure belli ac pacis*, II.XX.50.

[58] Adam Neuser (1530–76), one-time Minister of Heidelberg. Neuser rejected the doctrine of the Trinity and eventually converted to Islam after fleeing to Constantinople.

else to some judgements of God, whose workings we don't understand. Good men are often unhappy. Besides, a difficult death, accompanied by raging and screaming, being an effect of illness and constitution, may happen to the best Christian in the world. Further, mad people do not usually feel pain as much as they seem to, as is acknowledged by those who have recovered from the condition. As there have been and still are, among the Anti-Trinitarians as well as among the Turks, people living morally good lives, we ought to pity them, and appeal to God's leniency and mercy on their behalf.

I am no less displeased than you are, Sir, that *Socinus* seems to want to deny the natural knowledge of God, and that he makes the effort to avoid the passages of Holy Scripture that teach it in formal terms. It is also a strange doctrine to say that one can live in a holy way without knowing God. I like to think that one may have some apparent virtue which has no relation to God, but holiness, properly speaking, includes this relation of virtues to him who is the source of all purity and all perfection. Besides, an atheist may be a good man, morally speaking, either through disposition, custom or fortunate circumstance, but he cannot be completely so through a sound principle of right reason unless he has grasped that great point of finding a pleasure in virtue and an ugliness in vice which surpass all the other pleasures and displeasures of this life, which seems very difficult and quite rare. Although it is not altogether impossible that a happy education, a conversation, a meditation and a proportioned practice may lead a man to that point, he will always arrive there more easily with piety. Aside from this extraordinary disposition of mind, when our reasoning is confined only to the conveniences of this life, it cannot inspire sufficiently noble sentiments nor teach man his principal duties which regard the Supreme Lord of the universe, knowledge of whom makes us understand that his service can oblige us on many occasions to prefer the good of others to our own present interests, and to take a course which prudence would not always approve, if that great motive were to cease, and if we did not have the best and greatest of all masters, who we are happy to serve and who always pursues the common good. So the Socinians seem to debase both natural and revealed religion, in theory and in practice, and remove a good part of what is beautiful in them. But I must now end a letter which has become more longwinded than I thought it would when I began it. I am with all my heart, etc.

Your very humble and very
obedient servant
Leibniz

From Berlin, 2 December 1706

Index

Abraham 115, 290
Adam 77, 83, 264, 296
Adam Kadmon 342
Anaxagoras 91, 117, 120
angel 26, 34, 81, 99, 115, 177, 179–80, 183, 190–1, 198, 200, 220, 251, 278, 297, 300 n.72, 326 n.57, 328, 330
anomie 272
Anselm, St 28, 66–7, 72
antecedent will *see* God, antecedent will of
Anti-Trinitarians 198, 230–1, 343–4
Apocryphal books 228, 339
Aquinas, St Thomas 29, 38, 40 n.71, 44, 68, 72 n.43, 75, 86, 101, 105, 321
Aristotle 38ff, 73, 75, 106, 118, 120, 170–1, 304 *see also* Aristotelians
Aristotelians 39
arithmetic 99, 115, 277, 320
   binary 335
Arnauld, Antoine 45–6, 48, 320
astronomy 114, 207, 217, 336
atheism 104, 160, 234, 237, 251
atheists 23, 32, 41, 43, 95, 100, 102, 112, 284, 344
atom 133, 304–5
attrition 31–2, 144, 248
Augsburg Confession 44–5, 141, 288, 343
Augustine 101, 105, 112, 200, 230, 260 n.10, 263, 277, 282, 292, 294–5, 304, 311ff, 317

baptism 199, 248, 250, 298
Bayle, Pierre 110–11, 287

beatific vision 33, 49, 76
beauty 31, 33, 74 n.50, 300, 321
   of God *see* God, beauty of
   of things/the world 22, 76, 138, 151, 164, 217, 262, 285
Bellarmine, Robert 101, 228
Bible, the *see* Scripture
Boëthius 25
Boyle, Robert 28

Calvin, John 273
Calvinists 29
Cartesians 48, 55–6, 58, 68, 89, 122, 222
Catholics 46, 100, 198, 229, 231, 251, 318
charity 49, 79, 103, 123 n.12, 126, 135, 137, 142, 145, 147, 150–1, 153, 156, 158ff, 211, 234, 236, 241–2, 245, 249, 298, 310
China 90–1, 115, 332ff
Christianity 41, 48, 50, 93–4, 104, 126, 144, 175 n.19, 186, 217, 233–4, 237, 246, 332, 338ff, 342–3
Church
   Catholic 36, 44–5, 62, 71–2, 104, 122, 124–5, 154–5, 166, 225, 227 n.4, 228, 237–8, 240, 243ff, 251, 283, 308ff, 317
   Christian 234, 243, 287
   Greek 250 n.76, 308–9
   militant 252
   Roman *see* Catholic
   triumphant 252
   universal 35, 238, 243ff
Cicero 95, 115, 117, 207, 234, 245
concurrence *see* God, concurrence of

consequent will *see* God, consequent will of
continuum 33, 222
contrition 31–2, 144, 160, 231, 248, 321
Copernicus, Nicolaus 34
Council of Nicea 342
Council of Trent 39, 41, 44, 47, 50, 230, 241
creation 26, 38 n.62, 49, 217 n.78, 254
 continuous 22, 76, 87, 289, 331, 336
Cudworth, Ralph 204, 207

damnation 276, 296, 310, 314, 317, 320
Day of Judgement 186, 202, 300, 305, 317
deism 234, 237, 338
Deluge, the 49, 117
Descartes, René 23, 26, 38 n.61, 42, 45, 49, 60, 66–7, 85ff, 122 *see also* Cartesians
Devil, the 81, 101, 195, 316

eduction 26, 262
entelechy 106, 328–9, 331
enthusiasm 75, 176
Epicureans 262
eternal punishment *see* punishment, eternal
Eucharist 29, 43–4, 48, 107, 226, 242, 245, 249
Evangelicals 147, 167, 172, 215
evil 32, 75ff, 79, 136, 238, 263–4, 266, 268, 279, 282, 285, 289–90, 293, 295–6, 316
 cause/origin of 27, 78, 112, 255, 260, 276, 287, 292–3
 metaphysical 291–2
 moral 291–2
 permission of 83, 109, 111–12, 260, 292
 physical 291–2
 as a privation 78, 262, 271–2, 277–8
extension 37–8, 49, 106–7, 132, 222, 232

faith 32, 43, 79, 81, 83–4, 96ff, 101–2, 104–5, 113, 147, 158, 164, 166ff, 183, 196, 214–15, 241, 244, 247, 262, 287, 298, 321
 articles of 171, 241, 244, 312, 317–18
 Catholic 71, 124, 200
 Christian 25, 104
 nature of 221
Fall, the 77, 220, 288 n.38, 293, 296, 300 *see also* sin, of Adam
fate 253, 259
Flood, the *see* Deluge, the
flower of substance 307
freedom
 divine *see* God, freedom of
 human 27, 77, 79, 218, 222, 255, 259–60, 275, 296–7
 of minds 27, 75

Galileo, Galilei 48–9, 70
Gentiles 114, 178ff, 182, 192, 218
geometry 105, 114, 126, 216–17, 221, 279, 320
God
 antecedent will of 289ff, 295
 beauty of 151–2, 270, 321
 concurrence of 37, 76, 261ff, 289, 294
 consequent will of 290ff
 decretory will of *see* God, consequent will of
 essence of 43, 54ff, 67–8, 71–2, 76, 85–6, 171, 196, 198, 257, 260
 eternity of 25, 71, 257, 300 n.72
 existence of 22–3, 36, 54ff, 59ff, 63, 66ff, 72, 93–4, 99, 112, 231–2, 236, 257, 262, 288
 foreknowledge of 77, 256, 259 n.10, 260–1, 275–6, 290, 341
 freedom of 74–5, 257ff, 275, 288, 291
 glory of 78, 102, 138–9, 156, 158, 162, 249, 324

goodness of 76–7, 79, 85, 112, 135, 152, 163, 233, 236, 247, 277, 288, 290–1, 293ff, 300 n.72, 326 n.58
holiness of 251, 254, 259, 261, 294, 344
justice of 76, 78–9, 85–6, 104, 135, 200, 233, 254–5, 259 n.10, 284, 289, 293ff, 309, 320, 326 n.58
omnipotence of 25, 62, 71, 75, 82, 135, 198, 207, 233, 236, 254 n.4, 255, 288–9
omnipresence of 25
omniscience of 25, 71, 74–5, 82, 233, 236, 254, 256, 288–9
perfection of 57, 62, 67, 71ff, 75, 80, 85–6, 100, 111, 134–5, 139, 149, 151–2, 160, 163, 232, 247, 249, 293, 341
persons of 26, 61–2, 104, 171, 196ff, 203, 206ff, 230–1, 247, 341
providence of 76–7, 104–5, 108, 117, 120, 129, 134, 151, 166, 233–4, 237, 239, 253, 270, 283–4, 289, 294, 300 n.72
grace 78, 83, 104, 142–3, 151–2, 164, 201, 235, 237, 240, 242, 245, 247ff, 253, 255, 288, 295, 297–8, 323–4
auxiliary 27
of conversion 298
efficacious 264
of perseverance 264, 298
state of 79
sufficient 255, 264, 298
Grotius, Hugo 176ff, 184, 186–7, 209

harmony 40, 78, 109, 132, 138, 152, 255, 269, 279, 293, 295, 321
pre-established 295
universal 33, 111, 149
heaven 29, 103, 180, 186, 310, 320–1, 323
hell 31, 33, 125, 234, 237, 247–8, 310, 317, 320, 323

Helmont, Francis Mercury van 151, 156
Hobbes, Thomas 23, 25, 33, 46
Holy Communion 146, 249ff
Holy Scripture *see* Scripture
Holy Spirit 26, 84, 98, 118, 196ff, 205–6, 208–9, 230, 231 n.17, 242, 245, 247–8, 250
Holy Trinity *see* Trinity
Host 40 n.71, 44–5, 225ff, 250–1

idolatry 114, 177, 183, 185, 192, 251–2, 332, 335
immortality *see* soul, immortality of
imperfection of creatures 78, 209, 232, 236, 263, 265, 278, 282, 291, 293, 341
Incarnation, the 27–8, 43, 48, 62, 78, 104, 199–200, 206, 231–2, 237, 340
indulgences 249
infinity 82, 111, 207, 212, 219, 222, 277
innate ideas 296
intermediate state of souls 32–3, 317
Irenaeus, St 175, 177, 181–2
Israelites 115, 189, 190 n.106, 191–2

Jansenism 22
Jansenists 144
Jehoshaphat, Valley of 318–19
Jesuits 49
Jews 33, 178–9, 307, 333
joy 33, 138, 240, 249, 316, 322
justice 49, 74 n.50, 76, 79, 106, 131, 137, 140, 142, 145, 158, 162–3, 264–5, 267, 270, 283ff, 293, 320, 325–6
of God *see* God, justice of
Justin Martyr 118, 200

Kabbalah 328
kingdom of Christ 179–80

Last Judgement *see* Day of Judgement
Lateran Council 33, 105, 112

lazy sophism 260, 276, 291 n.52
Locke, John 222–3
logic 48, 68, 99ff, 206
Lord's Prayer 145
love 31, 78, 84, 87, 138–9, 147, 151,
    159–60, 197, 209, 247–8, 294, 313
  of God 62, 76, 79, 83–4, 89, 103,
    125–6, 132, 135ff, 139, 142ff,
    146–7, 149ff, 154–5, 158ff, 163–4,
    231, 233, 235–6, 241, 246ff, 276,
    312, 320–1, 323–4
Lucretius 301
Luther, Martin 146, 175, 179, 229, 282
Lutherans 215

Malebranche, Nicolas 87, 89, 285
Mary 30, 198, 342
mathematics 22, 49, 105–6, 128
matter 22, 26, 29–30, 38ff, 76, 90–1, 107,
    124, 129, 132ff, 170, 200, 262,
    304–5
mechanics 106, 128, 337
Messiah 328, 330, 342
metaphysics 22, 48–9, 119, 126, 206,
    216, 231, 336
metempsychosis 116, 119
middle knowledge 25, 257, 290
miracles 24, 28, 50, 97, 99, 104, 119, 195,
    210, 217, 221, 262
missionaries 50, 334ff, 339
Mohammedans 97–8, 338ff
More, Henry 85, 151
Moses 85, 90, 97, 116–17, 119, 189ff, 228
motion 22, 26, 36, 38 n.61, 40, 64–5, 73,
    87, 129, 134, 231 n.17, 261, 263,
    269, 285, 304, 306–7, 322
Muslims *see* Mohammedans
mysteries 25, 43–4, 48, 78, 96, 104, 118,
    169, 171, 196, 199–200, 207, 210,
    211 n.54, 218ff, 247, 341
mystical theology 73, 80, 103, 301
mysticism *see* mystical theology
mystics 158, 160

natural theology 93, 108, 114ff, 119, 338,
    341, 344
necessary being *see* God
necessity 25ff, 74 n.50, 129–30, 255ff,
    259, 276, 279, 289–90, 297
  absolute 63, 260, 276
  conditional 276
  of existence 58, 60
  hypothetical 259–60
  material 285
  metaphysical 215, 291
  moral 291, 293
New Testament 167, 221, 242 *see also*
    Scripture
Newton, Isaac 162, 222
Noah 28, 117
nothingness 81–2, 277–8, 336

Old Testament 333 *see also* Scripture
Origen 342
Origenists 317
original sin *see* sin, original

paganism 338
Paradise 27, 300, 328–9
Pascal, Blaise 95
Paul, St 78, 102, 180, 219, 241, 279, 282,
    298, 304, 312ff, 332
Penn, William 149–50, 156
perfection
  of God *see* God, perfection of
  of things 76, 78, 80, 89, 108, 125,
    130ff, 138–9, 159, 232, 236, 263,
    279, 289, 294, 324, 331
perfections 55, 59, 67–8, 71ff, 81, 86,
    163, 197, 201, 232, 278, 291
physics 22, 106, 285, 337
piety 49–50, 88–9, 102, 105–6, 142, 144,
    151, 162, 164, 211 n.54, 244, 249,
    253, 255, 287–8, 301, 322, 328
    n.9, 339, 344
Plato 24, 39–40, 74, 76, 113, 115, 118,
    120, 176

Platonists 27, 86–7, 91, 119, 277, 328, 342
Pliny 193, 342
Plotinus 118
Poiret, Pierre 151, 155–6
Pomponazzi, Pietro 102
Pope, the 34, 50, 146, 212, 228 n.4, 238, 243
prayer 85, 178, 189, 201, 238, 249, 252, 291 n.52, 310, 324, 343
prayers for the dead 249, 309–10
predestination 109, 139, 167
principle
    of action 36, 40
    of beauty 33
    of charity 156
    of contingency 257–8, 285
    of contradiction 100–1
    of individuation 38–9, 285
    of love 31
    of motion 36, 38, 40, 64, 120, 129
    of negation 278
prophecy 176, 179, 193, 195
prophets 97, 120, 176, 185, 191, 193, 228
Protestants 71, 166, 228, 231, 240–1, 243, 245–6, 249ff
providence *see* God, providence of
punishment 27, 30ff, 77, 109, 115, 117, 133, 136, 144, 183, 185, 187, 236, 247–8, 264, 284, 286, 291, 292 n.54, 293, 300, 308ff, 314, 322, 324
    eternal 30, 33, 324ff
purgatory 30ff, 248, 308ff, 313–14, 317
Pythagoras 114, 116, 119

Quakers 149, 151–2
quietism 152, 158, 160

real presence 44–5, 172
redemption 247, 300
Reformation, the 343
religion
    Christian *see* Christianity
    natural *see* natural theology
    revealed 108, 233, 237, 344
Remonstrants 71, 79, 340
resurrection
    of bodies 48–9, 303ff, 314
    day of 308ff
    of the dead 186, 306
    of Jesus 177
    time of the *see* resurrection: day of
revelation 43, 97, 99, 112, 119–20, 177, 217, 220, 236 n.26, 237, 244, 247, 328, 331
reward 109, 115, 133, 136, 151, 236, 248, 285

saints 81, 126, 153, 185–6, 251–2
salvation 31, 46, 104, 143–4, 147, 166, 171, 178, 199, 211 n.54, 220, 223, 227, 229–30, 237–8, 244, 248–9, 295, 299, 310, 321
    of Christ 30
    of heretics 31, 246
    of pagans 142, 323
    state of 142, 240–1
schism 146, 234–5, 238
Scholastics 22, 25, 29, 36, 39ff, 45, 47, 77, 87, 111, 144, 146, 170, 200, 340
Scripture 34, 62, 72, 75, 81, 84, 90–1, 97, 109, 143, 163, 166ff, 170ff, 197 n.7, 198, 200, 205–6, 209, 219–20, 227, 229–30, 234–5, 237ff, 244ff, 248, 254 n.4, 272, 278, 286–7, 294, 305, 317, 335, 339, 341, 344
Sherlock, William 204, 207
sin
    of Adam 32, 78, 277, 295
    author of 79, 259 n.10, 260, 271ff
    mortal 30ff, 144, 248, 266, 323–4
    original 27, 78, 82, 264, 278, 296–7
    punishment of *see also* eternal punishment
    venial 31–2

Socinians 26, 30, 71, 79, 109, 172–3, 205–6, 215, 230–1, 288, 338, 340–1, 344
Socinus, Faustus 198, 341, 344
Socrates 115
soul 33, 48, 62, 82, 89, 106, 120, 124ff, 132–3, 136, 152, 160, 199–200, 295–6, 300 n.72, 306ff, 328–9, 331, 342
  of Christ 40 n.71, 62, 202, 226, 229, 342
  immateriality of the 119–20
  immortality of the 23, 25, 94–5, 113ff, 128, 134, 176, 341
  origin of the 23 n.15, 264, 295–6, 331
  transmigration of the *see* metempsychosis
  of the world 39, 70, 74, 91, 106, 129, 133
space 22, 26, 29, 36, 38, 73, 82, 262
Spee, Friedrich 154, 160
Spinoza, Baruch 60, 121ff
spiritual body 306
spirituality 151
Steno, Nicolas 121ff
Stillingfleet, Edward 222–3
Stoics 39, 73, 91, 118
Strabo 90–1, 116
substance 29, 36ff, 44, 48, 62, 67, 71, 76, 79, 85, 89, 91, 104, 106–7, 119–20, 132ff, 163, 198, 203, 205ff, 212, 216, 219, 231–2, 236, 247, 249, 251, 254, 257–8, 261–2, 294–5, 307, 328

substantial form 29–30, 37ff, 48, 106, 304
superstition 114, 118, 240, 245, 251, 339

Tertullian 153, 168, 308
theodicy 283
traduction 23 n.15, 27, 264, 295
transubstantiation 29–30, 35ff, 39, 41, 43ff
Trinity 43, 48, 62, 99, 104, 118, 172, 198ff, 204, 206, 229ff, 237, 247, 340, 342
truths 49, 54, 56, 57 n.3, 59, 102–3, 108, 110ff, 120, 126, 132, 136–7, 149, 151, 159, 195, 211, 215, 234, 237, 258, 263, 289–90, 296
  contingent 74 n.50, 257 n.8, 258, 290 n.45
  eternal 59, 71, 74, 86, 89, 136, 149, 293

union of soul and body 37, 89, 124, 200, 210, 222, 231–2

Virgin Mary *see* Mary
virtues 85, 136, 145, 155, 158, 164, 266, 268, 285, 300 n.72, 344
void 87
Vorst, Conrad 25, 71, 231, 288, 341

Wallis, John 204, 207–8
world
  best 293, 295–6
  possible 269, 286, 290, 293
  soul *see* soul, of the world

Zwingali, Ulrich 29, 146, 229

www.ingramcontent.com/pod-product-compliance
Lightning Source LLC
Chambersburg PA
CBHW071757300426
44116CB00009B/1119